DATE DUE

The New Military

Changing Patterns of Organization

Research Studies Edited by

Morris Janowitz

Russell Sage Foundation

New York · 1964

THE CONTRIBUTORS

ALBERT D. BIDERMAN — Bureau of Social Science Research
Washington, D.C.

MAURY D. FELD — Center for International Affairs
Harvard University

OSCAR GRUSKY — Department of Sociology
University of California, Los Angeles

KURT LANG — Department of Sociology
State University of New York
Stonybrook, New York

MOSHE LISSAK — Department of Sociology
Hebrew University

ROGER W. LITTLE — U.S.A., Office of Military Psychology
and Leadership
United States Military Academy

JOHN P. LOVELL — Department of Government
Indiana University

RICHARD W. SEATON — Stanford Research Institute
Stanford, California

WILLIAM SIMON — Department of Sociology
Southern Illinois University

MAYER N. ZALD — Department of Sociology
Vanderbilt University

3

CONTENTS

5

PREFACE

RESEARCH SCHOLARS are chronically dissatisfied with the forms of scholarly communication and publications. In recent years there has been a marked increase in the volume of monographic research in the field of social organization which seeks to collect empirical data on important theoretical propositions. Scientific journals appear unable to devote sufficient space to the substantive and methodological detail of such research, while full book length publication of these materials is both excessively expensive and elaborate.

Thus *Studies in Social Organization*, of which this is the first volume, is an experiment to meet the changing needs of publication in the field of social organization research. The basic plan is to present, periodically, papers of substantial length which focus on a central theoretical, research, or policy issue. The objective is twofold. First, the social scientist is freed from arbitrary space limitations. Second, by bringing together a number of papers on a related theme, fragmented publication is avoided, and the results of sociological research are made more available to related disciplines and professional specialists.

Most of the papers presented in this volume are an outgrowth of the Inter-University Seminar on Armed Forces and Society sponsored by Russell Sage Foundation. The purpose of the seminar was to supply a focal point for discussion and research on the changing nature of military organization in the United States. Against the backdrop of *The Professional Soldier: A Social and Political Portrait*, over a three-year period, 1960 to 1963, a series of research papers was discussed that sought to probe the extent to which the military establishment and the military profession were adapting to the new requirements of international relations. The members of the seminar wish to acknowledge the generous assistance of Russell Sage Foundation, as well as the guidance and stimulation of Dr. Leonard S. Cottrell, Jr., who actively participated in their deliberations. By means of the resources of the Inter-University Seminar, it was possible for the members to carry out their research and analysis on an independent basis. Thus this volume is not the report of the proceedings of a conference or symposium, but rather the result of the ongoing work of a number of social scientists. There has been no attempt to present these papers as if they constituted a unified intellectual approach; instead they are related original research studies.

The sociology of military institutions has been beclouded by the question of "values," in particular, the values of the sociologist. The fundamental assumption which has guided my own work was that the

7

study of military institutions was a legitimate object of scientific analysis. For it to be a legitimate object of scientific analysis it has to be approached on a realistic basis. It was necessary to strive to overcome distortions that come from hidden and even explicit biases, or from the pressures of political objectives. The sociology of military institutions becomes a meaningful enterprise only when scholars can project themselves into the institutional life of the military. In any institutional sector there is no understanding without some ability to take the role of the other.

In American sociology it was once widely assumed that to study military institutions was an expression of a particular political or value point of view. How many times have sociologists said to me with profound naiveté and without realizing their bias, why study the military and thereby make it better. The naiveté is based on an exaggeration of the consequences of sociological research; the bias, in that it is a distortion to believe that a more effective military is more dangerous than an inefficient institution.

In the contemporary period, academic hostility toward the study of military institutions is absent. This point of view is absent not because it has been eliminated but at least it can no longer be voiced with intellectual respectability. The members of the Inter-University Seminar yield to none in their personal concern with peace—or in their general interest in the responsible application of knowledge to social problems. But intellectual issues are not solved by fiat, by committee reports of professional associations, or even by the discussion of values. To the contrary, the intellectual relevance of the sociology of military institutions has to be grounded in its content and in its scholarly character. It is with this goal in mind that these research studies were assembled.

The field of social organization has its unfolding character in the specific writings of individual scholars who make use of comprehensive and quantitative field techniques, but those interests dedicate them to an understanding which comes only by prolonged and direct contact with the complexity of social institutions. This series on organizations and professions is related to the work of the newly created Center for Social Organization Studies of the University of Chicago, which is an experiment in graduate education and research designed to assist individual scholarship on the comparative study of social organization.

MORRIS JANOWITZ

Center for Social Organization Studies
University of Chicago
April 15, 1964

Part One

INTRODUCTION

Introduction

ORGANIZING MULTIPLE GOALS: WAR MAKING AND ARMS CONTROL

Morris Janowitz

IF THE HUMAN COMMUNITY were ever to free itself of disease and illness, the world would not be without doctors. But it is probable that under the conditions of a medical utopia, doctors would be called by another name. In fact, the term "public health doctor" is an expression of the powerful contemporary effort to transform the medical profession and increase its capacity for preventive practice.

Likewise, a world without war would not be a world without soldiers, or "specialists in violence." But the role of the professional soldier, even in the initial halting steps toward arms control, is a subject which needs to be clarified by social science analysis and resolved by public debate. In fact, there are two very different models of the role of the military in the international relations of arms control and disarmament. One set of assumptions excludes the military. This approach focuses on the explicit negotiation of civilian political leaders searching for the terms of reference to initiate treaties or agreements as the prime mechanisms. From this point of view, the organizational aspects of arms control are secondary and present few special problems beyond the technical features of inspection and the like. The basic issues are the political, social, and psychological requirements in order to ensure the success of the diplomatic and negotiating process. In one version or another this is the approach that runs through the bulk of the literature produced by university-based social scientists when they have written on this topic.[1]

The second model, and the one on which this volume proceeds, does not exclude the military from a positive role in arms control and disarmament. In this view there is more to the problem than political, social, and psychological preconditions for bargaining and negotiating at the diplomatic level. There is an organizational aspect. International relations, including arms control and disarmament, involve all the

11

institutions of foreign policy, political, economic, and military. It is not enough to speak of policies without a concern for the organizations that must implement policy, since policy per se is not self-enforcing. For example, arms control, whether it be a crash program for the removal of missile bases in Cuba, or a nuclear test ban, involves adjustment and response by the many agencies of international relations, including especially the military.

Over the long run, successful systems of accommodation and arms control would reduce the size of the military; but in the very short run, such schemes are likely to require a shift in the pattern of military activity. From this point of view each step and each type of international accommodation require new involvements and adaptations by the military if the accommodations of arms control are to be stable, relatively enduring, and expanding in scope. Thomas C. Schelling is one of the few writers on the theory of arms control who make use of this approach.[2]

THE CONSTABULARY CONCEPT AND ARMS CONTROL

Thus it becomes highly relevant to examine the actual and potential capacity of the armed forces to adjust and adapt to the problems of managing the instruments of violence when national policy is designed to avoid general war, and manage limited war so as to avoid general war. Obviously, this is a multifaceted problem; political, strategic, and organizational. The sociological analysis of the military must also deal with this problem. But for this purpose the sociologist must have a conceptual standpoint if his research is to bear on these policy problems and not be overwhelmed by the sheer complexities and dilemmas of change in a military force.

The notion of the constabulary force is a sociological contribution to understanding this organizational problem. In *The Professional Soldier: A Social and Political Portrait*, the constabulary concept is defined in the following way: "The military establishment becomes a constabulary force when it is continuously prepared to act, committed to the minimum use of force, and seeks viable international relations rather than victory because it has incorporated a protective military posture."[3] The constabulary force concept encompasses the entire range of military power and organization, including the military contribution to arms control and disarmament.

The constabulary concept and its equivalents are organizational concepts. Of course, they can be linked to different patterns of strategic thinking, for example, the kind of strategic thinking which emerged

and professional solidarity? How is participation in arms control and disarmament being integrated with the other aspects of the management of violence?

For this purpose the question needs to be asked: What is the present state of the sociology of military institutions? Over the past five years there has been a marked increase in intellectual activity. This is hardly to say that the specialty has reached a level of competence appropriate for the research problems and basic policy issues to which it addresses itself. Moreover, the progress that has been made is not the result of a large number of research workers or large expenditures of funds. There are still only a handful of sociologists in the United States who can be identified as "experts," in contrast, for example, to the more than three hundred specialists in medical sociology.

In *Sociology and the Military Establishment* the author made an effort to integrate the limited research accumulated in the fifteen years since the close of World War II into an analysis of the military as a social system.[8] The purpose was to present an analysis of the military establishment that highlighted the similarities and the differences from other types of bureaucratic organization. By contrast, *The Professional Soldier: A Social and Political Portrait*, while grounded in the view of the military establishment as a large-scale organization, was an exploration in elite analysis. It presented a body of empirical data on social background, career lines, professional ideology, and decision-making of the ranking military leadership. The task was to elaborate the study of a profession from the standpoint of organizational and political analysis. The study of a profession without reference to its internal political dynamics is a desiccated model of reality.

However, the publication of *The Professional Soldier* raised a range of fundamental questions for research and national policy. The study was based on a decade of individual scholarship. Relevant empirical and quantitative data were collected and the book did include a reanalysis of some large-scale surveys. But it was still an "old-fashioned" personal intellectual enterprise. The volume could at best be accepted as a benchmark requiring further effort. The interest in the volume only served to underline the importance of continued research.

Thus in a sense the present state of the sociological study of the military profession and military institutions in the United States can be in part assessed by the new data and research that have been produced since the appearance of *The Professional Soldier*. In fact, paradoxically, despite the limited number of social science specialists, there are now available more data and more analyses of aspects of the military profession than on many other professional groups in the United States. In this connection the following observations are relevant:

First, *The Professional Soldier*, as well as works by Samuel Huntington, John Masland, Laurence I. Radway, and Gene Lyons, helped to stimulate a debate within the profession.[9] Also, self-scrutiny and self-evaluation are standard operating procedures among professional officers. This posture stands in marked contrast, for example, to the medical and education professions. Mainly, however, the revolution in military technology produced an overriding need to adjust the military profession, especially its educational procedures. The result was an increased interest among military officers in contacts with civilians and in the findings of civilian social research. The result of social science studies of the military profession was to make the military, over the short term, more interested and more available to additional systematic social science research.

Second, in recent years the armed services themselves have made greater use of social research to generate significant data about their internal organizational and personnel structures. All of the services make use of periodic sample surveys which produce relevant data for operational needs and are indispensable for research purposes. In addition, the needs of civilian control have led to additional important research efforts. In particular, in 1960 the Armed Forces Committee of the United States Senate undertook a massive study of military personnel by means of a university study committee on which the author served. These materials are essential aspects of this volume, since they supply unique data on educational background, career patterns, and retirement matters.

Third, a small group of civilian specialists, many of whom are represented in this volume, have displayed, by current standards of social research, a long-term interest in the sociological aspect of the military. Although these specialists are very young men, their ten to fifteen years of specialization make them veterans. While they are engaged in a research dialogue with the military profession, their interests are mainly scholarly and not the product of contract research. As a result of these considerations, four years after the appearance of *The Professional Soldier*, a collection of research studies in depth is available which puts to test and revision many of its central hypotheses.

Four broad categories serve to examine selected aspects of the military establishment undergoing change. The first is *managerial format and succession*. The military establishment, like any organization, develops an operating structure. This structure has undergone tremendous change in direct response to the new types of military technology which have produced a managerial format emphasizing decision-making and command. But for the military, it is impossible to analyze organizational format without reference to the consequences of a succession, or rotation system, which constantly shifts personnel. Second, the military establishment, like any other profession, must induct, train, and indoctrinate new generations and develop in them a sense of professional identity. The concept *professional socialization* seems appropriate, since it encompasses both the deliberate and the traditional aspects of this process. The third category is the area of *social cohesion*, especially under prolonged stress. Sociological analysis in this regard makes use of notions of primary groups, sociometric choices, and group loyalties, the elements of social microsystems, in order to help explain the performance of military units regardless of their specific military task. The fourth category is the area of *career commitment and retirement*. In the traditional military establishment, career commitments were formed early and remained effective for long periods of time, if only because of the difficulties of transferring to civilian employment. In the contemporary armed forces, professional commitment must be continually reenforced and the multiple goals of the military only serve to complicate the task of maintaining professional commitments. Because of the expanded size of the military establishment and because of early retirement, the changing character of the military includes a large and ever-expanding cadre of retired officers and enlisted men.

DIMENSIONS OF ORGANIZATIONAL CHANGE

a. Managerial Format and Succession

In analyzing the actual and potential adaptation of the military, an overriding sociological consideration is that the military is a profession that can be practiced in only one organizational setting. Professional innovation may start within the services or be stimulated from the outside, but since there are no solo practitioners or free professionals, innovation to be effective requires organizational change. Thus in the case of the military the analysis of profession and bureaucratic organization fuse.

It has long been recognized that the military has pioneered in the development of new mechanisms to rationalize its operating procedures. The uncertainties of war plus the technological environment of the profession have led, since the turn of the century, to a persistent drive toward "scientific" management. This proclivity has been resisted by heroic ideals and concerns with personal honor. But in the past decade the impact of thermonuclear weapons and the changing role of force in international diplomacy have only served to speed up and intensify the pressure for rational and scientific procedures in internal administration. Kurt Lang, in his study, "Technology and Career Management in the Military Establishment," analyzes the newer forms of career development and military management best described as "technocratic." Career management is a term the military use to designate their planned efforts to adapt the military career to changing requirements. In his analysis Lang delineates the consequences of new technology and of new organizational devices such as performance budgeting, cost accounting, automated personnel systems, and the like, on the professional career of the officer and enlisted man.

Despite popular stereotypes, in many areas the military establishment is the prototype of rationalized and advanced bureaucratic structure. By the single measure of educational attainment of members, it is in advance of many other sectors of institutional life. In terms of rank stratification it has moved farther toward a "middle class" or middle majority hierarchy and decline of an unskilled lower class than have most industrial sectors. Moreover, to the extent that bureaucracy is based upon criteria of achievement, to that extent it should be prepared to make use of personnel without regard to racial considerations. The armed forces have gone farther than any other institutional sector of society in incorporating and upgrading Negro personnel.

But the study of career development in the military requires identifying the disruptions and limitations of a scientific management approach. Specifically, refined personnel systems often tend to create confusion and organizational strain through excessive centralization. More fundamentally, the very image of the military as a technological organization has several disruptive aspects. The military in many of its functions is a primitive organization achieving its goals by sheer impact of weight of numbers and personal effort, and scientific personnel management often tends to weaken these capacities.

The constabulary concept with its wide range of organizational goals implies that the military establishment must develop higher levels of skill specialization. Nevertheless, because of the need to respond to unanticipated situations and the heavy emphasis on leadership development, the military has resisted modification in its rotation system. In the logic of the armed forces, rotation is assumed to be essential for developing broad professional perspectives and for maintaining a capacity to respond to a crisis. Thus the system of periodic rotation even among highly specialized personnel continues to be one of the noteworthy characteristics of the military and one whose consequences for organizational effectiveness are difficult to gauge and even more difficult to study systematically.

While the advantages and disadvantages of routinized rotation are being debated within the military establishment, it has become an approach that is exploited more and more in business corporations. The very large-scale nature of American business requires the equivalent of military systems of rotation. In studying the effect of rotation and succession, Oscar Grusky seeks to compare a military base and a relatively comparable business organization, with the result that for the first time there is a body of systematic data that permit some contrasts. A rather similar hierarchy of ranks operates in the military base and in the business firm under study, although they are only loosely comparable in other organizational aspects.

Because of the more routinized rotation and earlier retirement policies in the military, the military base revealed a marked homogeneous grouping at each hierarchical level. This finding was to be anticipated. The real problematic issue was the effect of rotation on the exercise of authority. Grusky is able to demonstrate that, as measured by the officer's feeling of the amount of authority he has, the longer he stays on the base the greater his sense of authority, especially at the top ranks. While this relationship exists in the business organization, it is less clearcut and operates mainly at the middle ranks. Thus the system of rotation in the military establishment conditions and weakens personal executive authority and encourages the development of a general acceptance of professional and organizational authority.

While no generalization can be drawn from these two specific comparisons about commitment, in the military establishment commitment is much higher than in the business organization. Furthermore, and striking, is the conclusion that length of tenure in a military installation is not related to strength of commitment but rather that the strength of commitment to the military organization is a function of underlying professional attitudes.

By use of comparative analysis it is also possible to examine systematically participation of military officers and business personnel in community life and the impact of rotation on such participation. The argument has been raised that regular rotation makes difficult social participation outside of professional duties. This issue of the "rootlessness" of organization personnel has special meaning for the military where the danger exists that the day-to-day pressures of a constabulary force tend to create a self-contained group removed from community integration and isolated from the values of society as a whole. Grusky's analysis reveals, as expected, that military officers participate more extensively in community affairs than do their counterparts in business. Because succession is anticipated, military personnel develop attitudes which are supported by internal administrative programs and which result in a compensation for the disruption of rotation. In effect, officers develop extensive forms of participation which reflect a self-concept that officers are active leaders. There appears also to be a social stratification effect. The officer tends more often than his counterpart in the business organization to think of himself as higher in the social status system (he is more likely to describe himself as upper-middle class as opposed to merely middle class). As a result, he displays the greater community involvement associated with higher social status.

b. Professional Socialization

Professional socialization focuses on the values that military personnel develop. For example, before 1939 it was a universal belief among the professional military that the outbreak of war was inevitable—that is, in the inevitability of major conflicts. This was one of the core orientations which officers came to hold. In *The Professional Soldier*, the proposition was offered and supported with limited but relevant documentation that, with the development of thermonuclear weapons, the military profession was no longer universally committed to this belief. In fact, a majority of selected officer groups no longer held this expectation. To the extent that this belief is no longer part of the self-conception of the military, to that extent it can be said that they have moved toward the constabulary concept of the management of violence.

The belief in the inevitability of major war is an expression of an "absolutist" point of view, while the rejection of this proposition is an indicator of a more "pragmatic" approach to the role of violence in international relations. Exploration of this proposition is of the highest priority for the study of the adaptation of the military to international relations. John P. Lovell, in his study, "The Professional Socialization of the West Point Cadet," probed this issue.

Central to his analysis is the dramatic finding that the inevitability of war—that is, all-out war—is held only by a minority (approximately one-third) of those who enter the military academy and that this point of view seems to decrease somewhat among those who graduate. One would, of course, expect important differences between the services and among different age cohorts. But these cadets still have a military professional outlook, in that most (80 per cent) agree with the proposition that "limited conventional war between the United States and Communist forces is likely within fifteen years." The inevitability is the continuation of the struggle in narrower and more limited military terms. But in this issue the attitudes of the West Point cadets are very similar to a comparable sample of Dartmouth undergraduates.

Lovell's study makes possible a deeper understanding of attitude change among these military cadets. There is relatively little change in strategic outlook, since the Academy does not or cannot enforce rigid adherence to a specific service outlook. Self-selection into the military seems more important. Undoubtedly, subsequent career experiences continue to operate in fashioning and refashioning such attitudes. Since the cadets' outlook reflects their civilian backgrounds, the resulting pattern of attitudes is not grossly unrepresentative of equivalent elements in civilian society. By contrast, the Academy modifies their specific professional interests, as between different specialties in the military. Undoubtedly, the Academy molds fundamental commitments to the military profession, but this impact can be studied only years after graduation.

The study avoided direct probing of political attitudes. The military would not permit such investigation. Equally important in a political democracy, it is assumed that in his professional role the military officer will be nonpartisan and it is improper for social scientists to violate this assumption, unless there is explicit evidence that the military officer does not adhere to this logic.

But Lovell's investigation is more than a charting of stability and change in attitude structure. He seeks to demonstrate some of the underlying organizational changes in the military academy as it faces the problems of training for the constabulary force. He discovers that the task of professional socialization becomes more complex, not only because of the required higher levels of academic and skill training, but also because of two other factors. First, the representativeness and the heterogeneity of the incoming cadets continue to increase so that the task of developing professional perspectives is compounded. Second, the sheer size of the Academy continues to increase, making the use of traditional interpersonal influence much more complicated.

Professional self-image alters only gradually under the impact of changing technology and changing patterns of international relations. One revealing source of information about long-term trends in the self-conceptions of the military is the content of the sponsored service journals. The military establishment, like other large-scale institutions, cannot operate merely on the basis of written directives and orders. It requires a forum of communication; namely, professional journals, where the basic issues of the profession are discussed within prescribed limits. M. D. Feld analyzes the key Army and Navy service journals for the period 1938 to 1959, recognizing that these journals have been transformed from primarily internal house organs to specialized media with outside audiences.

Throughout this whole period, the field grade officer was the most frequent contributor in the columns of the service journals. It is through the middle ranks that the discussion of issues of innovation is mainly pursued. While the field grade officer still predominates, the junior officer has suffered a marked decline in representation, and the new element is the growth in prominence of civilian contributors and the more frequent appearance by high-ranking officers. In terms of content, historical and narrow technical articles have declined, while broad conceptual articles dealing with applied strategy and civil-military issues have increased and set the basic elements of the professional self-image.

Feld's frame of reference for the content analysis derives from the technological environment within which the military establishment operates. He is concerned with the well-recognized transformation of the military establishment from a relatively self-contained organization (in his terms, primitive) to a complex and civilian interrelated agency (in his terms, a competitive organization). Findings on the Navy journal clearly indicated that the process of change had already started initially for this service before World War II. The Army, when confronted with the realities of technological change during World War II, fluctuated more sharply toward the competitive model during the post-World War II period, while the Navy continued its process of gradual change. Thus, as of 1958, the Navy had developed a self-image that was basically competitive and managerial but still embodied important and clearcut elements of the primitive approach, while the Army was still seeking a fusion of the traditional military self-conceptions with contemporary technological and constabulary requirements. In short, as reflected in their journals, a broad-scale change in professional identity in the Navy started early, was more gradual, and resulted in a more stable self-image, while in the Army change began later and produced more marked response and greater instability.

c. Social Cohesion

The assessment of the capacity of the military to adapt or resist change also requires analysis of the underlying microsystems or primary groups on which professional and organizational solidarity rests. This is true for any institutional setting. But if one is to speak of the intellectual contributions of sociology of military institutions to the broader discipline, it has been precisely in emphasizing the role of intimate face-to-face relations in influencing organizational performance. The intellectual residues of research during World War II as embodied in "Cohesion and Disintegration in the Wehrmacht"[10] and the attitude research of *The American Soldier*[11] highlighted the importance of cohesion as a basis for combat effectiveness. The dramatic discovery that group cohesion rather than ideological motivation is the basis for understanding contemporary military "morale" continues to be reaffirmed by subsequent research. But to speak of the contributions of cohesive primary group structures to organizational cohesion is not necessarily to overlook the variety of other factors, such as types of authority, status systems, incentives, internal communication processes, skill structure, and commitment to organizational goals, as well as the specific contributions of the ideological picture itself. To state the case in other terms, primary group solidarity is not enough. The groups must be articulated with and dedicated to the goals of the larger organization, for primary group solidarity can develop into a basis of opposition to military requirements.

Whether the task of a constabulary force involves limited war or the maintenance of a surveillance system for arms control, its capacity to resist prolonged stress is in question. The experiences of group cohesion in the Korean Conflict are relevant in this respect. Lt. Col. Roger W. Little presents in "Buddy Relations and Combat Performance," by means of sociometric analysis and participation observation, an intensive analysis of social solidarity in a rifle company engaged in defensive action at the forward edge of the battle area in Korea.

Under these conditions, primary group relations involved a diffuse attachment toward members of one's platoon, and a specific attachment to another single person with whom the soldier had developed a basis of mutual support. In a sense, the pressures of the military situation produced more simple primary groups based on a two-person system in contrast to wider networks of four to six or eight men as observed in World War II.

Military policies also tended to weaken and to narrow the basis of social solidarity. Because "Korea" was a limited war, intense rotation procedures were employed to equalize sacrifice. The result was a restriction of opportunity to develop personal loyalties. The actual exercise of authority also weakened primary group solidarity. Nevertheless, fundamental attachments persisted which, together with the contributions of small unit leaders, created a mutual support system that made it possible for this type of combat organization to achieve its specific and limited objectives.

Fundamentally, Roger Little implies that the task of maintaining group cohesion for constabulary units generally becomes more complicated and more difficult. Because of the limited involvement of the supporting society, there is greater necessity for reward based on actual achievement rather than on formal position. The need to modify authority toward a heavier reliance on consensus increases and becomes more overriding as the unit must rely predominantly on its own internal resources.

As a contribution to the social psychology of group formation, Little finds that when military primary groups are faced with external threats, the group response as cohesion weakens is not primarily the emergence of social isolates or individuals concerned with their own survival. It is not even the development of smaller cliques, although this may be a transitional phase. The group response is the persistence and emergence of two-person systems as the minimum social units of interaction which make possible the survival of the functional group and its ability to operate at least at a minimal level. A similar conclusion about the response of military groups under stress was reached by Richard Seaton in an extensive field experiment involving military work groups exposed to experimental stress on the icecaps of Greenland. He also discovered that the group response to stress and the weakening of cohesion produced the two-person defensive systems. Furthermore, as in the case of the Korean situation, Seaton found no diminution of diffuse attachments to members of the work team as a whole as a result of having undergone stress.

The experimental study of military work groups exposed to deprivation on the icecaps of Greenland is a rewarding undertaking which has all of the elements of a rigorous experiment in academic social psychology. But it needs also to be evaluated as a reflection of military values and military ethos. The experiment was presumably undertaken with policy objectives in mind to improve the capacity of the ground forces to operate in the extreme environs of the Arctic. But as one reads parts of the original reports and the final analysis, it is clear that this enterprise was another example of the traditional participation of the military in exploration, undertaken as an act in and of itself.

The experiment was comprehensive and detailed and far more meaningful than the typical laboratory research. The military establishment was prepared to make available abundant resources in the name of exploration and science. Thus a special field operation was undertaken in which men engaged in a work trek over icy wastelands under a variety of different experimental conditions in which the timing of the operation, the nature of the work task, and most dramatically, the amount of food intake were controlled. Under frigid conditions, elaborate physiological observations and repeated interviews and questionnaires were administered. The dramatic aspects of the experiment were the elaborate efforts to ensure the safety and well-being of the participants, and yet make certain that the experimental conditions were real and significant.

In the writer's opinion the experiment goes about as far in the physical manipulation of human beings as is compatible with scientific responsibility and human dignity. There was no deception of subjects. Again, the impact of the military situation and the nature of the environment made the experiment more real and therefore less manipulative.

At first glance this kind of research seems far removed from the organizational requirements for a constabulary force. And in a sense this is the case. But a careful appraisal of the conclusions indicates that when the constabulary forces operate under extreme environmental conditions, sheer levels of personal energy emerge as powerful determinants of organizational performance. Thus these experiments highlight the primitive nature of aspects of military organization even in a technological age.

d. Career Commitment and Retirement

The transformation of the military establishment hinges upon its ability to maintain a cadre of trained career officers. In managing such a cadre, the military, like any profession, must find a balance between serving the career needs of its members and meeting the requirements of the profession. This problem is of special importance for the military because it assumes that it has unique problems of recruitment and especially of retention of personnel. There are the risks and discomforts of the profession; there are the limited monetary rewards, especially for outstanding personnel; and there are the self-imposed definitions of the personal career required of a good officer.

Traditionally, the approach to handling recruitment and career commitment has been to train a small core of professionals in the service academies whose number could be expanded by reservists and civilian soldiers. The combination of special professional socialization at the academies and superior career opportunities produced lifetime commitment among these officers. Since World War II an expanded military establishment could no longer meet its officer needs by this formula. The armed forces have come to rely on the service academies less for sheer numbers and more for professional solidarity.

They have been forced to use as career officers men recruited from a variety of sources. It thus becomes a crucial question to determine the relative importance of the type of commission as compared with professional experiences in fashioning career commitments among military officers. Our underlying hypothesis was that while in the past, type of commission was the most important single consideration in fashioning long-term and intense career commitment, in the expanded military establishment actual career opportunities emerge as more important. In other words, the differences between academy and selected groups of nonacademy officers have declined, at least over the short run, in willingness to pursue a full military career.

This is just a specific case of the transformation of institutional life in modern society. With a broadening of the base of recruitment and with an increased degree of career specialization, education (prior socialization) declines in importance in determining professional commitments while actual career experience and in-service training (professional socialization) increases in importance. Sociologists seldom gain access to a profession on a broad enough basis to collect the essential data to test this significant hypothesis. For the military the relevant data are available from the study sponsored by the Armed Services Committee of the United States Senate, and are analyzed by Mayer Zald and William Simon in their essay, "Career Opportunities and Commitments Among Military Officers."

Since the services cannot rely on Academy graduates, they must be able to develop career commitments among a proportion of officers who are merely filling their obligations without any strong prior commitment. The data indicate that service academy graduates persist in their strong career commitments and correspondingly maintain a disproportionate access to higher career opportunities. However, for the Officer Candidate School and Reserve Officer Training Corps officers, the actual career opportunities that are provided to them, and facilitated by continuing in-service education, supply the basis for developing a professional commitment to the military establishment. These career opportunities can develop powerful professional commitments among the nonacademy officers. Most striking is the conclusion that the transferability of skills to civilian life does not decrease commitment to the military career. To the contrary, for men with all types of commissions, commitment to a military career is much more closely tied to a feeling that one's skill is actually being utilized.

These findings reaffirm the conclusion that to the extent that the military develops overritualized forms and fails to employ effectively its officers, to that extent it weakens professional attachment. The constabulary force requires specific civilian-type functions compatible with its resources such as emergency disaster functions; it must also develop a variety of garrison contests which operate as realistic military training for its personnel. Likewise, there is every reason to believe that programs of continuing in-service education become more and more important in satisfying professional needs. The military establishment has since the turn of the century been a vast training establishment and the emphasis on training increases. No experiment is more dramatic than the incorporation of advance degree programs by the Air Force in its missile bases in order to present positive and meaningful objectives for men who must perform a "fire department" type of assignment. But the importance of continuing education as a basis for professional self-esteem is not to be judged by selected and special educational programs, but the extent to which it has been diffused throughout the whole armed forces.

Again, this is not a new dimension but one that takes on new meaning because of the changes in skill and professional tenure. Military service for both officers and enlisted personnel is becoming more and more the first phase in a two-phase career in which the soldier leaves the military service in midcareer for civilian employment. Professional training and education prepare him not only for military service but for civilian employment after retirement. In this regard, we face the paradoxical situation that the officer or enlisted man with the most military-type skills has the least transferability to civilian employment. Thus it is clearly a requirement of the constabulary force that military personnel be trained and prepared for orderly transition to civilian life.

Albert D. Biderman, in "Sequels to a Military Career: The Retired Military Professional," presents a description of the dimensions of the problem—contemporary and in the future. Basically, the costs of military retirement are deferred costs of war and national defense. Current practices of continuous promotion or selection out, plus early retirement, increase the number of retired personnel. There are, of course, alternative possibilities in personnel policies. On the one hand, greater flexibility could be achieved (as is the case in the Royal Air Force) by short service of five to ten years to meet the need for junior officers who would then be separated with a lump sum payment rather than lifetime benefits. On the other hand, it would be possible to follow a policy of the retention of personnel who after fifteen or twenty years would not be eligible for promotion but who are needed for their special skills or experience. While both of these procedures would cut down the number of future retired personnel, it is difficult to anticipate all of the organizational consequences of such policies.

Biderman's study assumes a continuation of present policies and focuses on the legal and institutional barriers to transfer in an orderly fashion from military service to civilian employment. The problems of military retirement are destined to be compounded, since the contemporary total of 350,000 will increase steadily as career officers and enlisted men of the expanded forces of World War II complete their twenty years of service. The available data indicate that for a significant minority retirement involves a clearcut and measurable reduction in income and a loss of social status that is difficult to judge. The trend in the military is toward a more explicit recognition of this problem because, at a minimum, the social and economic consequences are certain to influence the recruitment of new cadres. But in its fullest scope, the issue is a societal wide one if the retired professional is to be incorporated into civilian life without political disruption.

Finally, an organizational analysis of the American military establishment requires comparison with the military of other nations and particularly with the military of the so-called "new nations." In particular, comparative sociology of the past decade has become concerned with distinguishing modernization from westernization. The military establishments of the new nations are based upon technology and organizational patterns rooted in western institutions. Thus the analysis of the armed forces of the new nations as they are evolving requires identifying their generic characteristics and those which are an expression of particular cultural and societal environments.

The military establishments of these new nations are centrally involved in internal order and political power. Thus it is necessary to explore on a comparative basis the ability of these military establishments to contribute to political stability and to reduce internal violence and internal war. As representative of the current interests of social scientists, Moshe Lissak presents a selected guide to the literature of revolutions and coups d'état in the developing nations. Through this literature it is possible to raise, if not answer, central questions about the management of conflict in the processes of social change in new nations. This literature, although still fragmentary, related to a crucial aspect of the military establishment in its constabulary dimensions because by means of military assistance it has become United States policy to mobilize the armed forces of the new nations and Latin America to assist in the modernization of their countries. It is already clear that the military's capacity to accumulate political power under these circumstances is greater than its ability to govern as a ruling group. The available research provides clues concerning the dilemmas a military oligarchy faces when it seeks to exercise direct national political power.

Elsewhere, the author has offered the following proposition: "The 'takeover' of power by the military in new nations has generally followed the collapse of efforts to create democratic-type institutions; the military has tended not to displace the single mass party authoritarian political regimes. After 'takeover,' the military regime faces the task of supplying national political leadership and of developing mass support for its programs. While this phase is only emerging, the evidence seems to indicate that, if the military is to succeed in this political goal, it must develop a political apparatus outside of the military establishment but under its direct domination."[12] In short, military regimes are at best incomplete and transitional.

ARMED FORCES AND SOCIETY

The focus in this volume is on the internal organization of the military. But the sociological analysis of the military encompasses the "armed forces and society," the role of the military in social, economic, and political change. It does not seem that the concept of the military as a pressure group, one conventional approach to this problem, is adequate, if only because of the vast resources at its disposal. For example, defense budgets have become an integral aspect of the domestic economy and under present management contribute that margin which constitutes the basis of economic prosperity. But it is precisely as a pressure group that the military operates in influencing political decisions about national defense policy. Unfortunately, there is very little continuing research on the mechanics of the military and related voluntary associations as pressure groups. In a democratic system, pressure groups are part of the political process if their activities remain within bounds; disclosure, legislative bargaining, and political party supremacy are the available devices of control. Moreover, no pressure group can be permitted to develop excessive political influence. In the case of the military, since it is an administrative agency of government, the requirement of political neutrality and adherence to civilian direction is supposed to operate to contain its political involvement. But it is the scope of the influence of the military that continues to be the central issue.

Again the concept of the constabulary is relevant, for the constabulary concept is seen as a professional formula designed to enhance effective political supremacy by the political parties and the organs of civilian government. The constabulary concept is designed to help modernize the balance between civilian supremacy and professional responsibility. It is a concept designed to enhance the self-regulating dimensions of the military profession. It does not assume that civilian supremacy will rest on self-regulation, but it does assume that civilian supremacy is greatly enhanced by such self-regulation.

In a democratic society the pressures of limited war and even the strains of maintaining operational readiness can contribute to weakening this process of self-regulation and the development of rigid and extremist political demands. Military men who are exposed to hardships, dangers, and frustrations run the risk of alienation from the large society. For example, military intervention in South Vietnam presents such a potential. Military management has responded vigorously in order to prevent such alienation, by speeding up the normal processes of rotation. Thereby the hardships that one person must endure are limited and the sacrifice diffused. As a result, there is great resistance to drawing possible parallels between American military intervention in South Vietnam and other similar historical engagements. It may be justified, especially if the comparisons involve the type of response that was produced in the French Army after World War II. But what are the consequences at the level of the military as a pressure group? This is a military operation in which each officer, regardless of rank, becomes a political agent and develops new political perspectives. In the language of the military, South Vietnam is producing a new "breed" of professional soldier. The impact of this military experience is only dimly perceived by the military itself and by civilian society. The categories and concepts of these papers may also be relevant for understanding the impact of this experience on the military profession.

NOTES

1. See particularly Wright, Quincy, William M. Evan, and Morton Deutsch, editors, *Preventing World War III*, Simon and Schuster, Inc., New York, 1962.

2. Schelling, Thomas C., "A Special Surveillance Force" in Wright, Evan, and Deutsch, editors, *op. cit.*, pp. 87–105.

3. Janowitz, Morris, *The Professional Soldier: A Social and Political Portrait.* The Free Press of Glencoe, New York, 1960, p. 418.

4. Millis, Walter, and James Real, *The Abolition of War.* Macmillan Co., New York, 1963.

5. Schelling, Thomas C., *op. cit.*, pp. 87–105.

6. *Ibid.*, p. 87.

7. *Ibid.*

8. Janowitz, Morris, *Sociology and the Military Establishment.* Russell Sage Foundation, New York, 1959.

9. Huntington, Samuel, *The Soldier and the State*, Belknap, Harvard University Press, Cambridge, Mass., 1957; Masland, John W., and Laurence I. Radway, *Soldiers and Scholars*, Princeton University Press, Princeton, N. J., 1957; and Lyons, Gene M., and John W. Masland, *Education and Military Leadership: A Study of the ROTC*, Princeton University Press, Princeton, N. J., 1959.

10. Shils, Edward A., and Morris Janowitz, "Cohesion and Disintegration in the Wehrmacht in World War II," *Public Opinion Quarterly*, vol. 12, Summer, 1948, pp. 280–315.

11. Stouffer, Samuel A., and others, *The American Soldier: Studies in Social Psychology in World War II.* Princeton University Press, Princeton, N. J., 1949.

12. Janowitz, Morris, *The Military in the Political Development of New Nations.* University of Chicago Press, Chicago, 1964, p. 29.

Part Two

MANAGERIAL FORMS AND SUCCESSION

Part Two

MANAGERIAL FORMS AND SUCCESSION

TWO MODES OF ANALYSIS are open to the sociologist when he studies the military establishment undergoing change. One approach is to focus on internal processes, with the result that his empirical findings tend to emphasize the similarity of military organization and other class organization: industrial, education, religious, and the like. This is the perspective that has come to be called organizational theory and in which military institutions are seen as one social system among many other social systems.

On the other hand, and by no means incompatible, is the approach that focuses on the goals and tasks of military organization. This is the approach of comparative institutional analysis. The intellectual concern is on the particular consequences of technology and military goals on military organization. The empirical results focus on systematic differences between various classes of organizations.

Clearly, most research on organization represents some admixture of these approaches. The work of the Inter-University Seminar has been to emphasize goal analysis and comparative perspectives. The realities of military institutions and especially the revolution in military technology, as well as the policy implication of the constabulary concept, lead in this direction.

When one seeks to study the special characteristics of the military as part of a strategy of comparative analysis, managerial format becomes a central concern. Managerial format encompasses the system of authority and communication patterns that are used to maintain control because the organization is dealing with such destructive instruments of violence. But to the outside observer this managerial format of control is juxtaposed to a system of routine rotation and succession in which personnel are continuously shifted from post to post. It is this automatic system of rotation that is so striking a feature of military life. The tension between the operating principles of organizational control and regularized rotation can best be seen in those units where rotation is modified for the key personnel who manage the most destructive weapons. For example, in the Strategic Air Command, during the period of reliance on manned bombers for strategic deterrence, special rules of tenure were applied to flying and highly specialized personnel. But the dilemmas of organization control versus the principles of systematic rotation pervade the entire military establishment.

Thus a first step in the analysis of the military at a time when both complex systems of nuclear weapons and limited war technology have been incorporated into the center of the command system, is to examine its managerial format, including the system of rotation. The managerial format system not only controls weapons systems; it is also a format for managing the career development of officers and enlisted men. In the language of the sociologist, what is the pattern of social stratification and mobility in the military? In the language of the military officer, what are the organizational consequences of career management that seek to use the devices of scientific management in the military setting: automated personnel, recordkeeping, psychological testing, cost accounting, and performance budgeting? The military establishment is being converted into a cost accounting system in which even the chaplain function is being managed by cost estimates and time budgets for burial and bereavement activities.

The available documentation based on operating statistics and sample surveys makes it possible to present a structural analysis of the military establishment as an advanced form of technocratic management in which skill levels and educational background are very high and the pressure for rational decision-making most powerful. But the analysis of the actual social organization of the military highlights the inherent limitations on a purely rational format, especially the inherent limitation that emerges in any highly centralized organization. Moreover, the military as a management organization—which strives for a merit basis for promotion—develops deep and identifiable dilemmas because many of the key activities are still accomplishment by primitive expenditure of energy or by sheer improvisation in the face of uncertainty or new environments.

But it is not only the primitive nature of military functions that impose limitation on organization and career management. Disruption and strain are linked to the rotation system which is assumed to be an integral part of career management. The rotation system has special importance for the military because the armed forces operate on the notion that they must recruit top leadership from within their ranks. The military function is seen as indivisible in this respect. To probe the consequences of rotation it was useful to compare the military with a business organization. The focus of the empirical materials that are presented is not the highest level of the command and management where basic issues of policy and strategy are influenced by rotation, but at the middle levels of the organization where career commitment, exercise of day-to-day authority and integration of the officer with the larger society are at stake. The research design did not encompass the question of personnel resignation. Nevertheless, the data indicate that the military establishment has been able to develop internal practices and policies which reduce, or at least contain, some of the disruptive consequences of regularized personnel rotation.

TECHNOLOGY AND CAREER MANAGEMENT
IN THE MILITARY ESTABLISHMENT *

Kurt Lang

THE ARMED FORCES, like all organizations, are responsive in varying
degrees to changing internal and external requirements. Developments in the technology of warfare, which have increased the range and
destructive power of weapons, and changes in the level of skill, force
adaptations in the structure of military organization. The broad outline
of historical change is unambiguous. Armed forces whose mainstay was
once a postfeudal aristocracy and whose officer corps functioned as
quasi-autonomous estates have everywhere been professionalized.

Among the attributes of a profession, as that term is commonly
understood, are an emphasis on objectively recognizable performance
criteria and self-surveillance by a body of colleagues to enforce standards.[1] Possession of skill that is easily acquired by anyone does not
qualify a group of practitioners as a profession. In addition, the professional label is a mark of prestige, which then justifies the exclusiveness
of the group possessing the skill. Professional career armies, like the
aristocratic armies they replaced, have sought to control entry. The
basic change has been the principle of selection. A decline in the number
of aristocratic officers took place in the armed forces of every modern
nation as the expertise requisite to effective performance gradually displaced ascriptive criteria based on social origin and family tradition.[2]

Despite an increasingly open recruitment policy, the military has
nevertheless continued to rely heavily on its own training institutions.
Experience in military academies or service as junior officers under close
supervision by superiors is designed to promote a unified outlook. Self-enforcement of a professional code of conduct, which incorporates the
value of disinterested service to society, also ensures a degree of insulation against outside intervention. Still another peculiarity of the profes-

* A special note of thanks is due the many officers and civilians in the military
establishment who freely shared their own insights and provided leads to much useful
data, and to Albert Biderman and Roger Little for their cogent comments on an
earlier version of this paper.

39

sion is that military skills, because of their nature, cannot be practiced outside the specific institutional context provided by the military establishment. The true military professional is the person who makes the military his primary lifetime commitment.[3] The enlisted man, whose contractual obligation to serve must be renewed after each term of enlistment, is excluded by this definition.

In order to understand the transformation in the military establishment, especially under the impact of the new technology of the past twenty years, it is necessary to broaden our focus beyond professionalism and professionalization. The military is a complex, large-scale organization in which professionalization has been subject to extensive bureaucratic management. Career management is the term employed by the military services to describe the process of explicit and planned adaptation of the profession to change. Examination of the processes of career management supplies a perspective for understanding the formal structure and the organizational realities of the military, both in a period of cold war and at the threshold of new forms of international relations, including possibly arms control arrangements.

At the surface, the newly emerging forms of career development and military management can best be described as *technocratic*, reflecting that revolution in technology that has affected the structure of society no less than it has the military establishment. Advanced "scientific" procedures developed in industrial, academic, and military laboratories are rapidly adopted by the military organization in attempts to attract, train, and retain men with essential military skills. The combined impact of the new requirements confronting the military establishment is to undermine, rather than support, the older forms of control typical of a self-contained profession and to bring to the fore a system of rationally managed career incentives.

Here we describe and analyze the broad organizational outlines of the military establishment as it seeks to apply the principles of scientific management, cost accounting, and performance budgeting. Statistics that reflect both administrative arrangements and actual patterns of personnel management on a service-wide basis provide our primary source of data. The emphasis is on those characteristics that can be observed in the aggregate; or, in other words, the emphasis is on the organization of the military establishment as a whole.

To be certain, the present structure is fashioned by former policies and can only be altered slowly by administrative decision. In fact, the heritage of the past has not simply produced three separate services, but each service itself represents a variety of fused military systems derived from gradual and constant adaptation to historical change. Wherever available, the data presented cover changes in each of the services over approximately a twenty-year period and similarly reflect the influence of service traditions as well as the contemporary requirements of service missions.

The influence of technology on an organization has limits and can easily be exaggerated. The fact that the military, like any organization, is a human system curtails the effectiveness of rational principles of organization. In particular, because of the heroic element of combat, the military is a unique mixture of rational organization and nonlogical traditions and sentiments. Thus while the emphasis in this analysis is on the broad organizational features of the military establishment and its personnel system, it is recognized that each element in the system produces organizational strains which key commanders must either resolve or learn to tolerate. One of the basic dilemmas is that involving the articulation of an orderly military career with the needs of the military service. This traditional dilemma continues as a central issue even when military careers are explicitly managed rather than taken for granted.

MANPOWER REQUIREMENTS

Military manpower requirements are fundamentally affected by the military mission. The armed forces of the United States are no longer concerned primarily with localized threats at national frontiers, but with a permanent threat of worldwide dimensions. Any local engagement can quickly lead to a confrontation of the major power blocs. Therefore the capacity for an instantaneous response with weapons of increased variety and firepower leads to the military requirement for a vastly expanded, permanent establishment ready for immediate action.

The severe cutback in the size of the armed forces after World War II still expressed the older concept of small standing forces as a base for mobilization in an emergency. Since Korea, the United States has maintained its armed forces at expanded strength with less oscillation in size. In contrast to previous eras, the cessation of active hostilities has involved a less drastic reduction of military forces (Table 1). Expanded standing forces require a larger core of career personnel with an extended commitment to military service and the continuous replacement of recruits whose military service is of short duration.

But much more far-reaching in their consequences than the higher numerical requirements are the qualifications of military personnel, especially those who make service in the armed forces their career. Very little is indeed gained if levels of experience and competence fall below

TABLE 1. TOTAL ACTIVE DUTY MILITARY PERSONNEL IN THE
UNITED STATES, 1916–1960

Period	Number	Ratio of Change[a]
Pre-World War I		
June 30, 1916	179,376	—
World War I peak		
November 11, 1918	4,315,239	24
Post-World War I low		
June 30, 1933	243,845	.06
Pre-World War II		
June 30, 1939	334,473	1.4
World War II peak		
May 31, 1945	12,124,418	36
Post-World War II low		
May 31, 1948	1,398,726	.12
Korean Conflict Peak		
April 30, 1952	3,685,054	2.6
Post-Korean Conflict		
June 30, 1960	2,476,435	.67

[a] Strength in the given period as ratio of strength in preceding period.

SOURCE: Statistics issued by the Statistical Services Center, Office of Secretary of Defense, August 19, 1960.

those consistent with efficient performance. Quantitative and qualitative requirements must somehow be equated.

The need in the military establishment for unskilled manpower has declined rapidly and the demand for technically competent manpower increased correspondingly. For example, in 1942 there were only two Army enlisted jobs in the Radar and Fire Control field; there were 27 in 1958, plus 72 jobs in guided missiles and 9 in atomic weapons, two fields in which there had previously been none. The more complex the technology, the more maintenance it requires. Thus according to estimates given before a congressional committee, the Air Force averaged 51.2 maintenance hours for each hour of flying time of the B-47 bomber. This increased to 115.6 hours for the B-52 and was judged to be even higher for the B-58 in 1959.[4] These requirements have produced a marked shift in the occupational structure of the armed forces in the direction of increased jobs in the electronics, technical, and repair fields (Table 2), which together accounted for 34 per cent of all jobs at the end of World War II, for 39 per cent during the Korean Conflict, and for 47 per cent by the end of 1958. Most of this gain was at the expense of ground combat assignments, which dropped during this same period from 24 per cent to 13 per cent of all enlisted jobs.

The allocation of higher proportions of manpower to technical functions occurs in all services, although not to the same degree. The Air Force stands out clearly as the most "technical" among the services,

TABLE 2. DISTRIBUTION OF ENLISTED JOBS BY MAJOR
OCCUPATIONAL GROUPS

Major Occupational Group	End of World War II	During Korean Conflict	December 31, 1958
	(Percentages)		
Electronics	6.2	9.6	13.5
Other technical	6.9	6.9	7.4
Mechanics and Repairmen	21.3	22.6	25.8
Total technical	34.4	39.1	46.7
Administrative and Clerical	15.3	20.8	20.6
Crafts and Services	26.7	22.7	19.4
Ground Combat	23.6	17.4	12.9
Total	100.0	100.0	100.0

SOURCE: Wool, Harold, "The Armed Services as a Training Institution" in Ginzberg, Eli, editor, *The Nation's Children*. Columbia University Press, New York, 1959, vol. 2, p. 166. Based on personnel assigned to units in all the services.

with a greater preponderance of "technical and scientific" personnel and "mechanics and repairmen" (Table 3). This technological concentration trend was already evident in World War II. In fact, the Air Force in its current classification scheme does not retain a category for "military-type occupations." Meanwhile, the Air Force's share of military manpower has grown steadily. As an auxiliary branch of the Army at the start of World War II, Air Corps units at that time accounted for about

TABLE 3. OCCUPATIONAL STRUCTURE OF SERVICES, ENLISTED
PERSONNEL, 1954

Occupational Group	Marine Corps	Army	Navy	Air Force
	(Percentages)			
I. Technical and Scientific	8.9	14.5	13.4	21.7
II. Administrative and Clerical	18.9	17.4	8.0	23.7
III. Mechanics and Repairmen	17.4	12.5	22.2	24.5
IV. Craftsmen	5.6	8.0	3.7	4.8
V. Service	6.2	10.4	6.4	20.7
VI. Operatives and Laborers	7.2	8.4	a	4.6
VII. Military-type Occupations Not Elsewhere Classified	35.8	28.8	46.3	a
Total	100.0	100.0	100.0	100.0
Proportion in Groups I and III	26.3	27.0	35.8	46.2

a Where no percentages are shown, services classify this type of personnel in alternate groups. (Author's comment: occupational classifications were not identical and hence distributions are approximations.)

SOURCE: U.S. President's Commission on Veterans' Pensions, *Veterans' Benefits in the United States: Findings and Recommendations*, April, 1956.

8 per cent of total military personnel, rising to approximately 20 per cent of the peak strength in World War II. During the Korean Conflict the Air Force stood at more than 25 per cent and by 1960 accounted for one-third of the total.

Overall shifts in military occupational structure also reflect strategic doctrines and images of future conflicts. The importance of a particular weapons system may change even within the broad historical context set by the technological revolution in warfare. Current strategic doctrine recognizes the need for conventional striking forces adequate for a variety of limited war missions and as a result influences the military definition of occupational categories. Thus the Navy, which ranks next after the Air Force in technological complexity, continues to classify nearly half its personnel in "military-type" occupations: duty on board a warship entails hazards and makes demands on naval personnel that have no exact civilian counterparts and Navy tradition insists on maintaining these differences. The Air Force, on the other hand, in discarding classification of the military-type category of occupation, is emphasizing the specific organizational competences that even air combat personnel must acquire. Combat personnel are considered specialists irrespective of the mission they fly. The irreducible minimum requirement for combat personnel is generally estimated to be about 10 to 20 per cent of total military strength.[5]

The use of sophisticated weapons—on the ground and at sea as well as in the air—dispels the image of combat assignments as basically unskilled enlisted assignments. Yet combat entails much more than technical skill in the use of arms. Combat operations place a premium on the independence and initiative of combat soldiers, while unconventional forms of war demand greater political awareness. Even enlisted ground personnel, when serving abroad as advisers to indigenous troops, are expected to assume many training and supervisory functions, display tact and diplomacy in dealing with other nationals, and exhibit an understanding of the strategic importance of their mission. For this reason, the Army explicitly seeks to describe ground combat as one of its most skilled enlisted career fields. But because many high quality personnel elect technical and administrative jobs, the combat specialty is faced from time to time with shortages of effective manpower, and there is some tendency to fill these assignments with men whose aptitude scores are below Army average.

The technological transformation and the emergence of new skill requirements have also affected the officer corps. Line officers continue to comprise the largest group, but they, too, must acquire higher levels of skill and the administrative background necessary for the direction of diverse elements in combat. As a Department of Defense study committee in the so-called "Bolte Report" stated, the "trend in recent years, caused by the use of complex weapons systems, has been toward increased specialization of line officers in order to retain within the line the knowledge required to command modern forces effectively."[6]

To compare the military occupational structure with the civilian labor forces would be useful even though such comparisons are difficult. Despite the nearly identical terminology for the major occupational groupings, the definitions and criteria for classification in the civilian labor force and military differ, and they differ even among the services. Subject to these limitations, a comparison of the occupational groupings of enlisted personnel with those of employed male workers in the United States reveals some points worthy of notice (Table 4).

First, in terms of enlisted men's occupational distribution, the military establishment stands out as one of the more technologically advanced sectors of American society. The military employs higher proportions of technical and scientific, administrative-clerical personnel, mechanics and repairmen, and service workers than are found in the male labor force. Likewise it employs significantly lower proportions of men in the categories "craftsmen" and "operatives and laborers." To these statistics, covering only enlisted personnel, must be added the scientific, technical, and administrative skills which are found in even greater concentration among officers.

Second, the military had a higher representation in precisely those occupational groups which, between 1940 and 1960, registered the greatest gains in the labor force—namely, professional, technical, and kindred workers; managers, officials, and clerical workers; and mechanics and repairmen. Change in the military occupational structure appears in certain respects to have anticipated change in the labor force. The decrease in the proportion of mechanics and repairmen in the armed forces during the Korean Conflict can be attributed to the peculiarly limited nature of the operations and reiterates the influence of limited war missions on the distribution of occupations. The decrease in administrative and service personnel of the armed forces after Korea probably represents a readjustment from the unusual expansion required to process a large number of short-term inductees, before quantitative manpower requirements during the Cold War had been stabilized. Some short-run changes may be more apparent than real, in that they follow from changes in definitions rather than from changes in functions. It can be said, however, that the military occupational distribu-

TABLE 4. ENLISTED MILITARY OCCUPATIONAL STRUCTURE AND COMPOSITION OF U.S. MALE LABOR FORCE

	ENLISTED MILITARY					MALE LABOR FORCE					
									Per Cent of Change		
Occupational Group	World War I	World War II	Korea	1954	Per Cent of Change from World War II to 1954	1940	1950	1960	1940–50	1950–60	1940–60
	(Percentages)					(Percentages)					
I. Technical and Scientific	3.7	10.4	12.7	15.8	52	6.1	7.3	10.3	20	41	69
II. Administrative and Clerical	8.0	12.6	18.1	17.1	36	9.9	11.8	13.6	20	15	37
III. Mechanics and Repairmen	8.5	16.6	15.3	18.3	10	2.4	4.2	5.1	75	21	113
IV. Craftsmen	13.0	5.9	4.7	6.0	2	12.7	14.4	14.4	13	0	13
V. Service	12.5	9.6	12.4	12.1	26	6.1	6.0	6.1	–2	2	0
VI. Operatives and Laborers	20.2	6.1	6.5	5.4	–11	26.9	28.2	26.8	5	–5	–4
VII. Military/Civilian-type Occupations Not Elsewhere Classified[a]	34.1	38.8	30.3	25.3	–65	35.3	27.0	19.2	–24	–33	–46
Total	100.0	100.0	100.0	100.0		99.4[b]	98.9[b]	95.5[b]			

[a] Civilian-type occupations with no counterpart in military job structure include: farmers, farm managers, and farm laborers; all self-employed proprietors and managers; and sales workers.

[b] Because of variations in the number whose occupation was not reported, the percentage is less than 100.

SOURCE: Military data from studies for the U.S. President's Commission on Veterans' Pensions, *op. cit.* Labor Force data from U.S. Bureau of Census.

46

tion, despite some irreducible differences that will persist, represents in many respects the direction in which the civilian labor force is moving.

Third, the civilian occupational structure reveals a decline in the number of self-employed managers and officials and of gainfully employed persons in the agricultural sector, all of which appear in our table as occupations with no counterparts in the military structure. This category consisted of farmers, farm managers, and farm workers; self-employed proprietors of all sorts; and sales workers. Persons having civilian skills have long been useful to the military: civilian surgeons and medical doctors, photographers, storekeepers, and so on have often participated in military operations. But the decline of occupations with no civilian-military counterparts both in the armed forces and in the labor force suggests increasing overlap between skills required in the two sectors. As a result, experience acquired during military service has increasing transfer value in a civilian career.[7]

SELECTION AND TURNOVER

To meet the new manpower requirements, the armed forces must recruit personnel either with the requisite skills or with aptitude for training. In past emergencies the armed forces have, as a rule, encountered little difficulty in meeting their quotas through some combination of voluntary enlistment and conscription. The primary problem was how to allocate the limited manpower reservoir between industrial production and agriculture, on the one hand, and military needs, on the other. In the present Cold War, however, the armed forces must obtain qualified personnel in large numbers and on a continuing basis. The military has evolved policies that seek to meet competition from the civilian sector for the same limited pool of qualified manpower.

The need for personnel who either already possess the skill to fill a variety of specific positions in the armed forces or have the aptitude for training in the particular skills has led to the imposition of higher standards of eligibility not only for officers but for enlisted cadres as well. All men who seek to enlist, and those drafted, must take tests from which their general mental ability and specific aptitudes are judged. Only limited quotas with marginal mental ability are accepted; they are eligible if the tests indicate some specific aptitude. Furthermore, many enlisted career fields now have minimal educational requirements, usually completion of high school, while a college degree is increasingly becoming the norm for officers.

At the same time, some physical requirements have in certain respects been lowered to take account of the actual duties a man will perform in his military assignment. In a related fashion in psychiatric screening, the military has modified definitions of neurosis because they were not valid indicators of subsequent performance. There is, however, increased psychiatric screening of active duty personnel in order to assess suitability for specific tasks, particularly, for example, the management of nuclear weapons. The mechanical application of physical and psychiatric standards tends to eliminate significant numbers of men who could effectively carry out a variety of assignments. Screening procedures are becoming increasingly geared to reduce "slippage," by selecting men for specific career fields and by more careful assignment.

Nevertheless, the armed services would probably encounter difficulty in filling their quantitative and qualitative requirements on a completely voluntary basis for an expanded establishment. While the Army alone is forced to use Selective Service as a replacement source, the mere existence of the system helps to generate volunteers for the other services. But many of the recruits procured under the pressure of a draft are not career-motivated and do not remain beyond the obligatory term. The presence of large numbers of short-term personnel means high turnover and chronic manpower problems even when quotas are met. Large cohorts of young recruits do not guarantee sufficient qualified personnel to man a career force, because turnover can cause deficiencies in the required levels of experience and technical competence.

Organizational equilibrium in this regard rather hinges on an optimal balance between turnover and retention. Turnover at the higher levels is necessary to maintain opportunities for those at the lower levels, and without compulsory attrition peacetime forces inevitably exhibit a tendency to "age." The skills of many men, recruited when different requirements prevailed, become obsolete, and many times they cannot be retrained in the new skills. Yet a new recruit or officer requires much more training before he becomes useful, especially in the highly technical jobs, whereas the broad perspectives demanded of middle and higher level managers presuppose long prior service.

The military seek to fill many positions from internal recruitment, with selection based on competitive achievement. But, for enlisted personnel, the bulk of the internal recruitment in effect takes place during the initial period of basic training. Priority in assignment to service schools is allocated to new recruits, on the basis of their aptitude scores, and selection is strongly conditioned by the existence of a service school quota at the completion of their basic training. The policy of selecting the most promising men for special training and marking them for rapid advancement has accompanied the policy of forcing out, in increasing numbers, personnel who cannot meet the stringent skill requirements and are unlikely to benefit from training. This creates wider opportunities for younger men with demonstrated competence. The goal of manpower management is more effective management of the assignments and careers of men in the service as a supplement to an increasingly flexible screening of prospective entrants.

The training period in service schools for various enlisted occupations ranges from an average of nine weeks in such fields as food service, security, and motor transport, to an average of twenty-eight weeks in electronics maintenance. Furthermore, enlisted men in technical assignments have been trained in military service schools more often than men in less technical jobs, ranging from 98 per cent of all electronics repairmen to about 40 per cent in the crafts or services. For most other technical personnel, mechanics, and repairmen, the percentages were about 75 or higher. Since service school attendance is preceded by a general orientation and processing and by other less specialized training, the total training investment in these specialities is extensive. The average cost, in the late 1950's, for training a two-year inductee was estimated between $11,000 and $14,000, not including the cost of transporting new men to fill vacancies created by loss of short-term personnel. Close to one-quarter of the military effort was being devoted to all kinds of training.[8]

The short military service expectancy of the new enlistee is, on the average, only about one-tenth the working expectancy of an eighteen-year-old civilian male worker entering the labor force. The shorter the utilization period, the smaller the return to the services for their investment. A short-term military establishment with a rapidly rotating base of poorly trained manpower will contain hidden costs. Critically low reenlistment rates in specialized career fields, as electronics, which call for the highest training investment, have resulted in present policy requiring an extension of service commitment in return for specialized training.

In view of this, the military is under great pressure to ensure the maximum use of trained personnel. Advanced data processing systems, together with the availability of air transport, have made possible a "By-Name-Assignment Program" of all personnel in a given service from one central location. For example, the Army program, under development since 1960, seeks to facilitate a more effective utilization of available skills. An enlisted man can be authorized, if he so desires, to transfer out of a surplus skill area into the area of one of his additional skills, where more promotion opportunities exist than in his primary skill area. Any increase in job satisfaction, as a result, might also be translated into higher reenlistment rates. The same program is also designed to enable a prospective reenlistee to secure a preferred assignment (including a service schooling) commensurate with his ability, training, and grade as long as this fits into overall service needs. But in a large and complex system, such personnel innovations introduce unanticipated rigidities. Because it is centralized at the Department of Army level, local authorities have little influence in adjusting the program to immediate organizational realities. While there are many exceptions, the approach tends to restrict horizontal mobility and consequently the chances for vertical mobility. Such blocked mobility contributes to the problem of retention.

Another managerial device for encouraging reenlistment is the system of granting special monthly bonuses of either $30 or $60 for "proficiency" to soldiers passing Army-wide tests devised for each occupational specialty and also receiving a favorable superior's evaluation. Initial experience with new managerial practices has been accompanied by rising reenlistment rates, but not all the improvement can *ipso facto* be attributed to these techniques. Other factors, to be discussed later, particularly civilian employment opportunities, probably set the range within which practices influence the flow of manpower in and out of the services.

The turnover problem, which threatens the balance between training investment and utilization, also affects officers. Retention of junior officers assigned to scientific, technical, and engineering duties has been considerably below optimum. In the Air Force lowest retention rates were indicated for science and engineering graduates who are not flying personnel and who are assigned to research and development specialties. In the Army retention was lowest for lawyers. Usually these positions are filled by individuals who acquire their training primarily outside the military organization.

Turnover problems among officer personnel are aggravated by the need to balance the requirements of training with those of education, as these terms are used by the military. Training involves the acquisition of a skill necessary for a specific job, while education relates to acquiring knowledge and skills for the officer career as a whole. Except in the highly technical functions, as an officer advances through the hierarchy, the ability to relate to the military as a whole becomes more important than the specialized experience acquired during early years of service as a junior officer. This places the emphasis on formal education (both in service schools and in civilian institutions) and on obtaining the kind of assignments that enable an officer to develop perspectives appropriate both to the exercise of organizational leadership and to the variety of liaison roles involved in the management of defense. Mobility into the top leadership nucleus, as Janowitz has shown, has been via assignments that offer opportunities for innovation and facilitate a broadening of outlook.[9] In the career development of officers education thus plays a more critical role than specific training.

The desirable progression of assignments by which qualified officers should seek to develop appropriate managerial perspectives has received formal recognition in career management plans. Recruitment into the higher military leadership positions is exclusively from within the organization, from among a reservoir of officer cohorts with varying years of service. The period of "major professional contribution"—as the Army's career planning guide for officers calls the period of service typically beginning about the twenty-fourth year of service—presupposes a long period of career development, in the course of which assignments geared to the development of an officer gradually give way to assignments that permit his maximum contribution to the service.

The progression of assignment is based on a system of rotation in which the officer and the enlisted soldier periodically are reassigned to a new post. Some hardship assignments are as brief as one year; some educational and staff assignments are as long as five years, but most are in the three-year range. There is a trend toward longer assignment but it is indeed very limited. The logic for rotation is powerful as a system for developing higher officers. Its impact on the system, however, is pervasive, since it forces the constant utilization of personnel who are new to their assignments. As a result, the solutions that must be developed tend to rely on a general formula rather than specialized ones. In so reducing the period of specialized in-service training, the policy forces a reliance on civilian experts in assignments where long training is a prerequisite. The preparation of each officer—or at least the majority—as a potential commander clashes with day-to-day organizational effectiveness. It causes additional strain because the assumption on which the practice is based does not, except in periods of unusually rapid expansion, articulate with the opportunity structure.

The career management system depends on a steady supply of new junior officers and on continuous selection procedures to create the vacancies necessary for their advancement. In 1960 the Bolte Committee study of career opportunities found that the officer personnel of all the services contained fairly serious bulges in roughly the sixteen-to-nineteen year category of prior service cohorts. These bulges were delayed effects of the unusually large intake of officers in World War II, many of whom remained in the service. In 1960 the Army and the Marine Corps also exhibited sizable bulges in the eight-to-ten year prior service cohorts—again delayed effects, but in this case of the Korean Conflict. In addition to specific historical reasons, some imbalances are part of a general pattern. Whatever the variations by service, component, officer procurement source, nature of the assignment, and so on, resignation rates following the obligatory tour of duty have generally been high. This has caused the most critical shortages to occur neither at the junior nor the senior officer level, but among those who began with low commitments to a military career and had not yet developed a future stake in career prospects and retirement benefits. Voluntary resignations decline with increasing length of service.

Among both officers and enlisted men, recognition of the benefits of continuing in military service increases with years spent in the service. For the enlisted man, the point of decision tends to occur at the termination of his first enlistment. The proportion of reenlistments among career personnel serving on second or subsequent enlistments has approached 80 per cent in most categories. In this process the quality of those retained is an issue. Data by Ryan point to an inverse relationship between military efficiency ratings and the willingness of an enlisted man for further service. Men with high efficiency ratings were least ready to reenlist.[10] The same inverse relationship between qualifications and career motivation exists for certain categories of officer recruitment. In 1954 one out of five of the Army's "distinguished" graduates of Reserve Officer Training Corps and Officer Candidate School, who were eligible for regular commissions, actually applied, a significant drop from the over 50 per cent who did apply in 1949.[11] According to Masland, available information about the Distinguished Military Graduates in the Army and Air Force and the Holloway officers in the Navy suggests that those who select an officer career are far from the very top of the college graduates.[12]

New selection and management procedures have led to some improvement in the quality of enlisted personnel (Table 5). The trend is away from "natural turnover," voluntary and self-selected, and toward managed or forced turnover, in which the military set standards and direct policies. Progressively larger proportions of men in each service fit into the average and above-average mental groups, in that they score above the thirty-first percentile on general qualification tests. Upgrading in the quality of the enlisted force has been most pronounced in the Air Force. The overall trend is particularly noteworthy because some of the most talented are drawn into the officer corps.

TABLE 5. ENLISTED PERSONNEL IN MENTAL CLASSIFICATION
AVERAGE AND ABOVE AVERAGE

Service	1943	1957	1959
	(Percentages)		
Army (Ground and Service Forces)	64.0	73.6	83.4
Air Force (Air Corps)	73.1	84.9	90.0
Navy	—	76.7	83.5
Marine Corps	—	80.2	84.2

SOURCE: Palmer, R. E., and others, *The Procurement and Training of Ground Combat Personnel*, War Department, Washington, 1948; and U.S. House of Representatives, Committee on Armed Services, *Hearings Before the Subcommittee on Utilization of Military Manpower*. 86th Congress, 2nd Sess. Government Printing Office, Washington, 1960.

Skill—that is, mental ability and aptitudes—has its social correlates, since the various tests do not merely measure innate traits but are also influenced by differences in social and educational background. Careful evaluation of manpower performance during World War II fully documents the fact that ineffectiveness from all causes (psychoneurotic breakdown, ineptitude, and the like) was less frequent among the more educated.[13] The return from the training investment is increased, and the probability of ultimate failure is decreased, if men accepted for military service have completed a minimal amount of education, or have already acquired some skill before entering the military service. Among 100,000 men inducted into the Air Force in 1956, over 10 per cent were discharged as unsuitable before the end of their four-year reenlistment. Only 20 per cent of those discharged had finished high school. They were also younger, with a high proportion of seventeen-year-olds, many of them no doubt school dropouts.

Improvement in the qualifications of military personnel can evidently be measured by their educational level. Educational statistics on enlisted men and officers in the Army, the only service for which trend data covering the years 1940 through 1961 were obtained, reveal a steady rise in the amount of formal schooling for all personnel (Table 6). Since the agespread within the armed forces is both narrower and more skewed toward youth than it is within the total population, military personnel would immediately manifest the effects of any national trend toward longer schooling. Comparison of the educational levels in the military with those of a civilian male cohort aged twenty-five to twenty-nine—the youngest cohort for whom the census supplies comparable statistics from 1940 on—indicates the possibility that military personnel may not just be reflecting an overall trend but, in some respects, anticipating civilian trends.

54 THE NEW MILITARY

TABLE 6. EDUCATIONAL LEVEL OF ARMY PERSONNEL ON ACTIVE DUTY AND OF U.S. MALE POPULATION 25 TO 29 YEARS OLD, 1940–1961

Educational Level	1940[a]	1944[a]	1950	1952	1959[b]	1960	1961
ENLISTED MEN (Cumulative percentages)							
College graduates	c	c		4	2	2	2
Some college	4	11		14	13	17	18
High school graduates	25	41		48	68	64	73
Some high school	59	70		76	88	91	96
Total Enlisted Men	100	100		100	100	100	100
COMMISSIONED OFFICERS							
College graduates		c		50	79	57	75
Some college[d]		67		76	98	89	97
High school graduates		82		97	99.8	99.5	99.8
Total Officers		100		100	100.0	100.0	100.0
U.S. MALE POPULATION 25 TO 29 YEARS							
College graduates	7		9			17	
Some college	14		20			31	
High school graduates	36		49			66	
Some high school	57		71			85	
Total U.S. Male Population 25 to 29	100		100			100	

[a] 1940 and 1944 data include Air Corps personnel. 1940 data based on white men in the Army as of December 31, 1941, who enlisted prior to July 1, 1940, and include mostly the peacetime Regular Army personnel.

[b] This column is based on Regular Army personnel only. It represents the latest year for which separate breakdowns permitting comparison with 1940 data were obtained.

[c] No data available on number of college graduates.

[d] Includes small number with registered nurse diploma.

SOURCES: 1940 and 1944 military from Stouffer, S. A., and others, *The American Soldier: Adjustment to Military Life*. Princeton University Press, 1949, pp. 59, 246.

1952 and 1961 military based on sample survey. Systems Development Branch, The Adjutant General's Office, Department of the Army.

1960 military from Statistical Services Center, Office of the Secretary of Defense, August 9, 1960.

U.S. male population 25 to 29 years old from U.S. Bureau of Census.

During this twenty-year period the number of Army enlisted men with high school diplomas increased by 39 per cent, while the increase among the male civilian cohort was only 30 per cent. The proportion of Army enlisted men who completed high school has thus come to approximate that among civilians, and this despite the fact that many enlist before graduation. Nor can the improvement, since it has also affected Regular Army personnel, be accounted for by the presence of large numbers of involuntary selectees. Certainly the enlisted force no longer represents a semiliterate or educationally deprived group. It is well on the way, in terms of education, to becoming a middle-level group.

A parallel trend is evident among officer personnel. Not only is a college degree becoming indispensable, but most striking is the increase in number of officers acquiring graduate and professional education beyond the bachelor degree. Many officers are sent to civilian universities for advanced degrees. The various military institutions of advanced education are also taking greater account of curriculum developments in civilian graduate and professional schools; much in-service professional education provides the equivalent of a higher degree.

Present differences in educational achievement among Army, Air Force, Navy, and Marine Corps personnel (Table 7) result from a number of factors. The superior educational level of Air Force enlisted men reflects its occupational requirements, but the Army and Marine Corps enlisted men rank higher in education than the men in the Navy. Similar proportions of Army and Air Force enlisted men continue school while in service; hence the higher Air Force ranking reflects its success, especially throughout World War II (and afterward), in recruiting a greater share of better educated men. By contrast, the comparatively low educational level of present Air Force officers is a delayed effect of World War II, when young men with no more than a high school education qualified for aviation training and an officer commission. The number of them who remained in the service caused an extensive educational deficit among Air Force regular officers in the years immediately after the war. The educational deficit among the middle officer ranks was

TABLE 7. ESTIMATED LEVEL OF EDUCATION OF MILITARY
PERSONNEL ON ACTIVE DUTY, FEBRUARY 29, 1960

Educational Level	Marine Corps	Army	Navy	Air Force	Total
	COMMISSIONED OFFICERS (Cumulative percentages)				
College graduates	59	57	70	49	57
Some college[a]	84	89	91	79	85
High school graduates	98	99	99	99	99
Total Officers	100	100	100	100	100
	ENLISTED MEN				
College graduates	[b]	3	[b]	1	2
Some college	6	17	5	18	14
High school graduates	63	64	51	81	66
Some high school	92	91	90	96	92
Total Enlisted Men	100	100	100	100	100

[a] Includes small number with registered nurse diploma.

[b] Less than .5 per cent.

SOURCE: Based on sample survey. Statistical Services Center, Office of Secretary of Defense, August 9, 1960.

still clearly evident in 1960, nearly twenty years after the outbreak of World War II. But officers who failed to acquire additional education and, partly for that reason, were passed over for promotion are being forced out and retired in large numbers as they reach the twenty-year point.

Despite the heritage of an educational deficit among personnel senior in time of service, the relationship between military rank and general education is, on the whole, positive (Table 8). Higher educational requirements are being enforced to raise levels of professional competence. Where the average education of one officer rank exceeds that of the rank above, the excess reflects differences in requirements at the time of entry, but the difference is being reduced by the additional education many officers obtain while in military service. The works of Masland and Radway[14] and of Janowitz[15] have documented, each in its own way, that "broadening" through education plays an increasingly

TABLE 8. LEVEL OF EDUCATION OF ACTIVE DUTY PERSONNEL BY RANK

	ARMY, AUGUST 31, 1961			
Educational Level	Field Grade Officers	Company Officers	Warrant Officers	Enlisted Personnel
	(Cumulative percentages)			
Graduate or professional work beyond the bachelor's	31	22	1	a
College graduates	54	72	4	2
Some college[b]	96	97	67	18
High school graduates	99.6	99.7	99	73
Total	100.0	100.0	100	100

	AIR FORCE, MAY 31, 1960												
Educational Level	Col.	Lt. Col.	Maj.	Capt.	First Lt.	Second Lt.	W.O.	M. Sgt.	T. Sgt.	S. Sgt.	A/1c	A/2c	A/3c
	(Cumulative percentages)												
Graduate or professional work beyond the bachelor's	33	29	20	22	16	17	1	a	a	a	a	a	a
College graduates	68	54	34	43	61	68	5	2	1	1	1	a	a
Some college[b]	95	94	87	89	93	94	53	31	24	18	17	15	13
High school graduates	99	99	99	99.7	99.7	99.9	99	89	86	81	84	77	58
Total	100	100	100	100.0	100.0	100.0	100	100	100	100	100	100	100

a Less than .5 per cent.

b Includes small number with registered nurse diploma.

SOURCE: Based on sample survey. Systems Development Branch, Adjutant General's Office, Department of the Army; Personnel Statistics Division, Comptroller of the Air Force, Headquarters U. S. Air Force.

TABLE 9. EDUCATION ACQUIRED BY PERSONNEL ON ACTIVE DUTY DURING THEIR MILITARY SERVICE[a]

Educational Level	ARMY, AUGUST 31, 1961			
	Field Grade Officers	Company Grade Officers	Warrant Officers	Enlisted Men
	(Percentages)			
Some graduate work	21	8	1	b
Earned college degree	19	11	2	b
Attended college for first time (no degree)	30	23	51	5
Completed high school	5	7	39	27

	AIR FORCE, MAY 31, 1960					
	Colonel	Captain	Warrant Officers	Master Sergeant	Technical Sergeant	Staff Sergeant
	(Percentages)					
Some graduate work	21	12	1	b	b	b
Earned college degree	18	18	3	1	1	b
Attended college for first time (no degree)	7	29	35	18	16	10
Completed high school	1	4	21	7	11	4

[a] Based on difference in per cent who had completed given amount education at present and at time of entry into military service.

[b] Less than .5 per cent.

SOURCE: Based on sample survey. Systems Development Branch, Adjutant General's Office, Department of the Army; Personnel Statistics Division, Comptroller of the Air Force, Headquarters, U.S. Air Force.

important part in the career development of general officers. Table 9 gives statistics on education acquired while in military service.

The same positive relationship between general education and military rank can be observed in the enlisted force. Men entering without high school diplomas usually acquire them during military service. While enlisted men continue to be, on the average, below the officer corps in level of education, the highest enlisted ranks have nearly all completed high school, with close to one-third having at some time attended college, including college work offered in the military. Those promoted to warrant officer rank tend to have even more education, though still less than commissioned officers. The grade hierarchy in the armed forces is, in this respect, a fair articulation of the skill hierarchy.

In sum, then, the upgrading of the skill level of military personnel is the combined consequence of selection procedures and of competence gained during military service. Selection procedures that emphasize education and experience acquired in civilian life can be expected to yield personnel with longer periods of utilization since they have less likelihood of subsequent failure. However, the reservoir of men lacking in formal educational qualifications contains significant numbers with high aptitude and even more with the capacity for training to perform many specific jobs. Stricter standards of selection would exclude those groups with the most favorable motivations toward service. The logical alternative to raising selection standards is to use in-training both as a method of developing talent and of weeding out the unfit. Even though civilian education acquired prior to entry into military service continues to be the one basic prerequisite for advancement within the military, in actual practice the qualifications that enable individuals to carry responsibilities at the middle and higher levels are being developed more and more in the course of, rather than prior to, their military career.

MILITARY SERVICE AND CAREER PERSPECTIVES

Men enter military service for a variety of reasons. Often their tour is to fulfill an unavoidable obligation. Yet military service also holds many inducements, the strength of which varies with the background and aspirations of the men. Some of these inducements are negative and result from the absence of other alternatives. Or military service may offer experience and training valued highly because it opens new opportunities to a variety of civilian careers. For still others, military service represents a positive choice made in response to the attractions believed to be inherent in a career in the armed services.

Most enlisted men as well as the majority of the officers are single at the time they enter military service. The prospect of several years away from home appeals more to young men who are still without the responsibility of their own family. Polls on the prestige ranking of occupations have also confirmed this idea; male teenagers rated both officer and enlisted men somewhat higher than did the national adult sample,[16] a difference that probably reflects more the romantic attraction of military service for some youths than a generational shift toward increasing military prestige. The higher prestige of military occupations among teenagers frequently gives way subsequently to more realistic assessments of the actual standings of alternative career opportunities. Changes in the family status of single men also create new demands and aspirations, so that military service loses some of its appeal.

Historically, one important source of the manpower for large standing armies has been the "surplus" populations from rural regions. Enlisted service, in particular, has offered men from these areas an escape from a restrictive and provincial milieu. Equally important is the lack of economic opportunity in such areas. Men with rural and small town backgrounds continue to be more favorably disposed to an enlisted career than their better educated and more sophisticated urban peers, but the supply of manpower from this source has diminished as the size of the rural population declines. However, the present advanced stage of industrialization produces its own type of population "surplus." Notwithstanding a nationwide trend to extend schooling and to reduce school dropouts, the larger age cohorts entering the adult labor force in the 1960's will lead to an absolute increase of young people whose civilian employment opportunities are severely circumscribed by deficiencies in education. Unemployment among young people without technical or professional skills has reached high chronic proportions in some urban areas. The Negro population, with its heavy concentration in unskilled jobs, has been especially exposed to such unemployment.

The experience, training, and career opportunities offered in enlisted service would be an answer to the aspirations of educationally deprived persons. The enlisted force, one of the last havens in the United States of a genuinely lower-class culture, provides an important avenue of social mobility to young men who have aptitudes but lack the formal education required for alternative careers. Yet the reliance on higher educational requirements tends to block those who would be most strongly attached to an enlisted career.

At the same time, the transfer value of military experience to civilian employment is, of course, responsible for many retention problems, with heaviest losses among personnel assigned in the electronics field. Over one-third of all civilian electronics technicians are estimated to have been trained in service schools, and the expansion of civil aviation following World War II was based on the pool of men trained by the Air Force.[17] A survey of veterans of past wars, conducted by the United States Bureau of the Census in 1955, further testifies to the occupational value individuals place on military experience. Four times more veterans said time spent in the service helped rather than hindered their subsequent careers.[18]

Still, most training offered in service schools is narrower and more specialized than that generally given in civilian schools. Some training provided by the military has been narrowed deliberately so that men could be taught more quickly and also so that the direct transferability to civilian employment of the skills so acquired would be reduced. Evidence collected by the services in a variety of studies, using both stated intentions and actual reenlistment figures, also points to a significant relationship between education and reenlistment. The more limited the prior education of trainees completing a service school, the more favorable their attitudes toward military life and the higher the value placed on the training received.

Data on the educational background of Air Force airmen's intention to reenlist indicate that in the contemporary period the military serves as a "second chance" for some who did not complete high school. A survey among airmen on active duty, as of May, 1961, revealed that high school graduation was unrelated to reenlistment intentions. The proportion of high school graduates in each of three groups—those who intended to reenlist, were undecided or did not intend to reenlist—was very close to the 81 per cent for the enlisted group as a whole. But there was a noteworthy difference between those airmen who completed their high school education before entering the Air Force and those who had an opportunity to get a high school diploma while in the Air Force. The intention to reenlist was higher among those who received their high school diploma while in the Air Force. In addition, it should be pointed out that this difference operated only among the first termers and not for the career airmen, since for the first termers the question of reenlistment is most problematic. For the career airmen, length of service, family considerations, and the like seem to be the important factors.

The utilization of Negroes by the armed forces further highlights the opportunities available for undereducated population groups. Prior to 1948, opportunities in the armed forces for Negroes were seriously curtailed by an official policy of segregation. Until the change in policy as a result of an executive order by President Harry S. Truman on equality of treatment and opportunity in the armed forces, Negroes had served mainly in separate units with limited functions. The representation of Negroes in the armed forces has since greatly increased (Table 10). In 1962 Negroes, who comprised 11 per cent of the United States population, and a slightly higher proportion of the age range eligible for military service, totaled about 8.2 per cent of all military personnel. Only among Army enlisted men does the percentage of Negroes exceed that in the population, although the percentage of Negroes in the Air Force is beginning to approach this level. But since fewer Negroes than whites meet the physical and educational and mental standards that the services apply, it is probable that higher proportions of eligible Negroes than whites enter the armed services.

Negroes are underrepresented at the officer level, especially at the higher ranks, partly as a result of the absence of opportunity for Negroes in the past. In 1962 each of the three service academies counted a number of Negroes among its student body. Yet admission of Negroes

TABLE 10. NEGRO PERSONNEL IN ARMED FORCES
(Per Cent of All Personnel)

Service	ENLISTED MEN			OFFICERS		
	1949	1954	1962	1949	1954	1962
	(Percentages)					
Marine Corps	2.1	6.5	7.7	0	.1	.2
Army	12.4	13.7	12.2	1.8	3.0	3.2
Navy	4.7	3.6	5.1	0	.1	.2
Air Force	5.1	8.6	9.1	.6	1.1	1.2
Per Cent of Negroes in U.S. Population			11			11

Source: President's Committee on Equal Opportunity in the Armed Forces, *Initial Report: Equality of Treatment and Opportunity for Negro Military Personnel Stationed in the United States,* June 13, 1963.

as officers on an equal basis with whites is of recent origin, so that most Negroes lack the seniority requisite for advancement. Whereas 3.2 per cent of Army officers were Negro, only one per cent of officers with twenty or more years of service were Negro. As of 1963, the only Negro to hold general officer rank was in the Air Force; one Negro had held such a rank in the Army.[19]

Characteristics of the Negro population, such as limited college attendance, which stand as a barrier to entrance into the officer ranks, make the educational and career opportunities of an enlisted career especially attractive. The progress made by Negroes in the armed forces by 1962 exhibits a mildly disproportionate concentration at the lowest NCO grade and the two grades below it; that is, E-3 to E-5 (Table 11). Very few Negroes, even relatively, are in the highest NCO grades; nor is there, with the possible exception of the Air Force, a disproportionate influx at the bottom ranks.

An executive order cannot wipe out, at once, every vestige of racial prejudice. Informal practices of discrimination by military personnel on base, during off-duty hours, and in communities where Negro troops are stationed, can still cause disadvantages for Negro servicemen and their families, especially since many military installations are located in the South. Yet the armed services have advanced farther than other institutions in eliminating segregation and achieving integration. On a service-wide basis, Negroes have been assigned to virtually all occupations, although they are still overrepresented in Service and other areas with limited promotion opportunities. In many technical fields, such as Electronics and Crafts in the Navy, or Electronics Maintenance in the Air Force, their participation, though increasing, continues to be limited. Educational disadvantages that might make Negroes available

TABLE 11. NEGRO PERSONNEL IN EACH RANK IN 1962
(PER CENT OF ALL PERSONNEL)

Rank	Marine Corps	Army	Navy	Air Force
	OFFICERS			
	(Percentages)			
Generals/Admirals	0	0	0	a
Colonels/Captains	0	.1	0	a
Lt. Cols./Commanders	0	1.0	a	2.5
Majors/Lt. Commanders	0	2.5	.1	.6
Captains/Lieutenants	.2	5.2	.4	1.7
First Lieutenants/Lts. (j.g.)	.4	4.3	.4	1.6
Second Lieutenants/Ensigns	.3	2.3	.2	1.5
Total Officers	.2	3.2	.2	1.2
	ENLISTED MEN			
	(Percentages)			
E-9 (highest)	.7	3.0	1.3	.8
E-8	.8	5.7	1.2	1.7
E-7	2.1	7.6	2.4	2.5
E-6	3.9	12.7	4.4	4.2
E-5	8.7	16.3	6.2	9.3
E-4	9.1	12.2	6.6	12.5
E-3	8.1	11.9	5.1	9.3
E-2	8.0	10.6	5.2	10.2
E-1	7.6	11.1	4.8	17.2
Total Enlisted Men	7.6	12.2	5.2	9.1

a Less than .5 per cent.

SOURCE: President's Committee on Equal Opportunity in the Armed Forces, *op. cit.*

for military service cause them to be, at the same time, unavailable for certain types of job opportunities in expanding skill areas.

The social base from which most officers are recruited differs considerably from that of enlisted men. Seven out of ten commissioned officers, but only one out of ten enlisted men, attended college before entering military service. This indicates the higher social origins of officers and also reflects the younger age at which most enlisted men begin their military service. Lack of formal education, if not remedied during the early years of military service, constitutes a barrier to promotion of most enlisted men into the ranks of commissioned officers and restricts the prospects for subsequent advancement. In this respect, the distinction between the officer career and the enlisted career is being sharpened by the increasing stress on academic education. Unless the educational requirements for professional status are obtained early in one's career, the prospects for achieving that status are considerably diminished.

Enlisted men are, in many ways, like skilled workers. Thus since academic education is rare among persons in blue-collar occupations, very few succeed in moving into the managerial or professional occupations. More typically, after reaching the top of their trade, they advance by moving into the self-employed business category or other business categories. But enlisted men—the skilled workers in the military—make this upward move primarily by leaving military service, except where there are special programs for commissioning enlisted personnel, particularly in technical specializations.[20]

Education furthermore conditions the relative attractiveness of an officer career compared to alternative civilian careers. Survey data analyzed by Zald and Simon show that officers who have not completed college have stronger career commitments than those who hold a degree.[21] However, since many officers earn their college degrees while in the service means that it would be misleading to conclude that there is a simple relationship between length of service and education, even for the recent past. The influence on career commitments of not having a college degree upon first entering military service persists even after an officer has made up the initial educational disability. Since a completed college education, preferably supplemented by graduate work, is one of the requirements of a successful military career, one would expect a committed officer to be strongly motivated to continue his education, and many do indeed earn a degree without weakening their commitment. Data from a periodic survey of Air Force officer personnel, taken in May, 1961, reveal that having a college degree *at the time of entry* into college is a better indicator of career commitment than *present* educational level. The relationship holds even when officers in the Regular Air Force, the Career Reserve, and the Noncareer Reserve are examined separately.

Further clarification of this issue can be obtained from Table 12, where the length of service of officers who retired between 1955 and 1959

TABLE 12. YEARS OF SERVICE PRIOR TO RETIREMENT, BY EDUCATION AMONG SAMPLE OF OFFICERS RETIRED DURING 1955–1959

Years of Service	Less Than High School Education	High School Graduates	Some College Education	College Graduates
	(Percentages)			
Minimal (20 or less)	20	30	41	46
Intermediate (21 to 29)	57	57	47	35
Extended (30 or more)	24	14	12	28
Total	100	100	100	100
Number of cases	398	836	1,064	744

SOURCE: Based on data from a mail survey by the University of Michigan of officers retired during fiscal years 1955–1959. Percentages do not total 100 because of rounding.

is classified by level of education of the officer. Careers are classified minimal career, 20 years or less; intermediate, 21 to 29 years, and extended, 30 years or more. Those officers who have limited education— less than high school—were characterized by a high concentration on intermediate and extended careers, and as educational level rose the proportion of minimal careers rose. Men who had limited education were seeking to build on their career investment in the military. However, those with college graduation, while they have the highest concentration of minimal careers, also had the highest concentration of extended careers. Since military rank and education are generally related and college graduates also held the highest permanent ranks at retirement, a large number, especially the academy graduates, having made a success of it, remained in the service.

Any current sample of retired officers, of course, reflects past promotion and separation policies. Under contemporary policies, large numbers of officers without educational qualifications are being passed over for promotion and as a result either have separated or been forced to retire with a minimal career. Therefore the pattern is certain to change. Officer procurement source is another determinant of his motivation toward a service career. The high retention rates of officers who graduated from the service academies (Table 13) support the finding of Zald and Simon, based on reported career intentions, that this category usually has the strongest career commitment.[22]

The service academy entrants are undoubtedly screened more carefully in the first place, and the years spent in the academy as lower

TABLE 13. JUNIOR OFFICER RETENTION RATES, SELECTED
CATEGORIES, 1960

(PERSONNEL CONTINUING ON ACTIVE DUTY BEYOND OBLIGATED TOUR OF SERVICE)

Selected Categories	Dept. of Defense	Air Force	Navy	Army	Marine Corps
	(Percentages)				
Academy graduates	83.6	82.7	80.6	88.2	85.7
ROTC graduates	32.9	33.0	22.8	34.3	36.9
Rated officers[a]	58.5	64.6	34.4	not applicable	40.7
Aviation cadets		(84.2)			
ROTC (rated)		(52.0)			
Officer Candidate School				68.8	
Direct appointments				26.2	

[a] Navy and Marine Corps figures are for regular officers only; statistics on retention of OCS officers and officers given direct commission obtainable only for the Army.

SOURCE: Department of Defense, Office of Assistant Secretary of Defense (Manpower, Personnel and Reserve), September, 1960.

classmen subject their motivation and aptitude to a severe test. Many who are unsuited to the officer profession or who discover that they prefer civilian careers are likely to be eliminated through natural attrition. Students at the academies are also exposed to service tradition, and friendships formed there will later facilitate their advancement in the military. The academies are therefore an important source of highly qualified officers. Every fifth United States Military Academy graduate on active duty in the Army in 1959 was a full colonel. In this group high retention and the likelihood of a successful career tend to reinforce each other.

The career potential of USMA graduates as a group does not, however, eliminate the influence of social background. On the contrary, when resignation rates are related to father's occupation, a persistent residual effect is clearly discernible. Cumulative statistics for the classes of 1938 through 1954 indicate that West Point graduates from a middle-class background (that is, father's occupation is classed as managerial, white-collar, or professional) have resigned about twice as frequently as graduates with a family tradition of military service. Among sons of officers, fewer than one out of twelve had resigned by 1958, compared with one out of six among the civilian urban middle-class group. Although the statistics cover only the classes through 1954, earlier data suggest that the difference is being accentuated. On the other hand, whether the father of a USMA graduate had himself been commissioned through the Academy or through some other source has no apparent effect on the likelihood of the son's resigning.[23]

In the past the service academies have been able to supply the armed forces with the core of required regular officers, but the proportion of academy-trained officers has declined in all the services. At the outbreak of World War II, 45 per cent of Regular Army officers were USMA graduates; eighteen years later (in 1959) the percentage was only 22.8. The presence of large numbers of reserve officers, many of them on extended active duty, further dilutes the academy-trained core. In fact, in 1959 academy graduates accounted for only about 8 per cent of all officers on active duty.

Since the end of World War II, the armed forces have placed greater reliance in terms of numbers on other officer procurement sources to supplement those commissioned through the academies than they did in the past. Department of Defense figures in 1963 show that the academies were providing about 5 per cent of the entire new intake, while the Reserve Officer Training Corps supplied about 40 per cent. Since Academy graduates tend to remain in service longer than non-Academy graduates, their concentration in the middle and higher ranks is naturally greater than indicated by these figures and likely to remain so. Moreover, in 1964 the Congress authorized substantial increases in the size of the service Academies.

Losses among ROTC officers, as Table 13 reveals, have been high in all the services.[24] Among Holloway-plan graduates, whose college education was financed by the Navy, very few applied for regular commissions upon completion of their obligatory tour of duty, and many who did, resigned shortly thereafter. Despite the high attrition rates among junior officers from this source, the Reserve Officer Training Corps continues to be important to the services as a source of educationally qualified officers recruited directly through the colleges. ROTC officers in 1959 accounted for over one-third of Army colonels and for about the same proportion of all Army officers. In the Air Force, ROTC contributed in 1960, about one-fifth of both active duty officer strength and of colonels. The type of officer most frequently commissioned through ROTC can be gauged from their major in college. Contemporary students in civilian universities who display an interest in becoming professional officers appear to be different in their career preparation field from the general male student population. Their enrollment in business administration is most extensive, while engineering chosen by one per cent of these students is a poor second.[25]

Most Officer Candidate School graduates in the Army, unlike ROTC officers, have been prior-service personnel and are not recruited directly through the colleges. The retention rate for Army OCS graduates during the fiscal year 1960 continued to be about twice that for officers recruited through ROTC, despite a slight improvement in ROTC retention figures over the years preceding. The OCS group probably has been better screened by natural attrition than the ROTC group and therefore contains a larger residue of persons strongly motivated toward an officer career. Similarly the improved retention of ROTC graduates may reflect greater selectivity imposed by cutbacks in the program.

Civilians with professional skills, for example, physicians and dentists, continue to be directly commissioned as officers. High attrition among this group is a result of their standing as professionals in civilian pursuits. Many of them will follow a more lucrative career outside the military establishment.

The military career is an avenue of social mobility for both officers and enlisted men, although men of relatively lower social origin appear to perceive the opportunities as greater. At the same time, the education and experience acquired during one's career become an increasingly important determinant for mobility potential. Organizational problems are created by the imposition of higher academic prerequisites for many positions and by the transfer value of skills in high demand within the armed forces for civilian careers.

FROM PROFESSIONALISM TO PROFESSIONAL MANAGEMENT

To the extent that the upgrading of skill levels has resulted in chronic shortages and periodic losses of personnel in certain categories, the military establishment has sought to solve recruitment and retention problems by expanding the opportunity and rank structure. In this way the military seeks to cope with rising career aspirations among those whom it endeavors to recruit and to retain. But the changes that take place in the grade structure represent more than a pragmatic response to outside competition. The development of managerial and technical expertise have stimulated a pattern of organizational growth by which the middle ranks have expanded more rapidly than the rest. The grade distribution has had to accommodate to the new roles and specialties that have grown up within the military, many of which have their counterparts in civilian institutions. As a result, the rank structure ceases to be a direct expression of a simple hierarchical authority structure.

The increased requirements for all types of professionally trained personnel create a moderate increase of officers in proportion to enlisted personnel. But growth in the proportion of officers among active duty personnel has been neither continuous nor dramatic (Table 14). Basic

TABLE 14. TRENDS IN PROPORTION OF OFFICERS AMONG ACTIVE DUTY PERSONNEL, 1923–1960

Year	Dept. of Defense	Marine Corps	Army Commands	Navy (excluding Coast Guard)	Air Force Commands
			(Percentages)		
June 30, 1923	9.5	5.8	10.6	8.9	9.7
June 30, 1933[a]	10.3	7.4	10.1	10.9	10.6
June 30, 1939	8.3	7.1	7.1	9.6	11.2
May 31, 1945[b]	10.4	7.7	8.4	9.7	16.8
June 30, 1948[c]	11.7	8.1	12.3	10.8	12.6
April 30, 1952[d]	10.1	7.0	9.0	9.7	13.0
June 30, 1960	12.8	9.5	11.6	11.3	15.9

[a] Post-World War I low of total military personnel.
[b] World War II peak of total military personnel.
[c] Post-World War II low of total military personnel.
[d] Korean peak of total military personnel.
SOURCE: Statistical Services Center, Office of Secretary of Defense, August 19, 1960.

service structure has remained relatively intact. Reductions in officer ranks during periods of general retrenchment have been less drastic than cutbacks in total military personnel. Moreover, technology has produced consistent differences among the services. Since 1939 the number of officers has been consistently highest in the Air Force, where they now account for nearly one-sixth of the manpower.

Upward expansion of the grade structure has been accompanied by a blurring of the traditional distinction between the military professional qualified to exercise line authority and other professionals whose skills, though equally necessary to the military establishment, have in the past been considered subsidiary to the regular "line." The officer proportions shown in Table 14 refer to all officers, including warrant officers, who are specialists and not commissioned, and "limited duty" officers, who are commissioned from the enlisted ranks but only for technical duties related to their enlisted specialty and therefore cannot be promoted beyond the rank of lieutenant colonel or commander. Both these categories represent the top achievement categories for enlisted careers.

The emergence of skill on all levels of military organization tends, on the one hand, to emphasize formal education but, on the other hand, to weaken the distinction that divides enlisted men from officers in terms of technical expertise. This is officially recognized in the pay schedules. The basic pay of the two highest NCO grades now exceeds that of junior officers and even more so when increments for length of service are added. This overlap is significant in light of a general policy designed to eliminate overlapping pay scales as premiums for seniority. A similar overlap exists in many civilian industries between the pay of highly skilled blue-collar workers earning more than young professionals whose full earning power has not yet been realized. The emergence of a middle stratum within the military points up a blurring of the sharp line that formerly separated the career of an enlisted man from that of an officer, in much the same way as distinctions between skilled blue-collar and lower white-collar occupations are weakening.

This trend to recognize skill by extending the enlisted rank structure upward has increased the proportions in the middle grades (Table 15). In 1935 the two lowest grades, private and private first class, accounted for three-quarters of all Army enlisted personnel. By 1962 about one-fourth of all enlisted men in the Army and about one-fifth in the Air Force occupied these bottom ranks. In fact, the amount of reduction at the base and expansion at the top of the enlisted grade structure reflects again, in striking fashion, the relative importance of the new technology for the several services (Table 16).

TABLE 15. GRADE DISTRIBUTION OF ENLISTED PERSONNEL OF
U.S. ARMY AND AIR FORCE

Rank (from high to low)	1935	1945	ARMY	AIR FORCE	ARMY	AIR FORCE	ARMY	AIR FORCE
			1948		1952		1962	
			(Percentages)					
E-9							.2	.5
E-8	.8						1.0	1.2
E-7	.9	1.5	5.0	6.8	3.0	5.3	4.0	5.2
E-6	1.3	2.9	5.1	6.1	5.4	6.4	8.4	9.4
E-5	3.6	8.3	10.3	13.4	11.4	15.0	14.6	20.2
E-4	9.4	14.3	14.8	16.4	22.6	18.8	21.5	19.9
E-3	9.0	20.9	19.4	18.4	28.5	21.3	24.4	22.8
E-2	25.5	29.8	28.2	27.8	20.4	26.9	11.7	17.9
E-1	49.5	22.3	17.3	11.2	8.6	6.4	14.1	3.0
Total	100.0	100.0	100.0	100.0	100.0	100.0	100.0	100.0

SOURCES: 1935 data from Secretary of War, *Annual Report*, 1935.
1945 data from U.S. Army, Adjutant General's Office, cited in Stouffer, S. A., and others, *op. cit.*
1948, 1952, and 1962 data from Statistical Services Center, Office of Secretary of Defense. Percentages do not total 100 because of rounding.

TABLE 16. GRADE DISTRIBUTION OF ACTIVE DUTY MILITARY
PERSONNEL, 1962

Rank	Marine Corps	Army	Navy	Air Force
	(Percentages)			
Generals/Admirals	.4	.5	.4	.3
Colonels/Captains	3.9	4.9	5.9	3.6
Lt. Cols./Commanders	9.2	11.7	11.9	8.9
Majors/Lt. Commanders	15.2	16.6	18.2	22.0
Captains/Lieutenants	27.7	31.2	26.4	38.4
Lieutenants/Lts. (j.g.) and Ensigns	43.6	35.1	37.2	26.8
Total Officers	100.0	100.0	100.0	100.0
E-9 ⎫	.4	.2	.3	.5
E-8 ⎪	1.4	1.0	1.3	1.2
E-7 ⎬ non-coms	21.2 ⎰ 3.8 ⎱ 28.2	4.0 ⎰ 34.6	6.7 ⎰ 36.5	5.2
E-6 ⎪	4.6	8.4	10.9	9.4
E-5 ⎭	11.0	14.6	15.4	20.2
E-4	37.6 ⎰ 17.1	45.9 ⎰ 21.5	42.8 ⎰ 18.7	42.7 ⎰ 19.9
E-3	20.5	24.4	24.1	22.8
E-2	23.0	11.7	17.4	17.9
E-1	41.3 ⎰ 18.3	25.8 ⎰ 14.1	22.6 ⎰ 5.2	20.9 ⎰ 3.0
Total Enlisted Men	100.0	100.0	100.0	100.0

SOURCE: Statistical Services Center, Office of Secretary of Defense, 1962.

The demand for unskilled men has declined so markedly that almost all privates are new recruits who have not yet completed specialist training. Those who remain in service can expect promotion as soon as they complete training and gain experience. An enlisted force with an optimum experience level would therefore exhibit a most pronounced bulge in the middle ranks.

Modification of the traditional enlisted grade structure with its broad base of unskilled privates and consecutively smaller strata of enlisted leaders is largely a consequence of the new skill requirements, especially in technical fields. Yet the upgrading of the specialist has disturbed the clearly visible connection between rank and supervisory authority, which the rank hierarchy was designed to articulate. Before World War II, enlisted technicians ranked as privates or privates first class, but held technical ratings with additional pay. By 1948, the enlisted technician held a rank practically indistinguishable from that of the supervisory noncommissioned officer, who was a leader of men and not a specialist or technician. During and following the Korean Conflict, the Army felt it necessary to take steps to reestablish the prestige and authority of the supervisory ("command") NCO, whose rank once had been an explicit mark of leadership qualities. This meant a separation between the career of the specialist and that of the NCO leader.

When the Army in the late 1950's, through its NCO-specialist program, reintroduced the distinction between an NCO-grade and a specialist grade, the number of NCO's was reduced from 62 per cent to 25 per cent of all enlisted personnel. This reduction gives some indication of the proportion of technicians in the higher ranks. Yet training is so general that in practically all areas every man with some skill has been given a grade to distinguish him from the unskilled trainee. Even the "ordinary" rifleman has been granted recognition as a specialist. Changes in the grade allocations to the infantry rifle company have given NCO leaders at least a parity in rank with specialists over whom they may have to exercise supervisory authority (Table 17). Despite this upgrading in rank, even among ground combat personnel, the table of organization of the rifle company still provides fewer grades above the E-4 level than one finds presently in the overall enlisted grade distributions of the Navy or Air Force.

Thus the rank structure of ground combat units probably helps to account for shortages and high turnover in this career field. For example, the Marine Corps, which has the fewest NCO openings of all the services (Table 16) has also consistently shown (with only one exception since 1955) the lowest reenlistment rates. Career regulars in the Marines

TABLE 17. AUTHORIZED ENLISTED GRADE DISTRIBUTION IN
INFANTRY RIFLE COMPANY, 1941–1960

Rank (from high to low)	1941	1944	1947	1950	1960
			(Percentages)		
E-9					0
E-8					1
E-7		1	a	2	2
E-6		2	2	9	8
E-5	a	9	11	10	17
E-4	1	9	10	26	30
E-3	9	3	14	41	41
E-2	37 ⎫	⎫	⎫	11 ⎫	0
	⎬ 90	⎬ 77	⎬ 62	11 ⎬ 22	
E-1	53 ⎭	⎭	⎭	0 ⎭	0
Total	100	100	100	100	100

a Less than .5 per cent. Percentages do not total 100 because of rounding.
SOURCE: U.S. Army Tables of Organization for respective years.

who are serving second and subsequent enlistments likewise have lower reenlistment rates than career regulars in the other services.

The expansion of career opportunities for enlisted men by the addition of two new "supergrades" (E-8 and E-9) was explicitly meant for the NCO leader. These two grades, designed for men with leadership responsibility, reestablished the chain of command even though some promotions, it was anticipated, would ultimately go to positions requiring an "unusual" amount of technical competence and "some" supervisory responsibility. Permanent promotions have also once again become available to NCO's, but not to specialists. Soldiers appointed in permanent NCO grades are given warrants in recognition of the special contribution they make to the service. The experience of these men is of high value, and their morale as well as their retention is the subject of considerable concern.

Pay differentials among military ranks have, on the whole, been compressed since World War I. Enlisted men especially can anticipate higher real earnings than they could at the beginning of the present century. The rise in their pay has kept reasonable pace with that of industry, especially when additional allowances and fringe benefits are considered.[26] The trend toward narrowing pay differentials was reversed in the effort of the 1958 Officer Pay Act to bring the remuneration of general officers more in line with that given at comparable levels in industry. Legislation in 1963 was aimed primarily at increases for the middle officer ranks who might be deciding whether or not to remain in the service.

But as in the case of enlisted ranks, professional military management has permitted the expansion of the middle levels of the hierarchy. Here the establishment of additional grades for a very small number of general officers has been much less important than the proportionate increase of officers in the "upper middle" ranks (Table 18). The increasing proportion of lieutenant colonels and colonels (or their Naval equivalents, commander and captain) reflects the increased requirements at these specific levels of responsibility. Since the large intakes during periods of expansion usually occur at the lowest ranks and many of

TABLE 18. ARMY AND NAVY OFFICERS ON ACTIVE DUTY BY GRADE, 1920–1962

Rank	1920	1945	1948	1952	1962
	ARMY (Percentages)				
Generals	.4	.2	.6	.4	.5
Colonels	4.1	1.3	5.3	3.6	4.9
Lt. Cols.	4.7	3.4	12.3	9.6	11.7
Majors	14.9	8.3	15.9	12.9	16.6
Captains	35.9	23.4	30.2	27.6	31.2
Lieutenants	40.0	63.4	35.7	45.9	35.1
Total Officers	100.0	100.0	100.0	100.0	100.0
	NAVY (Percentages)				
Admirals	1.3		.6	.4	.4
Captains	4.4		6.2	3.9	5.9
Commanders	7.6		11.4	8.7	11.9
Lt. Commanders	14.4		15.6	16.0	18.2
Lieutenants	32.8		24.1	32.6	26.4
Lts. (j.g.) and Ensigns	29.5		42.1	38.4	37.2
Total Officers	100.0		100.0	100.0	100.0

SOURCES: 1920 data from Janowitz, Morris, *op. cit.*
1945 Army data from Stouffer, Samuel A., *op. cit.*
1948, 1952, and 1962 data from Statistical Services Center, Office of Secretary of Defense.

those inducted serve only during the emergency, the rank distribution of regular officers tends to be inflated during periods of retrenchment. Thus 1920, a year of retrenchment, should be compared with the year 1948, rather than wartime 1945.

The career progression of officers has become highly institutionalized. Advancement is controlled by a system of career management designed to assure a constant supply of professionally qualified officers at all levels of the hierarchy. The necessity of recruiting middle and higher professional leadership from officers who enter each service at the lowest officer grade presses toward an essentially pyramid-shaped grade structure. Inherent in the pyramidal grade structure is the steady narrowing of opportunity as one approaches the top of the organization. Unless wartime emergency suddenly creates more openings, opportunities for younger officers during periods of stability depend upon the number of vacancies produced by processes of natural attrition and retirement. The resignation of many officers after their obligatory duty serves in this respect as a "safety valve." But it is problematic whether the number of vacancies thus made available is sufficient to guarantee advancement prospects satisfactory to ambitious junior officers who are otherwise highly qualified. As a consequence, peacetime military establishments that gear promotion to seniority exhibit a tendency toward stagnation. Under the conditions prevailing in the 1920's and 1930's, it was not at all unusual for regular officers to retire after long years of service with the rank of captain in the Army or lieutenant in the Navy.

The present officer career management structure of the services has sought to create more promotion opportunities for qualified young officers. Higher authorizations at some officer grades have accompanied a deliberate policy of forcing into early retirement officers who fail promotion after specified times in grade. Additional vacancies produced by forced attrition permit accelerated promotions for some even before they reach the prescribed time of service in grade. The more favorable grade structure has improved opportunities for both regular and extended active duty officers, and as a result, promotion though more selective, also comes more rapidly. To be sure, the rank of captain (lieutenant in the Navy) was still the modal rank in the 1962 officer grade distribution. But this includes all categories, such as noncareer reserve officers not expected to extend their service beyond the obligatory tour. They contribute disproportionately to the lowest officer grades. The increases in the middle-level ranks are nevertheless such that the pyramid comes more and more to look like a flask.

It is evident, therefore, that even though officer grade allocations are subject to direct statutory controls, the system has many elements that permit flexibility. The continued presence on active duty of large numbers of reserve officers concentrated at the lower ranks, in particular, enables each service to maintain a rank distribution of regular officers much more favorable than that authorized (Table 19). Some reserve officers later obtain regular commissions and still others remain on extended tours of duty until they reach the retirement point. But as a group they not only lack seniority and experience as professional officers; judged by educational attainments they are inferior in quality to the regulars.

TABLE 19. GRADE DISTRIBUTION OF REGULAR AND RESERVE
COMMISSIONED OFFICERS, 1960

Rank	Marine Corps		Army		Navy		Air Force	
	Reg.	Res.	Reg.	Res.	Reg.	Res.	Reg.	Res.
	(Percentages)							
Generals/Admirals	.6	a	1.2	a	.7	a	.8	a
Colonels/Captains	5.7	.1	12.0	.6	8.7	.5	8.8	.5
Lt. Cols./Commanders	12.6	.7	19.6	6.9	15.4	5.6	15.8	3.0
Majors/								
Lt. Commanders	2.1	1.4	17.7	16.2	22.9	8.0	24.2	16.7
Captains/Lieutenants	38.2	11.9	30.9	32.4	28.9	17.5	34.0	38.7
Lieutenants/Lts. (j.g.)								
and Ensigns	20.7	85.8	18.6	43.9	23.4	68.5	16.5	41.2
Total	100.0	100.0	100.0	100.0	100.0	100.0	100.0	100.0
Proportion of total-commissioned								
officers	.69	.31	.42	.58	.65	.35	.40	.60

a Less than .5 per cent.

SOURCE: Department of Defense, 1960. Percentages do not total 100 because of rounding.

A rational system of personnel management is governed by the assumption that the interests of individual officers are to be subordinated to service needs. Problems of morale, however, produced by management policies not acceptable to an overwhelming number of officers, must receive equal consideration with the manpower needs of the military establishment. If a rigorously enforced policy of competitive promotion threatens to force out qualified officers, professional *esprit de corps* will suffer serious impairment. Therefore, no account of existing vacancies is taken in selecting regular officers up to the rank of major; only qualifications are considered. In fact, judging by 1960 selection rates, any qualified officer who chose to remain in service stood an excellent chance of attaining at least the rank of lieutenant colonel (or the Navy equivalent) because of the large number of junior officers who resign after a minimal tour.

Yet a uniform officer career management structure, founded on the principle that every professional officer given the chance to develop the appropriate perspective is a potential manager, must also accommodate itself to the increasing diversification of skill requirements. Included within the officer corps are many men whose status as professionals, and therefore as officers, derives from special competences that do not, even when developed further, prepare them to assume responsibilities central to military management. Their presence dilutes the homogeneity of outlook that should mark officers as a single distinct profession and forces a diversification of the career lines of officers.

This distinction between line officer and specialist is most explicit in the Navy. The Navy's promotion system is geared to the advancement of unrestricted line officers, the only ones qualified to command at sea. Categories outside the unrestricted line, consisting of engineering duty officers, aeronautical engineering duty officers, and special duty officers in such fields as communications, intelligence, law, and public information are clearly recognized. Staff corps officers, a third category, are commissioned in or assigned to the Chaplain's Corps, the Civil Engineer's Corps, the Supply Corps, and the various medical service corps. The advancement of officers not in the unrestricted line is linked to the advancement of those qualified for seagoing command by a "running-mate" principle, which preserves the integrity of the rank structure but prescribes distinct career lines. The Navy, too, was the first to introduce the "limited duty" officer, by which highly skilled enlisted specialists were commissioned as officers in their specialty, usually after about ten years of service, and thus frequently were retained in the Navy for an additional twenty years. They could not, however, advance beyond the rank of commander.

The Air Force formally recognizes a fundamental distinction between officers holding an aeronautical rating and nonrated officers who do not and, like the Navy, prescribes different patterns of utilization for the two categories. But unlike the Navy, where the new specialist categories were designed to uphold the preeminence of the unrestricted line officer, the qualified nonrated officer may also be utilized in an operations career area, where he is directly involved in the manning and managing of the weapons systems. The development of missiles especially will diminish the central importance of aeronautical ratings and weaken the distinction between rated and nonrated personnel. Meanwhile, all rated officers in the Air Force are required to develop a technical or a scientific and engineering field in addition to their operations career area. The Army probably maintains the most unified pattern of career development, with technical career patterns that represent a variant of an overall career plan applicable to all regular officers. In spite of increasing specialization, there is some reluctance to abandon the traditional notion of a military professional skilled in handling men during wartime operations.

Because the officer corps actually embraces personnel with widely different experience and career perspectives, utilizing varied skills, it experiences the persistent dilemmas of maintaining a unique and uniform profession while accommodating within its single uniformed hierarchy elements of other professions. Thus certain professional categories—at present primarily medical and dental officers liable for compulsory service—are exempt from forced attrition. Likewise, the practice of granting commissions to other specialists and the utilization of large numbers of reserve officers means that many military officers are not necessarily military professionals in the strict sense of a full career commitment. Military service can provide these officers with experience useful in subsequent careers; yet many of them view their service as a deferment of primary occupational goals.

Similarly, the availability in the civilian labor force of many professional men with skills necessary to the military has led to the increased use of nonuniformed personnel, directly employed by the defense establishment, by the particular services, or by civilian contract agencies. As Table 20 shows, the number of such civilians has grown more rapidly

TABLE 20. UTILIZATION OF CIVILIAN MANPOWER

Service	Civilians	Military	Ratio Military/Civilian
	(In Thousands)		
Department of Defense (June 30, 1939)	163.5	486.4	3.0:1
Department of Defense (June 30, 1946)	879.9	2,495.2	2.8:1
Department of Defense (December 31, 1959)	1,234.0	2,487.2	2.0:1
Army (December 31, 1959)	500.8	876.3	1.75:1
Navy and Marine Corps (December 31, 1959)	366.3	781.5	2.1:1
Air Force (December 31, 1959)	366.9	829.4	2.25:1

SOURCE: Statistical Services Center, Office of Secretary of Defense, January 29, 1960.

than the personnel in military uniform. In some scientific categories, military employment accounts for a sizable proportion of all professional personnel, and their professional experience is frequently indispensable to the management of the armed forces. These men are not subject to reassignment and rotation, so that their comparatively long tenure in specific activities enables them to exercise considerable influence, even though formal responsibility continues to rest with officers in actual command.

Nevertheless, the largest proportion of civilians employed in the defense establishment and the services are not professionals. A variety of service functions, many relatively menial tasks, are assigned to nonuniformed personnel. The purpose of this policy is to relieve military personnel as far as possible of nonmilitary tasks, including kitchen duty, and to free them for assignments that civilians cannot fill. With so many civilians providing services, a large number of outsiders become directly involved in military activities and the entire management structure becomes increasingly complex.

CONCLUSION

Interpenetration of the civil and the military sectors has deeply modified the insularity of the military profession. The new skill requirements, the growing importance of academic rather than strictly military education, modifications of the military rank hierarchy mirroring changes in civilian society, and a diversification of military careers are all elements in this process. One can speak of these developments in their entirety as a "civilianization" of the military; yet the militarization of society provides an equally apt image, describing dependence of the military on the total national resources as a base of mobilization.

Obviously, there are specific personnel requirements that can be met only to the degree that the military mobilizes, trains, and manages manpower directly under its control and in its organizational logic. Basically these are the requirements of combat. A special force of men trained to carry on under enemy fire and prepared to go instantly to locations far removed from their permanent residence is indispensable to the success of many military missions. In addition to combat personnel, the modern military establishment requires increasing numbers of technical specialists at all levels, many of them in uniform but others as civilians. The use of civilians in some tasks can increase the effectiveness of the combat force, but when troops are engaged in active hostilities or performing sea-going duties, even "civilians" in military employ must be subject to military discipline. To this extent, then, combat requirements remain unchanged.

The presence of all kinds of technical specialists with distinct career patterns does, however, tend to dilute the homogeneity of outlook on which professional *esprit* was founded. Neither the combat soldier nor the specialist need be committed to a lifetime military career. Age tends to limit the effectiveness of combat personnel and even of combat leaders. After ten or fifteen years most of them must move to other assignments in order to make room for younger personnel. By contrast, the skill of the specialist, civilian or military, who often functions outside the regular line of command, may continue to be in high demand by the military, despite the fact that he fails to qualify for higher managerial responsibility. Hence personnel procedure can be modified so that he need be subject neither to forced attention nor continuous rotation.

The relatively small group of military managers, selected by a process of internal recruitment on the basis of career commitment and demonstrated potential for higher management, represent the core of the profession. For them military service is a lifetime career. Thus military requirements call for a relatively large group of men committed to a limited career, serving sufficient years to man the various specialist assignments (including those of combat), to be released at an age young enough to enter a second career in which skills acquired in military service can be gainfully employed. As a common outlook based on similarity of skill and experiences decline for the officer corps as a whole, the maintenance of the professional core assumes fundamental importance.

No longer are officers, by virtue of officer status, merely military professionals. The new nature of military service drastically alters the significance of being an officer. For many it is less a professional commitment than a phase in a longer occupational career. The entire military establishment in many respects ceases to be the world of a profession but becomes instead geared to the mobility needs of individuals. While this change mirrors a developing pattern in American life, it also poses special problems for the effectiveness of a military force. Rational organization and automated personnel systems are designed to allocate resources and improve the organizational effectiveness of the contemporary military establishment. That technocratically oriented military leaders would emphasize new personnel systems, new management techniques, and new organizational formats is to be expected in a period of rapid technological change. The sheer management of the armed forces is unthinkable without constant innovation in these sectors. Yet these same practices and programs also have disruptive impacts.

The military professional confronted with an unpredictable and uncontrollable external environment has traditionally responded with a drive for internal order and internal consistency. The range of strategic alternatives narrows as the number and destructive power of weapons systems increase; conventional definitions of victory and defeat become ambiguous. The technology of weapons systems requires the most rationally constructed control devices; yet there is a point at which military management can become overconcerned with an ideological effort to impose order and its managerial practices cease to be devices for solving specific organizational problems. This creates a new danger: old-fashioned military rituals can be supplanted by a modernized cult of scientific management.

Technology has created new career fields, and the division of labor in the military—given the number of personnel involved—is probably more complex than any other institution's, with the possible exception of space exploration. More complex and more sensitive devices of coordination are required. But the military to the extent that it is a combat organization has also many primitive characteristics. Its effectiveness depends not only on a formal structure that recognizes internal complexity but also on the sheer weight of its aggressive numbers.

Innovations in military management can easily become dysfunctional. In fact, the very image of the military as a technological organization, operating on a rational principle, essential though it may be, has its disruptive aspects. The introduction, for example, of new elaborate classification schemes of military specialties and occupations often bear little relationship to reality and the way in which personnel must be utilized. The result of overrefined systems is to create confusion and organizational strain. Despite the explicit rules for officer career management systems, individual officers and their sponsoring superiors still exercise considerable initiative in selecting their assignments, but the process of justification becomes more complex. Assignment of enlisted personnel "by name assignment" is less personalized than the term suggests. The local commander is unable to reward demonstrated exceptional skill with much flexibility. He must operate as a branch manager, using as best he can the resources allocated by a central manpower agency.

As long as there are still many elements of military organization that are not highly technological, men with only general aptitude can and ultimately must be used. Questions must continually be raised concerning the consequences of highly centralized personnel policies on operating military units. When personnel agencies divert men with specific technological skills to service units, these units receive a surplus of advanced skills and there is wastage as well as chronic morale problems among those whose skills are not effectively utilized. Likewise, centralized personnel agencies can drain off talented personnel from units without a technological image (such as infantry) and they have, as a result, a reduced capability for using innovation in weaponry.

No doubt, many of these problems can be seen as transitional, and there is certainly a limit in the capacity of a military organization to use its manpower effectively. The crux of the matter is that career and military management, when used as a device for serving the officer and enlisted man, can become excessively technocratic and create new inflexibilities. The military's downgrading of testing and selection in recent years indicates an area of successful counterbalancing innovation against a partially perfected innovation. But the failure to modify the system of excessive personnel rotation bears witness to the fact that the persistence of traditional formats is even more difficult to handle.

NOTES

1. Goode, William J., "Community within a Community: The Professions," *American Sociological Review*, vol. 22, April, 1957, pp. 194–200.

2. For discussions of this transformation see Vagts, Alfred, *A History of Militarism*, 2d ed., Meridian Books, New York, 1959; Goerlitz, Walter, *Der deutsche Generalstabs: Geschichte und Gestalt, 1657–1945*, Verlag der Frankfurter Hefte, Frankfurt am Main, 1950; Girardet, Raoul, *La société militaire dans la France contemporaine, 1815–1939*, Libraire Plon, Paris, 1953; and Janowitz, Morris, *The Professional Soldier: A Social and Political Portrait*, The Free Press of Glencoe, New York, 1960, for the peculiarly American version.

3. Huntington, Samuel P., *The Soldier and the State*, Harvard University Press, Cambridge, Mass., 1957, chap. 1; also Etzioni, Amitai, *A Comparative Analysis of Complex Organizations*, The Free Press of Glencoe, New York, 1961, pp. 16–20.

4. U.S. House of Representatives, Committee on Armed Services, *Hearings Before the Subcommittee on Utilization of Military Manpower*. 86th Congress, 2nd Sess. Government Printing Office, Washington, 1960.

5. *Ibid.*

6. U.S. Department of Defense, Ad Hoc Committee to Study and Revise the Officer Personnel Act of 1947, *A Concept of Career Management for Officer Personnel of the Armed Services: A Report and Recommendation to the Secretary of Defense*, December, 1960, p. 12.

7. President's Commission on Veterans' Pensions, *Veterans' Benefits in the United States: Finding and Recommendations*, April, 1956.

8. U.S. House Committee on Armed Services, *op. cit.*

9. Janowitz, Morris, *op. cit.*

10. Ryan, F. J., *Relation of Performance to Social Background Factors of Army Inductees*. Catholic University Press, Washington, 1958, p. 68.

11. U.S. House of Representatives, *Career Incentives Act of 1955*. 84th Congress, 1st Sess. Report No. 90, March 8, 1955.

12. From an unpublished paper, cited by S. P. Huntington, "Power, Expertise and the Military Profession," *Daedalus*, vol. 92, Fall, 1963, p. 792.

13. Ginzberg, Eli, and others, *The Ineffective Soldier*. Columbia University Press, New York, 1959, 3 vols.

14. Masland, John W., and Laurence I. Radway, *Soldiers and Scholars: Military Education and National Policy*. Princeton University Press, Princeton, N. J., 1957.

15. Janowitz, Morris, *op. cit.*

16. Public Opinion Surveys, Inc., *Attitudes of Adult Civilians Toward Military Service as a Career*, Princeton, N. J., 1955.

17. Wool, Harold, "The Armed Services as a Training Institution" in Ginzberg, Eli, editor, *The Nation's Children*. Columbia University Press, New York, 1959, vol. 2, pp. 158–185.

18. President's Commission on Veterans' Pensions, *op. cit.* The exact question was: "Looking back, how has the time you spent in the Armed Forces and the training, skills, and experience you acquired there affected your employment and progress in civilian life?" The answers were as follows:

    14.7 per cent: Helped me considerably.
    26.2 per cent: Has been of some benefit.
    50.1 per cent: Not much effect either way.
    2.7 per cent: Was a temporary handicap but what I learned helped me later.
    6.3 per cent: Has been a handicap or disadvantage.

19. President's Committee on Equal Opportunity in the Armed Forces, *Initial Report: Equality of Treatment and Opportunity for Negro Military Personnel Stationed in the United States*, June 13, 1963.

20. Statistics on the "second careers" of retired enlisted men are not available. According to a mail survey of nearly four thousand officers who had retired between 1955 and 1960, only about 5 per cent were operating their own business. See the report by the Study Committee of the University of Michigan to the Committee on Armed Services of the U.S. Senate, *A Study of the Military Retirement Pay System and Certain Related Subjects*, Ann Arbor, Mich., June 27, 1961, Appendix 2.

21. See pp. 264–265 of this volume.

22. See p. 268.

23. U.S.M.A. Superintendent's Curriculum Study, *Report of the Working Committee on the Historical Aspects of the Curriculum for the Period 1802–1945*, July 31, 1958.

24. See also the Zald and Simon paper, pp. 257–285 of this volume.

25. An analysis by Julian G. Franks (unpublished) of data from NORC Study No. 431: "Great Aspirations, Career Plans of America's June 1961 Graduates."

26. President's Commission on Veterans' Pensions, *op. cit.*

THE EFFECTS OF SUCCESSION: A COMPARATIVE STUDY OF MILITARY AND BUSINESS ORGANIZATION

Oscar Grusky *

T HE PROBLEM OF SUCCESSION is the organizational equivalent of the
larger societal problem of generations.[1] The replacement of personnel in complex organizations is a continuous process, just as the cycle of
life and death is an inevitable feature of human existence. This study is
concerned with a comparative analysis of the effects of succession on a
military installation and a large business firm.

The study of succession, sometimes called occupational or administrative succession, has been pursued from two vantage points. One approach locates the problem exclusively at the top of the organization
hierarchy.[2] Such a viewpoint offers the distinct advantage of a focus
upon those elites that are generally most accountable for the direction
and implementation of organizational objectives. A second approach
emphasizes that the proper study of succession should be broadened to
include the effects of personnel circulation through positions at all
levels in the hierarchy.[3] By this approach the concepts of occupational
mobility and administrative succession tend to be fused and career
mobility in an organizational setting is seen not only as essential for
leadership development, but, at the same time, as creating problems of
organizational continuity in the performance of its critical functions.
Succession, as we shall use the term, is meant to refer to the processes
associated with the movement of members out of the organization and
their replacement by new members.

Comparative analysis of military and industrial organization suggests
that military organization has reached a stage of bureaucratic develop-

* I regret that I cannot name the Air Force officers whose overall aid and attempts
to educate me about the base and about the military establishment as a whole were
virtually indispensable. I am also grateful to the officers and managers who provided
the basic data for the research. Most of the data on business managers were gathered
during the tenure of a Ford Foundation Faculty Research Fellowship in Social
Science and Business. I wish to thank Don Baker for research assistance. Morris
Janowitz first suggested that I make this study and provided continuing intellectual
stimulation.

83

ment which seemingly anticipates the future movement of other complex systems. Concepts now commonly applied in industry, such as line
of command, staff-line, the development of oral briefing, and others,
were derived from military experience. It is already evident that the
highly bureaucratized patterns of career succession in the military have
spread to large industrial corporations. Still, the degree of bureaucratization of careers is greater in military than in business organization.
Four factors have contributed to the extensive organizational control of
the military over officer career patterns: the nature of its mission, its
size, complexity, and geographical dispersion. The intense political and
social implications involved in the management of violence require
careful control over the training particularly of those in executive positions. The distribution of goods and services for profit does not require
the same degree of close control. The sheer size of a centralized military
establishment necessitates control by extensive rules and regulations.
There were about 2,450,000 men under arms and 343,000 officers on
active duty in 1962. Research indicates that large size in itself may not
require an unusually large administrative apparatus, but size is positively related to complexity of organization and the more complex the
system the greater the demand for a large administrative staff.[4] The
many component parts of the military mission and the related necessity
for locating military units all over the world combine to emphasize the
overall complexity of the United States military establishment. However, it should be kept in mind that because the military is both a unified
and highly centralized system it is not strictly comparable to business
organization. Rotation in the military is from one unit to another
within a single establishment. The business executive may either transfer
from one unit to another within the corporation or move to another
firm. Hence in business two different modes of succession exist whereas
there is one in the military. We have assumed arbitrarily that the military
base may be considered to be equivalent to the business firm. We justified this decision on the grounds that both units of study have clear and,
we think, parallel organizational identities within their respective institutional contexts as well as within the local community in which they
are situated. Interdepartmental transfers, either in the military base or
business organization, were not considered in this study. Instead, our
focus was on movement into and out of the military base and the
business firm.

Assuming that "Military career lines are highly standardized, as
compared with other professions,"[5] and some comparative data will be
presented to test this contention, what are the effects of this bureaucrat-

ization? Two independent studies have shown that large, and therefore more bureaucratized, organizations have greater rates of executive succession than small organizations.[6] Kriesberg has pointed out that this may mean that career patterns are different in the small and large systems. The small organization is more likely to be manned by "home-guards" or "locals," whose careers are characterized by relatively little movement from place to place. Larger organizations are more likely to be dominated by executives who are "itinerants," moving frequently from organization to organization.[7] Military systems are of theoretical significance to organization theory because all those of executive rank are, of necessity, itinerants. Thus military systems are desirable objects of investigation for the student of succession because they represent a relatively extreme career situation. Military rotation policies require officers to change their assignments after a given period of time. This period may be one year in hardship areas, but more typically two, three, four, and at times, five years. Hence executive succession at all military installations is highly routinized and frequent.[8]

A number of studies of small organizations have indicated that succession is disruptive, typically producing low morale and conflict among the staff.[9] It is likely that in highly bureaucratized organizations such as the military where succession is closely regulated, these disruptive responses are muted. By standardizing career experiences the organization systematically prepares the manager for future moves. Comparisons of business firms and military installations facilitate the study of the effects on succession of differential degrees of organizational control.

Three problems formed the central interest of our study. First, we were concerned with the structural context in which succession takes place. What are the organizational correlates of the two types of succession, bureaucratic and less bureaucratic? Second, we were interested in the consequences of succession for organizational commitment. How does rotation influence the orientation of the military officer to his present organizational assignment? Third, we were interested in adjustment to community life. How does the military officer adapt to the transient nature of his family life? Is he truly "rootless" or does his behavior reflect an alteration in the conventional patterns of integration found in stable settings?

No single unit could hope to be typical of either industrial or military organization, although military organizations have a common format. In both cases, it was the cooperation on the part of the host institution in permitting the study, and, to a lesser extent, geographical location, that dictated our choices. It is probably unnecessary to say that access for research purposes to either of the two types of organization is not always readily available. The data on the industrial firm were collected in 1960; that on the military installation in 1962. In both instances the research techniques applied were diverse. They included exploratory interviews, observation, perusal of official documents, and questionnaires. The latter represented the source of the most systematic data.

A questionnaire was distributed to all 2,198 managers (as defined by the firm) of the United Utility Corporation (a fictitious name), the largest single enterprise of a major public utility holding company in the United States. Approximately 75 per cent, or 1,649 usable, signed schedules were returned. A comparison by salary, sex, and position of the distributions of the sample with that of the total population of managers in the firm revealed a very close correspondence.

On the basis of observation, a six-level corporate hierarchy was initially distinguished, as follows: I. Top Management; II. Upper-Middle Management; III. Middle Management; IV. Lower-Middle Management; V. Lower Management; VI. First-Line Supervisors. The last group consisted almost completely of females, who were not included in the present study. Two managers in the firm (one Level III, and the other Level IV) independently placed each of the 318 management positions in the corporation on one of the six levels, applying the criterion of amount of official authority associated with the position.[10]

The United Utility Corporation has several branches, most of which are located within the confines of a single metropolitan area, a format that increases its relevance for comparison with the military base. The largest proportion of managers are situated in a single building, the general headquarters. Length of time with the organization, which we shall use as a measure of succession, refers in most cases to service within the numerous departments of the United Utility Corporation. The large majority of the managers (84.7 per cent) started in nonmanagement positions and worked up the hierarchy. In this respect, as in others, the firm may not be typical of most large business enterprises.

The military installation was a United States Air Force base. Although not of the combat type, it was adequate for our purposes with respect to its overall form. Specifically, the rotation problems of the base were characteristic of military installations. Hence we could properly assess the effects of these on officer behavior. Of the 629 questionnaires distributed to the entire complement of officers, 11 were returned as unreceived and 556, or almost 90 per cent, were completed and returned.[11] A comparison by military rank and aeronautical rating of the questionnaire sample and the total officer population revealed a close correspondence. Such an unusually high rate of return, exceeding even the high return of the business managers, may have been partly a function of the endorsement of the study by the Commanding Officer. Such support was unquestionably more effective than the corresponding support by the President and Board Chairman of United Utility, reflecting perhaps an important difference between civilian and military authority systems. The fact that the military questionnaire could not be signed may also have facilitated a higher rate of return.[12]

There is some limited evidence that organizations with markedly different authority structures may respond in different ways to executive personnel changes.[13] A comparison of the authority structure of the industrial firm and the military installation was therefore desirable. Table 1 presents such a comparison. In order to have a sufficient number of cases in each category we found it necessary to combine top executives and upper-middle management (both to be called Top Executives) on the one hand, and Generals and Colonels on the other. Moreover, lower management and supervisors (to be called First-Level Management), and Captains, First and Second Lieutenants were combined for the sake of convenience. The business organization had a higher proportion of top managers and middle managers than the Air Force base. On the other hand, the latter had considerably more lower level management. Nevertheless, as shown in Table 1, there was overall similarity in the two structures, considering the fundamental differences in their official objectives.

Further indication of structural similarity was revealed from the questionnaire data. The business managers and Air Force officers were asked: "In general, how much do you personally have to say about how

TABLE 1. MILITARY VERSUS BUSINESS ORGANIZATION:
HIERARCHY OF AUTHORITY LEVELS

Military Installation *1962*		*Business Firm* *1960*	
	Per cent		*Per cent*
Generals	.5	Top Executives	1.6
Colonels	4.6	Upper-Middle Management	6.7
Lt. Colonels	10.0	Middle Management	14.4
Majors	23.5	Lower-Middle Management	40.2
Captains	55.3	Lower Management	36.3
First Lieutenants	4.8	First-Line Supervisors	.8
Second Lieutenants	1.3		
Total	100.0	Total	100.0
Number of cases	*631*	*Number of cases*	*1,240*

things are decided in your department?" The responses permitted were: "I have a great deal to say," "I have some say," or "I have no say at all!"

In one sense, in both settings, there is an overall pattern of similarity (Table 2). The order in the percentage responding, "I have a great deal to say" was not markedly different between the two hierarchies; for the military, at the top the percentage was 92 and at the bottom 21 per cent; by comparison the range for the business firm was from 82 per cent at the top to 34 per cent at the bottom. However, the pattern of gradation was not without differences. In the case of the military a sense of authority was closely linked to rank, and increased rank by rank. For the busi-

TABLE 2. MILITARY VERSUS BUSINESS ORGANIZATION:
PERCEIVED AUTHORITY OF EXECUTIVES AT VARIOUS LEVELS
OF THE HIERARCHY[a]

Per Cent Responding: "I have a great deal to say."	Military Installation		Business Firm	
	Per cent	Number of cases	Per cent	Number of cases
Colonels and Generals (Top Executives)	92	26	82	101
Lt. Colonels (Middle Management)	65	55	44	174
Majors (Lower Middle Management)	49	138	32	492
Captains and Lieutenants (First-Level Management)	21	332	34	455

[a] Item: "In general, how much do you personally have to say about how things are decided in your department?"

ness firm, while first level of rank was slightly higher than the comparable level in the military, it was comparable to the next, the lower-middle management level. In fact, the third, the middle management, was only slightly higher. In short, the pattern of the business firm showed limited spread at the lower and middle ranks and a larger gap to the top level. Thus the military revealed a greater degree of hierarchicalization, and since degree of hierarchicalization of authority is one index of bureaucratization, these data may be taken as support for the assumption of greater bureaucratization in military than in business organization.

THE STRUCTURE OF SUCCESSION

Two ends of a continuum describing rates of succession have been suggested. On one end, the maximum rates of succession in an organization would be represented by the hypothetical case in which all the members of the system are replaced daily, hourly, or even more rapidly. The French Army in the middle of the eighteenth century approximated this extreme. Because of an abundance of officers, practices were created that encouraged rapid succession and minimum effectiveness. The historian Walter L. Dorn, described the situation thus: "The incredible number of officers with their elaborate baggage and servants, who frequently became entangled with marching columns, reduced the mobility of the army in the field. The Quartermaster-General had often to mobilize the resources of an entire city to provide for them. Actual service occupied only a small proportion of the officers. To create opportunities for all of them, one struck upon the expedient of rotating Lieutenant-Generals and Marshalls 'du jour,' just for the day. The commands of the line and the flanks were passed on from one officer to another from one day to the next."[14] The other extreme form would be represented by an organization in which the members remain throughout their lifetimes. Among industrial organizations, the Japanese factory is illustrative of an extremely low rate of succession at all levels in the hierarchy. Abegglen notes that in the Japanese factory, unlike its American counterpart, the employee commits himself and the firm correspondingly feels committed to him for a lifetime relationship.[15] A factory employing 4,250 persons in Osaka was described by the author. In this firm only five or six persons, or about one per thousand, leave the company each year, and these for extreme behavior, such as habitual thievery.[16] Most organizations, naturally, would be situated somewhere between these two radical types.

Table 3 compares the rates of managerial succession among business managers and officers of the military installation studied. It is readily apparent that their differences were considerable. Almost half (45.5 per

TABLE 3. MILITARY VERSUS BUSINESS ORGANIZATION: LENGTH OF TIME IN THE ORGANIZATION OF EXECUTIVES

Length of Time in the Organization	Military Installation	Business Firm
	(Percentages)	
1 year or less	45.5	2.1
2 years	18.8	2.0
3 years	15.7	3.9
4 years	14.4	4.6
5 years or more	5.6	87.5
Total	100.0	100.1
Number of cases	554[a]	1,219[b]

[a] 2 cases were not ascertained.   [b] 21 cases were not ascertained.

cent) of the Air Force officers had been at their base a year or less, while only slightly more than 2 per cent (2.1 per cent) of the business managers had been with the firm for a comparable period of time. Correspondingly, almost nine out of ten of United's managers had at least five years of service with the Corporation, while only about one officer in twenty (5.6 per cent) stationed at the military installation had a similar length of service.

Both the high rate of succession of the Air Force base and the low rate of the business corporation maintained themselves at every major hierarchical level. At the top executive level, all but 7 per cent of the business managers had at least five years' service with the firm, while only one-third of the Colonels and Generals had equivalent experience with their organization (Table 4). The Chairman of the Board of the business firm had been with the firm for thirty years and had occupied his present position or that of President for thirteen years. In contrast, the Commanding Officer of the Air Force base had a three-year tour of duty. A similar situation prevails at most military installations, although normal tours of duty occasionally may be slightly greater.

Continuing with our comparison of the succession rates of our two research sites, Table 4 indicates that the discrepancy between the two institutions on this variable can be found at the lower levels of management as well as at the higher ones. Considering for the moment only those business executives with five years of service or more, we found that at every hierarchical level over eight out of ten of the managers held the maximum of organizational experience. If the criterion of organizational experience is raised to fifteen years or more with the firm, hierarchical differences among business managers emerge clearly. Almost half (48 per cent) of the top level executives of United had been with the company that length of time. This reduced to 22 per cent for middle management and 16 and 17 per cent for each of the two lower-level strata. A greater proportion of senior officers, that is, Colonels and Generals, were likely to have had five or more years' experience at the base than officers of lower rank. Whereas one-third of the top level officers (N = 9) had this amount of experience at the base, fewer than 2 per cent of the company grade officers, Captain and below, had equivalent experience. Moreover, it was at the lowest rank level that the largest percentage of officers had one year or less experience. Hence two propositions were supported by our analysis thus far: (1) The military installation studied was confronted with more rapid succession than the business firm at every level of the management hierarchy. (2) In both types of organization, the rate of succession tended to be somewhat lower among the top executives of the organization. (However, the small

TABLE 4. MILITARY VERSUS BUSINESS ORGANIZATION:
LENGTH OF TIME IN THE ORGANIZATION OF EXECUTIVES
AT VARIOUS LEVELS OF THE HIERARCHY

Length of Time at Various Levels of Hierarchy	Military Installation	Business Firm
Colonels and Generals (Top Executives)	(Percentages)	
1 year or less	33	4
2 years	26	1
3 years	4	2
4 years	4	—
5 years or more	33	93
Total	100	100
Number of cases	27	99
Lt. Colonels (Middle Management)		
1 year or less	36	2
2 years	20	1
3 years	24	2
4 years	15	6
5 years or more	5	89
Total	100	100
Number of cases	55	175
Majors (Lower Middle Management)		
1 year or less	30	4
2 years	17	2
3 years	20	5
4 years	23	6
5 years or more	10	82
Total	100	100
Number of cases	138	494
Captains and Lieutenants (First-Level Management)		
1 year or less	54	—
2 years	19	2
3 years	14	2
4 years	12	3
5 years or more	1	93
Total	100	100
Number of cases	334	447

number of top-level officers at the military base gave us considerably less confidence in the second proposition than the first.)

The purpose of showing that the two research sites were different with respect to their rates of succession was to prepare the way for our primary concern, the consequences of the bureaucratization of succession. Effects in two areas were indicated, organizational homogeneity and strength of executive control.

Rapid succession is associated with greater homogeneity among organizational members. Bureaucratic control involves the widespread application of rational, universalistic criteria in dealing with members of the system. Hence general indexes of bureaucratization are the extensiveness of rules, the degree of hierarchicalization, impersonality, and the focus on managerial expertise.[17] The opposite type of control, the nonbureaucratic, implies the absence of those factors. In the less bureaucratic form, social control is more personal and the uniqueness of the organization and its chief administrators is paramount.

The more rapid succession of officers at the military installation meant that the *range* of executive experience in the organization was much less among this group than among the business managers. Most of the officers at the Air Force base had two years or less experience, while most of the business managers had at least five years' experience in the organization and almost half of the top level managers had at least fifteen years. Therefore it appears that a concomitant of rapid succession may be decreased executive homogeneity with respect to experience in a particular organizational setting. But the military officer rotates through an establishment which has a basic format and a high degree of organizational standardization. At the same time, the socialization for higher position of all managers, business and military, requires constant exposure to a large number of organizations. The crucial difference would seem to be this: The business executive is more likely than his military counterpart to be able to count on staying with an organization for a long enough period to implement major innovations.

In general, rapid succession encourages executive homogeneity with respect to universalistic criteria. Data on age and seniority may be cited illustratively. Table 5 represents the age distribution of executives of the United Utility Corporation and the officers of the Air Force base. Be-

TABLE 5. MILITARY VERSUS BUSINESS ORGANIZATION:
AGE DISTRIBUTION OF EXECUTIVES

Age Distribution	Military Installation	Business Firm
	(Percentages)	
Under 35 years	49.4	33.4
35 to 44 years	45.3	43.8
45 to 54 years	4.9	14.7
55 years and over	.4	8.1
Total	100.0	100.0
Number of cases	*554*[a]	*1,226*[b]

[a] 2 cases were not ascertained.   [b] 14 cases were not ascertained.

cause of military retirement policies, the officers were, on the whole, much younger than the business managers. In general, age and rate of executive succession should be directly related.[18] Thus the finding that the military installation had a higher rate of succession than the business firm may actually tend to underestimate slightly the true relationship to be found were age to be adequately controlled.

Table 6 compares the age distribution of executives of the military and business organization at each level of the authority structure. A greater proportion of older executives, that is, those fifty-five and older, was

TABLE 6. MILITARY VERSUS BUSINESS ORGANIZATION: AGE DISTRIBUTION OF EXECUTIVES AT VARIOUS LEVELS OF THE HIERARCHY

Age Distribution at Various Levels of Hierarchy	Military Installation	Business Firm
Colonels and Generals (Top Executives)	(Percentages)	
Under 35 years	—	9
35 to 44 years	74	41
45 to 54 years	22	32
55 years and over	4	18
Total	100	100
Number of cases	27	101
Lt. Colonels (Middle Management)		
Under 35 years	—	27
35 to 44 years	85	48
45 to 54 years	13	18
55 years and over	2	7
Total	100	100
Number of cases	55	175
Majors (Lower Middle Management)		
Under 35 years	5	40
35 to 44 years	88	42
45 to 54 years	7	13
55 years and over	—	5
Total	100	100
Number of cases	137	495
Captains and Lieutenants (First-Level Management)		
Under 35 years	80	34
35 to 44 years	19	45
45 to 54 years	1	12
55 years and over	—	9
Total	100	100
Number of cases	335	455

found consistently in the business firm.[19] Also relevant is the finding that the Air Force officers were considerably more homogeneous with respect to age than the business executives. Note that 80 per cent of the Captains and Lieutenants were under thirty-five, almost nine out of ten (88.3 per cent) of the Majors and Lieutenant Colonels were in the same thirty-five to forty-four age bracket, and finally, about three-fourths of the top level officers (74.1 per cent) were similarly located in a single age category. The business executives failed to approach this exceptional degree of homogeneity at any level in their structure of authority. Reflected strongly in these data is the systematic selection and promotion policies typical of the present American military system. Military recruitment is tied closely to age, and promotion up to field grade rank is linked just as closely to length of service.[20] Data from United Utility Corporation indicated that here, too, length of employment with the firm was positively related to amount of upward career mobility.[21] Table 7 examines the relationship between hierarchical position and seniority (the number of years of service in the corporate or military establishment) for the two samples.[22] It is evident that the military sample is more homogeneous than the business managers at *every* hierarchical level. One hundred per cent of the senior military executives had fifteen or more years of seniority compared to only 48 per cent of their business counterparts. At the middle management level, the comparison is 96 per cent to 22 per cent in the maximum seniority category. Among those we have termed lower middle management, we find 99 per cent of the officers grouped in the two highest seniority categories compared to only 65 per cent of the business managers in the same group. The degree of homogeneity among the military officers at the first level of management is brought out most clearly if this group is differentiated more sharply by rank. Seven out of seven Second Lieutenants had four years or less of military service, 78 per cent of the First Lieutenants were in the same category, and 93 per cent of the Captains had either between five or nine or ten through fourteen years of seniority. This close relationship between rank and seniority was not matched by the business managers.

A comparatively slow rate of succession in the business firm studied seemed to function to produce homogeneity through shared experiences in the organization. The significance of leadership homogeneity for administration has been noted by Selznick: "Another developmental problem is that of creating an initial homogeneous staff. The members of this core group reflect the basic policies of the organization in their own outlooks. They can, when matured in this role, perform the essential

TABLE 7. MILITARY VERSUS BUSINESS ORGANIZATION:
SENIORITY OF EXECUTIVES AT VARIOUS LEVELS IN THE HIERARCHY

Seniority at Various Levels of Hierarchy	Military Installation	Business Firm
Colonels and Generals (Top Executives)	(Percentages)	
0 to 4 years	—	7
5 to 9 years	—	5
10 to 14 years	—	40
15 years or more	100	48
Total	100	100
Number of cases	27	99
Lt. Colonels (Middle Management)		
0 to 4 years	—	11
5 to 9 years	—	13
10 to 14 years	4	54
15 years or more	96	22
Total	100	100
Number of cases	55	175
Majors (Lower Middle Management)		
0 to 4 years	—	19
5 to 9 years	1	16
10 to 14 years	43	49
15 years or more	56	16
Total	100	100
Number of cases	135	494
Captains and Lieutenants (First-Level Management)		
0 to 4 years	14	7
5 to 9 years	48	21
10 to 14 years	37	55
15 years or more	1	17
Total	100	100
Number of cases	334	447

task of indoctrinating newcomers along desired lines. They can provide
assurance that decision-making will conform, in spirit as well as letter,
to policies that may have to be formulated abstractly or vaguely. The
development of derivative policies and detailed applications of general
rules will thus be guided by a shared general perspective."[23] Such functions, essential to business organization, ostensibly are replaced in
military systems by bureaucratic forms.

The high rate of succession in the military installation militated
against the creation of homogeneity through shared experiences in the
particular organization of which the officer is a part. Instead, the bases

for homogeneity would seem to lie with the similarity of the officers'
military training, social values, the hierarchy of authority, age, sex, and
other nonparticularistic factors. In the military, the nature of the particular installation is less important to administration than the fundamental similarities of each base. Rapid succession may be both a cause
and a product of organizational uniformity.

Rapid succession is associated with limitations on executive control. It
is frequently argued that in an organization where few executives can
anticipate long periods of service and most can look forward to relatively short tenures in that particular organization, the ability of the
executive to implement major policy changes is greatly weakened. By
contrast, failure to rotate creates powerful barriers to innovation by
entrenching traditionalistic perspectives. Continuous rotation clearly
fashions the pattern of organizational innovations in military systems,
especially at the operational level. All too frequently, the first year of a
three-year tour of duty is spent familiarizing oneself with the idiosyn-
crasies of the base, the second in implementing a number of relatively
limited rule changes, the third in setting the base in order in anticipation
of departure. Moreover, where civilian employees have long tenures and
military officials are frequently rotated, we would expect the former
group to tend to absorb a disproportionate amount of influence on the
implementation of policy and policy-making. Nor is such a situation
conducive to identification with the commanding officer of a military
base. The performance of General Curtis E. LeMay in welding the
Strategic Air Command into a highly effective and adaptable force was
undoubtedly related to the fact that he was left in command for over
eight years rather than the normal shorter tour of duty.[24]

When asked: "What officer of General rank, past or present, do you
admire most?" the 497 military officers who responded selected 118
different generals. Less than one per cent selected their own commanding
officer. For these officers, the system of rotation produced attachments
not so much to one well-known leader but to one of many lesser known
leaders. It is only in the small unbureaucratized organization or in the
large complex system unified through a single overriding objective, as in
combat, that a specific leader is closely identified with the organization
as a whole.[25]

One concrete aspect of the consequences of rotation can be seen in the
data linking length of service in the organization and perceived authority; that is, the amount of authority the person believes he has. These
data are presented in Table 8, which reveal differences between the
military and the business setting. When officers who had been stationed

TABLE 8. MILITARY VERSUS BUSINESS ORGANIZATION:
LENGTH OF TIME IN THE ORGANIZATION AND PERCEIVED
AUTHORITY AT VARIOUS LEVELS OF THE HIERARCHY

Per Cent Responding:
"I have a great deal to say."

| *Military Installation* | *Length of time in the Organization* | | | |
| | Less than 2 years | | 2 years or more | |
	Per cent	*Number of cases*	*Per cent*	*Number of cases*
Colonels and Generals	75	*8*	100	*17*
Lt. Colonels	55	*20*	71	*35*
Majors	49	*41*	50	*96*
Captains and Lieutenants	17	*179*	26	*152*

| *Business Firm* | Less than 5 years | | 5 to 14 years | | 15 or more years | |
	Per cent	*Number of cases*	*Per cent*	*Number of cases*	*Per cent*	*Number of cases*
Top Executives	83	*7*	80	*45*	83	*47*
Middle Management	25	*20*	43	*116*	51	*39*
Lower-Middle Management	13	*91*	31	*324*	56	*79*
First-Level Management	31	*32*	34	*340*	35	*75*

at the base for more than two years were compared with officers at the base for less than two years, a greater proportion of the former felt that they had a "great deal of authority." This held true for all ranks, perhaps most clearly among the uppermost ranks. Although the small number of cases compels qualifying our comments, it appears that knowledge of the military base plus the integration of the officer into its organizational structure, served to strengthen perceived authority. In the business organization, the same relationship was present, but it operated more selectively with respect to the rank structure. At the very top level of management, perceived authority did not increase with length of service, nor were the differences very great at the bottom level. It was only in the middle ranks that there was a marked increase in perceived authority with length of service. Hence, it would appear that frequent succession conditions personal executive authority. The highly bureaucratized system, by routinizing the succession process, modifies the authority of the person through reliance on the authority of the total complex organization.

SUCCESSION AND ORGANIZATIONAL COMMITMENT

Two "types" of succession have thus far been described. The first, represented by the business firm, is characterized by a comparatively slow rate of succession, particularly among the top executives. The integration of the top level group, as well as to a lesser extent, the lower level stratum, is encouraged through shared experiences that take place within the context of a single corporation. The second kind of succession, typified by the military installation, is defined by continuous and regular changes among occupants of all of the positions in the system. Military organization is viewed as a collection of separate and structurally identical installations and a military career may be defined as a journey, with regularly spaced intervals, from one fundamentally equivalent bureaucratic organization to another.

The resulting career patterns should yield different types of commitment to the organization and to its subunits. The present study permitted us to compare the degree of commitment of the officials of the two organizations. We assumed tentatively that differences in commitment might be attributed, in part, to differences in succession experiences. By commitment we refer to the nature of the affective relationship of the member toward the organization as a whole and toward the department. Commitment was measured in these areas by means of two three-item Guttman scales.[26]

Tables 9 and 10 present the major findings. The outstanding differences between the two institutions were the consistently stronger commitment of the officers and the differential effects of organizational experience. When controls for numerous variables were applied, such as education, age, and rank, these differences remained.

We have already suggested that bureaucratic career patterns tend to produce a limited identification with the chief executive. The present findings suggest that affect is transferred from the leader to the organization. Bureaucratic career patterns emphasize the influence of the organization and the profession rather than that of the individual. Accordingly, we find in Table 9 that length of service in the organization was not directly related to strength of commitment to the military installation. Those officers with more than four years of organizational experience on the base were as strongly committed to the organization and to their department as those officers with less than two years' experience. On the other hand, the pronounced lower rate of career succession of the business managers may have been responsible for the strength of their commitment increasing steadily with length of time in the organization. Only 29 per cent of the business managers with less than five years' experience compared with almost half (48 per cent) of those with fifteen or more years' experience in the organization had favorable attitudes toward the firm. Likewise, positive commitment to the department was on the whole positively related to length of time in the organization.

TABLE 9. MILITARY VERSUS BUSINESS ORGANIZATION:
RELATIONSHIP BETWEEN LENGTH OF TIME IN THE ORGANIZATION
AND TWO INDEXES OF COMMITMENT

Military Installation	*Length of Time in the Organization*					
	Less than 2 years		2 to 3 years		4 years or more	
	Per cent	*Number of cases*	*Per cent*	*Number of cases*	*Per cent*	*Number of cases*
(a) Favorable attitude toward the organization	53	*252*	52	*191*	57	*111*
(b) Favorable attitude toward the department	67	*252*	62	*191*	68	*111*
Business Firm	0 to 4 years		5 to 9 years		10 to 14 years		15 years or more	
(a) Favorable attitude toward the organization	29	*149*	29	193	34	*613*	48	*231*
(b) Favorable attitude toward the department	40	*147*	51	194	50	*613*	55	*236*

TABLE 10. MILITARY VERSUS BUSINESS ORGANIZATION: INDEXES OF
EXECUTIVE COMMITMENT AT VARIOUS LEVELS OF THE HIERARCHY

Indexes of Executive Commitment	*Military Installation*		*Business Firm*	
	Per cent	*Number of cases*	*Per cent*	*Number of cases*
Colonels and Generals (Top Executives)				
(a) Favorable attitude toward the organization	67	*27*	65	*97*
(b) Favorable attitude toward the department	81	*27*	56	*97*
Lt. Colonels (Middle Management)				
(a) Favorable attitude toward the organization	69	*55*	42	*170*
(b) Favorable attitude toward the department	74	*55*	49	*173*
Majors (Lower-Middle Management)				
(a) Favorable attitude toward the organization	61	*139*	28	*486*
(b) Favorable attitude toward the department	68	*139*	42	*484*
Captains and Lieutenants (First-Level Management)				
(a) Favorable attitude toward the organization	47	*335*	34	*448*
(b) Favorable attitude toward the department	62	*335*	58	*452*

Three major findings are shown in Table 10: (1) It presents additional support for the previously reported stronger commitment of the Air Force officers. In all comparisons a greater proportion of military officers than business managers were favorably oriented toward the organization and subunit. (2) It suggests the greater importance for strength of commitment of hierarchical position in the military than in the business firm. Although by no means unimportant to business organizations, hierarchicalization in the military setting was more uniform and hence more closely predictive of attitudes. (3) In both institutions, commitment to the subunit (department) was considerably greater than commitment to the organization. (See also Table 9.) The lone exception was among the top business executives.

The data presented, which demonstrated a stronger organizational commitment among military officers than among business managers, may challenge the assertions of those military analysts who have maintained that the rapid rate of military succession has led to declining officer morale.[27] Succession in a highly bureaucratized context may, in most cases, call forth a highly adaptive series of responses. Rather than always disrupt social relations, rapid succession, if routinized, may be associated with the emergence of new patterns of adaptation.

SUCCESSION AND INVOLVEMENT IN COMMUNITY AFFAIRS

Theorists of mass society have insisted appropriately on the importance of community associations as mediating links between the nation-state and the otherwise alienated, powerless citizen.[28] According to some, C. Wright Mills was the most prominent proponent of this view, the rising importance of bureaucratic organization threatens to atomize the middle class and thereby weaken their social power.[29] In fact, however, the new middle classes do not lessen their participation in voluntary associations. On the contrary, as W. H. Whyte has suggested, Organization Man may be more likely than his predecessor to be involved in community life.[30]

Our research situation enabled us to examine these apparent effects of bureaucratization by comparing the community participation of military officers and business managers. Two approaches to the effects of succession on community involvement may be distinguished. The first, which sees succession as socially disruptive, argues that the high rate of succession associated with the bureaucratic career pattern prevents the manager from planting his roots in the community. Rapid succession should militate against frequent participation in voluntary associations because it promotes a transient orientation toward such involvement. Therefore, by this approach, officers of the military installation should be less likely to be involved in community affairs than the business managers of the firm studied. An alternative orientation, stemming from the theory of bureaucracy, leads to the opposite hypothesis. Frequent succession, a standard attribute of the bureaucratic career pattern, is highly routinized and therefore normally anticipated. The anticipation of change enables the highly mobile manager to deal with his transiency by means of a series of adjustive responses.[31] We speculated that one such response was to quickly become a part of the local community in a new assignment by joining voluntary associations. In effect, awareness of transiency generates a strong desire to become socially involved. Hence, the hypothesis that military officers would be more likely to be involved in community affairs than business managers.

Our measure of community involvement was the number of memberships in various community voluntary associations.[32] Data were collected from both samples pertaining to four types of organizations: church groups, fraternal organizations, neighborhood clubs, and sports clubs. In three of these four the Air Force officers demonstrated a greater overall proportion of memberships: church groups, 33 to 29 per cent, neighborhood clubs, 54 to 47 per cent, and sports clubs, 42 to 29 per cent. The business managers were more likely, to a slight extent, to be members of one or more fraternal organizations, 30 to 28 per cent. (Officers are not permitted to be members of political clubs while on active duty.[33] Hence, comparisons of this type were not feasible.) Sixty-one per cent of the total military sample belonged to three organizations or more, while only 31 per cent of the business managers reported memberships in an equivalent number of organizations. Table 11 indicates that when length of time in the organization was controlled, the same pattern of differences was maintained. Of 15 comparisons that could be made, 13 were in the direction supporting the proposition that a greater proportion of military officers than business managers were likely to be members of voluntary associations. Wright and Hyman's report of the Denver study of associational membership showed no systematic relationship between length of time in the community and incidence of membership in voluntary associations.[34] Contrary to this report, and consistent with Zimmer's findings, the data reported in Table 11 indicated that among military officers such a relationship did exist.[35] The pattern suggests clearly that frequency of affiliation was positively related to length of time in the specific military organization (and hence in the community). Only fraternal organizational memberships violated the overall trend. The pattern was less clear among busi-

TABLE 11. MILITARY VERSUS BUSINESS ORGANIZATION: LENGTH OF TIME IN THE ORGANIZATION AND PARTICIPATION IN VOLUNTARY ASSOCIATIONS[a]

| | Length of Time in the Organization | | | | | |
| | Less than 2 years | | 2 to 3 years | | 4 years | |
Members of One or More Organizations	Military Installation	Business Firm	Military Installation	Business Firm	Military Installation	Business Firm
	(Percentages)		(Percentages)		(Percentages)	
Church Groups	27	24	31	29	43	30
Fraternal Organizations	26	32	23	20	22	32
Neighborhood Clubs	40	24	54	29	63	50
Sports Clubs	35	24	49	29	50	30
Political Clubs	–[b]	4	–	9	–	5
Three Organizations or More	52	28	71	16	81	33
Number of cases	153	25	111	71	68	128

[a] The overall proportion of memberships in each type of association was as follows (military organization first): Church groups, 33 per cent and 29 per cent; fraternal organizations, 28 per cent and 30 per cent; neighborhood clubs, 54 per cent and 47 per cent; sports clubs, 42 per cent and 29 per cent; political clubs, business managers only, 6 per cent; three organizations or more, 61 per cent and 31 per cent. Number of cases was slightly different for each type of association.

[b] No data on this item were collected from the military officers.

ness managers. While church, neighborhood, and sports group memberships increased with length of time with the firm, fraternal and political club memberships did not, nor did overall frequency of total memberships.

One among several problems in comparing our two samples lay in the relationship between length of time in the organization and length of time in the community. Among the military officers, this problem could be ignored as the two variables were perfectly and positively correlated. Not so with the businessmen. A manager may have been with his present firm a short time, but still be a long-time community resident. For-

TABLE 12. MILITARY VERSUS BUSINESS ORGANIZATION: SOCIAL CLASS SELF-CONCEPTIONS AT VARIOUS LEVELS OF THE HIERARCHY

Social Class Self-Conceptions	*Military Installation*	*Business Firm*
	(*Percentages*)	
Colonels and Generals		
(Top Executives)		
Upper and Upper Middle Class	52	38
Middle Class	41	57
Lower and Working Class	7	5
Total	100	100
Number of Cases	*27*	*99*
Lt. Colonels		
(Middle Management)		
Upper and Upper-Middle Class	48	31
Middle-Class	44	59
Lower and Working Class	8	9
Total	100	99
Number of cases	*54*	*174*
Majors		
(Lower Middle Management)		
Upper and Upper-Middle Class	43	17
Middle-Class	51	64
Lower and Working Class	6	19
Total	100	100
Number of cases	*137*	*490*
Captains and Lieutenants		
(First-Level Management)		
Upper and Upper-Middle Class	36	9
Middle Class	55	59
Lower and Working Class	9	32
Total	100	100
Number of cases	*327*	*448*

tunately, however, this factor should have worked against the pattern reported of greater community participation among officers than among business managers.

Several studies have demonstrated a positive relationship between social stratification and incidence of affiliation with voluntary associations.[36] Position in the system of stratification of the association is positively correlated with position in the community's stratification system, as Table 12 demonstrates. Class self-conceptions were determined by this item: "If you were asked to use one of these names (upper, upper middle, middle, lower middle, working, and lower class), to which social class would you say you belonged?" In both samples, the proportion of persons identifying themselves as members of the upper and upper middle classes increased directly with level in the organizational hierarchy. Once again the greater importance of the rank hierarchy in the military setting was revealed. The converse proposition, namely, that the proportion of persons identifying themselves as members of the lower and working classes was inversely correlated with hierarchical level, held in perfect order only for the military population. Parenthetically, Table 12 also revealed a consistent tendency for military officers at every rank level to identify themselves as members of higher class levels. Although the differential decreased with downward movement in the hierarchy, military officers were more likely than business managers to place themselves in the upper and upper middle classes. Despite the fact that our sample of military officers did not suggest any narrow social class alignment, it nevertheless pointed toward a greater homogeneity of perspective in the military than in the business firm studied.

Table 13 compared voluntary association memberships in the two samples within social class groupings. In ten of thirteen comparisons, a greater proportion of military officers than business managers were members of voluntary associations. Two of three exceptions again referred to fraternal organizations. Memberships in this type of association seem to be stressed more heavily in business.[37] On the other hand, the greater stress in the military on physical fitness undoubtedly accounts in part for the officers' more frequent memberships in athletic organizations.

The relationship between hierarchical level and participation in voluntary associations is shown in Table 14. The greater community involvement of the military sample was once again sustained in seventeen of twenty comparisons. (It was impossible because of the limitation in number of cases to control simultaneously for socioeconomic level,

TABLE 13. MILITARY VERSUS BUSINESS ORGANIZATION:
VOLUNTARY ASSOCIATION MEMBERSHIPS, SOCIAL CLASS
SELF-CONCEPTIONS CONTROLLED

Members of One or More Organizations	Military Installation	Business Firm
Upper and Upper-Middle Class	(Percentages)	
Church Groups	37	35
Fraternal Organizations	30	41
Neighborhood Clubs	61	52
Sports Clubs	48	26
Three Organizations or More	68	44
Number of cases[a]	214	214
Middle Class		
Church Groups	31	29
Fraternal Organizations	28	30
Neighborhood Clubs	53	48
Sports Clubs	41	32
Three Organizations or More	58	31
Number of cases	162	716
Lower Middle, Lower, or Working Class		
Church Groups	30	25
Fraternal Organizations	27	24
Neighborhood Clubs	45	48
Sports Clubs	34	26
Three Organizations or More	54	24
Number of cases	44	250

[a] Number of cases for each type of group varied slightly.

rank, and length of time in the organization.) It should be noted that executives of United Utility Corporation were actively encouraged by superiors to join community associations. In this sense, United resembled the absentee-owned corporation in "Bigtown," a community studied by Pellegrin and Coates.[38] In this study, the authors observed that "Executives are expected to belong to civic organizations and serve on committees as part of their jobs."[39] A comparable policy encouraging affiliation with local organizations was not discovered at the military installation. The clearest association between corporate level and associational membership was found for political organizations. Only the top business executives, to any significant extent, belonged to political clubs.[40]

Thus, the pattern of involvement in local community affairs differed consistently in the two research sites. Officers apparently responded to their assignments, which were of brief duration, by quickly tying themselves into local community activities. Rapid succession, instead of

TABLE 14. MILITARY VERSUS BUSINESS ORGANIZATION: EXECUTIVE PARTICIPATION IN VOLUNTARY ASSOCIATIONS AT VARIOUS LEVELS IN THE HIERARCHY

Members of One or More Organizations	Top Executives		Middle Management		Lower-Middle Management		First-Level Management	
	Military Installation	Business Firm	Military Installation	Business Firm	Military Installation	Business Firm	Military Installation	Business Firm
	(Percentages)		(Percentages)		(Percentages)		(Percentages)	
Church Groups	42	32	33	31	43	32	30	24
Fraternal Organizations	31	45	35	29	31	30	26	27
Neighborhood Clubs	58	51	75	52	70	47	45	45
Sports Clubs	56	30	48	36	45	27	40	32
Political Clubs[a]	—	16	—	4	—	4	—	4
Three Organizations or More	85	53	62	35	76	32	54	25
Number of cases[b]	26	102	52	178	138	497	332	459

[a] No data were collected on this item from the military officers.
[b] Number of cases for each type of group varied slightly.

producing a withdrawal from community life, was associated with an active and continuing search for extensive social involvement.

SUMMARY AND CONCLUSIONS

Although we have deliberately focused on differences between military and business organization, it is apparent that all organization officials in our society share certain characteristics. They occupy well-defined positions in a hierarchy; interpersonal skills are critical to their career advancement; they are concerned with salary and prestige as measures of worth; and they seek to maintain ties to the local community and to the society as a whole. However, these many similarities ought not obscure the fact that organizations have markedly different objectives and structures and that these necessarily produce different patterns of behavior among their executives.

We have assumed that bureaucratic career patterns were more typical of military than business organization. And we did find that rapid succession, typical of highly bureaucratized systems, characterized the military installation to a much greater extent than it did the business firm. Moreover, not surprisingly, we found consistent evidence of greater hierarchicalization in the military site.

It was the consequences of rapid succession, however, which concerned this exploratory study most of all. How do organizations and their members respond to highly routinized and rapid succession? The limited evidence was examined in four problem areas: executive homogeneity, control, commitment, and community involvement.

Because bureaucratic control necessitates the extensive application of rational criteria for selection and promotion of personnel, homogeneity among executives with respect to numerous social characteristics tends to result. Accordingly, we found at each rank level greater uniformity in age, length of time in the organization, and seniority among the military officers than among business managers.

Routinized succession conditions the exercise of organizational control. Rapid succession in the military inhibits strong identification with the chief executive. The data collected for this study indicated that length of tenure at the military base increased the perceived authority of the officers, including those at the highest ranks. Length of tenure also increased perceived authority in the business setting, but not at the top ranks. Thus it appears that in the military, bureaucratic forms of rotation, regardless of the organizational objectives they serve, weaken personal executive power and encourage the development of a general orientation toward organizational authority.

More favorable orientations toward the organization and the specific department were found in the military setting than in the business organization. In the military system, and unlike the business firm studied, length of experience in the particular installation was not systematically related to the strength of these attitudes. Instead, the more favorable orientations to the organization and the subunit could be seen as tied closely to the greater standardization of assignment and greater strength of professional commitment in the military.

Evidence supporting the hypothesis that frequent succession inhibits extensive participation in community life was not found. Instead, the opposite pattern prevailed. Military officers, despite their short time in the community, were found more likely to be members of various community voluntary associations than were business managers. The findings were viewed as suggestive of a pattern of adaptation to bureaucratic succession. Military officers, knowing full well that their assignment to a given base was temporary, apparently responded by rapidly integrating themselves into the local community through memberships in numerous voluntary associations.

NOTES

1. Mannheim, Karl, *Essays on the Sociology of Knowledge*. Oxford University Press, New York, 1952, pp. 276–280.

2. Gouldner, A. W., *Patterns of Industrial Succession*, The Free Press, Glencoe, Ill., 1954; Guest, R. H., "Managerial Succession in Complex Organizations," *American Journal of Sociology*, vol. 68, July, 1962, pp. 47–54; McCleery, R. H., *Policy Change in Prison Management*, Governmental Research Bureau, Michigan State University, East Lansing, Mich., 1957; Dale, Ernest, "Du Pont: Pioneer in Systematic Management," *Administrative Science Quarterly*, vol. 2, June, 1957, pp. 25–29; Grusky, Oscar, "Administrative Succession in Formal Organization," *Social Forces*, vol. 39, December, 1960, pp. 105–115.

3. Warner, W. L., and J. C. Abegglen, *Occupational Mobility in American Business and Industry, 1929–1952*, University of Minnesota Press, Minneapolis, 1955; Levenson, Bernard, "Bureaucratic Succession" in Etzioni, Amitai, editor, *Complex Organizations: A Sociological Reader*, Holt, Rinehart, and Winston, New York, 1961, pp. 362–375.

4. Anderson, T. R., and Seymour Warkov, "Organizational Size and Functional Complexity: A Study of Administration in Hospitals," *American Sociological Review*, vol. 26, February, 1961, pp. 23–28.

5. Janowitz, Morris, *The Professional Soldier: A Social and Political Portrait*. The Free Press, Glencoe, Ill., 1960.

6. See Grusky, Oscar, "Corporate Size, Bureaucratization, and Managerial Succession," *American Journal of Sociology*, vol. 67, November, 1961, pp. 261–269; and Kriesberg, Louis, "Careers, Organization Size, and Succession," *American Journal of Sociology*, vol. 68, November, 1962, pp. 355–359.

7. Hughes, E. C., *Men and Their Work*, The Free Press, Glencoe, Ill., 1958, p. 129; Gouldner, A. W., "Cosmopolitans and Locals: Toward an Analysis of Latent Social Roles—I," *Administrative Science Quarterly*, vol. 2, December, 1957, pp. 281–306.

8. Hanson W. Baldwin reports this study: "An informal survey made last spring of a 20 per cent random sample of officers in each grade assigned to Headquarters, First United States Army, on Governors Island, indicated that the average officer had 17 years of commissioned service, acquired eight military occupational specialties, made 12 PCS (permanent changes of station), had 26 major assignments (not including minor additional duties), and made at least 16 moves (combat zones excluded) that required uprooting of his family," *New York Times*, Western Edition, October 21, 1963.

9. Gouldner, A. W., *op. cit.* (note 2); Whyte, W. F., "The Social Structure of the Restaurant Industry," *American Journal of Sociology*, vol. 54, January, 1949, p. 304; Grusky, Oscar, "Role Conflict in Organization: A Study of Prison Officials," *Administrative Science Quarterly*, vol. 3, March, 1959, pp. 463–467.

10. Interrater reliability was .904 (p<.0001). When the raters were brought together to examine disagreements, none of which deviated by more than one level, complete agreement was arrived at when the criterion was restated and the duties of the position discussed. Corporate level was related both to salary (Cramer's $V = .58$, p<.0001 and perceived authority $V = .21$ p<.0001). A description of Cramer's V may be found in Blalock, H. M., Jr., *Social Statistics*, McGraw-Hill Book Co., New York, 1960, p. 230. Since the study of the military installation and the business firm were both based on a nonrandom sample, the application of statistical tests is problematical. Our interpretations of the findings are based on patterns of differences and not on statistical tests. In every case our interpretations should be viewed as highly tentative.

11. In both samples, questionnaires were distributed by the institution but mailed on completion directly to the University of California, Los Angeles.

12. Pelz found that identification of response by code on a questionnaire did not produce more cautious responses than when the respondent was anonymous. See Pelz, D. C., "The Influence of Anonymity on Expressed Attitudes," *Human Organization*, vol. 18, Summer, 1959, pp. 88–91.

13. Etzioni, Amitai, "Authority Structure and Organizational Effectiveness," *Administrative Science Quarterly*, vol. 4, June, 1959, pp. 43–67.

14. Dorn, W. L., *Competition for Empire, 1740–1763*. Harper and Row, Publishers, New York, 1963, pp. 86–87.

15. Abegglen, J. C., *The Japanese Factory*. The Free Press, Glencoe, Ill., 1958, pp. 11–25.

16. *Ibid.*, p. 12.

17. For a statement that applies these four factors, see Blau, P. M., *Bureaucracy in Modern Society*, Random House, New York, 1956, p. 19.

18. Grusky, Oscar, *op. cit.*

19. The youth of the Air Force Officers, a favorite gibe during World War II, cannot match that of the French Army of the middle of the eighteenth century where the colonel of fourteen or sixteen was not at all rare. See Dorn, W. L., *op. cit.*, p. 88.

20. Janowitz, Morris, *op. cit.*, pp. 6–64.

21. See my "Career Mobility and Organizational Commitment," paper presented at the annual meeting of the American Sociological Association, Los Angeles, 1963.

22. Seniority in business in order to be properly equated with military seniority ought to be construed as meaning total length of time in the business world. Actually, as we noted, it refers in this case to its customary reference, number of years in the employ of the corporation.

23. Selznick, Philip, *Leadership in Administration*. Row, Peterson and Co., Evanston, Ill., 1957, p. 105.

24. Huntington, S. P., *The Common Defense*, Columbia University Press, New York, 1961, p. 311.

25. Business novels provide some illustrations. These comments were ascribed to Avery Bullard, chief executive of Tredway Corporation, in Cameron Hawley's famous novel, *Executive Suite:* "When he did come for lunch, there was no man in Millburgh, even the president of the Susquehanna National Bank, who could escape the temptation of bragging to his wife that he had lunched that day at the table next to Avery Bullard's." And one of Bullard's vice-presidents described him as ". . . a great man . . . He was the greatest man I've ever known." See *Executive Suite*, Houghton-Mifflin Co., Boston, 1952, p. 31.

26. The Guttman scale of Attitude toward the Organization was based on three items worded as follows: (1) "Do you feel that the men who ran the Base (Company) recognize your ability and what you are able to do?" (2) "How well do you feel that the men who run the Base (Company) understand your problems and needs?" (3) "In general, how well do you think the Base (Company) is run?" The responses were dichotomized. The coefficient of reproducibility for the business managers was .96 and for the Air Force officers .94. For the items comprising the Guttman scale of Attitude toward the Department, the term "department" was substituted for Base or Company. The coefficient of reproducibility for the business managers was .95 and for the Air Force officers also .95.

27. Baldwin states: "There are far too many transfers and shifts—so many that a great many service officers feel that they never stay long enough at any one job to master it properly." He cites illustratively the case of a Major Wood who resigned ostensibly because of the rapid succession he experienced—thirty-three moves in thirteen years. *New York Times*, Western Edition, October 21, 1963.

28. Kornhauser, William, *The Politics of Mass Society*, The Free Press, Glencoe, Ill., 1959; Nisbet, R. A., *The Quest for Community*, Oxford University Press, New York, 1953.

29. Mills, C. Wright, *The Power Elite*. Oxford University Press, New York, 1951, p. 262.

30. Whyte, W. H., Jr., *The Organization Man*. Doubleday Anchor Books, Garden City, New York, 1957, chaps. 20 and 21.

31. Litwak, Eugene, "Voluntary Association and Neighborhood Cohesion," *American Sociological Review*, vol. 25, February, 1960, pp. 258–271; Fellin, Phillip, and Eugene Litwak, "Neighborhood Cohesion Under Conditions of Mobility," *American Sociological Review*, vol. 28, June, 1963, pp. 364–376. Our findings are consistent with those of Litwak, who found that bureaucratic managers were more likely than entrepreneurs to integrate quickly into a neighborhood.

32. Respondents were asked to list the names of associations to which they currently belong. Associations to which only their wives belonged were not solicited. Examples of each type of organization were provided. Unfortunately, we had no measure of extent of involvement in each association.

33. Of course, this is not unique to the United States military system. Alfred Vagts quotes Lorenz von Stein, noting that in 1868 members of the English army were not allowed "to institute or take part in any meetings, demonstrations, or processions for party or political purposes in barracks, quarters, camps, or elsewhere." *A History of Militarism*, W. W. Norton and Co., New York, 1937, p. 169.

34. This is an oversimplification and should be qualified. Although there is a marked difference in associational memberships between urban residents and rural *farm*

residents, the reported differences between urban and rural *non-farm* residents were not great when degree of urbanization of the county was controlled. However, relevant to the present case, Wright and Hyman found that the more urbanized the county in which the urban resident was located the smaller the proportion of persons with no associational memberships. See Wright, C. R., and H. H. Hyman, "Voluntary Association Memberships of American Adults: Evidence from National Sample Surveys," *American Sociological Review*, vol. 23, June, 1958, pp. 284–294.

35. Zimmer, B. G., "Participation of Migrants in Urban Structures," *American Sociological Review*, vol. 20, April, 1955, pp. 218–224.

36. These are reviewed in Wright and Hyman, *op. cit.*, pp. 288–289.

37. For example, see Dalton, Melville, *Men Who Manage: Fusions of Feeling and Theory in Administration*, John Wiley and Sons, New York, 1959, pp. 178–181.

38. Pellegrin, R. J., and C. H. Coates, "Absentee-owned Corporations and Community Power Structure," *American Journal of Sociology*, vol. 61, March, 1956, pp. 413–419.

39. *Ibid.*, p. 416.

40. Rossi found that business executives in Mediana (a fictitious name) tended to avoid any community participation where possible community conflict might be involved. He observed: "Participating in political affairs is acceptable only when the element of hostility and possible opposition are moved from the scene, preferably in advance." See Rossi, P. H., "The Organizational Structure of an American Community" in Etzioni, Amitai, editor, *Complex Organizations*, p. 306.

Part Three

PROFESSIONAL SOCIALIZATION

Part Three

PROFESSIONAL SOCIALIZATION

ORGANIZATIONS, and especially military organizations, have an existence which extends beyond that of the active career of their individual members. Year by year, a new generation of personnel is recruited who must be indoctrinated and assimilated into ongoing operational patterns. At the same time some of the men must be prepared for leadership positions from which they can change and adapt the organization.

Thus a third step in a comprehensive analysis of the extent to which the military is adapting toward the constabulary force concept, centers on the mechanics of professional socialization. Socialization initially meant the social processes by which an infant interacts with his parents and comes to incorporate their values and attitudes. But it has become commonplace to point out that despite the crucial impact of childhood experiences, socialization and internalization of new values continue throughout a person's complete life cycle. Socialization no longer refers to childhood, but is linked to the continuous processes of personal development and change. As a result, students of organizations and professions have come to be concerned with professional socialization—the process by which personnel incorporates those values and perspectives essential for a particular skill group.

The broadening of the terms of reference of a concept such as socialization runs the risk of creating both popular and intellectual confusion. However, the concept *professional socialization* has the advantages of fusing together under one category a wide range of different institutional practices which serve to fashion attitudes and values in military personnel. The process of socialization into a profession is a gradual and slow process, but one that can be deeply affected by particular significant and highly charged events. The essential relevance of the concept is that it permits the student of institutions to relate the pressures and requirements of the profession to the needs and aspirations of the recruit. It is part of an approach for charting changes in attitudes and for focusing

115

on those attitude patterns that are important for the performance of professional roles.

But there is an incompleteness in this perspective, since the analysis of attitudes and values proceeds at the manifest level. The materials that are accumulated do not probe the hidden and unconscious meanings of men as they express their aspirations. In order to gain a broad institutional overview of attitude formation and attitude change, there is a foreshortened intellectual perspective. Research on professional socialization in general and the research studies on the military profession of the Inter-University Seminar do not make possible a deep understanding of the prime movers or even of the clusters of innovating deviants who, as they pass through the processes of professional socialization, have responded in terms of powerful personal motives.

There are three types of data relevant for the study of professional socialization: direct participant observation, questionnaires or interviews, and content analysis of documents. In varying combinations, these three approaches have been used in the two research studies that are presented. One study is an intensive investigation of a specific but crucial aspect of professional socialization—the impact of military academy experience on officer cadets. The other is a longer-range historical model in which the contents of the service journals are used to chart changes in the self-image of military professionals.

Both studies are designed to answer specific empirical questions. The four years of socialization at West Point do not have as much impact on strategic and broad professional perspectives as might have been anticipated; attitude change which takes place is more in specific career interests. In terms of long-term changes in military self-image, the content analysis study confirms the long-held hunches that the Naval establishment started to change toward a technological self-image earlier and more gradually than the Army. The Navy has been able to avoid the sharp fluctuations that have complicated the professional identity of the ground forces.

It is not enough to note changes. But both studies are concerned with analytical considerations in the process of professional socialization. The purpose is to help pose questions about effectiveness. The socialization of the West Point cadet must be seen in the light of the fact that the Academy continues to draw on a more and more heterogeneous population, that the size of its operation has greatly increased, and the values that it must transmit have become more and more diffuse. The academies are faced with incompatible demands; they must emphasize their unique characteristics in order to develop commitments to the military career; yet they must produce graduates who are part of the mainstream of American life. For these questions, the empirical data have special relevance. Because the military academy does not produce monolithic strategic attitudes or radical changes in professional perspectives, its operation remains compatible with the political notions of officer cadets training in a democratic society. In other words, the military academy has become a relatively open institution. Like other educational institutions, it will produce men whose professional interests change somewhat in the course of their careers, for example, in their commitment to the military. From this point of view, the resignation rate is not a demonstration of the weakness of the institution, but of its effective integration into American society. The data to be presented leave unanswered the question whether among those who remain there is a cadre of innovative types that will be able to participate in the shaping of the emerging constabulary force.

The trend analysis of the service journals—as one revealing indicator —highlights other dilemmas of professional socialization. In particular, the findings confirm the decline in the role of junior officers—more so in the Army than in the Navy—as a responsible agent of authority. Creative assignments as portrayed in the service journals emerge at the field-grade level. The service journals both reflect organizational reality and mold self-conceptions. Since professional socialization continues on after military academy, there is every reason to believe that the "shock" of the first assignments become crucial in determining retention or resignation.

THE PROFESSIONAL SOCIALIZATION OF THE WEST POINT CADET

*John P. Lovell**

> At the period of adolescence, when character is plastic and impulse wayward, before the stereotype has set, control and constraint are the essential forces for impressing permanent form upon young manhood. If the material can be removed from contaminating impurities, fused in the furnace of hard work, and kept in its mould until it has set, the best has been done that education can do for character, provided the mould is a noble one.[1]

THIS QUOTATION by a West Point professor, written over a half century ago, presented his description of West Point as an "ideal" system for rigid and effective socialization of cadets in a formative "mould." From current impressionistic notions about the totality of institutional life at the United States Military Academy, one might continue to believe that West Point cadets experience profound change of attitudes in the direction of conformity to a common "mould." Likewise, one might believe that cadets from military backgrounds have already experienced some socialization into military life, while those from civilian background would undergo marked changes in the direction of attitudes held by cadets from military backgrounds. It was the purpose of this study to

* The author wishes to express his appreciation to the former Superintendent of the U. S. Military Academy, Maj. Gen. (now Lt. Gen.) William C. Westmoreland, the former Commandant of Cadets, Brig. Gen. Richard G. Stilwell, the West Point Academic Board, and their staffs and student body, for extensive cooperation during 1961 and 1962 that made the present study possible. The cooperation of Dean Albert I. Dickerson, Dean William S. McNaughton, and Professor Laurence I. Radway, and others of Dartmouth College, made possible the comparative survey. The author received many useful suggestions from Professors Ralph K. Huitt, Harry Scoble, Leon D. Epstein, Carlisle P. Runge, Charles Anderson, Thomas L. Thorson, Lewis A. Froman, Nelson Polsby, Peter Rossi, and James A. Davis. Professors Bernard C. Cohen, James L. McCamy, Morris Janowitz, William T. R. Fox, Christopher Wright, Percy H. Tannenbaum, Laurence I. Radway, Milton Hobbs, Col. G. A. Lincoln, Col. Russell K. Alspach, Captain Harvey A. Garn, Dr. Sidney Forman, Dr. Joseph E. Marron, and Dr. Judith Cates made comments and suggestions at various stages of the development of the study. Only the author is responsible for errors of fact or judgment.

Portions of the research for this study were supported by funds from the National Security Studies Seminar (sponsored by the Carnegie Corporation) of the University of Wisconsin; the Institute of War and Peace Studies, Columbia University.

probe such questions by describing and analyzing the patterns of attitude change at West Point on the basis of direct empirical research.

There were many reasons to question the idea of the military academy as a total institution with a comprehensive impact of implanting traditional military values on its student body, although this idea may have been more applicable in the past. The empirical results of this study clearly do not support a conclusion of comprehensive impact.

During an Academy education, the cadet experiences only slight changes in his orientation toward his professional role and in the perspectives with which he views the use of force in international relations. Even more important, there is no single attitude pattern on these matters, either at the beginning or at the end of his four-year education. Initially, cadets from military backgrounds tend to have somewhat different professional orientations and "strategic" perspectives from cadets with civilian backgrounds. These differences are diminished by the cadet experience, in that the attitudes of both types of cadets converge rather than cadets with military backgrounds merely influencing the civilian. In contrast to the relative stability of professional orientations and strategic perspectives, important changes take place in the preference which cadets have for particular branches of the Army in which their careers will develop. Attitudes related to interpersonal patterns of cadet life, out of which professional attachment to the military develops, are also subject to significant change.

In addition, it is the purpose of this study to explore the organizational factors which help to account for this pattern of attitude change and professional socialization. The military profession is not characterized by a monolithic value structure which remains unchanged. To the contrary, a variety of research indicates a shift in recent years in the professional orientation of the American military from a "heroic" to a "managerial" emphasis. Different segments of the West Point faculty emphasize aspects of either heroic or managerial orientation, or a mixture of both. Likewise, strategic military perspectives mirror differing perspectives within the civilian society. Thus the value system of the academy environment, far from being monolithic or harmonious, has been increasingly varied and diffuse since the end of World War II. Moreover, the recruitment patterns have been changing so as to incorporate an ever more heterogeneous student population, and one whose increase in size serves to undermine the uniformity of the institution. Nevertheless, equally striking is the high degree of continuity of the institution's character in spite of these various sources of change.

It should be unnecessary to add that a more comprehensive survey which included additional measures of social and political attitudes would have yielded a more exhaustive description of the process of professional socialization. The measures that were selected for inclusion in the present study were those related to specific issues in professionalization in the military ones and that would be unlikely to offend the respondent's sense of propriety. (Therefore cadets were not asked their preference of political party, for example, a commitment they are expected not to voice.)

Research methodology for the present study is discussed in detail in the technical appendix. The limitations of a cross-sectional design, which was employed in the present study rather than a longitudinal design, are well known but merit further emphasis. The present study is essentially a search for evidence of the effects of the process "professional socialization."[2] Such evidence has been provided by comparisons of the responses of samples of West Point freshmen, sophomores, juniors, and seniors to a series of attitude measures. The inference has been made that such comparisons reveal "change" or the basis of "change" in attitude over the four years of exposure to the socializing influence of the West Point environment. Obviously, such inferences must be made with the greatest caution, because a number of variables other than length of exposure to environment might account for differences of responses of different groups.[3]

In every instance where differences in attitude have been found in gross comparisons across class samples, an effort has been made to confirm the *replicative consistency* of the finding by comparing the responses of homogeneous subgroups of the classes. Secondly, the criterion of *internal consistency* has been applied to the findings; that is, support for the validity of a particular finding has been assumed to be weakened unless the pattern of responses for that item recurs in the responses to similar items.[4]

A second important limitation of the design of the present study is the span of cadet experience encompassed by the cross-sectional measures. The questionnaire utilized in the study was administered to cadets late in November, 1961. Freshmen respondents had already been exposed to nearly five months of cadet life; senior respondents had more than six months' experience remaining. The importance or lack of importance of these five months of freshman year and six months of senior year to the process of professional socialization cannot be estimated from the survey data of the present study.

CADET ATTITUDES: STABILITY AND CHANGE

Professional Orientation

The process of professional socialization at West Point has been analyzed principally in terms of two sets of concepts provided by Janowitz in *The Professional Soldier:* "heroic leader" and "managerial" orientations toward professional roles, and "absolutistic" and "pragmatic" strategic perspectives.[5]

The "heroic leader" is "a perpetuation of the warrior type," in contrast with the "military manager," who "reflects the scientific and pragmatic dimensions of war-making" and has "effective links to civilian society."[6] The integration of "heroic leader" and "military manager" is essential to the maintenance of cohesion within the profession. Yet changing technology and increasingly complex organizational relationships have forced the military to reassess various professional goals and practices. The process of reassessment produces continuing tension between the "heroic leader," oriented toward the preservation of a traditional professional self-image, and the "military manager," oriented toward the modification of the image in the direction of greater emphasis upon expertise equal to the tasks of large-scale management.[7]

What is the impact of the West Point socialization experience upon the professional orientations of cadets? Is the impact upon cadets from military backgrounds the same as the impact upon cadets from nonmilitary backgrounds? Are the professional orientations of cadets related to their preferences of the branch of service in which they will serve? A simple battery of questions was used in the present study as an index of professional orientation. Cadets were classified as "heroic," "managerial," or "mixed" according to criteria described in the appendix to this study.

Comparisons by Class and by Military-Nonmilitary Background

Approximately one-third of each class sample falls into each category of professional orientation (Table 1). While no profound changes over the four years are indicated, the data suggest that a slight shift away from "heroic" orientation toward "managerial" orientation takes place between the junior and senior years. Socialization also produces increased homogeneity of orientation among cadets of military and nonmilitary backgrounds (Table 2). As freshmen, nearly half of cadets from military backgrounds are "managerial" in orientation; only 22 per cent of the military sample are "heroic" in orientation. On the other hand, 39 per cent of the freshman sample from nonmilitary backgrounds are

TABLE 1. PROFESSIONAL ORIENTATION OF CADET FRESHMEN,
SOPHOMORES, JUNIORS, AND SENIORS

	Class			
Professional Orientation	Freshman (1965)	Sophomore (1964)	Junior (1963)	Senior (1962)
	(Percentages)			
Heroic	35	31	37	29
Mixed	32	39	31	37
Managerial	33	30	32	34
Number of cases	197	255	242	253

TABLE 2. COMPARISONS OF PROFESSIONAL ORIENTATIONS OF
FRESHMAN, SOPHOMORE, JUNIOR, AND SENIOR CADETS FROM
MILITARY AND NONMILITARY BACKGROUNDS[a]

	Father's Occupation	
Professional Orientation	Military	Nonmilitary
Freshman	(Percentages)	
Heroic	22	39
Managerial	47	28
Sophomore		
Heroic	23	33
Managerial	31	30
Junior		
Heroic	35	38
Managerial	31	32
Senior		
Heroic	28	27
Managerial	33	35

[a] Only heroic and managerial orientations are depicted; the percentage of each group in the "mixed" category equals the difference between 100 per cent and the sum of the heroic and managerial percentages for that group. Data for cadets who listed someone other than father as head of household are omitted.

"heroic" in orientation; 28 per cent of them have "managerial" orientations. By the junior year, however, the percentages of cadets with "heroic" and with "managerial" orientations are virtually the same for cadets from military and from nonmilitary backgrounds. The homogeneity remains during senior year, when both groups become slightly less "heroic" in orientation.

Relationship Between Orientation and Branch Preference

The relationship between professional orientation and the branch of service preferred by the cadet was also explored. The branch of service in which a West Pointer will serve subsequent to graduation is selected by him during his senior year. According to his standing in the class, he has the opportunity to compete for vacancies which are allocated according to a quota system determined by the Department of Defense. For the present study, cadets were asked to indicate in which branch they would choose to serve if all were equally available to them. Their responses, the actual branch choices of the Class of 1962, and the Defense Department quotas for that class are listed in Table 3.

TABLE 3. CADET BRANCH OF SERVICE PREFERENCE

Branch[a]	Preference[b] November, 1961				Actual Choice[c] April, 1962	
	Freshman	Sopho-more	Junior	Senior	Senior	Dept. of Defense Quota
	(Percentages)				(Percentages)	
No preference	7	3	1	0[d]	—	
Air Force	27	22	20	16	11	
Marines	2	4	3	4	2	13[e]
Navy	1	2	0[f]	0	0	
Armor	11	15	17	14	11	8–12
Artillery	14	12	17	27	31	26–38
Engineers	22	14	15	9	11	13[e]
Infantry	15	26	25	27	31	30–42
Signal Corps	1	2	2	2	5	5[g]
Number of cases	212	270	248	265	598	

[a] The branches are listed in the order in which they appeared in the questionnaire administered to cadets.

[b] Figures represent percentage responses to the question, "*Assuming* that *all branches and arms of the service listed below* were equally available to you, if you were asked to make your 'branch choice' today, in which branch or arm would you choose to serve?"

[c] The actual branch choices of the senior class and the Defense Department quotas which limited those choices were obtained from the Personnel Office, USCC, West Point, N. Y.

[d] Less than .5 per cent.

[e] The quota of 13 per cent is for AF plus Marines plus Navy.

[f] Less than .5 per cent.

[g] Reduced from 9.5 per cent to meet small demand.

Important changes in cadet branch preferences may be noted in comparing the responses of the four classes. Nearly 50 per cent of the freshman sample selected either the Air Force or the Engineers as branch preferences, whereas fewer than 25 per cent of seniors actually chose those branches. On the other hand, Infantry and Artillery, selected by only 29 per cent of the freshman sample, were the choices of 62 per cent of seniors.

Branch preferences reflect professional orientations and the differences in demands made and rewards offered by the various branches of service (Table 4). Infantry, the top preference of the cadet with "heroic" orientation, tends to be the branch where the officer role most closely resembles that of the charismatic leader whose exploits liven the annals of military history. Air Force and Engineers, the branches ranking highest in the preferences of "managerial" oriented cadets, require considerable involvement by the officer in technology and place relatively

TABLE 4. BRANCH PREFERENCES OF CADETS ACCORDING TO THEIR PROFESSIONAL ORIENTATION AND ACADEMIC ACHIEVEMENT

Academic Achievement	Professional Orientation	Class	Number of Cases	Branch Preference					
				A.F.	Engr.	Arty.	Armor	Inf.	Other
				(Percentages)					
Top Third	Managerial	Freshman	34	29	26	9	6	12	18
		Senior	41	27	24	34	7	5	2
		All	154	27	27	18	8	10	10
	Mixed	Freshman	33	24	24	12	12	18	9
		Senior	42	5	24	26	14	26	5
		All	154	14	21	21	14	24	6
	Heroic	Freshman	29	14	28	7	10	28	14
		Senior	21	14	14	33	14	19	5
		All	118	16	20	14	17	25	8
Middle and Lower Thirds	Managerial	Freshman	31	26	26	19	13	10	6
		Senior	45	22	0	36	13	18	11
		All	152	32	9	21	13	15	9
	Mixed	Freshman	30	40	17	13	7	10	13
		Senior	52	8	2	15	21	48	6
		All	176	17	9	14	19	33	9
	Heroic	Freshman	40	22	13	20	20	15	10
		Senior	44	16	2	16	16	41	9
		All	183	17	7	16	16	34	10

less emphasis upon charismatic leadership of the traditional "heroic fighter" type. Armor and Artillery occupy somewhat intermediate positions, requiring a fair amount of technological expertise but providing many opportunities for leadership of the charismatic variety.

Differences in academic achievement provide further explanation of the changes in branch preference during socialization. Cadets in the top third of their class, to whom all branches are likely to be available when branch selection is made during senior year, are less likely to change their branch preference over the four years than are cadets in the middle and lower thirds of the class. For cadets in the middle and lower thirds of the class the shift is likely to be away from Air Force and Engineers, where the quotas are small and likely to be consumed by those in the upper third of the class, and toward Infantry, with the largest quota of any branch.

Strategic Perspectives

The American tradition of civil-military relations requires the military man to implement the policy guidelines outlined for him by civilian leadership. Nevertheless, American foreign policy finds the military man deeply involved, directly or indirectly, not only in the implementation but in the formulation of policy.[8] Therefore the perspectives of the military professional toward the use of force in international relations are of particular interest.

Janowitz has suggested that two schools of thought compete among American military professionals as a basic approach to the problems of international politics, "absolutists" versus "pragmatists." These two schools represent two points along a continuum rather than polar opposites. "Each theory," according to Janowitz, "has its own philosophy of long-range political goals, a conception of politico-military strategy, an image of enemy intentions, and an estimate of the uncommitted nations."[9]

In order to set the present discussion in a framework which has utility for the general study of attitudes toward international politics, the paradigm which Janowitz formulated is expanded here and presented as Table 5. At the extreme right of the continuum is the type which Janowitz calls the "absolutist." Because both ends of the continuum represent extreme or "absolute" positions, the "absolutist" might better be called the "activist" to distinguish him from his polar opposite, the "pacifist." The "absolutist," or "activist," is one whose basic predisposition is toward the seeking of tangible, forceful, immediate, and total solutions to the problems of foreign policy which confront the nation. Compromise or coexistence with Communist nations is viewed by the "absolutist" as impossible; since compromise is impossible, war is inevitable. Therefore the full energies of the country should be directed toward preparing for the inevitable conflict. Such preparation may involve some reliance upon alliance systems; but allies are not to be trusted very far. And so-called neutrals, in the view of the "absolutist," are not to be trusted at all; if they are unwilling to commit

TABLE 5. STRATEGIC PERSPECTIVES: A CONCEPTUAL SPECTRUM

Issue	"Pacifist" Approach	"Pragmatic" Approach	"Absolutist" Approach
War	All wars can be eliminated, through demonstration of peaceful intent	Some types of conflict are likely to continue indefinitely; we must be prepared for all contingencies	Thermonuclear war is likely; warfare in some form is inevitable so long as there is Man
U.S. political-military strategy	Work for world government	Mutual security	Gibraltar defense
U.S. military strategy	Unilateral disarmament	Graduated deterrence	Massive retaliation
Communist intentions	Defensive—potential friends	Expansionistic	Intent on world domination
Motivation of neutrals	Desire to promote world stability	Incapacity to make a commitment—potential allies	Desire to get something for nothing —potential enemies

themselves to the cause which America espouses, they should be regarded as enemies.

Toward the middle of the continuum is the "pragmatic" approach to international politics. The "pragmatist" is not willing, as is the "absolutist," to concede that major war is inevitable; however, he considers limited war in some form to be highly probable, and advocates a policy of preparedness for all contingencies. Unlike the "absolutist," the "pragmatist" believes that the limitation of war's objectives and scope is strategically feasible and desirable. The "pragmatist" regards the Communists as expansionistic, though not necessarily irrevocably committed to world conquest. He is more likely to regard neutrals as potential allies than as potential enemies.

At the extreme left of the continuum is a group which Janowitz omitted from his discussion, since it was a type not found to any significant extent among the military professionals of his study. The extreme "pacifist" of our typology is one who believes that all wars can be eliminated, if men will devote their full energies to the pursuit of peace. Communists are regarded as equally capable of peace as are non-Communists, provided peaceful intent is made clear to them. American policy emphasis, therefore, should be on disarmament rather than armament, on promoting international stability rather than upon emphasizing nationalistic objectives.

Freshmen and Senior Perspectives Compared: West Point and Dartmouth

A series of items was constructed to provide a scale along the strategic perspectives continuum; construction of the scale is discussed in the technical appendix to this paper. The items were administered to all four classes of cadets and to a sample of freshmen and seniors at Dartmouth College. The items included in the scale provided data for the analysis of four aspects of the strategic perspectives of respondents: attitudes concerning the likelihood of war, attitudes about the motivations of neutral nations, attitudes about Communist intentions, and attitudes about the desirability of limiting military objectives.

The attitudes of the Dartmouth samples are not necessarily representative of those of male freshmen and seniors at Dartmouth.[10] Nevertheless, comparisons such as those in Table 6 highlight the continuity of cadet attitudes from freshman to senior year by pointing up the similarity of the attitudes of West Point freshmen and seniors in contrast to those of peers from a civilian college.

A great majority of both the West Point and Dartmouth samples felt that war in some form between United States and Communist forces within fifteen years was likely. Over three-fourths of each of the four samples believed that a limited conventional war between forces of the United States and those of Communist nations would occur.

However, when the question of nuclear war was considered, West Point cadets responded quite differently from Dartmouth students. Approximately two-thirds of the sample of West Point freshmen and seniors indicated that a limited nuclear war between United States and Communist forces within fifteen years was likely; in contrast, that view was held by only one-third, approximately, of the sample of Dartmouth freshmen and seniors. Thirty-five per cent of the sample of West Point freshmen and 24 per cent of the sample of West Point seniors believed that allout war involving the United States and Communist nations was likely within fifteen years; only 12 per cent of the sample of Dartmouth freshmen and 9 per cent of the sample of Dartmouth seniors shared that belief.[11]

Nearly 60 per cent of the samples of West Point freshmen, West Point seniors, and Dartmouth freshmen attributed the pursuit of a policy of neutrality by a nation to Communist influence in that nation's government. Approximately the same percentage of Dartmouth seniors disagreed with this view. Between 80 and 90 per cent of the samples of West Point freshmen and seniors, in contrast to 73 per cent of the sample of Dartmouth freshmen and 58 per cent of the sample of Dart-

TABLE 6. STRATEGIC PERSPECTIVES OF FRESHMEN AND SENIORS AT
WEST POINT AND AT DARTMOUTH COLLEGE:
RESPONSES TO INDIVIDUAL SCALE ITEMS[a]

Scale Item	Response Category	West Point Fr.	West Point Sr.	Dartmouth Fr.	Dartmouth Sr.
		(Percentages)			
Allout war is likely within 15 years	Agree	35	24	12	9
	Disagree	65	76	88	91
Limited nuclear war between the U.S. and Communist forces is likely within 15 years	Agree	64	69	30	31
	Disagree	36	31	70	69
Limited conventional war between the U.S. and Communist forces is likely within 15 years	Agree	82	91	76	84
	Disagree	18	9	24	16
Neutrality is caused by Communist influence in the neutral nation's government	Agree	58	57	57	35
	Disagree	35	39	39	55
	No opinion	6	3	4	11
The Korean Conflict was a good illustration of the fact that the Communists are determined to conquer the world	Agree	89	82	73	58
	Disagree	7	16	21	38
	No opinion	4	1	6	4
The Korean Conflict was a good illustration of a conflict in which U.S. and U.N. forces were denied victory unnecessarily	Agree	51	61	44	39
	Disagree	33	32	41	50
	No opinion	16	7	15	11
Number of cases		*217*	*274*	*202*	*94*

[a] A number of related items, eliminated during the scaling process, were included in the questionnaire; these items are described in the technical appendix to this study.

mouth seniors, described the Korean Conflict as "a good illustration of the fact that the Communists are determined to conquer the world." Finally, over half of the West Point cadets queried felt that United States and United Nations forces had been "denied victory unnecessarily" in the Korean Conflict; roughly 40 per cent of the Dartmouth cadets questioned asserted the same view.

The overall pattern that emerges from these comparisons is that West Point cadets tend to be more "absolutistic" in their strategic perspectives than their Dartmouth peers, but at both institutions seniors are less "absolutistic" than are freshmen (Table 7). Approximately 50 per cent of each sample falls into the category of "medium absolutism." However, one-fourth of West Point freshmen and one-fifth of West

TABLE 7. STRATEGIC PERSPECTIVES OF FRESHMEN AND SENIORS
AT WEST POINT AND AT DARTMOUTH COLLEGE:
PERCENTAGE DISTRIBUTION OF SCALE TYPES

Absolutism	West Point Freshmen	West Point Seniors	Dartmouth Freshmen	Dartmouth Seniors
	(Percentages)			
High	25	20	5	3
Medium	52	50	54	46
Low	14	20	31	41
Nonscale	9	10	10	10
Number of cases	197	253	203	93

Point seniors are in the "high absolutism" category, in contrast to one-twentieth of the sample of Dartmouth freshmen and one of the Dartmouth senior sample in 33. Likewise, there are proportionately fewer West Point cadets of the "low absolutism" type than are found among Dartmouth students.[12]

Perspectives of Cadets with Military and Nonmilitary Backgrounds

It is interesting to note that proportionately more cadets from non-military backgrounds than from military backgrounds initially possess "high absolutist" perspectives; also, fewer cadets from nonmilitary backgrounds than from military backgrounds possess "low absolutist" perspectives as freshmen. Of the sample of freshmen from nonmilitary backgrounds, 27 per cent are in the "high absolutist" category and only 12 per cent in the "low absolutist" category (Table 8). In contrast, 22 per cent of the sample of freshmen from military backgrounds fall into the "high absolutist" category and 19 per cent into the "low absolutist" group. The senior with military background differs little in strategic perspective from the freshman with the same background. However, among cadets from nonmilitary backgrounds there is a decrease from freshman to senior year in the percentage of "high absolutists" and an increase in the percentage of "low absolutists"; by senior year, 18 per cent of the nonmilitary sample are in the "high absolutist" category and 24 per cent in the "low absolutist" group. During junior and senior years, the differences between cadets from military and nonmilitary backgrounds are slight. The impact of the West Point experience upon the strategic perspective is slight and the changes that occur, as noted earlier in the discussion of professional orientation, seem to reflect an increase in homogeneity attributable to socialization.

TABLE 8. STRATEGIC PERSPECTIVES OF CADETS FROM
MILITARY AND NONMILITARY BACKGROUNDS[a]

Strategic Perspective	Father's Occupation	
	Military	Nonmilitary
	(Percentages)	
Freshmen		
High absolutism	22	27
Low absolutism	19	12
Sophomore		
High absolutism	17	25
Low absolutism	26	13
Junior		
High absolutism	19	23
Low absolutism	19	21
Senior		
High absolutism	19	18
Low absolutism	18	24

[a] Medium absolutism and nonscale types are not depicted; for each group these types equal the difference between 100 per cent and the sum of the high and low absolutism percentages for that group. Data for cadets who listed someone other than father as head of household are omitted.

Strategic Perspective and Professional Orientation

A final question about strategic perspectives was probed: Is strategic perspective linked to professional orientation? The distribution of strategic perspectives is virtually the same for cadets with "heroic" and "managerial" orientations (Table 9). Cadets with "mixed" orientation are slightly more inclined toward the "low absolutism" end of the continuum than are their "heroic" and "managerial" peers. For the cadet at least, strategic perspective and professional orientation are independent dimensions of attitudes.[13]

TABLE 9. RELATIONSHIP OF PROFESSIONAL ORIENTATIONS AND
STRATEGIC PERSPECTIVES OF CADETS

Strategic Perspective	Professional Orientation		
	Heroic	Mixed	Managerial
	(Percentages)		
High absolutism	22	19	24
Medium absolutism	52	50	49
Low absolutism	17	22	16
Nonscale type	10	8	10
Number of cases	*310*	*331*	*306*

Interpersonal Patterns

In contrast to professional and strategic attitudes, significant changes take place during cadet socialization in the expressed satisfaction that cadets derive from various extracurricular activities, and in their secondary career preferences.

Activity Preferences

The distribution of top activity preferences of samples of the four classes of cadets is indicated in Table 10. During freshman year, the cadet is not yet fully assimilated into the organized activities of the Academy; club activities and organized athletics are activities from which a higher percentage of upperclassmen derive top satisfaction than do most freshmen. Related to the lack of integration of the freshman into the cadet community, and to the severe anxieties which the *rites de passage* of "plebe year" induce, is the preference by proportionately greater numbers of the freshman sample than of the samples of upperclassmen for escaping from the institutional role by "just being alone."

Senior year is the time when the Academy attempts to effect the transition of the cadet to the junior officer role by increasing his responsibilities and his privileges. As a cadet officer or noncommissioned officer, the cadet senior performs administrative duties and supervises the activities of fellow cadets. He is given some opportunity to structure his own academic schedule through elective courses. Restrictions on the times he is required to be in his room for studying are relaxed. And he has greater opportunity to get away from the Academy on weekends and during nonduty hours. The consequences of increased responsibilities and increased privileges awarded to the senior seem to be that "escape" activities, such as being alone, or dating, become proportionately less important, whereas individual academic and professional activities, and the exchange of ideas in bull sessions with his fellow cadets become more important to him.

Alternative Career Preferences

Indications by cadets of careers which they would seriously consider if they were unable to pursue a military career provide an indication of the kinds of vocations that interest cadets and of changes in these interests during the socialization process (Table 11). Interest in engineering and scientific research outweighs that for any other vocational area among the freshman sample; such emphasis is consistent with evidence presented elsewhere that a military education and a military career are more attractive to young men with a high aptitude and interest in the

TABLE 10. SINGLE EXTRACURRICULAR ACTIVITY THAT GIVES
CADETS THE MOST SATISFACTION: TOP PREFERENCES OF
THE FOUR CLASSES

Activity	Freshman	Sophomore	Junior	Senior
	(Percentages)			
Organized				
Club	4	11	10	11
Athletics	21	37	34	26
Individual				
Academic or professional activity	9	6	5	20
Bull sessions	7	5	5	11
Athletics	0	2	5	4
Dating	24	24	25	15
Just being alone	19	9	6	4
Other	16	8	9	8
Number of Cases	70	104	93	97

TABLE 11. ALTERNATIVE CAREER PREFERENCES OF CADETS[a]

Career Field	Freshman N=222	Sophomore N=278	Junior N=261	Senior N=276
	(Percentages)			
Interpersonal Activity				
Business or industrial management	21	47	48	56
Law	24	29	36	33
Politics	17	19	22	25
College teaching	18	31	31	35
High school or elementary school teaching	18	32	26	31
U.S. Foreign Service	26	40	41	47
Impersonal Activity				
Engineering	56	68	69	59
Scientific research	39	42	40	34
Each of all other fields	Less than 20 per cent of each class			

[a] Figures represent responses, as percentages of each of the four class samples of West Point cadets, to the question, "If you were unable to pursue a military career, which of the following career fields would you *seriously consider* entering?" No limitation was placed on the number of alternatives which a given respondent might select.

engineering sciences than to those with other vocational orientations. The evidence further suggests that military activity is least attractive to young men with a high aptitude and interest in the fine arts; career areas in the fine arts interest less than one per cent of the freshman sample.[14] Moderate interest by freshmen is expressed in fields such as the U.S. Foreign Service, law, and business or industrial management. Areas such as teaching, politics, medicine, and religion are attractive to between 10 and 20 per cent of the freshman sample; fewer than 10 per cent are interested in any other area.

The alternative career preferences of upperclassmen reflect a pattern of increased diversity of interest in comparison with freshman preferences. Although interest in the relatively impersonal activities of engineering and scientific research remains fairly stable, a considerable expansion of interest occurs in careers characterized by interpersonal activity.[15] Over half of the senior sample express an interest in business or industrial management; nearly half are interested in the Foreign Service. Interest in teaching and in law also is proportionately higher than it was for freshmen. Particularly noteworthy is the interest in politics and its increase during cadet socialization. The nonpartisan posture of the military professional apparently denotes neither lack of interest nor of aptitude for politics.

SOURCES OF STABILITY AND CHANGE

The stability and the changes of cadet attitudes during socialization seem to be related to aspects of West Point recruitment practices and the value structure of the institutional environment. The base of recruitment to West Point has been broadening; recruitment has also become more selective, however. At the same time, the Academy has grown, and the institutional value structure has become more diffuse. The relative heterogeneity of the contemporary cadet population and the arena of competing values relative to professional self-image in which the cadet finds himself provide conditions for stability of the cadet's professional orientation and strategic perspective during his socialization at West Point. However, in those facets of behavior where the rewards and punishments of the institutional system dictate a high degree of conformity, such as posture, decorum, and institutional lingo, the cadet's high adaptability permits him to perceive the cues accurately and to make the appropriate response quickly. The cadet changes his branch preference, his activities preference, or his secondary career preferences as new limitations are imposed upon him by the environment, new opportunities are made available to him, or new experiences broaden his knowledge.

Trends in West Point recruiting patterns and changes in the Academy value structure are of interest both for helping to explain cadet socialization patterns and for the evidence they provide about changes in composition and values that are taking place in the American military profession as a whole.

Recruitment Patterns: Broadened Representation, Increased Selectivity

Representativeness. One of Janowitz's basic hypotheses about the American military profession over the past fifty years is that the military "elites" have been "shifting their recruitment from a narrow, relatively high, social status base to a broader base, more representative of the population as a whole."[15] West Point recruitment patterns since World War II give additional support to this hypothesis.

The percentage distribution of father's occupation among the classes entering the Military Academy from the years 1945 through 1960 is presented in Table 12. A decline in both professional and business-white collar representation, and an increase in representation from

TABLE 12. FATHER'S OCCUPATION OF CADETS ENTERING THE MILITARY ACADEMY FROM 1945–1960

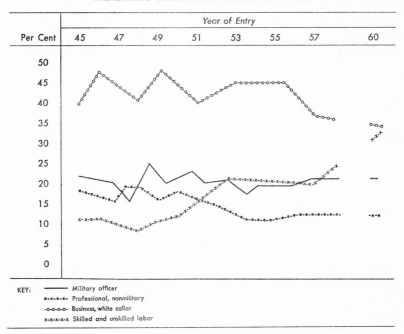

KEY:
——— Military officer
-•-•-•- Professional, nonmilitary
-o-o-o-o- Business, white collar
x-x-x-x-x Skilled and unskilled labor

SOURCE: Data for the years 1945–1957 are from USMA, Superintendent's Curriculum Study, *Report of the Working Committee on the Historical Aspects of the Curriculum for the Period 1802–1945*. West Point, 1958, Appendix 23. The broken lines indicate that data for 1958 and 1959 were not available. Data for 1960 are from Research Division, Office of the Director of Admissions and Registrar, USMA, *Relationship Between Selected Background Variables and Three Criteria of Success*, Research Note 61–4, West Point, 1961.

skilled and unskilled labor backgrounds since the war are indicated.[16] The combined professional and business-white collar representation in the early years after the war comprised roughly 60 per cent of entering class strengths; but by 1960 the figure had dropped to roughly 40 per cent of the entering class strength. Sons of skilled and unskilled laborers, approximately 10 per cent of the entering class representation in the early years after the war, by 1960 comprised nearly 30 per cent of the entering class strength. Farmers' sons have represented fewer than 5 per cent of the members of each class since World War II; this group is not reported in Table 12.

The percentage of cadets whose fathers are military officers has remained relatively constant at approximately 20 per cent over the past fifteen years. The percentage of cadets whose fathers are now or have been at some time military officers is higher; 36 per cent of the Class of 1965 are in that category. An additional 25 per cent of that class have fathers who are or have been enlisted men, although fewer than 2 per cent of cadets entering the Academy since the war have had fathers on active duty as enlisted men or warrant officers.[17] The number of sons of West Point graduates has fluctuated between 6 and 9 per cent of the entering strength of recent classes.[18] Continuity of professional pursuits from one generation to the next is relatively common. Rogoff found that 18 per cent of University of Pennsylvania medical students had fathers who were physicians. In a related study, Thielens found that 50 per cent of medical students had doctor relatives; 51 per cent of law students had lawyer relatives.[19]

Rogoff found that a much greater proportion of students whose fathers were M.D.'s began thinking in terms of a career in medicine at an earlier age than did students with no relative in medicine.[20] A similar finding concerning the cadet's decision to enter the Military Academy was encountered (Table 13). Forty-four per cent of the cadet sample whose fathers pursued nonmilitary occupations and who had no West Point relatives first seriously considered applying for an appointment to West Point at age fifteen or earlier. Approximately 60 per cent of those who either had West Point relatives or whose fathers were in the military first considered the decision to come to West Point at age fifteen or earlier.

Another measure of representativeness is religion. While data on religious affiliation of classes entering the Academy during the entire period since World War II are not available, the religion of childhood and current religious preferences of samples of contemporary classes of West Point freshmen and seniors are listed in Table 14. Comparative data are provided of the religious affiliations of the total American civil

TABLE 13. AGE AT WHICH THE DECISION TO ENTER WEST POINT WAS FIRST SERIOUSLY CONSIDERED BY CADETS, AND MILITARY BACKGROUND

Background	Decision Age 15 or Earlier	After 15
	(Percentages)	
Father, military Cadets have West Point relatives	83	17
Father, military Cadets do not have West Point relatives	63	37
Father, nonmilitary Cadets have West Point relatives	59	41
Father, nonmilitary Cadets do not have West Point relatives	44	56
All Cadets N=946	51	49

TABLE 14. CHILDHOOD RELIGION AND CURRENT RELIGIOUS PREFERENCES OF WEST POINT FRESHMEN AND SENIORS

Religion[a]	West Point Freshman		West Point Senior		U.S. Total[b] 119,333,000 (14 years and over)	Top Army Leaders[c]
	Child-hood	Current	Child-hood	Current		
	(Percentages)					
Jewish	2	2	2	2	3	0
Roman Catholic	29	30	29	30	26	11
Protestant, Total	65	61	65	54	66	89
Episcopal	9	9	9	11	3	40
Other traditional	20	19	20	14	15	23
Pietistic	29	24	28	20	34	18
Other Protestant	7	8	8	9	14	8
Other	d	d	d	d	1	0
No Religion	4	5	3	13	3	0
Number of cases	223		276			166

[a] "Other traditional" includes Presbyterian, Lutheran, Congregational, and Evangelical and Reformed; "Pietistic" includes Baptist, Methodist, and Disciples of Christ.

[b] U.S. Bureau of the Census, *Statistical Abstract of the United States: 1962.* 83d ed. Washington, 1962, pp. 46–47.

[c] Janowitz, Morris, *The Professional Soldier.* The Free Press, Glencoe, Ill., 1960, pp. 98–99.

[d] Less than .5 per cent.

population as of 1957, and of Army top leadership as of 1950. The cadet religious preferences resemble those of the total civil population more than they do those of Army top leadership. Undoubtedly these data reflect part of a trend within the military profession toward increased representativeness.

Episcopalianism, the core religious faith of the American military profession historically, is slightly overrepresented at West Point, although the percentage affiliation among cadets is not nearly that found among Army top leadership. However, in the past, incorporation into the military profession and upward social mobility have been accompanied by some change of affiliation toward Episcopalianism.[21] Episcopalianism has served as one basis of group cohesion; the ritual and formality associated with the Episcopal service are similar to ritual and formality integral to the officer's daily professional life. Therefore, it may be that as cadets continue up the career ladder the percentage affiliation with Episcopalianism will increase and affiliation with other faiths, especially "pietistic" denominations, which among major faiths represent the sharpest contrast to Episcopalianism, will decrease.

A third measure of representativeness is race. Although the nation's Military Academy, in contrast to a vast number of other institutions of higher learning, has admitted Negroes since shortly after the Civil War, only a total of 80 had been admitted through the year 1961.[22] Obviously, a number of factors other than the Academy screening process—factors such as handicaps in prior education, and unfavorable opportunities to compete for congressional appointments—have contributed to the relative dearth of Negro representation at West Point historically.

Of the estimated 1,781,000 males in the United States between the ages of eighteen and twenty-four who were in college or professional school in 1961, approximately 6 per cent were nonwhite.[23] Of the 17 Negroes who joined the Corps of Cadets with the classes of 1962 through 1965, 11 remained as of January, 1962, comprising 0.4 per cent of the total Corps strength.[24] Although the 17 Negroes who were admitted represent a tiny fraction of the total Negro population, they comprise 21 per cent of all Negroes ever admitted to West Point. In other words, the Negro is not represented at West Point in proportion to his numbers nationally, but the West Point student body is more nearly representative in terms of race than in the past.

The Janowitz study revealed that top Army leadership of 1950 came predominantly from rural backgrounds, and disproportionately from the South, although the trend since the turn of the century has been toward increasing urban representation in the profession and toward bringing regional representation more in line with the distribution of the population as a whole.[25] Data on cadet backgrounds reveal a continuation of these trends toward increased representativeness.

A comparison of the rural-urban backgrounds of cadets from civilian environments with the distribution of the U.S. civilian population in

1960 is made in Table 15. Data available on the size of hometown of cadets suffer from a number of limitations; the data do not reveal geographic mobility, access to metropolitan areas, important differences that may distinguish communities of identical size, and other aspects of community environment that might be meaningful. Gross comparisons of population distributions, however, suggest that the current cadet population from nonmilitary environments is fairly representative of the urban-rural distribution of the civilian population as a whole. Figures for cadet backgrounds represent a sharp decline in the percentage of recruits into the military profession from rural backgrounds; Janowitz found that 66 per cent of Army top leadership came from rural origins. However, as he points out, the figure is nearly in line with the percentage of the national population living in rural areas at the time when most of

TABLE 15. RURAL-URBAN HOMETOWN BACKGROUND OF CADETS FROM CIVILIAN BACKGROUNDS

Type of Hometown	U.S. Population, 1960[a]	West Point Class of 1964	West Point Class of 1965
		(Percentages)	
Rural	30	24	26
Urban area under 50,000	34	36	40
City of 50 to 100,000	8	10	9
City of 100,000 or greater	29	29	25
Number of cases	—	480	565

[a] U.S. Bureau of the Census, *Statistical Abstract of the United States: 1962*. 83d ed. Washington, 1962, p. 21. The current urban definition is used.

the contemporary military leaders were born. On the other hand, Janowitz makes an important distinction between the rural origins of the military elite, and the predominantly urban origins of business elites.[26] That important distinction remains. The rural or small town background is still characteristic of a majority of cadets from civilian backgrounds, in contrast to the urban background characteristic of business elites. Cadets from military backgrounds, who comprise slightly over 20 per cent of the total cadet population, are, of course, the group whose backgrounds are least representative of the backgrounds of the total American population.

The regional backgrounds of the Class of 1964 at entry are compared to the distribution of the fifteen to nineteen age group of the total population as of 1960 (Table 16). Since congressional representation is principally by population and since 85 per cent of appointments to

TABLE 16. REGIONAL BACKGROUNDS OF THE WEST POINT
CLASS OF 1964

Region[a]	Class of 1964[b]	U.S. Population, 1960 15 to 19 Age Group
	(Percentages)	
Pacific	9.9	11.4
Mountain	3.7	4.0
West North Central	8.3	8.5
East North Central	14.5	19.3
South Central	13.6	17.9
South Atlantic	20.0	15.8
Middle Atlantic	21.8	17.3
New England	8.3	5.6

[a] Standard Census Bureau regions are indicated, except that South Central is sometimes further divided into East South Central and West South Central.

[b] Research Division, Office of the Director of Admissions and Registrar, USMA, *Relationship Between Selected Background Variables and Three Criteria of Success.* Research Note 61–4, West Point, 1961.

West Point annually are made by United States Senators and Representatives, it follows that the cadet population will closely resemble that of the total U.S. population. Since the distribution of the fifteen to nineteen age group differs little from the distribution of the total population, the former also necessarily resembles the distribution of cadet backgrounds.[27] It is interesting to note that some overrepresentation occurs, not of the traditionally overrepresented South, but of the eastern coastal regions of New England, the Middle Atlantic states, and the Southern Atlantic states. The overrepresentation of these regions is attributable to the concentration there of the homes of noncongressional appointees. Noncongressional appointees are of two types. The more numerous category is the competitive appointment. Fifty-seven per cent of the competitive appointees in the Class of 1964 were sons of military officers, in contrast to 16 per cent of congressional appointees from such backgrounds, and 7 per cent of other noncongressional appointees from military backgrounds. A majority of sons of military officers of the Class of 1964 listed hometown addresses in the eastern coastal regions, where their fathers (mostly field grade or general officers) are stationed.[28] The second category of noncongressional appointment is the "additional appointment," by which the Military Academy is authorized to select candidates for admission to fill vacancies not filled through regular congressional and competitive channels. The evidence suggests that the Academy has utilized these appointments primarily to attract promising athletes, mostly from the East coast, to West Point.[29] Ninety-eight per cent of additional appointees of the Class of 1964 were high school varsity lettermen in contrast to only 60 per cent of congressional appointees and 55 per cent of regular competitive appointees who were lettermen.[30]

Selectivity. Although the social base of recruitment to West Point has been broadened, higher standards of admission make the recruitment highly selective from a mental, physical, and emotional point of view.

In May, 1957, the Military Academy adopted a recruiting program based upon what they termed a "whole man" concept, designed to improve the quality of recruits and to reduce resignations from the Academy by taking into account in the screening process, qualities in addition to educational achievement which seemed to be important attributes of the military leader.[31] Educational admission standards were also raised, shortly thereafter.[32] These programs aimed at improving the quality of West Point recruits have met with some success. In recent years the percentage of cadets who have graduated from high school in the upper fifth of their class has steadily increased. Sixty per cent of the Class of 1963, 63 per cent of the Class of 1964, 74 per cent of the Class of 1965, and 78 per cent of the Class of 1966 graduated in the upper quintile of their high school class. The number of those who enter West Point with outstanding high school athletic records is unusually marked in recent years, although athletic ability has long been a hallmark of the cadet. Typically, the cadet has been active in other high school activities as well. Thirty-seven per cent of the Class of 1965 had been club presidents, 11 per cent had been editors of school publications, 16 per cent had been debate team members.[33]

In a study of college seniors by the National Opinion Research Center, although West Pointers were not included in the sample, self-descriptions by those who indicated a preference for a military career are suggestive of the kind of self-image that is likely to typify the West Pointer as well. "Ambitious," "forceful," "energetic," "hard-driving," "athletic," "dominant," and "easy-going" were adjectives of self-description which seniors bent upon military careers used to significantly higher degree than did the total senior sample. Likewise, the adjectives "intellectual," "moody," "cultured," "quiet," "fun-loving," "shy," and "outgoing" were selected to a significantly lower degree by military aspirants than by the sample as a whole.[34]

Not only has the Academy higher academic standards now but younger recruits than in the recent past. The seventeen to eighteen age-at-entry group comprises over 70 per cent of the Corps of Cadets today, as compared to 40 per cent or fewer during the period 1938 to 1948. Studies comparing age of entry to the Academy with various measures of subsequent adaptability suggest that the younger cadet is more successful in adjusting to professional socialization than is the older cadet. The seventeen to eighteen age-at-entry group has had a lower rate of dropouts from the Academy, a higher mean standing at graduation, and even a considerably better record at achieving the rank of general officer.[35]

Institutional Environment: Diffusion of Values

From the point of view of cadet socialization, the facet of the contemporary West Point environment that differs most from what was characteristic of the Academy until about the time of World War II is the diffuse nature of the value system which the contemporary environment embodies. The diffusion of values which has taken place is attributable to three factors: adjustment of the Academy to changing professional requirements of nuclear weaponry and worldwide military assistance-type operations, adaptive efforts by West Point to compete successfully for top caliber recruits with institutions such as the new Air Force Academy, and changing practices and relationships stemming from the sheer growth of the institution.

Changing Professional Requirements

The *modus operandi* of West Point historically was the "Thayer System," a prescribed system of training and education.[36] Discipline was the core of the system: discipline of the mind, body, and emotions.[37] The heart of the educational program was mathematics, which was believed to provide an intellectual discipline that was transferable to all other intellectual endeavors.[38] Physical training stressed discipline of the body and the development of skills appropriate to the officer-gentleman, such as fencing and riding. Emotional discipline was transmitted particularly through the *rites de passage* of "plebe year," in which one established his legitimacy as a member of the Corps by practicing strict obedience to his superiors, unswerving dedication to the professional code of honor, and willingness to place duty before personal pleasure.[39]

The simplicity of the assumptions upon which the "Thayer System" rested was challenged as early as the turn of the century. However, revision of the system followed the impact of two world wars and the advent of nuclear weapons.[40] It became apparent to many military leaders during or soon after World War II that the postwar era would make unprecedented demands upon the military profession, not only in terms of skills, but in terms of breadth of vision and adaptability to diverse situations.[41] Momentum slowly gathered for reassessment of the Military Academy in the light of these new demands.

Competition for Recruits

The pressure for reassessment was speeded by the opening of the Air Force Academy in 1955. Air Force officials indicated that the new institution would foster a "modern" image, designed to present a sharp contrast to the older academies, particularly West Point.[42] Since all of the service academies compete for a limited pool of young men able to meet certain standards, and willing to consider a military career, when access to the pool was granted to a new competitor, the older academies necessarily took stock of their own potential for maintaining a steady input of promising candidates.

The self-assessment that had begun at the Academy as a result of changing professional requirements and changing problems of recruitment came to a climax in the Superintendency of Major General Garrison Davidson. Upon assuming the post in 1956 General Davidson announced that "the time had come for a more searching and fundamental review of what our goals should be and how best to attain them."[43]

Among the more important changes instituted were provisions for broadening the curriculum and making it more flexible, to give students selective opportunities for specialization in subjects of their special interest; a movement away from the once sacrosanct "daily recitation" system; more emphasis in summer tactical training on realistic training for combat and less on drill, ceremony, and VIP-type tours; greater privileges allotted to cadets—particularly greater opportunities for seniors to leave the Academy grounds during free time.[44]

The consequence of these changes is not the replacement of an old value system with a new one, but a diffusion of the values that the environment embodies. Today as they have for generations the Gothic architecture, the emphasis in statue and plaque upon the brave deeds of former graduates, the ceremonial ritual, the nineteenth-century cut of the uniforms, the institutional customs and lore all reflect traditional "heroic" values of the service. Furthermore, a portion of the contemporary faculty and alumni remain committed to these values to the point of regarding changes which have been implemented in the past ten years as dangerous departures from traditional practices, undermining the basic foundations of Academy strength. On the other hand, the emphasis upon modern weapons strategies and techniques, the concern for the theoretical and practical problems of the atomic and space requirements, and even the modernity of the facilities and equipment of the new academic building reflect "managerial" values emphasizing planning, flexibility, and innovation. These newer values also have their champions among faculty members and alumni. Probably the largest group of faculty and alumni, however, occupy a middle ground, deeply committed to West Point traditions and customs, but cautiously receptive to innovation.

The indoctrination which the cadet receives today contains the inherent ambivalence of the diffuse value system. Change is justified to him in terms of tradition. The cadet is told that "West Point is changing. But these vast improvements have been achieved only by this striving for perfection of those who have gone before—traditionally known as the Long Grey Line."[45] Emphasis upon the intangible rewards of service and sacrifice for one's country is balanced with reminders that three-fourths of Academy graduates today can expect to receive postgraduate schooling at government expense. Appeals to team spirit, comradery, and conformity to group mores are made simultaneously with entreaties to develop a "capacity for critical and original thought."[46]

Institutional Growth

Additional diffusion of values in the West Point environment has been the product of sheer growth. Life at West Point during most of the Academy's history had a familial quality. Cadets knew all other cadets and all of the faculty. Although a certain aura of formality and impersonality was maintained, in accordance with military decorum, the cadet's relations were highly personal. His behavior was dictated far more by the informal customs and mores of the society in which he found himself than by codified rules of conduct.

But the Military Academy has grown. Sylvanus Thayer graduated in a class of 15 cadets, Ulysses Grant in a class of 39, Douglas MacArthur in a class of 93, Maxwell Taylor in a class of 102.[47] By the 1930's, with Corps strength authorized at approximately 1,400, the graduating classes were over 200 in size. During World War II, the authorization of Corps strength was raised to the present figure of approximately 2,500. Plans authorized by Congress call for increasing the size of the Corps of Cadets to 4,417 in the near future. The staff and faculty have also grown; whereas in 1900 there were only 74 commissioned officers assigned to duty at West Point, today there are nearly 600.[48]

Institutional growth has bred increased diversity, both among cadets and among faculty. Rarely today does any single social or extracurricular activity involve more than a small portion of the Corps or the faculty. In 1911, the cadet could choose from among six extracurricular activities. A half-century later, cadets are involved in 57 extracurricular activities, reflecting the diversity of interests of cadets and the multiple units into which the Corps divides for spare time associations. The faculty, in turn, has grown so large that nearly all social functions are held within departmental groupings, or in groupings by the USMA classes in which the faculty members graduated.

New educational policy requires all permanent professors on the Academy faculty to pursue graduate work to the successful completion of the doctorate and to take sabbatical leaves. Between sabbaticals, they are to visit in other service installations for at least three months. This policy is designed to have the effect of maintaining a constant input of fresh ideas from civilian institutions of higher learning and from other parts of the military profession. But additional effects of the policy will be increased specialization and further diversity of outlook among the faculty.

CONCLUSIONS

As Everett C. Hughes has emphasized, the term "profession had its origins in the notion of a group that has taken a vow."[49] Under the impact of modernization and industrialization, the "secularization" of professions takes place and the sacred-like character of professional groups is transformed. The difference between professional groups and other social groups becomes blurred, partly because the conception of professional responsibility diffuses throughout society. Professional socialization is no longer consecration to beliefs and values that distinguish the professional group from other groups, but rather a process of adapting the values and beliefs held rather widely in the society to the specialized roles associated with a skilled profession.

Changes at West Point are part of this process of social change. To be sure, West Point retains a number of significant traditional features that are essential for the military profession. These specialized practices distinguish the military academy from a civilian college or university. The basic trend, however, has been toward a decrease in the differences between the U.S. Military Academy and civilian institutions of higher learning.

Given this trend, the empirical findings of this study become understandable. Socialization at West Point produces only slight impact upon professional orientations and strategic perspectives of the cadet. There is some increase in homogeneity of attitudes among cadets, as evidenced by the diminution from freshman to senior years of differences between attitudes of cadets from military backgrounds and those from nonmilitary backgrounds. By contrast, attitudes which relate closely to the common experiences of most cadets and are linked to their specific career interests are subject to considerable change during socialization. For example, important changes occur in the preferences that cadets express for the branch of service in which they hope to serve and for the extracurricular activities that provide them the most satisfaction.

These conclusions must, of course, be qualified by the limitations of the design of the present study, particularly since this is a cross sectional study rather than one designed to follow a single class through the four-year period. Moreover, measures employed in the present study focused upon selected aspects of the socialization process. Facets of socialization such as the commitment to a career in the service developed at West Point, the professional skills acquired, friendship patterns and the like were omitted from the present analysis because of limitations of time and resources. In an effort to relate the present study closely to prior research, the emphasis has been upon professional orientation and strategic perspective, with some attention to interpersonal attitudes.

Nevertheless, on the basis of these findings, it would be misleading to argue that the young officer cadet who graduates from West Point in the 1960's has been unaffected by his military academy experience. A process of professional socialization has begun which will continue after graduation and throughout the course of his career. The basic point is that this process takes place in an educational environment closely related to and therefore compatible with the civilian educational environment and in an atmosphere that accommodates diverse values in preparation for the diversity of professional roles.

TECHNICAL APPENDIX:

SURVEY DESIGN, SAMPLING PROCEDURES, AND METHODOLOGY

In a discussion in December, 1960, with the author of his proposal for the present study, the Superintendent of the U.S. Military Academy granted him permission to undertake the study, on the condition that any cadet participation be voluntary and involve no use of scheduled training time. Subsequent correspondence and discussion with the Military Academy staff led the author to make a number of modifications in his initial research design. Among the most important of these were the abandonment of a longitudinal study of the freshman class, which was to supplement the cross-sectional study of the four West Point classes, and the postponement of the initial measurement of attitudes of freshmen from the first few weeks of training to November, the fifth month of cadet life for freshmen. As a limited basis of comparison with cadet attitudes, a survey of the attitudes of a sample of freshmen and seniors at a civilian college was added to the design. Dartmouth College was selected as the source of this sample.

Colonel G. A. Lincoln, chairman of the Department of Social Sciences at the Military Academy, pointed out to the author the many similarities between the Dartmouth and West Point "socialization structures" that would be advantageous in terms of controlling the maximum number of variables. Dartmouth and West Point are both all-male institutions. Dartmouth has approximately 2,900 students; West Point has approximately 2,500. Both schools have a broad geographic representation, although Dartmouth draws somewhat more heavily from New England than does the Academy. Both schools maintain a vigorous athletic program. Both campuses are relatively isolated geographically; each campus is a storehouse of tradition, going back to Revolutionary War days.

In order to get an adequate sample of cadets without being able to communicate with potential respondents in person, the author sent a copy of the survey instrument, with a cover sheet explaining the general nature of the inquiry and asking for cooperation, to each member of the Corps of Cadets.[50] Because cadet time is heavily scheduled, the author desired to get the survey instrument to the cadet at a time when he would be most likely to take time to complete and return it. Therefore survey instruments were distributed to cadets through Academy internal distribution channels, just prior to Thanksgiving; cadets were asked to return the completed survey to the author the following week. This gave them a holiday plus a weekend of free time to complete the instrument, should they so desire. Responses were obtained from more than one thousand cadets, representing approximately 40 per cent of the total cadet population.

Because the sample was self-selected from the total cadet population, the possibility of a systematic bias of the sample must be considered. As a check for evidence of such a bias, a comparison was made of the distribution of key variables in the total population of each class. These comparisons are presented in Table 17. A blank column under a class heading for a given variable indicates that data were not available for that class for that variable.

A close similarity in the representation of the various types of hometown exists between the freshman and sophomore samples and total populations. Considering the fact that current religious affiliation is indicated for the class total populations in comparison with childhood

TABLE 17. THE DISTRIBUTION OF KEY VARIABLES; COMPARISONS OF PERCENTAGES OF WEST POINT CLASS SAMPLES (S) AND TOTAL POPULATIONS (P)[a]

Variable	Fr. S N=223	Fr. P N=725	So. S N=278	So. P N=629	Jr. S N=263	Jr. P N=512	Sr. S N=276	Sr. P N=601
Size of Hometown[b]								
Rural	18	20	15	18	19		18	
City 2,500 to 50,000	32	31	31	28	33		33	
City over 50,000	29	27	30	30	26		28	
Military, or moved often	22	22	23	23	22		21	
Religious Affiliation[c]								
Protestant	65	65	68	67	68	69	65	66
Catholic	29	33	27	32	28	30	29	32
Jewish	2	2	1	1	1	1	2	2
Other	4	–	4	–	3	–	3	–
Father's Occupation[d]								
West Point officer	8		11	8	9		8	
Non-West Point officer	14		12	12	14		13	
Military enlisted man	1		3	2	1		3	
Professional	11		13	11	10		9	
Business, white collar	33		35	33	38		37	
Skilled unskilled labor	27		22	30	24		25	
Other	6		4	4	4		5	
Academic Standing								
Upper third	49	33	45	33	47	33	43	33
Middle third	34	33	30	33	28	33	32	33
Lower third	17	33	25	33	25	33	26	33
Age at Entry[e]								
17 years	27	26	34	27	30	28	27	
18 years	53	50	40	43	43	39	38	
19 years	12	15	16	18	18	20	17	
Over 19 years	8	9	10	11	9	13	17	

[a] All data for class samples are based on responses to questions contained in Part III of the survey instrument, which is described in Appendix II of the author's unpublished Ph.D. dissertation, "The Cadet Phase of the Professional Socialization of the West Pointer: Description, Analysis, and Theoretical Refinement," University of Wisconsin, 1962.

[b] Hometown data for class total populations are based on data obtained from USMA, Information Office.

[c] Data on religious affiliation for class total populations were obtained from the office of the USMA Assistant Protestant Chaplain, in the spring of 1962.

[d] Data on the sophomore class total population are based on data contained in USMA, Office of the Director of Admissions and Registrar, "The Characteristics of the Class of 1964," West Point, n.d.

[e] Total population data were compiled from USMA, Office of the Director of Admissions and Registrar, "The Characteristics of the Class of 1963," "The Characteristics of the Class of 1964," "The Characteristics of the Class of 1965," 4, 12, and 19 pp., respectively.

religious affiliations of the samples, no evident bias is suggested by the comparison. The only comparison of "father's occupation" available was between sample and total population of the sophomore class; some underrepresentation of the skilled and unskilled labor group is suggested by the comparison; otherwise, the figures for sample and total population are very similar.

It is likely that the figures for the academic standing of the class samples in part reflect inaccuracy of the cadet's perception of his own relative academic proficiency. However, it also is likely that the academically successful student is more inclined to take the time to respond to a survey than is the less successful student. It appears, therefore, that the samples are biased in favor of representation of the academically successful cadet.

Also the samples appear to be slightly biased in favor of the representation of the younger cadet. Assuming that the younger cadet and the academically successful cadet are disproportionately represented in the samples, one must conclude that the attitudes of any one class sample (for example, sample of freshmen) may not accurately reflect the attitudes of the class as a whole. However, comparisons *between classes* (that is, cross-sectional comparisons) of attitudes are relatively unaffected by biased distribution of the above independent variables in the samples because the direction and magnitude of bias is approximately the same for each class.

Dartmouth Samples

A slightly shorter version of the survey instrument used at West Point was administered to samples of Dartmouth freshmen and seniors in January, 1962. The author believed that it was desirable to explain the questionnaire to the Dartmouth students in person, even though this had not been done at West Point, in order to get an adequate response. As at West Point, responses at Dartmouth were voluntary and anonymous.

No effort was made to ensure that the Dartmouth samples would be representative of the classes from which they were chosen. On the contrary, extensive cooperation from the departments of Military, Air, and Naval Science made possible the weighting of the samples heavily toward representation of students in military programs of some type, thereby further reducing differences in experience represented in the West Point and Dartmouth samples. Eighty-two per cent of the Dartmouth respondents indicated that they expected to perform military service as officers upon completion of college. The author's interest in the Dartmouth samples was not in their approximation of the total student population from which they were drawn, but in their usefulness as sources of comparison with the responses of the West Point samples. That is, the author was interested in differences noted between the responses of West Point cadets and those of the Dartmouth samples as evidence of differences of socialization experiences during the college

years, rather than as evidence of differences of recruitment patterns at
the two institutions.

From a comparison of the distribution of key variables between the
West Point and Dartmouth freshman and senior samples, it is obvious
that the Dartmouth samples served imperfectly the purpose for which
they were intended. Fewer of the Dartmouth samples have come from
military environments, or have changed hometown frequently, than is
true of the West Point samples. There is a higher percentage of Catho-
lics and a lower percentage of Jews in the West Point samples than in
the Dartmouth samples. There are relatively fewer Dartmouth students
than West Point cadets whose fathers are military men, or laborers, and
relatively more who are professionals or businessmen. The mean age of
the Dartmouth freshman and senior groups is less than that of the West
Point freshman and senior groups, respectively.

Construction of an Index of Professional Orientation

During September and October, 1962, the author conducted interviews with members of each department of the Military Academy
faculty. Officers were asked to assign a general priority (top, middle,
low) to 27 attributes or skills that might be important to the professional
officer in terms of the anticipated demands of the military officer's role
during the next fifteen years. Reference to the basic descriptive outlines
by Janowitz of the "heroic leader," the "military manager," and the
"technologist" led to the inclusion of items in the list peculiar to each
of the three types.[51] Technological specialists in the officer corps are
recruited principally from non-Academy sources; no officer interviewed
displayed a technological orientation. Analysis of interview responses
led to the elimination of "technologist" items, and the refinement or
elimination of remaining items. A final list of 16 items describing "characteristics of a career" was included in the questionnaire sent to all
cadets.

Cadets were asked to indicate the two characteristics that would be
the most important to them in terms of the satisfactions they would
expect of a career, regardless of how characteristic or uncharacteristic
the items might seem to be of a *military* career. Each item was given an
a priori classification, on the basis of the Janowitz findings and the
officer interviews, as "heroic" or "managerial." After plotting cadet
responses on a 16 by 16 frequency matrix, with rows and columns
indicating the first and second choice, respectively, of each cadet (which
choice was "first" and which was "second" was determined arbitrarily
and has no bearing on the analysis), it became apparent that some

items were selected with such universality that they would not distinguish the "heroic" from the "managerial" orientation. These items were redesignated "nondiscriminating." For each remaining item, the percentage of the second choices accounted for by items similarly classified was computed. Items were successively regrouped until the maximum amount of discrimination between "heroic" and "managerial" items was achieved (Table 18). The "nondiscriminating" grouping consists of items principally accounted for by other "nondiscriminating" items, with a percentage accounted for by "heroic" items approximately equal to that accounted for by "managerial" items. Both "managerial" and "heroic" items are also, in most cases, accounted for principally by

TABLE 18. ITEM CLASSIFICATION, PROFESSIONAL ORIENTATION INDEX

Item of First Choice[a]	Percentage of Second Choice Accounted for by:		
	Nondiscr. Items	Heroic Items	Managerial Items
The most important aspects of a career, in terms of satisfaction, are that it is:	(Percentages)		
Nondiscriminating			
Rewards initiative (M)	58	16	26
Provides satisfaction from proving oneself (H)	60	24	16
Demands knowledge of foreign systems (M)	62	20	18
Provides fellowship (H)	54	21	25
Requires managerial skill (M)	69	12	19
Presents challenging problems (H)	53	24	23
Heroic			
Demands spiritual strength (H)	38	51	11
Requires faith in the "American way of life" (H)	60	28	12
Requires subordination of self to profession (H)	42	38	20
Demands a colorful, aggressive personality (H)	70	22	8
Demands concern for fellow human beings (M)	58	27	15
Managerial			
Provides a full family life (M)	44	18	38
Affords financial security (M)	54	12	34
Demands broad cultural interests (M)	57	13	30
Provides opportunities for graduate schooling (M)	52	8	40
Provides opportunities for scientific research (M)	39	11	50

[a] The letter in parentheses after each item represents the group to which the item was assigned prior to the refinement which led to the above grouping. The selection of these items and the refinement process are explained in greater detail in the pages immediately preceding and following this table.

"nondiscriminating" items, since a few of the latter items account for well over half of the total alternate choices. But each "managerial" item is far better explained by the "managerial" category than by the "heroic"; and each "heroic" item is better explained by the "heroic" category than by the "managerial."

Cadet respondents were classified as "heroic," "managerial," or "mixed," if they had given at least one "heroic" and no "managerial" response, at least one "managerial" and no "heroic" response, or either a "heroic" and a "managerial" response, or two "mixed" responses, respectively.

Construction of a Strategic Perspectives Scale

A series of items designed to provide a measure of "strategic perspective" was included in the questionnaire which was administered to the West Point and to the Dartmouth samples (Table 19). By means of

TABLE 19. QUESTIONNAIRE ITEMS FROM WHICH THE STRATEGIC
PERSPECTIVES SCALE WAS CONSTRUCTED

1. How likely are the following types of events to take place within the next fifteen years? (Indicate the likelihood of *each alternative* by checking the appropriate column.)

Categories:	Practically inevitable	Quite likely	Possible but quite unlikely	Practically no likelihood
Allout war in which U.S. and Communist forces strike at each other's homeland with nuclear weapons.				
Limited nuclear war in which elements of U.S. and Communist forces fight each other on some foreign soil using nuclear weapons.				
Limited conventional war in which elements of U.S. and Communist forces fight each other on some foreign soil without employing nuclear weapons.				
Hostilities in which the U.S. and Communist nations back opposing sides, but themselves engage only in support or advisory roles.				
Hostilities which find portions of the Communist bloc allied with the U.S. to fight a common enemy (Communist or non-Communist).				

2. The Korean Conflict has been cited by various persons to support various arguments. To what extent do you agree or disagree with the following assertions about the Korean Conflict? (Indicate the extent of your agreement or disagreement with each assertion by checking the appropriate column.)

Categories:	Strongly agree	Agree	Disagree	Strongly disagree	No opinion
The Korean Conflict was a good illustration of:					
A conflict which confirmed the worth of the United Nations as an instrument of collective security.					
The fact that the Communists are determined to conquer the world.					
The fact that our military objectives must be coordinated with and limited by our foreign policy objectives.					
A conflict in which U.S. and United Nations forces were denied victory unnecessarily.					

3. Various factors have been advanced to explain why some nations in the world today have chosen to pursue a policy of "neutrality" or are "noncommittal" in the Cold War. In general, *which of the following factors seem to you to be among the significant causes of the choice of neutrality by these nations?* (Indicate the extent to which you consider each factor significant or insignificant by checking the appropriate column.)

Categories:	Very significant	Quite significant	Quite insignificant	Very insignificant	No opinion
Geographic location; lack of moral fiber; desire to contribute to world stability; lack of economic and/or military power to decide otherwise; desire to get something for nothing; Communist influence in the nation's government; political naiveté.					

a Guttman scalogram analysis program, which dichotomized the items, a scale of six items was constructed (Table 20). Respondents were assigned to one of the seven possible "pure types" or, if more than one error existed in a pattern of responses, the respondent was classed as a "nonscale" type.[52] The seven groups of scale types were collapsed into three groups, choosing cutoff points to make the groups as nearly equal in size as possible. These groups were designated "high," "medium," or "low" absolutists, according to the degree of agreement with the items in the strategic perspectives scale.

TABLE 20. THE STRATEGIC PERSPECTIVES SCALE

Content of Item	Per Cent Agree	Responses Included in "Agree" Category	Item Reproducibility
Neutrality is caused by Communist influence in the neutral nation's government	14	Strongly agree	92.2
Allout war is likely within 15 years	24	Strongly agree Agree	91.5
Limited conventional war between the U.S. and Communist forces is likely within 15 years	41	Strongly agree	90.9
Limited nuclear war between the U.S. and Communist forces is likely within 15 years	55	Strongly agree Agree	91.6
The Korean Conflict was a good illustration of a conflict in which U.S. and U.N. forces were denied victory unnecessarily	64	Strongly agree Agree No opinion	85.8
The Korean Conflict was a good illustration of the fact that the Communists are determined to conquer the world	84	Strongly agree Agree No opinion	93.3

Scale reproducibility: 90.8

NOTES

1. Larned, Charles W., "West Point and Higher Education," *Army and Navy Life*, vol. 8, June, 1906, p. 18.

2. "Professional socialization" refers to the process by which members of a profession learn the values, attitudes, and behavior appropriate to their roles within the profession. This definition has been patterned after one discussed at length in a terminological appendix to the collection of studies of socialization in the medical profession. Merton, Robert K., George G. Reader, and Patricia L. Kendall, editors, *The Student-Physician*, Harvard University Press, Cambridge, Mass., 1957, p. 287.

3. The compositions of the four-class samples according to the distribution of selected variables are compared in the appendix to this paper; the samples in turn are compared to the total populations from which the samples are drawn. The samples appear to be slightly biased in favor of the representation of the cadet in the upper third of his class, and the cadet who entered the Academy under the age of nineteen. However, the biases are consistent across the four-class samples; therefore, it appears that cross-sectional comparisons will not be affected by the systematic biases of the total sample, although the responses of any one class sample for a given item may not accurately represent the attitudes of the class as a whole.

4. For an extensive application of these criteria, see Selvin, Hanan C., *The Effects of Leadership*, The Free Press, Glencoe, Ill., 1960.

5. Janowitz, Morris, *The Professional Soldier*. The Free Press, Glencoe, Ill., 1960.

6. *Ibid.*, p. 21.

7. *Ibid.*, pp. 21–36.

8. Hilsman, Roger, *Strategic Intelligence and National Decisions*, The Free Press, Glencoe, Ill., 1956; and Millis, Walter, *Arms and Men: A Study in American Military History*, G. P. Putnam's, New York, 1956.

9. Janowitz, Morris, *op. cit.*, p. 264.

10. Dartmouth was selected as the source of a comparative sample to keep as many environmental factors constant as possible. The sample was drawn heavily from that portion of the Dartmouth student body expecting to perform military service as officers upon completion of college (82 per cent of the sample fell into this category), further minimizing the differences between the West Point and Dartmouth samples in order to focus upon the key variables of West Point versus non-West Point socialization. In spite of these similarities between the West Point and Dartmouth samples, however, certain differences, discussed in some detail in the appendix to this paper, remain.

11. The percentages of agreement by samples of the general public to the American Institute of Public Opinion poll question, "Do you think we are likely to get into another world war in the next five years?" on seven occasions between 1955 and 1960 were 48, 32, 34, 24, 23, 18, and 34, respectively. Reported in *Public Opinion Quarterly*, vol. 25, Fall, 1961, p. 488.

12. Relationships among situation, personality, and learning were investigated by Stern, Stein, and Bloom, using a "stereopathy-authoritarianism" scale to classify personality types. In reliability studies conducted at a number of different institutions, "West Point cadets appeared to be equally divided between authoritarians and rationals, whereas samples of psychologists, theological students from liberal Protestant denominations, and Reed College students were just as predominantly divided between antiauthoritarians and rationals." Stern, George G., "Environments for Learning" in Sanford, Nevitt, editor, *The American College*, John Wiley and Sons, New York, 1962, pp. 690–728. The study was reported originally in Stern, George G., Morris I. Stein, and Benjamin S. Bloom, *Methods in Personality Assessment*, The Free Press, Glencoe, Ill., 1956.

13. The relationship between strategic perspective and a number of other variables was explored, but is not discussed here because the explanatory value of these variables—which included prior service, age of the decision to come to West Point, regional background, father's occupation, religious preference, military achievement (cadet officer or nonofficer), and academic achievement—was low.

14. See Lopez, Ramon R., "A Study of Male High School Seniors' Attitudes Toward the Army and of the Relationships Between These Attitudes and Dominant Value Orientations." Unpublished Ph.D. dissertation, University of Chicago, 1961.

15. Janowitz, Morris, *op. cit.*, p. 10.

16. "Professional" includes medical doctors, dentists, lawyers, clergymen, scientists, and engineers. "Business-white collar" includes sales managers, sales representatives, insurance agents, business executives, store proprietors, the self-employed, realtors, accountants, contractors, and public school teachers. "Skilled and unskilled labor" includes foremen, skilled technicians, clerical workers, public workers such as postmen, common laborers, and the unemployed.

17. Sons of enlisted men are not indicated. Historical data are from USMA, Superintendent's Curriculum Study, *Report of the Working Committee on the Historical Aspects of the Curriculum for the Period 1802–1945*, West Point, 1958, Appendix 23. Data for the Class of 1965 are from USMA, "The Characteristics of the Class of 1965," West Point, n.d. Mimeographed, 19 pp.

18. USMA, Office of the Director of Admissions and Registrar, "Class of 1963"; "Class of 1964"; and "Class of 1965." West Point, no dates, three pages each. And consult the USMA Association of Graduates publication, *Assembly*, vol. 21, Fall, 1962, p. 3.

19. Rogoff, Natalie, "The Decision to Study Medicine" and Thielens, Wagner, "Some Comparisons of Entrants to Medical and Law School" in Merton, Reader, and Kendall, *op. cit.*, pp. 109–129 and 131–152, respectively.

20. Rogoff, Natalie, *Ibid.*, pp. 111–114.

21. Janowitz, Morris, *op. cit.*, pp. 97–101. Allinsmith, Wesley, and Beverly, "Religious Affiliation and Politico-Economic Attitude," *Public Opinion Quarterly*, vol. 12, 1948, pp. 377–389; Pope, Liston, "Religion and Class Structure" in Bendix, Richard, and S. M. Lipset, editors, *Class, Status and Power*, The Free Press, Glencoe, Ill., 1953. p. 319.

22. Data obtained from USMA, Information Office, January, 1962.

23. U.S. Bureau of the Census, *Statistical Abstract of the United States: 1962*, p. 116.

24. USMA, Information Office, January, 1962.

25. Janowitz, Morris, *op. cit.*, pp. 85–89.

26. *Ibid.*

27. The disproportionate representation of less populous states in Congress which occurs because of the method of equal representation in the Senate does not produce a systematic bias in the regional distribution of cadet origins. To illustrate this point, the Mountain and West North Central regions are overrepresented, in comparison to population distribution, in Congress, but underrepresented at West Point.

28. Distributions of a number of variables, including father's occupation, by type of appointment to West Point are made in USMA, "The Characteristics of the Class of 1964," West Point, n.d., mimeographed, 12 pp. Hometown addresses of the Class of 1964 were obtained from USMA, Information Office.

29. Of the 57 players listed on the football roster in *The Army Gridiron Magazine*, November 4, 1961, 60 per cent came from New York, Pennsylvania, or New Jersey. For a candid argument in justification of recruiting athletes to West Point, see a discussion by the former Academy athletic director and head football coach, Earl M. Blaik, with Tim Cohane, *You Have to Pay the Price*, Holt, Rinehart, and Winston, New York, 1960.

30. USMA, "The Characteristics of the Class of 1964."

31. The Academy now "scores" candidates for admission by assigning weights to high school athletic participation, participation in extracurricular activities, school honors or elective positions, favorable comments in confidential reports from high school principals and teachers, and scores on the College Board examinations. USMA, *Annual Report of the Superintendent*, West Point, 1957, p. 3.

32. The raising of educational standards was stimulated by the results of a study which revealed that a high percentage of attrition from the Academy came from those whose College Board Scores at entry had been near the minimum limit then acceptable. Research Division, Office of the Registrar, USMA, "Pre-USMA Academic Environment and Selection." West Point, February 12, 1960, 11 pp. Mimeographed.

33. Office of the Director of Admissions and Registrar, USMA, "Class of 1963"; "Class of 1964"; "Class of 1965." *Assembly*, vol. 21, Fall, 1962, p. 3.

34. Unpublished data compiled by Julian Franks from data originally collected for a study by James A. Davis, senior study director, *Great Aspirations, Career Plans of America's June 1961 Graduates*. Study No. 431, National Opinion Research Center, Chicago, 1961.

35. Superintendent's Curriculum Study, USMA, *op. cit.*, Appendix 23.

36. Sylvanus Thayer was a graduate of both Dartmouth College and West Point and was Superintendent of the Military Academy from July, 1817 to July, 1833. He is usually credited with having implemented the basic format of operation which served the Academy virtually unchanged until recent years.

37. A West Point professor, Colonel Charles W. Larned, made this point in a lengthy defense of the "Thayer System" in 1906 against the influences of what he called "modern secular education." Larned warned, "If in the development and guidance of the intellect and faculties there be no co-ordinate discipline and distinct moral direction—a harmonizing with the eternal verities—there must result degeneration." Larned, Charles W., "West Point and Higher Education," *Army and Navy Life*, vol. 8, June, 1906, pp. 9–22.

38. The official Board of Visitors, after their inspection of West Point training and education in 1820, said of mathematics that "nothing is more necessary to form the complete and accomplished officer, nothing so effectual in strengthening every faculty of the mind." *Report of the Board of Visitors to the Military Academy at West Point*. West Point, 1820.

39. It is interesting that the West Point "plebe system" has been maintained in the same basic form since the systematization introduced after World War I. See Richardson, Major W. R., "The 4th Class System," *Assembly*, vol. 21, Winter, 1963, pp. 6–9, and vol. 22, Spring, 1963, pp. 10–13.

40. When General Douglas MacArthur became West Point Superintendent shortly after World War I, he was determined that the Military Academy accommodate itself to a radical change in the world. But he encountered considerable resistance to innovation from the faculty among whom, MacArthur observed, "Conceits, sentiment, blind worship have sustained outmoded offshoots of tradition too long." Ganoe, William A., *MacArthur Close-Up*, Vantage Press, New York, 1962, pp. 30–31. Ganoe was MacArthur's Chief of Staff at the Military Academy during this period.

41. Janowitz, Morris, *op. cit.*, Hammond, Paul Y., "Effects of Structure on Policy," *Public Administration Review*, vol. 18, 1958, pp. 175–179.

42. Masland, John W., and Laurence I. Radway, *Soldiers and Scholars*. Princeton University Press, Princeton, N. J., 1957, pp. 100–128, 169–249.

43. USMA, "Annual Report of the Superintendent." West Point, 1957, p. 12.

44. USMA, "Annual Report of the Superintendent, 1957–1962," *Assembly*, vols. 16–22.

45. USMA, "Bugle Notes 1961." West Point, 1961, p. 3.

46. Westmoreland, Major General William C., "Address Before the Tennessee Valley Chapter, Association of the U.S. Army, Huntsville, Ala., February 15, 1961." West Point, typed, 12 pp.

47. Association of Graduates, USMA, "Register of Graduates, 1961." West Point, 1961.

48. Public Information Office, USMA, "Brief Historical and Vital Statistics of the Graduates of the United States Military Academy, 1802–1952," West Point, 1952, mimeographed, 23 pp.; Westmoreland, Major General William C., "Plain Talk," *Assembly*, vol. 21, Winter, 1963, p. 1, and vol. 22, Spring, 1963, p. 1.

49. Hughes, Everett C., "Professions," *Daedalus*, vol. 92, Fall, 1963, pp. 655–668.

50. The survey instrument is reproduced as an appendix to the author's unpublished Ph.D. dissertation, "The Cadet Phase of the Professional Socialization of the West Pointer: Description, Analysis, and Refinement," University of Wisconsin, 1962.

51. Janowitz, Morris, *op. cit.*

52. For a detailed discussion of this procedure, see Henry, Andrew F., "A Method of Classifying Non-Scale Response Patterns in a Guttman Scale," *Public Opinion Quarterly*, vol. 16, 1952, pp. 94–106.

THE MILITARY SELF-IMAGE IN A TECHNOLOGICAL ENVIRONMENT

Maury D. Feld

THIS PAPER explores the implications of technological change for the self-image of the military professional. In addition to developing a set of concepts, it seeks to make use of the contents of the service journals over the past thirty years as an indicator of changing notions of professional identity. I have chosen technology because developments in that area have clearly demonstrable consequences. Technological developments have results that can be observed, counted, and described. At a given moment a tool, previously unknown or unavailable, comes to be employed. Its presence or absence is verifiable in concrete terms. In 1914, for example, the German Army had heavy artillery in significant quantities and the French Army did not. Questions of belief, acceptance, and comprehension are immaterial. In this, technological change differs from changes in organization, ideology, or authority structure.

TYPES OF TECHNOLOGICAL CHANGE

The kinds of technological change affecting a military system can be ascribed to three general areas. First, there is the kind of innovation that involves instruments which are conventionally and exclusively military in use, such as the submarine snorkel or the recoilless artillery piece. Second, there are those innovations which are adopted in a nonmilitary environment for reasons independent of military considerations, but which nevertheless have a profound effect on the development and operations of armed forces. The Bessemer process and the canning industry can be cited as examples. Third, there are innovations which are developed in a nonmilitary environment, but whose application becomes consciously military. The theory of ballistics and the development of nuclear weapons can be cited as instances of this kind of innovation. In the interests of brevity, these three categories will be referred to as *arsenal, industrial,* and *laboratory* developments, respectively.

159

Arsenal Developments

In the case of *arsenal* developments, the distinguishing characteristic is that they represent obviously desirable improvements of some conventional instrument. The instruments they modify are already familiar and acceptable to all military men. The research which led to their development could not conceivably have taken place with any other objectives or under any other sponsorship.

Industrial Developments

On the other hand, industrial developments correspond to a form of change which takes place in virtual independence of military needs or objectives. Their acceptance by society is by and large unrelated to their military utility. They are undertaken because they seem theoretically interesting or generally useful. The research which produced them would have taken place had there been no state of warfare or an armed force. Their advantage represents a windfall dividend gained by the organization through its incidental feature of belonging to some society.

Laboratory Developments

Finally, laboratory developments have the distinguishing characteristic of being undertaken for the purpose of a technological revolution. They are, in one way or another, either incomprehensible or unacceptable to the established military professional. Their utility is apparent to the innovator rather than the consumer and generally they must be imposed on the soldier by some third party. Nevertheless, they are developed with some specific military application in mind. Laboratory research, therefore, is normally sponsored by other than military agencies on the assumption that it represents an approach which the armed forces are inherently incapable of undertaking. Implicit in this is the understanding that the resulting innovation will be resisted by the official agencies and that some extraordinary pressure may be necessary for its adoption. In the contemporary transformation of the military establishment, the armed forces seek to overcome their resistance to technological change. Thus, the military itself may support and sponsor laboratory developments.

Both the arsenal and the industrial concepts represent relatively manageable modes of innovation as the required process of adjustment does not of itself involve any radical changes in the structure of military organization. In the case of arsenal developments the novelties are both foreseen and desired. Moreover, since the process of development is entirely under military control, the acceptance or rejection of specific ideas is generally routine procedure. In the case of industrial developments, the innovations take place independently of military considerations. Their acceptance or rejection, therefore, is arbitrary and fortuitous. Neither of these lines of technological research foresees any application outside of the social and institutional setting which has sponsored it. Neither is normally subject to pressures and procedures over which the parent body has no control.

Laboratory developments, on the other hand, in order to be effective must gain the support of individuals other than those actually involved in the process of inaugurating and carrying them through. They begin as the exclusive concern of strictly nonmilitary persons, but the ultimate success of this development process requires that it be actively advanced by influential members of some armed force, and that its particular techniques be actively incorporated into the official body of standard institutional expertise.

There is value in contrasting this situation with that which has been designated as industrial development. While improvements in the techniques of metallurgy and food preservation are of obvious interest to the armed forces and may even be sponsored by them, there is no conventionally pressing need to incorporate the techniques involved in such advances into the accepted image of a professionally competent officer. If the capacity for such improvements is recognized in the society with which the armed force is affiliated, the military may subsidize research and set up agencies to inspire a more effective military utilization of results. But fundamentally it will agree that this process is essentially a civilian concern and that it would take place in any case short of coercive prohibition, and perhaps even then. The end product is designed for a civilian market and is subject to its demands. Its military utility is incidental.

The evolution of ballistic theory and the development of nuclear weapons, on the other hand, were undertaken with specific military applications in mind. The experiment could have been a success yet the project a failure purely on the basis of its rejection by the institution to which it was offered. The failure would not have resided in the specialized activity of the developers but in their incidental efforts to convert members of the military establishment to their point of view. From this it can be implied that the emphasis of laboratory specialists is not primarily on the transformation of their own techniques but on the modification and even subversion of the traditional self-sufficiency of the professional military image. The discoveries of the laboratory specialist are designed to demonstrate that the existing expertise in the military body represents a haphazard and inadequate approach to the problems with which it must deal.

Arsenal developments finally are completely under military control from authorization to acceptance or rejection. An armed force may pay the penalty of defeat for refusing to adopt an improvement within its grasp; for retaining a muzzle-loading musket, for example, when breech-loading rifles are available. But the decision is entirely its own. Within the context of its society there is no other potential customer, and no other body of experts to dispute the propriety of its choice.

OFFICER IMAGE AND TECHNOLOGICAL CHANGE

These three approaches imply a particular kind of relationship of individuals to the armed forces they serve. Officers involved in the process of technological change may be regarded as innovators, deviants, or marginal men. These descriptive terms imply not only that the organization is being served in a particular way, but also that the manner of service is related to the organization's self-image and to the relationship which it believes to exist between it and society.

The individuals responsible for arsenal developments have already been accepted as part of the military establishment. The fate of their particular product does not *prima facie* affect their position in the military. The adoption or rejection of proposals may, of course, determine short-term success or failure in a chosen career, but they are assured of a post. In joining the arsenal, the military technician accedes to the institutional decision-making process and is presumably resigned to the inherent risks. Loyalty to the organization is considered to be a stronger motive than devotion to research. The arsenal concept accordingly permits an armed force to allow some of its members to be *innovators* without running the risk that they may become *deviants*.

Industrial developments, on the other hand, are undertaken by individuals who have neither the desire to apply nor the attributes of being acceptable to the organization. They are members of a class which is by definition nonmilitary and their skills, even when accepted at their highest evaluation, will never be included within the official definition of professional military expertise. A career soldier who specializes in such procedures will invariably be a *deviant*, although at times a useful one. He might perform a valuable service in bringing remote though pertinent information to the attention of the proper authorities. But insofar as his interests centered on such matters, his professional capacities and his career prospects would be regarded as impaired, and he himself would be regarded as the kind of example to be discouraged.

The protagonists of laboratory developments, for their part, occupy the position of *marginal* men. They represent individuals who have undertaken to make their characteristic talents essential to the armed forces without in any real sense applying for admission to them. The decision to accept such skills as being either deviant or innovatory is one which the armed force has to make according to its conception of the specific merits of each particular case. Every laboratory development claims to be simultaneously a radical improvement of military techniques and an outright subverter of established military traditions. A professional officer in identifying himself with programs of this kind makes a critical decision. If he is successful in gaining acceptance of the novelty as essential to the proper performance of military missions, his career prospects are greatly enhanced. If he fails, he suffers the penalty of having openly aided influences which have been officially recognized and rejected as hostile to the established order.

In applying these concepts to the military, it might be said in formal terms that we are here dealing with two contrasting models of organizational outlook, one, like the guardian class in Plato's *Republic* views itself as the sole and exclusive elite agency in its society, the only body capable of rational behavior; the other, committed to a pluralistic vision of society and accordingly viewing itself as one among many collaborating bodies of rationally motivated experts. The first type will be referred to henceforth as *primitive*, the second as *competitive*.

Primitive military organizations characteristically consider themselves to be the embodiment of rational practices. They select as leaders only the genuinely rational and superior applicants; rejected candidates and nonapplicants are thus inferior to members of the organization.

At any given moment, therefore, a primitive organization represents the fullest possible realization of its potential strength. Insofar as numbers and knowledge are concerned, it has nothing to gain from any further dealings with the outside world. Since the organization, moreover, is the embodiment of rationality, there is no higher form of existence than official behavior. All members of the military, by the fact of their membership, possess these superior qualities. The total absorption of all its members in the institutional routine is, therefore, a rational objective. The round of drills, rituals, and disciplinary measures results in a range of refined characteristics according to which every member can identify himself with the organization and be recognized as such by every other member.

By definition, therefore, a primitive armed force confines its activities to the body of its actual members. The organization regards itself as the state of nature, and the outside world as the possibility of corruption and the fall of man. Consequently, insofar as the organization has the power, certain characteristics or virtues considered desirable become by definition a natural military monopoly. This includes not only the military virtues but any factor which might affect the existence of the armed force as a self-sufficient monopoly. Thus, for example, the ownership of land, literacy, the right of assembly have in the past been claimed as the exclusive privileges of military leaders who embody the primitive outlook. Such privileges do not necessarily increase military efficiency, but their preemption makes it difficult for nonmembers to achieve an independent bargaining position.

The primitivist approach systematically includes an image of the outside world which is essentially negative in nature. It describes and regulates its external environment in terms of the absence of those very traits which it believes to be essential for the maintenance of a coherent social scheme. Nonmembership, inferiority, and disorganization are equivalent terms.

The competitive approach, on the other hand, holds that no single profession or organization has a monopoly of effective and rational behavior. Society, insofar as it leads to interaction among its members, develops distinctive bodies of operational criteria and systematic rules, and it is on the basis of skill and mastery in such areas, rather than on the simple fact of membership in one social group or another, that the attribution of rationality is determined. Thus there are rational and non-rational soldiers just as there are rational and nonrational members of other professions. The term is descriptive of occupational proficiency rather than the primitive outlook of social affiliation.

This being the case, a competitively oriented organization has few built-in inhibitions against recognizing the existence of rational individuals who do not belong to the organization. And as a rationally oriented body, it is prepared to admit the existence of some individuals in the outside world who are, according to its own definitions, acceptable as members or active collaborators. If such individuals are civilians, it is either because, at a given moment, the organization has no need for their services, or because it is unable to provide them with sufficient inducement to join.

With such assumptions, it is impossible for a competitively oriented organization to assume attainment of the optimum level of efficiency, except, perhaps, in a purely military sense. But it is not easy to give a precise definition to the term "purely military." Indeed, given the assumption of the existence of a plurality or rational groups, an armed force has no "purely military" method for determining whether or not it is taking full advantage of the available range of rational skills. Characteristic expertise relates only to its own operations, and every other system of rational procedures is equally self-sufficient. Unless members of other professions can be persuaded to make their knowledge available to the competitively oriented armed force, it is in no position to evaluate the potential utility of such a contribution.

Active collaboration rather than isolated self-sufficiency is, therefore, the guiding objective of a competitively oriented organization. To the extent that they are able to cooperate with other groups of experts, competitively oriented experts themselves achieve an adequate degree of understanding of the outside world.

Now it can be objected that, as formal organizations, armed forces are unique and lacking, therefore, in criteria for measuring the achievements of nonmilitary groups. In a primitively oriented sense this statement is perhaps true. But it can be argued that with the competitive principle once accepted, an armed force becomes increasingly more heterogeneous and more similar in form and composition to the society supporting it, and that the cumulative result of competitive orientation is an accelerating tendency toward the expansion and diversification of the elite group. The greater the range of skills encompassed by its activities, the better the ability to appreciate the potential contribution of outside groups.

Primitive and competitive orientations accordingly carry with them their own particular adaptation to technological change. A strict *arsenal* approach to development activities is the necessary condition of primitive military control. The kinds of changes which might directly affect military techniques are explored under the exclusive sponsorship of the armed forces. Research outside its control is considered to have little or no direct bearing on the problems of the profession. There is no foreseeable reason for the organization to adjust its internal structure to changes taking place in the outside world.

An armed force which, on the other hand, is prepared to respond consciously to external developments in techniques is an expression of the competitive model, although in this respect it could be either passive or active. As a passive agency it would adopt the *industrial* approach; not collaborating directly in the rational pursuits of nonmilitary professionals but also not suffering from any inhibitions in taking advantage of them. The *industrial* approach is characteristic of a period of organizational transition in which the primitive approach is recognized as untenable but the competitive orientation has not yet been fully accepted. As an active competitive agency, the military would adopt the *laboratory* approach and officially sponsor the research and development processes to modify its own proper professional standards. Military efficiency would be equated with the inclusion of the greatest possible range of nonmilitary skills within the context of the organization, and active leaders of the armed forces eager to demonstrate their receptivity to technological change.

Many areas of critical technological change will harbor a conflict between proponents of arsenal type development and proponents of the laboratory approach. The attitude of a particular armed force toward these protagonists will be determined by the image it holds of itself as either a primitive or a competitively oriented body. As the former, it will admit as innovations only those techniques developed in its own arsenals, and treat as deviants the adherents of any type of externally developed change. This does not mean that change from without will be unacceptable, but rather that the proponents of such changes may be penalized in their career prospects even when successful in the advocacy. A competitively oriented organization, on the other hand, will seek to balance the developments of independent experts with its own internally generated process of change. It will institute programs to encourage the widest possible range of outside professional contacts among its personnel.

PRIMITIVE VERSUS COMPETITIVE MILITARY ORGANIZATION

The five basic hypotheses of *The Professional Soldier*, by Morris Janowitz, can be examined in the light of these contentions and translated in these concepts of primitive versus competitive military organization. The combination will, I believe, indicate possible lines of empirical investigation into the operations of military organizations.

1. Changing Organizational Authority

The shift from domination to manipulation and persuasion entails a transformation in the organization's self-image from that of an autonomous homogeneous body to that of a holding company exploiting the most rewarding combination of enterprises attainable. Under the primitive approach, a strictly prescribed mode of development had obtained with the organization laying down rigid criteria for the kinds of innovation it was willing to accept. Change in general, and particularly unforeseen change, was considered undesirable. The process of modification, therefore, would be entrusted exclusively to individuals satisfying the organization's standards of indoctrination and control, with no improvement acceptable unless it gave the appearance of having been officially anticipated. Individual skills involved would be considered characteristically military in a manner satisfying the force's contention that it was the sole valid judge of the meaning of the results. It is symptomatic of the primitive-arsenal approach that developments of obvious military applicability are rejected on the grounds that they are detrimental to the spirit which unifies and inspires the armed force. A list of prominent cases ranging from firearms to the guided missile documents this response. The attitude inherent in this reaction is that the cohesion and effectiveness of an armed force rests on an orthodoxy of practice and belief. The techniques and the ideals of the profession are presented as a single immutable whole.

Competitive-laboratory developments, on the other hand, represent breakthroughs into areas previously unfamiliar to the professional soldier. This fact in itself prevents the organization from applying its own criteria to assessment of the changes involved. The experts under consideration would have to be treated as autonomous agencies with offers of special benefits in return for making their services freely available. The relationship between a given armed force and its specialists would be of mutual advantage and the atypical nature of experts overtly recognized in the formal relations between them and members of the organization. Instead of rigid discipline, inducements such as civic honors, notably high salaries, and appeals to patriotism would be employed to achieve the desired results. It would be indeed an article of faith, subscribed to by both parties, that rigid compulsion frustrates development.

2. Narrowing Skill Differential Between Military and Civilian Elites

The primitivist approach implies a sharp either/or distinction between arsenal and other modes of development, so that the possibility of confusion between innovators and deviants is for all practical purposes eliminated. Only that research which is officially sponsored and internally staffed can yield acceptable results. There is inherent in the arsenal approach a tendency to accept only anticipated consequences, and by this mechanism the organization's self-image of a self-sufficient monopoly is maintained. The skills it does not command are therefore by definition antithetical to the ideals of the primitive armed force. The unauthorized innovator is almost inevitably treated as a deviant.

The competitive approach, by contrast, systematically seeks out those very skills it perceives to be absent in its table of organization. An obviously efficacious industrial or scientific technique represents a challenge to systematic military development. Recognized nonmilitary experts are viewed as promising "crash-programs" and "breakthroughs" which will radically extend the state of the art. The professional value of the soldier increases to the extent that he is sensitive to the possibilities of technical improvement inherent in his surrounding society. There is therefore a career premium attached to a demonstrated familiarity with the prevalent range of civilian expertise, and a tacit assurance that personal commitment to any established nonmilitary specialty will result in the career rewards of innovation rather than in the penalties of deviancy. The laboratory model includes this innovation of concepts and data based in the social sciences as well.

3. The Shift in Officer Recruitment

The sharp contrast between military and nonmilitary behavior inherent in the primitive approach leads the organization toward the recruitment ideal of a self-sustaining caste. The dominant personnel preoccupation is that of preserving the system from the contamination of the nonmilitary world. Soldiers are therefore sought among those classes which seem least likely to be influenced by forces of social change over which the armed forces exercise no direct control. In reciprocal fashion those elements of society in least contact and sympathy with the general process of social change turn to the armed forces as promising an environment in which their traditional values will be cherished and protected from the threat of obsolescence.

A general and naive suspicion of unanticipated change provides a common ground. Under the primitive model, the military seem to operate on the assumption that the narrower the social base of officer recruitment, the greater the certainty of the enforcement of a standard pattern for the belief and behavior of the individuals involved. The maintenance of a rigid orthodoxy becomes progressively more difficult as the number of active personnel increases. The officer caste, therefore, is drawn from a self-conscious and deliberate minority group. In such a system, deviancy is relatively simple both to recognize and to define. The determined deviant individual, moreover, has no motivation for undertaking the strenuous and risky effort of entering and persisting in a military career.

Under the competitive approach, however, the efficiency of the organization is assumed to increase with the widening of the range of encompassed skills. Armed forces are therefore encouraged to operate on the broadest possible recruiting base and individuals are given reason to believe that men with esoteric attitudes, backgrounds, and skills will have real prospects offered to them by a military career. Military organizations come to be regarded as especially representative institutions, open and receptive to a wide variety of talent.

4. Significance of Career Patterns

The primitive approach is characterized by the belief that the military profession represents a unique and exclusive way of life, one which is diametrically opposed to the habits and customs of the outside world. As such, it is an ideal to be pursued by military members. Within this context, therefore, there is a hierarchy of career patterns, ranked according to the degree in which they are considered to permit the realization of pure military conduct. Cavalry officers were, for example, traditionally considered to be more military than artillery men or engineers. The latter suffer from a dependence on techniques and instruments developed and employed in the nonmilitary world. As a practical matter, advancement prospects are directly allocated on the basis of the degree of "purity" attached to a given military assignment, and the scale is so clearly defined that every officer knows fairly well what to expect. This has the consequence, either deliberate or unconscious, of enforcing custom. Officers, on the one hand, realize that the branch of service is evaluated according to its demonstrated adherence to tradition. On the other hand, traditional branches clearly offer the best prospects for promotion. The best connected and most typical recruits are accordingly the ones that gain admission to these branches. Marginal types can only hope for commissions in unorthodox services. Moreover, since the inner elite is by and large made up of members of the traditional branches, official policy favors their outlook and techniques.

In a competitive system, on the other hand, no such hierarchy can exist. The contribution of each branch is measured not in pure military terms, but according to the estimate of the range and fruitfulness of general techniques which it is able to encompass. Entrance into the inner elite is to a large part determined by a demonstrated breadth of contacts and sympathies with the prominent members of the nonmilitary world. Under these circumstances, accordingly, the least traditional branches can compete if only because their members are likely to have fewer inhibitions in adapting to emerging military problems. In any event, there is no pure military type to serve as a hierarchic model, except perhaps the rather contradictory ideal of a dedicated and loyal soldier who has the capacity when necessary to free himself from all considerations of established military tradition and standard military procedure.

5. Trends in Political Indoctrination

Honor and tradition are the reigning standards of the primitive approach. An armed force tends to regard itself as a self-sufficient body apart from the general society. Its corporate behavior is designed to reinforce and maintain its own idiosyncratic code. Legitimate political objectives correspond to the social and economic conditions represented by the official military doctrine of requirements, privileges, and responsibilities. The officer who satisfies organizational standards satisfies all the criteria of political orthodoxy. A soldier, on the other hand, whose background and behavior are in some degree atypical, is a probable subversive. In one sense, then, a primitivist officer can be described as apolitical. So long as the established pattern of his own organization is unaffected, he is likely to have no interest in the competition for status and power taking place in the outside world. On the other hand, he can be regarded as intensely politically oriented, in that any nonmilitary intervention in military policy may be taken by him as a threat both to his society and to his existence and as a justification, therefore, for an open and all-out military attack on the interfering agencies. The values he is committed to preserve are those of his organization and in that cause there are no inhibitions as to the kind and degree of intervention he is prepared to practice in the nonmilitary world.

A competitive organization, by contrast, accepts the legitimacy of the application of nonmilitary standards to the conduct of military operations. This is not merely because it assumes that military acts have political and social consequences and that to a significant extent the organization is responsible for these consequences. It stems also from a prudent desire to hedge bets. Professional competence according to the competitive approach is directly related to the awareness of professional limitations. The rational outlook is a product of conscious specialization, and depends upon the interaction with authorities from diverse fields. The participation of nonmilitary experts in the formulation of military plans provides an assurance not only that a number of rational approaches will be put to work on the particular problem but also that the necessary specialization of individual experts will be neutralized by the unrestricted collaboration of a multiplicity of independent minds.

But active collaboration is also an essential ingredient of professional self-esteem. In a competitively oriented environment, general utility .

rather than parochial self-sufficiency is the dominant criterion. The specialist in one particular field needs, in order to achieve his full professional stature, some form of assurance that his behavior has been found rational by the general community of experts and that the manner in which he pursues his profession gives the greatest possible degree of encouragement and stimulus to theirs.

Membership in this community of experts entails adherence to its own special etiquette. Each participant is expected to understand and restrict himself to his particular role. According to the logic of military technological development, the competitively oriented officer is a consumer as well as a producer of results. If nonmilitary skills are to improve and extend the range of military operations, they must be free to develop according to their own inner criteria. The organization encourages disinterested researchers and adapts their results to the solution of its particular problems. It agrees with the general assumption that to impose its own particular outlook on the course of investigation would be to deprive itself of the resources of objective science. On the political and technical level, the competitively oriented officer seeks the kind of relationship that enables him to understand the problems of nonmilitary techniques and to collaborate sympathetically in underwriting and applying their discoveries.

Do these considerations illuminate the tensions presently operating within the American military establishment? The establishment's awareness of the tremendous technological resources of modern society present it with multiple alternative courses of development, not only with respect to the instruments it employs but also the forms of organization adopted. Every step in the direction of increased efficiency entangles the armed force in a complex of attendant problems arising from the fact that new skills may be thereby required, or that established professional standards are thereby rendered obsolete. The organization is confronted with a conflict of values. It can take the fullest possible advantage of the technological resources of its society and relegate the maintenance of its own characteristic professional standards and identity to a position of secondary importance. Or it can claim that its major role is to produce professional soldiers with characteristic military skills which have the fullest possible scope for rational application. In that case the professionals can refuse or modify techniques or instruments that might radically modify the organizational climate.

The result of such choices can be analyzed from two directions: what the armed forces feel they are expected to be and what they would like to be; namely, the self-image of the professional. When, as in the case of a primitively oriented body, the two coincide, the problem is not too serious. When, as in the case of a competitively oriented force, the professional soldier feels that he is expected to be a member of a body of rationally oriented experts recognized as such by the general professional community, the problem becomes more complicated. For the general community of the professionally educated, little value is placed on the intense form of parochial allegiance which appears to be so essential to military life. The civilian concept of military professionalism is likely to be drawn on the model of scientific objectivity and moral neutrality, while the military ideal of a professional soldier has the tendency to include the assumption of a deep commitment to certain moral and group values.

The argument is reduced to the contention that, to the degree that an armed force remains primitive it loses its efficiency, and to the degree that it becomes competitive it loses its identity. The fact that both primitive and competitive orientations can adapt themselves to technology, the one in the arsenal form, the other in the laboratory, does not affect the situation. Their characteristic limitations are transferred into new fields. The result in reality is a personal and organization effort to fuse orientations and create a viable balance.

The course of contemporary military technology provides some evidence for this contention. The assignment of specific areas of research and development to particular branches of service has frequently resulted in the elevation of the instruments involved into a kind of ultimate value. Primitive values are wedded to the most familiar machine. The retention of a particular kind of weapons system becomes an end in itself. The primitive organization treats as inconceivable the claim that its distinctive mission could be better carried out, or even carried out in any form, by any other instrument. To the extent that technological expertise is defined as part of the professional role, the relevant skills and practices are ritually associated with the instrument around which they were originally evolved. If, on the other hand, the laboratory approach is adopted and research and development is entrusted to purely scientific and technological bodies, the armed forces may be regarded as lacking in the expertise necessary for responsible control. The control of intercontinental missiles is a crucial case in point. Military experience provides only a partial basis for asserting a special understanding of such instruments. The individual military officer can enter the weapons system after assimilating himself to the class of experts that originally developed it. But to control even the missile requires more than technical expertise; it requires a military posture to guarantee local security and to ensure compliance with strategic commands.

Perhaps the differences are essentially related to the concept of control. From the primitive point of view it is the military organization that must be controlled. That condition realized, the environment presents no problems. From the competitive point of view, on the other hand, various organizations merely represent alternative devices for controlling the general environment. Diplomacy, economic policy, or even education, for example, may be considered to be just as effective as military action in the attainment of a desirable international order.

ROLE OF SERVICE JOURNALS

There are a variety of empirical approaches to studying long-term shifts in professional self-images, from primitivist to competitive. If one wants to employ relatively quantitative data, the contents of the service journals, studied by systematic content analysis, supply indicators of changing self-conceptions and efforts to fuse the component elements. For this purpose, two journals were studied over the past thirty years. For the Navy, the sponsored journal was the *U. S. Naval Institute Proceedings;* for the Army, it was the *Infantry Journal—Combat Forces—Army,* the three names through which the ground force publication evolved. This time sample has the double advantage of covering the period of professional transformation and of selecting for intensive study years without overt military hostilities.

In terms of role concept and professional ideology which took place in the officer corps of the United States armed forces somewhere between 1936 and 1959, the basic hypotheses of this paper can be stated explicitly. In the pre-World War II period the prevalent ideology of the armed forces as manifested in their professional journals contained strong elements of a primitive orientation. The post-World War II era has witnessed an intensified development of the competitive outlook with its managerial professional ideology. Before World War II the stress was on the stability of the military environment and the maintenance of institutional efficiency through the conscientious performance of routine assignments. The conceived role of the armed forces was not so much that of adjusting to changes in the outside world as that of continually perfecting itself in the execution of its natural military role.

Since World War II, the armed forces have been increasingly involved in the continuous process of adjusting to the manifold of changes— technological, economic, political, and sociological—in the world which surrounds them. Professional discourse centers not so much on the perfection of performance in routine assignments as on the anticipation of significant changes in the world arena and on the formulation of decisions which will have to be made.

According to these hypotheses the service journal would reflect the shift in the concern of the officer corps of the United States. In the framework of this analysis it can be said to have become more professional in the intervening period; by more professional is meant more rational in the bureaucratic and organizational sense. The possible range of military events has become increasingly complex. Armed forces were at one time expected to be prepared for, at most, two or three kinds of war. Now they are expected to maintain a capability for all responsibilities between arms-control enforcement and total war. But the striking conclusion is that the hypothesis was in part wrong. Before World War II, the Navy had already changed its self-concept by weakening its primitivist military component and incorporating important elements of the competitive outlook.

At this point it is appropriate to advance some observations about the institutional role played by service journals. Sponsored periodicals are by no means an exclusive feature of the armed forces. Almost every professional body maintains something of that nature as part of its organizational apparatus, and generally as a constituent part of its educational activities.

To operate effectively, organized professionals generally maintain an apparatus for the recruitment and training of prospective members. They also support at least one publication for the dissemination of common ideas and experiences. Every organized profession, in short, has its seminary, academy, or graduate school, and every profession has its journal.

The organization of professional education is much older and seems much more natural than the professional practice of sponsoring a periodical. The existence of an educational organization staffed and administered by senior members provides a profession with a means both of determining the acceptability of applicants and of instilling in them critical standards, essential factual background, and a sense of professional cohesion.

The reason for existence of professional journals seems less striking. Why should the professional be expected to contribute articles to professional journals? And why should publication of his writings take place in a medium supervised by the profession of which he is a member? There is an obvious difference between the two institutions: graduation from the proper school automatically confers professional status; publication of one's writings does not.

Doctors, lawyers, soldiers, scientists, and members of other organized or regulated professions do in general write for one another. When they write as professionals, their work is submitted to journals sponsored by the profession and edited or supervised by senior members. In writing for publication, therefore, members of the regulated professions are subjecting themselves to yet another form of organized control.

From this point of view, publication can be regarded as a postgraduate form of professional policing. It enables the organization to appraise and reward the activities of mature members. Efforts which conform to established standards and which deal with subjects of professional significance are guaranteed an appreciative audience. The professional who has works published is authoritatively presented as a person whose activities and thoughts merit the serious attention of his peers. The military, like any other highly trained, rationally oriented professional body realizes the value of disseminating rapidly and in a universal manner significant developments in techniques and doctrines. It needs some vehicle for emphasizing significant issues.

But there is one respect in which soldiers do differ from other professionals. The United States military establishment is a more comprehensive institution. Doctors, lawyers, and many other professionals are not encompassed by an institutional structure which takes upon itself the task not only of assigning to each member a particular role but also of furnishing him with the equipment and information regarded as necessary to his position. With regard to information at least, most professionals are relatively free and independent performers. In both the giving and receiving of information they have wide latitude in setting their own standards and practices. Professional soldiers, however, operate within a structure which not only defines official behavior but provides a copious and detailed flow of printed instructions on how they are to perform. It also makes use of a set of checks and procedures designed to ensure that official literature is read by its designated audience.

If the military organization furnishes its members with the details and doctrines pertinent to their particular assignments, what justification is there for a professional journal? The existence and promulgation of official doctrine does not necessarily imply that there is no room for further discussion. But since the journals themselves are officially sanctioned, a question arises about the role such discussion is assumed to play. For both the United States Army and the United States Navy, as concrete examples, there are two distinct bodies of printed literature edited and written predominantly by members of the profession:

1. Manuals and directives assigned to every active member on the basis of his particular assignment (assigned literature).
2. Journals made available to every interested party, active or inactive, professional or layman, on a general and unregulated basis (sponsored literature).

The examination of assigned literature is the scope of this paper. In many respects, however, its function is clear. It is an instrument of efficiency and control, a sort of impersonal and complex command. In short, it tells the officers what they *need* to know.

THE MEANING OF SPONSORED LITERATURE

Sponsored literature obviously must also respond to a need of the organization. Particular articles in a sponsored channel can, at best, be justified by the fact that they tell soldiers what they *might want* to know. The sponsored journal, as a whole, it is assumed, reaches areas of professional interest inaccessible to official publications. But this assumption does not provide us with clearcut criteria for assessing the significance of or reason for printing particular articles. If the information contained is considered vital to organizational effectiveness, why was it not circulated through official channels? If the information presented is of peripheral interest, why, in an organization devoted to discipline and decisiveness, publish it at all?

Sponsored literature is, unlike the body of assigned literature, an area of voluntary contributions. This does not mean that some contributors may not have been invited to submit articles, but that if invited they generally were in a position to refuse. A journal made up entirely of command performances would be a specimen of assigned literature. Sponsored literature provides the soldier with the opportunity of displaying his ability and impressing his superiors on subjects and under circumstances which are in general of his own choice. His choice must, of course, conform in some essential respects to that of established authority and practice. But the soldier who has articles published, nevertheless, operates to some extent outside of regular channels. He not only provides ideas and information to his peers; he also—and especially in the lower grades—provides them with a model of a certain kind of professional autonomy as well as competence.

The military profession therefore sponsors and maintains a considerable number of professional journals, designed for an audience of professional soldiers. All three services of the United States armed forces, for example, have their official or quasi-official publications, and many of the subordinate branches also have journals of their own. Contributors are solicited from active duty officers. Like all other professional journals, the published contents are expected by the editors to express personal and presumably original points of view.

Editorial content in a service journal is not a form of command. A published article may be disregarded. However, professionals are expected to read their journals not in order to be told what to do, but rather to be informed as to what is important to think about. Thus, for the purposes of this analysis of professional self-image, it is especially important to study sponsored literature. The prevalent military self-image is that of a man of action, yet the concept of professionalization entails a notion of rational behavior. The complete soldier, therefore, is an individual who under appropriate circumstances does without hesitation what he is told, and at other times is a creature who carefully examines the situation before deciding upon a course of action.

TRENDS IN CONTENT OF SERVICE JOURNALS

Two journals, *Infantry Journal—Combat Forces—Army*, and *U. S. Naval Institute Proceedings*, were analyzed for the periods 1936–1938, 1947–1949, and 1957–1959. Because of its comparatively recent origin, the U.S. Air Force had no sponsored publication for the first two sample periods. Both journals that were studied have a quasi-official status. They are sponsored, supervised, and edited by representatives of the services they profess to serve. Final responsibility and control has always been in the hands of a senior retired officer. Editorial standards can, therefore, be presumed to conform to the professional standards and objectives of the organization. This does not at all mean that published articles were intended to be accepted as official statements of doctrine. But the presumption does exist that printed material was viewed as indicative of the beliefs, interests, and problems considered useful and proper for the various ranks.

The first measure of trends in content was the relative distribution of articles by military and civilian authors. Crude though this measure may be, it can be taken as an indicator of the relative emphasis on a primitive versus competitive orientation. The extent to which a journal revealed an exclusive reliance on military authors would be a measure of organization exclusiveness (primitive outlook), and a resistance to competitive relations with civilian society.

The trend comparison between the Army and the Navy sponsored publication on this measure is most revealing. As in so many other content categories, the Navy revealed a remarkable stability throughout the three periods from 1936 through 1959, with roughly 75 per cent of the articles in each period written by military personnel (Table 1). Moreover, in comparison with the Army, it is clear the technological base of the naval establishment produced at an earlier period incorporation of civilian figures and movement away from the primitive model. The Army journal in 1936–1938 was decidedly more exclusive in that over 90 per cent of its articles were written by the military. The Army trend is one of wide fluctuation, reaching a low point in the 1947–1949 period in which the percentage of military dropped to two-thirds and civilian contributors reached one-third, a figure in excess of that for the Navy. The short-term change was a response to new politico-military conditions with an exaggerated shift toward the competitive model even beyond that of the Navy. The search for a new equilibrium can be seen by the fact that by 1957–1959 during the period of maximum retrenchment, civilian contributions to the Army journal declined sharply to 16 per cent. The "primitivist" component was strengthened temporarily. While these civilian contributions were not as low as before World War II, they are decidedly lower than in the Navy. Thus, in the long run, the Army has moved toward a more competitive approach of civilianization, but by this measure paradoxically during the period studied had not yet reached that of the Navy.

The second content trend in the service journals relevant for professional identity was with the type of subject matter contained in these publications. A simple classification into broad professional, narrow professional or technical, and human interest articles is relevant for this type of analysis. Broad professional refers to articles of apparent interest to all officers, such as historical accounts, for example, errors of the Korean Conflict; morale building (the objectives of leadership); mission defining (the role of the Navy in the Cold War); applied strategy (controlled retaliation). Narrow professional or technical refers to specific tactical and technical problems of direct interest to particular groups of specialists, for example, anti-tank mine simulation. Human interest articles are addressed to the military not as soldiers but as members of a certain socioeconomic group, for example, fishing in Alaska, investing for retirement.

Both the Army and the Navy organs reveal a similar trend during the period of increased emphasis on broad professional content, and a decline in narrow technical and human interest material (Table 2). The

TABLE 1. ARMY AND NAVY SPONSORED LITERATURE, 1936–1959:
DISTRIBUTION OF MILITARY AND CIVILIAN AUTHORS

Distribution of Articles	1936–1938	1947–1949	1957–1959	Total
	(Percentages)			
Army				
Military Contributors	91	66	84	
Civilian Contributors	9	34	16	
Total	100	100	100	
Number of articles	224	267	291	782
Navy				
Military Contributors	76	77	74	
Civilian Contributors	24	23	26	
Total	100	100	100	
Number of articles	397	351	324	1,072

TABLE 2. ARMY AND NAVY SPONSORED LITERATURE, 1936–1959:
DISTRIBUTION OF TYPES OF CONTENT

Types of Content	1936–1938	1947–1949	1952–1959
	(Percentages)		
Army			
Broad Professional	68	85	80
Narrow Professional	28	7	16
Human Interest	4	7	3
Total	100	100	100
Navy			
Broad Professional	67	83	83
Narrow Professional	24	15	14
Human Interest	9	2	2
Total	100	100	100
	BREAKDOWN OF BROAD PROFESSIONAL ARTICLES		
Army			
Historical	29	28	12
Morale Building	14	15	15
Mission Defining	—	9	10
Applied Strategy	25	33	43
Total	68	85	80
Navy			
Historical	37	44	27
Morale Building	14	13	12
Mission Defining	8	11	9
Applied Strategy	8	15	35
Total	67	83	83

concentration of broad professional material rose respectively for the Army 68 to 80 per cent, and from 67 to 83 per cent for the Navy. Narrow technical communications declined and found outlets in the more specialized journals, reflecting the increased division of labor in the military. Human interest material became practically nonexistent. The format that emerged is one more compatible with a managerial oriented profession.

These categories highlight again the greater stability of naval institutions. The evolution toward broader professional perspectives was gradual and in a steady trend in the naval publication. The Army sponsored publication showed greater fluctuations for the 1947–1949 civilianization period, when narrow professional articles dropped very sharply to only 7 per cent of the content but rose again to 16 per cent in 1957–1959, to a level comparable to the Navy.

If the total category of broad professional articles is further subdivided into four component groups (a) historical, (b) morale building, (c) mission defining, and (d) applied strategy (Table 2) the pattern of stability and change emerges more clearly. These categories further highlight the shift from a primitive orientation to a competitive model. Historical material as presented in these journals is more an expression of organizational solidarity and fundamental virtues than creative problem solving. Thus in both services the sponsored journals showed a decrease in concern with historical material; in the case of the Army from 29 to 12 per cent; and in the case of the Navy from 37 to 27 per cent. On the other hand, both journals show an increase in concern with the applied strategy to a point at which this emerged as the dominant category in the 1957–1959 period with 43 per cent in the case of the Army and 35 per cent for the Navy. Applied strategy is an expression of the competitive model to the extent that it is involved in relating military strategy to technological and political developments.

In addition, these broad professional articles help to probe the extent to which each service has been able to develop a fusion between the primitivist and the competitive orientation. It should be noted that in both journals the concentration of morale-building articles—a concern with fundamental group values—has been about equal and has remained persistent. Moreover, the concern with history as a reflection of primitivist values remains at a higher level in the Navy journal as compared with that of the Army. Although the Navy initiated efforts toward a competitive model earlier, the contemporary 1957–1959 period reveals a clear-cut persistence of a core interest in traditional concerns. The Army, by contrast, began the process of adaptation later and in the course fluctuated to a greater extent.

The third measure in content trends analyzed the rank of the contributors during the time period under investigation. (For purposes of comparison in Table 3 the breakdowns by rank are presented for all contributors, civilian as well as military.) A number of observations can be made about these data if the ranks are broken down into four cate-

TABLE 3. ARMY AND NAVY SPONSORED LITERATURE, 1936–1959:
RANK DISTRIBUTION OF CONTRIBUTORS

Service	1936–1938	1947–1949	1957–1959
	MILITARY AND CIVILIAN CONTRIBUTORS (*Percentages*)		
Army			
Enlisted	2	3	7
Lieutenant-Captain	35	4	14
Major-Colonel	48	47	46
General	6	12	17
Civilian	9	34	16
Total	100	100	100
Navy			
Enlisted	2	3	2
Ensign-Lieutenant	29	13	14
Lt. Commander-Captain	41	54	51
Admiral	4	7	7
Civilian	25	23	26
Total	100	100	100
	MILITARY CONTRIBUTORS ONLY		
Army			
Enlisted	2	5	8
Lieutenant-Captain	38	6	17
Major-Colonel	53	71	55
General Officer	7	18	20
Total	100	100	100
Navy			
Enlisted	3	4	3
Ensign-Lieutenant	39	17	19
Lt. Commander-Captain	51	70	69
Admiral	7	9	9
Total	100	100	100

gories of enlisted men; company-grade officers (Lieutenant-Captain; Ensign-Lieutenant), field grades (Major-Colonel; Lieutenant Commander-Captain), and general officers or admirals. (a) As in the case of the other content measures, there is much greater stability of rank levels in the sponsored literature of the Navy than in the Army, reflecting actual stability in the rank distribution as well as organizational conceptions about rank relations. (b) It was to be expected that the bulk of the writing was done by the middle-level ranks. In both services the field-grade officer is the most frequently represented. The percentage of field-grade officers who are the backbone of the contributors remains relatively stable. For the Navy, it rose gradually during the period as a whole (51 to 68 per cent of military contributors). For the Army, there is a marked fluctuation for the period immediately after World War II, but stability for the overall period. (c) Enlisted personnel are represented in both organs. For the Navy it is a stable token representation of around 2 or 3 per cent, which reflects the Navy recognition of the existence and accepted position of the enlisted men; while in the case of the Army the percentage has risen from token representation before the war to almost 10 per cent, reflecting the increased concern with the position of the enlisted man in the ground forces. (d) The great variation that has taken place is the decline of company-grade officers in both services, reflecting the broadening professional conceptions of the journals as well as the crisis of the position of the junior officer. In the case of the Army, the decline is much sharper and much more subject to fluctuation. (e) One would have expected an increase in representation of generals and admirals, reflecting the increased importance of new politico-military tasks which involve high ranking personnel. Using these measures, there is an increase of generals in the Army publication (7 to 20 per cent) but the Navy has remained relatively stable (7 to 9 per cent).

RANK AND AUTHORSHIP

It can be argued that these trends are influenced by changes in the actual distribution of ranks during the period. This is not the case, as can be seen from the data on rank distribution in Table 4. In the Army the concentration on junior officers increased from roughly three-fifths to two-thirds, while their representation declined in the sponsored journal; the increase in contributions of general officers is not a result of their increased concentration, since this figure remained stable as between 1938 and 1959. With the noteworthy decline in concentration of flag officers, the distribution of ranks in the Navy remained virtually unchanged and also constituted a pattern toward which the Army moved.

A more direct method of presenting these data is to calculate an editorial quotient; namely, a ratio of the percentage of published articles by a given rank to that rank's representation in the Army or Navy officer corps for that period, as presented in Table 5.

TABLE 4. DISTRIBUTION OF RANK: ARMY AND NAVY, 1938–1959[a]

Rank	1938		1948		1959	
	Per Cent	Number	Per Cent	Number	Per Cent	Number
Army						
Flag	.5	66	.6	348	.5	485
Field	41	5,138	34	22,811	35	31,812
Junior	58	7,310	66	50,301	64	58,322
Total	100[a]		100		100	
Navy						
Flag	01	83	.6	261	.5	299
Field	35	3,054	33	13,685	36	23,712
Junior	64	5,589	66	27,283	64	42,363
Total	100		100		100	

[a] Columns do not necessarily add to 100 per cent because of rounding.

TABLE 5. TRENDS IN EDITORIAL QUOTIENT, 1938–1959

Rank	1938	1948	1959
Army			
Flag	$14 \left(\frac{.07}{.005}\right)$	$30 \left(\frac{.18}{.006}\right)$	$40 \left(\frac{.20}{.005}\right)$
Field	$1.29 \left(\frac{.53}{.41}\right)$	$2.09 \left(\frac{.71}{.34}\right)$	$1.57 \left(\frac{.55}{.35}\right)$
Junior	$.66 \left(\frac{.38}{.58}\right)$	$.09 \left(\frac{.06}{.66}\right)$	$.27 \left(\frac{.17}{.64}\right)$
Navy			
Flag	$5 \left(\frac{.05}{.01}\right)$	$15 \left(\frac{.09}{.006}\right)$	$18 \left(\frac{.09}{.005}\right)$
Field	$1.54 \left(\frac{.54}{.35}\right)$	$2.12 \left(\frac{.70}{.33}\right)$	$1.92 \left(\frac{.69}{.36}\right)$
Junior	$.59 \left(\frac{.38}{.64}\right)$	$.26 \left(\frac{.17}{.66}\right)$	$.30 \left(\frac{.19}{.64}\right)$

These data serve to confirm and amplify the foregoing conclusions. They highlight even more sharply the marked decline in the representation of junior officers in both services and point, in addition, to some recovery of representation in the last time period as the services strive to find a new professional identity for junior personnel. The position of the middle-level field grade officer is seen as more than stabilized, as these measures reveal a clear increase in prominence. Most noteworthy is that, by these measures, the upward trend in the representation of generals and admirals appears more pronounced.

These trends in frequency of appearance need to be related to the contents of articles. What shifts have occurred in the types of articles written by the different ranks? For the Army, the data show that in the earlier period, the junior officers wrote primarily in the category of narrow professional, technical articles. As their prominence declined the junior officers continued and even increased their concern with narrow professional, technical articles. In short, there was a widening of the divergence between the professional model of the junior officer and the field grade officer in ground force sponsored literature. In the Navy, by contrast, while junior officers were heavily involved in writing narrow professional, technical articles, this type of writing did not predominate in the earlier period nor did it increase with time. The junior naval officer had other professional images, since he wrote frequently about history, morale building, and even broad professional articles, and this pattern has remained relatively stable through the period under investigation. In short, the model of the junior officer in the Navy did not diverge as sharply from that of the field grade officer.

The type of content the officer produces in sponsored literature, it is assumed, is a measure of his professional self-image and the competence the profession attributes to different ranks. Thus it appears that the Army has been inclined to develop a professional identity in its junior officers, as if they were members of a distinct category with special responsibilities and special experiences, while the Navy has treated its junior officers as a kind of apprentice to the roles of commanders and captains. In the Army, the experience of platoon leaders and company commanders seems to be considered little more than "mere experience." By contrast, in the Navy, the experience of the junior officers seems to have general significance to the organizational and professional problems of the Navy. In a sense, this is another expression of the Navy's greater ability to fuse primitivist orientations into its competitive and managerial elements, since in the primitivist model the experiences of the junior officers are of concern to the organization as a whole.

For the field grade officer, the trend in content has been toward greater emphasis on conceptual materials in both services and particularly in the areas of applied strategy. It is through the field grade officers, and civilians, rather than through the highest ranking officers, that the professional issues of adjusting military means to national goals are discussed. But even at this middle management level, there persists a difference between the Army and the Navy literature. In the Army, field grade officers concerned with historical material have sharply declined, while this concern of field grade officer continues in the naval journal. Again, the Army's striving for a competitive and managerial model seems to allow less opportunity for reflection of past accomplishments as part of the professional model, while naval counterparts still make use of this preoccupation.

The closer a service approaches the managerial model, the more extensive, intense, and customary does the range of its interactions with the outside world become. Many of these contacts are encountered by the top-ranking generals and admirals, but these contacts also pervade the entire rank structure. It would appear that top-ranking officers would carry the editorial burden of writing or at least signing articles dealing with basic strategic, technical, and politico-military affairs. And it is true that their presence has increased particularly in the Army sponsored literature. In a statistical sense they are overrepresented, but they are not and cannot become the most frequent contributors. To do so would convert the sponsored communication into an assigned communication. They must rely on the middle-ranking officer, particularly the staff officer, who has fuller command of the details, and on civilians as part of the process of managerial administration.

IMPORTANCE OF PROFESSIONAL WRITING FOR CAREER ADVANCEMENT

It is possible to speculate about the importance of professional writing in sponsored channels for career advancement. Under the professional image of the older heroic and primitivist model, a common and universally applicable set of standards of military proficiency was assumed, and the demonstration of this proficiency was the basis for professional success. The contributions by an officer of any rank were designed to demonstrate mastery of his particular assignment and thereby his usefulness to the whole profession. Mastery in general, rather than the significance of the particular problems, was stressed. Professionalism was regarded as a capacity to cope with the problems of military life. A scheme for more effective garbage disposal merited as much space as an examination of the role of armored vehicles in modern warfare. The emphasis was on military duty as a unique way of life rather than on the armed forces as an instrument for coping with particular social and political problems.

Under these circumstances, writing for publication by a military officer was considered desirable because it helped stress the universality of such standards and brought them to the attention of the broadest possible professional audience. Officers, junior and senior, hoped that their published writings would help their career advancement; not as innovators, however, but rather as individuals actively engaged in making established systems more efficient. The risk of deviancy was limited because the problems discussed were already well established as part of the institutional routine. Publication brought the author to the attention of important officers; it also demonstrated that he was devoting himself to the development of his overall competence rather than to the cultivation of specialized skills.

In terms of the competitive model, with its managerial outlook, the assumption is that every assignment has its own particular criteria of efficiency. Therefore, proficiency in a given assignment does not necessarily qualify an officer for promotion to another assignment. A variety of additional, often intangible, criteria become operative, such as the capacity for growth. The problems and approaches of one assignment may appear to have no direct relationship to those of its successor. Under these circumstances publication becomes less a device for enhancing an officer's chances for promotion.

Sponsored literature in the new context is less concerned with stimulating individual contributions to general standards of proficiency. Publication is rather devoted to the dissemination of information in the interests of professional solidarity and group cohesion. The officer writes less to glorify his own particular assignment and more to educate and influence those other officers involved in the processes of policy formation, coordination, and implementation.

Under the managerial model, general and flag rank officers contribute articles in order to educate one another and to inform the lower ranks about the complex problems which they know are being handled at higher levels, and with which the lower ranks have no direct experience. Middle-grade officers contribute articles to demonstrate that they are applying the directives of their superiors to particular problems—but in a fashion which they hope is creative and not merely mechanical. Junior officers have fewer opportunities to apply such high level principles. Therefore, they retain a residue of their traditional role of demonstrating that, notwithstanding the new emphasis on conceptual problems, there is still a place for a professional interest in purely technical matters and for being concerned with fundamental military values.

Our analysis has focused on content; but this is incomplete since the full significance of the contemporary sponsored literature involved an understanding of changes in the audience as well. The professional journal is typically addressed to other professionals and in a sense to other specialists. This was the case with *Infantry* and *U. S. Naval Institute Proceedings* before World War II. The shift toward the competitive model has also involved the development of multiple audiences. *Army* is edited in part for the benefit of the Association of the United States

Army. The *U. S. Naval Institute Proceedings*, although to a lesser degree, tends to serve the interests of the more professionally minded members of the Naval League. (The Naval League has its own house organ, *Navy*.) Retired military personnel, academic university personnel concerned with defense establishment matters, and informed citizens are now audiences that must be addressed, but without losing the interest of the military professional.

In the pre-World War II period, sponsored journals stressing the history and narrow professional techniques of the service reinforced the professional sense of tradition and continuity. They provided a professional forum for the problems to be covered in future assigned literature, for example, field manuals and the like. In writing a serious article for publication, the professional soldier was presenting his reflections upon the instructions which had been provided to guide him in the performance of his official duties. These reflections were useful for his peers and they supplied information to higher ranking officers about the strengths and weaknesses of the military system.

The newer publications continue to serve to some extent the same functions, but unlike their earlier counterparts the contemporary journal is less committed to the exploration and improvement of official routine. This is perhaps because the framework of improvement has shifted from an arsenal to a laboratory model. New devices ranging from operational analysis to performance budgeting are employed for these objectives. The sponsored journal places a stronger emphasis on bringing to the attention of the officer problems and procedures outside his normal professional pattern. The sponsored journal is at the frontier of the military establishment, serving to indicate the areas where innovation is or should be in process rather than how it is being accomplished. For better or for worse, the journal serves the military imagination rather than the military routine. The articles published in the old-style-sponsored journal did not extend much beyond the doctrine and routine accepted and promulgated by the military service. The articles published in the managerially oriented journal are expected to open up new and unexplored areas for military speculation and reflection.

The journals once operated, as the arsenal, for the technical development. By contrast, managerially oriented publications are oriented toward the exploration of the innovative aspects of organizational experience and, that, at the level of doctrine and mission defining. They have become analogous to laboratory-type developments. Laboratory developments, however, involve skills which, properly speaking, are not military. The professional engaged in them is only incidentally a member of some armed force. His contributions to the military journals are meant to popularize rather than stimulate his accomplishments.

In summary, it is possible to speak of the transformation of the content and approach of sponsored military literature and to use these materials to probe the basic changes in professional self-image in a technological environment. First, there is the underlying change that pervades both services as they move from a primitive self-conception to a competitive or managerial orientation. In simplest terms, the old model of sponsored literature was a professional journal written by and for military personnel. Its audience was conceived as a body of general practitioners. It was a journal in which field grade officers predominated but where junior officers also had an important role. In its content, historical and narrow professional technical articles were as important as conceptual-type articles. The newer approach is that of a journal in which specialists write for the edification of the general professional community as well as for all interested members of the general lay public. While the field grade officer still predominates, the junior officer has suffered a marked decline. Civilian contributions have grown in prominence, while papers by high ranking officers appear more frequently. Historical and narrow technical articles have declined, while the broad conceptual articles, dealing with applied strategy and civil-military issues set the basic element of the self-image.

Second, the divergence between the services is as important as the basic pattern of change. The naval journal clearly indicates that the process of change had already started for this service before World War II. The Army, when confronted with the realities of change, fluctuated more sharply toward the competitive model during the post-World War II period, while the Navy continued its process of gradual change. Thus, as of 1959, the Navy had developed a model which was basically committed to the competitive and managerial approach but still embodied important and clear-cut elements of the primitive approach, while the Army still was seeking a fusion of the traditional military heroic self-conceptions with contemporary politico-military requirements. If the service journals are a relevant indicator, the Navy has undergone a less radical change in professional self-image than the Army. The Navy has followed a pattern of increased professionalization by stimulating conformity to existing patterns while modifying them slowly. The Army has engaged in a drastic and unstable search for new bases of professional identity.

Part Four

SOCIAL COHESION UNDER PROLONGED STRESS

Part Four

SOCIAL COHESION UNDER PROLONGED STRESS

A FOURTH PERSPECTIVE in a sociological approach to military institutions is to focus on primary group relations. The objective of this approach is to probe the factors that contribute to and weaken social cohesion, since social cohesion is assumed to be essential for permitting the military to react to crisis and at the same time is an essential element in its capacity to change.

The intellectual contribution that has resulted from sociological investigations of the military has been mainly in this area of the analysis of microsocial systems. To speak of the analysis of military institutions has come to mean for many social scientists, to study primary groups and small unit formations. And truly, the military is an ongoing natural laboratory where training and operations create, fashion, and refashion basic loyalties and put primary group solidarity to test. The special quality of military life is rooted not only in the dangers that men must expose themselves to, but also in the high levels of solidarity that are generated. Issues of organizational climate and patterns of social cohesion immediately confront the sociologist concerned with change in the military.

It is not strange, therefore, that the results of sociological thinking on primary groups in the military have come to have a pervasive impact in the social sciences. Organizational analysis—theoretical and practical —has come to encompass routinely informal social processes and the primary groups structure for all institutional sectors; military or civilian, profit-seeking or nonprofit, private or public. These empirical findings serve to caution the administrator against overemphasis of ideological variables in accounting for organizational effectiveness. "Morale" is no longer a vague dimension of organizational behavior grounded in personal attitudes. Even in the smallest unit there is an "iron framework"

191

of organization which serves as a basis of social control. However, the contribution of these research findings to military primary groups has often been overinterpreted and overextended to the point of creating a "human relations" theory of organization which fails to give sufficient emphasis to authority, power structure, the environmental context, and organizational goals sufficient scope.

Thus primary groups cohesion per se does not account for organizational performance; to the contrary, the loyalties of primary groups and the needs to maintain them can develop into a basis of opposition to the larger organization. The task of social research is, therefore, to investigate the articulation of primary groups with the larger organizational structure in which they operate.

The dynamics of primary groups can best be studied when the organization is under pressure. The cross-section attitude study and the morale survey, although they may serve as a useful administrative and research tool, are not an effective standpoint for confronting the basic issues of social cohesion. Such research is not easily planned; instead, it is necessary to take advantage of organizational events as natural experiments or to stage large-scale field experiments. In assessing these problems, the Inter-University Seminar had two separate but related bodies of unique data: the direct and personal observations of a trained researcher at the battlefront in Korea, and the result of an elaborate field experiment in Greenland of men confronted with the experimental stress of underfeeding.

It would be simple-minded to extrapolate from these situations to the requirements of the constabulary force, although analogues are present. Some types of constabulary forces are likely to be widely scattered, require self-contained command structures and strong inner personal controls among key personnel, and are likely to be exposed to prolonged stress. These studies are case studies of primary groups under stress and constitute objects of inquiry in themselves. Nevertheless, they converge in their findings and implications. Both are of general relevance because they focus sharply on the grim realities of the environmental context in contradistinction to purely laboratory studies. In both cases, we are dealing with highly primitive social environments, despite the presence of complex technology.

An overriding generalization begins to emerge which can be stated in two alternative formats. First, the structure of military-type primary groups under conditions of prolonged stress has a dual aspect. It consists of a diffuse attachment to all the members of the basic primary unit who are designated as buddies. At the same time it involves for most of the members the selection of another single person for basic support—psychological and functional. But these sociometric attachments are private and unannounced and often unreciprocated, for to make them explicit would weaken broader diffuse attachment. All are buddies but one particular person is more so than others. Alternatively, the pressures of prolonged stress do not produce a disintegration of units into social isolates concerned with their own survival and well-being. Instead, as long as the tasks confronting the group remain relatively manageable, nuclear or granular, two-person subsystems emerge—be they implicit and unreciprocated—which contribute to the organizational effectiveness of the unit.

The literature of small group experiments presents a pattern in which social cohesion is grounded in reciprocated choices. This may reflect the types of research instruments used, or the ideological bias of the "human relations" investigators who assume mutuality as the basis of social cohesion. It may also be that military units under stress have a different structure from civilian units. However, these studies, like previous studies of military cohesion, may have the result of deepening our understanding of civilian groups by calling attention to the positive contribution of implicit and diffuse sociometric patterns. The danger still rests in overgeneralization. All of the materials on military small groups deal either with combat or field-type or training units. The dynamics of control headquarters and coordinating units remain unstudied.

BUDDY RELATIONS AND COMBAT PERFORMANCE

Roger W. Little

INFANTRYMEN IN COMBAT frequently refer to one another as "buddies." Some with long experience would even say that "it takes a buddy to cover the ground." By this they mean that their social relations are equal in importance to their tasks in the organization. A sociologist, pausing briefly among men like those in the Korean Conflict, would be likely to assume that they referred to specific members of their squad or platoon, easily charted on a sociogram. If he lived among them long enough, however, he would learn that the term "buddy" had two distinct meanings. In a singular sense, the buddy relationship was intensely personal and intimate, fostered by conditions of actual and expected stress. But the word was also used as a general term to describe all the men in the same unit with whom one shared the risks and hardships of combat. Although often at odds with the authority system, the network of interpersonal relationships formed by buddies contributed to operational effectiveness by establishing and enforcing upper and lower limits to role performance.

It was important, of course, that buddies, as primary groups, supported the organization because they comprised its foundation. A study of military organization would be incomplete without a projection of the meaning of these relationships to the larger organization.

Primary group solidarity does not automatically ensure that an organization will perform effectively. This has been long recognized by students of organization. Studies of industrial organization have noted that cohesive primary groups can at times supply the basis for group opposition to the goals of management. Such a response is dramatically encountered in the correctional institution where solidary inmate groups are organized in opposition to the authorities. Thus the focus of this paper is not on the detached analysis of primary group relations in the military context. To the contrary, it is concerned with how the buddy system, as encountered in the Korean situation, articulated with the structure and goals of military command. In this case, we are dealing

195

with two very different environmental situations: that of combat and that of the reserve rear area. The task is to understand why in combat the primary group relations—the buddy system—operated to support organizational goals to a greater extent than in the reserve areas.

Several sociologists have reported on primary groups in military organization since World War II, but few had opportunity for continuous observation of a single combat unit in the field. The author was able to make such a study while living with a rifle company from November, 1952, through February, 1953. His role was that of an observer of technical aspects of combat operations.[1]

The combat conditions encountered by this company, as well as its composition in terms of personnel and equipment, were the same as any other rifle company in Korea during that time. The period of observation covered three consecutive tactical situations: (1) a reserve bivouac with intensive patrol activity in forward areas; (2) a defensive position on the forward edge of the battle area with intermittent patrolling; and (3) withdrawal into reserve for retraining and the reception of replacements.

Combat activity at this time was relatively passive compared to earlier periods of the Korean Conflict. Enemy contacts took the form of brief, sharp engagements, interrupting a longer time perspective of standing guard at dug-in positions ("fighting bunkers") with a persistent expectation of enemy infiltration. Offensive combat actions by Americans were primarily in the form of patrols to the forward edge of the enemy battle area for the purpose of detecting changes in deployment. An awareness of the presence of a real enemy with a potential for destruction was maintained by frequent, sudden, and saturating mortar barrages.

In at least three specific ways the composition of combat units in Korea differed from those of World War II. First, there was a higher degree of youthful homogeneity among these troops. Ninety per cent of the platoon that the author observed were twenty-three years of age or less. Sixty-one per cent were in the age group from eighteen to twenty-one years. Only one man was a college graduate (and he was an enlisted man who had volunteered for assignment to a rifle company after being rejected for intelligence duties). Three others (including the officer platoon leader) had attended college for two years or less. Thirty per cent were high school graduates, and the remainder had less than a high school education.

Second, the duration of membership in the organization was determined by a concrete measure of individual experience rather than a

His Buddy Has Been Killed in Action

A grief-stricken American Infantryman whose buddy has been killed in action is comforted by another soldier. In the background, a corpsman methodically fills out casualty tags. Naktong-Ni Area, August 20, 1950

national goal (such as "Victory" in World War II). "Rotation" was a policy of the Department of the Army designed to require periods of service in Korea in inverse proportion to the degree of risk and hardship to which individuals were exposed. The policy was implemented by establishing zones of relative risk and crediting each individual with "constructive months of service" (commonly referred to as "points") for the period that his unit was located in a specific zone. Men assigned to infantry battalions on the line received the maximum of four points compared to men at stations in Japan, for example, who received the base credit of one point for each month of service.

Thus when two or more men joined the company together, their rotation status would be the same as long as they remained with the company. The number of points was not affected by promotion awards, punishments, transfers, or any factor other than the individual's period of service with the company, or larger unit, within the same zone of risk. This policy provided every man with an individual goal which could be achieved without activities involving greater risk than that to which all other members of the company were exposed.

Third, almost one-fourth of the platoon consisted of native Korean soldiers. The "ROKs" (for "Republic of Korea") were originally assigned during a period of shortage of American replacements, but remained after the need was filled.[2] They were distributed among the four squads. An American soldier was assigned as a sponsor to each Korean with the expectation that the ensuing relationship would be comparable to that of American buddies, but this kind of friendship rarely developed. The sponsor relationships were adhered to only on guard posts or when the American was reporting to an officer from a command level higher than the company.

The ROKs constituted a social system of their own, distinct from that of the Americans in the unit to which they were assigned. Rigid policies from higher echelons restricted their activity to specific combat tasks which tended to make their roles more specialized than those of the Americans. The Koreans were not required to go on patrols, they did not "pull K.P." when the company was in reserve, nor were they ever assigned as assistants on the automatic rifle. They segregated themselves in the chow line. On work details they exchanged tools with one another but rarely with an American unless the latter initiated the exchange. The Americans seldom differentiated them by name, and never mentioned them as specific "buddies." When the squad moved as an integral unit, the Koreans walked at the rear of the column.

There were, however, major similarities between the U. S. Army in the Korean Conflict and in World War II. The basic organization of infantry units was the same as in World War II with only minor changes made in weaponry. Tactical formations were identical. The conditions of infantry life—harsh, primitive, and "close to the ground"—were the same as in World War II. The faces had changed but the story remained much the same.

The methods used by the author were very simple. He selected one platoon in order to get to know the members as individuals and to recognize them in the chow line or on work details. He talked to each one alone at least twice, and subsequently in the presence of his companions at their positions, in the bunkers, or at chow. In the solitary interviews, he encouraged each man to talk about his "best friends" and asked him which, if any, he considered a buddy. The men were reluctant to designate one or more specific persons as a buddy. Once they had made a choice, however, they talked extensively about him, although the man designated rarely reciprocated the choice. Next, an attempt was made to find pairs of men who consistently went to chow together, or exchanged tools more frequently on work details, assuming that such observations would validate their choices in the interviews.

The data on buddy choices indicate the following. Of 39 men in the platoon, 9 were Korean soldiers and not interviewed; 30 men were interviewed and observed. Twenty-one men designated only one other person as a buddy. Four men made no choices. Five men designated two other persons as buddies. Of these five, three designated each other or reciprocated one another's choice.

Thus it appeared that a primary aspect of the social system of the platoon was a network of interpersonal linkages. Everyone was a buddy, but one man was usually more so. The one man toward whom the choice was directed, however, did not usually return the choice verbally. Buddy choices were private decisions and consequently never threatened the solidarity of the squad or platoon. The resulting relationships were thus a molecular or granular type of primary group.

But an interview or conversation about "buddies" always elicited additional comments about a context of solidarity in which distinctions among individuals did not appear. Even though a buddy choice was not reciprocated, there was another level of significance at which everyone in the squad seemed to have a centripetal effect, tending to draw all members into a system of consensus. Thus buddies also constituted a status group at a specific echelon of risk and involved by implication the larger organization to which they were assigned.

THE CONTEXT OF BUDDY CHOICES

The buddy role was an expectation of mutual loyalty and reciprocity attributed to another person at the same relative level in the organization. Behavior in the buddy role could be observed when opportunities existed for free choice of companions. These opportunities were limited by the "Table of Organization."

The formal positions men held in relation to one another comprised a scheme of interaction that would occur if the platoon moved as an integral unit, as in a parade. The pattern would also be used in an attack formation, a factor frequently mentioned as a basis for restricting buddy choices to the same squad.

There were other occasions when companions could be chosen freely, the most spontaneous occurring in the "chow line." Platoon integrity was maintained in reporting for meals but it was possible to exchange places in line with a man from another squad. Work details (digging and building field fortifications) were performed by squads, but within the squad it was possible to exchange tools more frequently with one man than another. Although patrols were composed of men drawn from all squads of the platoon, the buddy of a man designated by the platoon leader could volunteer to accompany the man selected. And finally, a man from one squad could visit a man in another squad at night when the unit was in reserve, although this was more difficult when the squads were on the line.

Buddy choices were always made in a situation of stress which provided opportunities for the offering or acceptance of help. "Old men" offered help as a sponsor, coach, or as the companion of another "old-timer" who had been through the same combat experiences. "New men" accepted help as novices or as companions of other new men.

Here are some of the ways buddy choices were made.*

As a companion to another new man:

> I was in the 1st Squad when I made my first buddy. I was sent to the command post to get him. We were both new guys, and it's easier for two new guys to buddy than to get in with the old ones. The first few nights we pulled listening posts together. We were so close that we would read each other's letters. That way we got to feel that we were in the same family. I think that what really made us buddies, though, was that we were new men together.

* Names used in interview material are pseudonyms, allocated as follows: Those beginning with "A" to platoon headquarters, "B" to 1st Squad, "C" to 2nd Squad, "D" to 3rd Squad, and "E" to 4th Squad.

As a novice sponsored by an "old man":

> Camp introduced me to everyone in the squad, and stayed with me that
> night because I was a new man. He told me a lot about each man in the
> squad, about the Chinese and their tricks. Then he told me that there
> would be days when we would feel like brothers, other days that we would
> hate each other, but that feeling that way was all just part of the job.

As a sponsor:

> From the first time that I saw Dion on Sandbag, I liked him. That night
> I volunteered to take his place on listening post because he was a little
> jumpy. I wasn't being a hero; I just felt that I'd rather go myself than let
> someone go who was jumpy. Now no matter what happened he'd still be
> my buddy.

As a companion for another "old man":

> When I joined the squad, Baum was *it*. Now he's the only one who was
> with us at Sandbag Castle. We depend on each other. I don't think that
> he would bug out, but if he did, it wouldn't make much difference. The
> only thing that would break us up would be if one of us was killed or left
> the company. Bell has been buddying with us but he's still a new man and
> hasn't been through any of the things that Baum and I have been through.

NORMS OF THE BUDDY RELATIONSHIP

From comments of these men and others, and the way they behaved,
a set of norms that seemed to guide the behavior of buddies can be
formulated.

First, a buddy had to "understand" in a deeply personal sense.
Buddies became therapists to one another. Infantrymen were most likely
to encounter situations provoking unusual and deviant emotional reactions. One man said of another whom he had chosen as a buddy, "Our
minds seem to run together."

> A buddy understands you and is interested in your story. Some big
> mouths talk as if everyone is interested in their story but they're not.
> You've got to find a guy you like and he likes you, then you're buddies
> and you know he'll listen to you when you want to talk. A buddy shares
> everything; if you don't get mail, he lets you read his.

The more one buddy told another, the more each depended on the other.
And whatever buddies heard or learned of each other, they kept to
themselves.

Second, although one man might think of another as a buddy, he
seldom stated it publicly or boasted of the attachment. Only when the
chips were down would his choice be displayed.

> You've got to make every man in the squad your buddy to get things done. You've got to get down and work with them and get them to feel that they can depend on you to stick by them. But I can never show that one man is my buddy because a lot of guys may think that I'm a buddy.

This norm recognized that the nature of the battlefield was such that he might need another buddy when the publicly designated one was not available. The rule tended to unite buddies subjectively with the squad or platoon as an integral unit, as it would be required to function in a combat formation.

Third, buddies did not boast of individual combat skills or compare combat proficiency. To do so was to suggest that obligation to the organization was more important than loyalty to one another.

> In the bunker the men don't talk much about combat. When they do the old men like Camp and Chap call them "war daddy" and they shut up. Clay is like that. Most of the time they talk about places back in the States or incidents around the company. It's a lot better to talk about things like that until you've really had some combat behind you.

The man who often boasted or expected recognition for his combat skills was considered the one most likely to forget, in a combat crisis, that he had a buddy and that buddies had to depend on each other.

Fourth, buddies never put one another on the spot by demanding a choice between loyalty as a buddy and obligation to the organization as an infantryman. One man did not volunteer for a patrol unless he had first obtained the concurrence of the person he considered his buddy, and then both volunteered at the same time. Usually one had been selected and the other felt compelled to volunteer because, on patrols, events were most likely to occur in which they would need each other.

> Buddies have to talk when they get the chance, and you're never sure when you'll get the chance. When on a patrol all the sweat is on the way out, when you're spread out and can't say anything to anyone. When you get to the objective you can say something to your buddy. Maybe you were afraid on the way out. You feel better after you've told someone. It could happen to anyone, and your buddy would understand even if no one else did.

Finally, in a crisis and if forced to make a choice, a man would think first of his loyalty to a buddy, and second of his obligations to the organization. If a man was wounded he expected his buddy to care for him until the "medic" arrived, even though the buddy had been taught to continue in the attack. "Bugging out" was an even more extreme form of deviating from the organizational task; deserting the field and leaving one's companions to continue in the fight. The attitudes of most men toward "bugging out" were expressed like this:

> I always wanted to shoot the guy who bugged out on me, and I would anybody but my buddy, Dion. Lots of times fellows do things when they're scared that they don't do at any other time. But I don't like to think of that happening.

Of the 26 men who made buddy choices in the platoon, 20 stated that even if the buddy should "bug out," they would remain buddies without any change in the relationship. Of the remaining six men, three stated that they were not sure that it would make a difference, while only three were certain that it would break the relationship. (Four men made no buddy choices.)

DEVIANT ROLES: THE DUD AND THE HERO

In each platoon there were two deviant roles which some men assumed. Usually it was enough to have one dud and one hero to a platoon, because the role itself was more important than the number of men occupying it. They were extreme types in their contribution to the organization. The hero did too much. The dud contributed the minimum necessary to get by. Men who were classified as duds or heroes could not make buddies, or lost them quickly.

The dud was a person who refused to do his share. He was not called a dud because he lacked skill, or was awkward, or nervous. To such men the others always gave more help and attention. The dud was deliberately undependable, and would not try. Indeed, he was crafty in avoiding the tasks that had to be performed together or not at all. He knew how to hide by lingering in the chow line, or by dallying on the work detail. He was rarely available when a patrol was being selected. In each case he made more work for the others. They had to do his share, not because the dud lacked ability, but because he refused to use it.

Frequent attendance at sick call was often interpreted as characteristic of the dud:

> When a man goes on sick call a lot, he misses out on things that happen to the squad. Then when he comes back he can't talk about it as if he had been with us. When he's gone someone else has to take his place, and that means more work for everyone else and no sweat for him. When he does come back, if the doctor didn't do anything for him, the guys think that he's been aping off. Crum just can't get close to the guys anymore, but he doesn't care because he has so many points and will rotate soon.

The dud had a rough time until one of two things happened. Sometimes he came around and began to do his share, yielding to the pressures exerted on him, but he never lived down his past. He could become an acceptable member of the squad—and be a buddy—only at the price of living with his old record, and being constantly reminded of it with jokes and nicknames. When the bitterness and rejection were gone, the reformed dud continued to serve a useful purpose; new men learned, from his reputation, that "aping off" was more easily forgiven than forgotten.

More often, however, the dud became increasingly isolated from the other men in the squad. He was seldom present when the squad worked together on a patrol, or on detail. Consequently, he had little to say when such activities were being discussed. He often became the butt of jokes in the bunker or chow line. Eventually he would abandon any pretense of being a member of the squad and direct all of his efforts toward getting a transfer. The irony of it was that when he did "get out," he was transferred to the rear as a driver or a cook's helper, at an echelon of less risk and more comfort.

The opposite role was that of the "hero." Unlike the dud, the hero wanted to do *more* than his share for the organization. In doing so he made it necessary for others to follow, or at least to expose themselves to additional risk.

> A guy who is just trying to show that he's not scared and sometimes trying to show up the other men. He's not braver. You shouldn't stick your neck out unless you have to. If someone gives me an order, we'll do it but we aren't going to take any unnecessary chances. If a guy gets a medal for doing his job it's O.K. But if he's taken a chance or exposed his men, he's no hero because he's made it more risky for everyone.

The hero frequently boasted of his courage and aggressiveness. He clamored for intensive combat. Like the dud, the hero appeared to be thinking first of himself, and only secondarily of the other members of the squad or platoon. No more than the dud could he be depended upon to act as one bound by his loyalty to a buddy.

Although buddies used the term "hero" in a negative sense, the organization provided a special, positive meaning for the term. From the organization point of view a hero was a person whose action had been officially recognized as making an exceptional contribution to the mission of the organization. A decoration or an award was the organization's mark for a hero, to be perceived by the recipient's peers as a reward for a deed well done and an inspirational symbol toward which others might strive.[3]

But a man who received an award often seemed to feel an obligation to deny that he had "earned" the medal. For example:

> Sergeant Alex was calling Earl out of his bunker to give him orders every five minutes. Earl objected and Sergeant Alex called him "our little hero" because he got the Bronze Star on Sandbag Castle. Earl got mad and said that he had never asked for it; they *gave* it to him. He told me that he wished that he'd been someplace else when it happened.

Although the hero was as isolated from his peers as the dud, it was easier for the hero to "reform" and become acceptable. It usually happened as a matter of course that he boasted less of combat experiences. As the number of "old men" in the platoon dwindled, he assumed the role of an "oldtimer" himself and found that role more satisfying. As he took on their sentiments, he volunteered less frequently. Sometimes the hero found this change too difficult. When the tactical situation failed to provide opportunities for him to live up to his ideals, he tended to withdraw, apparently into a world of his own.

The range of behavior defined by the roles of dud and hero has an implication for the larger organization. The role of the dud defined the minimal performance standards of a member. Below those limits, his failure to perform involved a distortion of the functional integrity of the unit. The negative definition of the hero's role tended to discourage episodes of reckless, aggressive behavior which would exceed the support capability of the larger organization, and enabled it to function with predictable routines.

COMBAT ROLE MOTIVATION

Despite the defensive value system which they developed, the tendency to restrict the aggressive activities of one another and to deprecate the symbols of the organization, the fact remains that buddies performed their roles effectively. They might have talked about what they would do if one of them bugged out, but no one ever did. They endured life in this harsh and primitive environment. What made them do it?

There are three major explanations of the way men perform in combat roles.

The first asserts that their performance is motivated by identification with some formal symbols of a particular organization or its traditions. For these men, however, the Army began with their buddies and extended little farther than the platoon and company. Beyond these levels the organization was as meaningless as it was complex. Men from one company seldom made contacts with men from other companies—even other platoons of their own company—so that their uniqueness in terms of unit identifications rarely came into play.

It may be that at some remote point in history (a favorite explanation of military historians) this condition was different, especially when outfits had fewer members, and units bivouacked and fought in close proximity. Then men of one company became acquainted with men of another, and their membership in different units would be one of the distinctions they made. Even the men of this company, who expressed or displayed no identification with the regiment while with the company, would be heard boasting of their membership, wearing the regimentals, and using distinctive calls, while in the rear or in Japan at rest centers. But while actually in combat, at this time and place in the Korean Conflict, membership in a particular unit appeared to have little effect on combat performance.

A second explanation would contend that men behave in a particular way in combat to "live up" to the code of "being a man." In these terms the man most respected in combat was the one who typically acted independently, aggressively, and with great enthusiasm. The least masculine person would be totally dependent on his fellows and least likely to act independently or with initiative. But this conception of masculinity did not operate either. This is certainly not to say that buddies did not "act like men," but that they had a different conception of masculinity, developed under constant threat to their lives. They thought of the man who acted independently as one who could not be depended upon in a combat skirmish. The hero exposed others to unnecessary risk, thought of himself (if anyone) first, and his buddies second, and forgot that buddies must fight together or not at all.

A third explanation is in terms of abstract values or the symbols of the larger society, such as patriotism, the flag, or "our way of life." It may be true that these factors have some inspirational influence when used by themselves in attempts to motivate the combat soldier. But such values and symbols were never talked about directly nor were they used to account for the failures of some men to perform adequately. A man accepted his position in the outfit as a matter of fate—it was "the way the ball bounced"—rather than a citizen's duty.

There is one way in which this explanation may have even greater validity. We can say that an important motivating force in the combat role was the soldier's relationship to some meaningful element of the larger society, especially his family. Real and symbolic activities of the organization based on this relationship were effective. It was not enough that he heard about patriotism, the flag, and our way of life in the abstract and general way of indoctrination. He had to hear about them from persons who represented those values to him intimately, persons whose evaluations of his behavior as good or bad were of great significance to him.

THE PRIMARY GROUP AND COMBAT ROLES

These explanations all failed to identify personal relationships as having an independent significance in military organization. The point of departure was an assumption that all members of the organization shared the same norms and sentiments, a consistency attributed to habituation and leadership. However, following World War II, one military observer and sociologists, generally, accorded greater prominence to the significance of the primary group.

Marshall, a military historian, discerned a deviant pattern in the reluctance of riflemen to fire. From interviews with combat infantrymen assembled in rear areas after the event, he concluded that only 15 per cent of the participants in a combat event had fired their weapons at either enemy positions or personnel. He noted that the most active firers were usually in small groups working together. However, he attributed this deviance to personality characteristics rather than recognizing it as a normative standard of organized deviance.[4]

Stouffer and his colleagues in *The American Soldier* presented a systematic and extensive collection of studies of the attitudes of individuals representing the social relations and activities of many combat units.[5] The discrepancy between the sentiments of officers and enlisted men as status groups was thoroughly demonstrated, although an inadequate effort was made to analyze the social structure within which these attitudes were generated. The responses were also generalized over a period of time and not related to specific combat events. These studies represent an excellent general description of the military population of World War II and of their attitudes toward salient features of their experiences with military organization.

The function of the primary group under the stress of combat was more specifically defined by Shils and Janowitz in an analysis of the effects of Allied psychological warfare on the *Wehrmacht*. Continued effectiveness of the individual combat soldier was concluded to be a function of his immediate primary group, to the extent that it "met his basic needs, offered him affection and esteem from both officers and comrades, supplied him with a sense of power, and adequately regulated his relations with authority. . . ." The acceptance of secondary symbols was of significance only "to the extent that these secondary symbols became directly associated with primary gratifications." There was also recognition of the significance to the primary group of the continued functioning of top command and supply echelons.[6]

Popular literature of World War II also contained significant descriptions of primary group situations. Notable among these was the work of Mauldin, the cartoonist, whose characters, Willie and Joe, became stereotypes of the infantryman, as well as objects of identification. Prominent among the sentiments depicted was the mitigating effect that risk had on differences between status groups. Willie and Joe were consistently closer to their company commander than they were to their status peers at battalion headquarters.[7]

Thus at the beginning of the Korean Conflict the significance of the primary group for combat role motivation was well established. However, isolated from the relational context in which it developed, the conception of the primary group tends to be broad and undifferentiated. Within such a context, the term "buddy" has two levels of meaning. Specifically, it identifies interpersonal choices and primary group relationships. Generally, it describes status group peers in military organization. The conception of buddies as status group peers can be extended to an explanation of military organization as a social system.

SOLIDARITY AND THE SOCIAL SYSTEM

Buddy relationships were established and maintained within the context of military organization as a social system. In this system, one aspect—the chain of command or system of authority—was the primary point of reference. All important offices in the chain of command beyond the squad were occupied by officers; officers and authority being frequently thought of together. The chain of command is a system of positions, however, and the authority is in the position.

Thus only a person who had a command relationship with another "in the performance of duty" could legitimately require compliance with an order. An officer could not "prefer charges" against a subordinate who was not under his command. He could merely make a written complaint to the subordinate's commander, who would then decide whether an offense had been committed, and if so, administer the punishment or refer the complaint to a higher echelon for determination. A staff officer or a first sergeant had legitimate authority only insofar as it was derived from their commanding officers. Hence authority was an element of the position, not of the social rank of the person who occupied the position.

The chain of command is, however, a deceptively simple scheme of the operation of the company. Division of all members into two status groups, and the distribution of rank corresponding to position held, tended to reinforce the chain of command. Increasing the risk to which all members of the company were exposed weakened the chain of command.

The battlefield situation was the prototype relationship between officers and enlisted men throughout military organization. Dominating all else was the probability that in a combat event and as a result of the officer's command, some members of the formation would be killed or wounded. Second, in the intensive system of interpersonal relationships existing among those who moved out in the attack, was a potential for collective defiance of the task demanded by the organization. Third, there was the problem of adequate reward for those who conformed and moved forward in the assault. Survival, the greatest reward, was a chance of the situation rather than something to be dispensed by the commander. The organization could offer nothing more than symbols of compliance in the form of decorations for valor.

The platoon leader occupied the lowest position of all officers in the chain of command. As the degree of risk increased, the intensity and frequency of the platoon leader's interaction with enlisted men increased, and, correspondingly, significant interaction with status peers decreased. The more he participated in their activities, the more he tended to share the sentiments of the men he commanded, and his willingness to use the sanctions available to him diminished correspondingly.

Yet the situations in which his authority was required were more crucial than those encountered by commanders at higher echelons. First, the chances were greater that the men he commanded would deviate from his orders because the risks of compliance were greater. Second, he was intimately associated with the men he commanded. Third, the sanctions at his disposal were of no immediate value if defiance occurred in the assault. The rifleman who refused to advance could only be punished by repeated threats of sanctions to be imposed when the battle was over.[8]

Besides these problems in using authority, the commander had to make punishment appear more unpleasant than the risks of combat. For a rifleman, tried by a Summary or Special Court Martial, only a fine would have been a penalty. If there was a sentence of confinement, the offender would be transferred to a rear echelon stockade to serve out his sentence, and this would be a reward rather than a penalty. The result was to make sanctions and courts martial more effective in prospect than in deed.

Authority was thus likely to fail if used alone. It worked only because it was supported by "manipulations:" indirect or symbolic acts which induced implicitly the desired behavior.[9] Such acts had the objective of creating a condition of generalized individual compliance with the ideals of the organization. They may have taken the form of an elaborate ritual such as a parade. They may have been as subtle as occasional breaches in the rigid limits of the social order by visits to the sick, or informal welfare inquiries while on formal inspection tours. They might have been as pointed as the presentation of an award for an exceptionally aggressive action, or for a wound incurred in the organization's battle.

The elaborate system of regulations and conventions applicable to officers as a status group functioned as a resource for manipulation. We have mentioned that authority was invested in positions, not in the status group attributes of the occupants. However, the association between status group membership and degree of authority was reinforced by permitting only officers to occupy significant positions in the chain of command. Thus even if a platoon had no officer, the platoon sergeant could not be the platoon leader unless he was made an officer. If there were no officers in the company, the first sergeant would command but he would not be the company commander. Hence there was a consistent relationship between the authority of these positions and their monopolization by officers as a status group.

There were procedures to ensure that the officer viewed himself—and was perceived by enlisted men—as having a relatively greater investment in the larger organization than in his platoon and the men with whom he lived. These procedures began when he arrived in the Division and continued until he reached his platoon. At each echelon he was introduced to his superior commanders personally and indoctrinated with the values of the organizational level through which he was passing. Even while isolated from his peers and living on the line with his platoon, the protocol of inspections maintained his identification with the larger organization.

When officers were together, as in the reserve period, their sentiments were the ideals of the organization. They were more intimately involved in the ceremonial activity of the organization, referring often to the traditions or abstract symbols of the organization. Technical competence was identified with status group solidarity. Initiative, aggressiveness, and tactical proficiency were the attributes they used in evaluating one another and the enlisted men.

The effect of continued solidarity with the superior status group was to develop in the officer a conception of himself as having "status potency," that is, the capacity to induce compliance by virtue of his status group affiliation alone. Although officers were provided with the right to invoke more severe sanctions than noncommissioned officers, ideally the "good officer" (among officers) was one who could get results without employing any sanctions. So long as his status potency was recognized he was seldom required to administer punishment.

When status potency failed and sanctions were required, he was sensitive to the evaluations of his status group peers. So long as he could contain the offense and punishment to his own unit, the apparent loss of his status potency was not recognized. Serious offenses, however, required that he relinquish his responsibility to a higher echelon. The subsequent trial procedure entailed an investigation by colleagues and a consequent evaluation of the effectiveness of his status attributes. Status potency and attempts to maintain the image of the good officer thus tended to mitigate the use of the sanctions actually available.

The mobility pattern among officers also fostered identification with the larger organization, for they rarely remained in the rifle company throughout their tour of duty in Korea. Enlisted men usually remained in their initial assignment and rarely moved to positions of less risk except within the company. Officers were initially assigned to a rifle platoon, then moved to the weapons platoon, where they did not have to lead patrols. The next step was to company executive officer and the management of supply and administration. One officer might become company commander, but the others would probably move to a staff position or service unit to complete their tours.

The battlefield situation itself often provided a manipulative resource in the form of the "status legend," an exaggerated descriptive narrative of a combat experience, varying according to the status vantage point of the observer. Status legends were confined to battalion or more remote commanders. The legend originated in a context of ambiguous feelings toward the commander, then an event occurred that structured the men's attitudes toward the commander even though he might not have recognized the event as important. His behavior during the event was subsequently evaluated and elaborated by persons at varying status levels. Thus formulated, the story was passed on from oldtimer to replacement, becoming a durable element in the sentiments of the unit, surviving long after the commander's departure and the membership of the unit had changed completely.

Positive status legends often referred to the commander's democratic eccentricities, his concern for human life, or his tolerance of deviations from the policies of the larger organization. Such positive legends assured the commander of warm, affectionate responses and willing cooperation from his subordinates. Other legends, however, tended to create an aura in which the commander's every step was critically and negatively evaluated. Whether positive or negative, the status legend expressed the troops' conception of their commander in battle, in an extension of behavior expected in his position.

The differentiation of officers as a status group was the organizational response to a problem of control. In the rifle platoon—the point at which control was crucial—there was a tendency for the effectiveness of specific sanctions to be dissipated. The willingness of officers to use the sanctions available to them was compromised by their solidarity with the men under their command. Traditions and procedures which reinforced the officer's solidarity with other officers ensured his fidelity to the norms of the larger organization.

Rank and Authority

Within the chain of command the relative importance of each position was indicated by the rank stipulated for the position. Thus each squad leader should have been a sergeant, the platoon sergeant a master sergeant, and the company commander a captain. Rank also carried perquisites as rewards for the persons who occupied such positions to ensure their fidelity to the organization at a cost of increasing the social distance between themselves and men with relatively less rank.

The lowest position in the chain of command was the squad leader. His fidelity, like that of the platoon leader, had to be maintained; but unlike the platoon leader, he was an enlisted man. At this time, in Korea, squad leaders did not have enough rank to differentiate them from other members of the squad. There were time-in-grade requirements which few men were able to meet before they rotated. Occasionally men with the stipulated grade but without combat experience came in as replacements and were assigned as squad leaders. Then the acting squad leader was "bumped" and had to move down a notch as did everyone else in the squad. The effect was to reduce the significance of formal social ranking within the squad and platoon, and to increase the informal importance of seniority.

Many men were reluctant to accept positions of increased authority when they knew that the organization could not give them rank with the positions. The prospect that an acting squad leader would be "bumped" by a replacement squad leader also limited his effectiveness in the role. An acting leader's relationships with his peers was always threatened when he attempted to exert the authority of the position without the corresponding rank. Hence few men were motivated to move up to higher positions when mobility involved little probability of reward but almost certainly the weakening of relationships with the peers to whom they might be compelled to return.

The uncertainty of rank tended to exaggerate the significance of the position held within the squad. Although the rank for the job might not be available, the job had to be done. In the order of rank formally prescribed by the organization the squad leader was followed by his assistant, then in descending order, the automatic rifleman and his assistant, and six riflemen. But members of the squad thought of this sequence as indicating the order of seniority and the mobility pattern within the squad rather than a hierarchy of rank or skill.

Although the grade did not "count for much" in the platoon or company, it was expected to be a source of prestige in the larger society, through the family and the work group. Promotion disappointment became increasingly severe as the rotation date approached. The rank held at discharge was expected to affect civilian employment opportunities. Men who had been performing in a higher position had frequently written letters to family and friends, describing their responsibilities and mentioning the stipulated rank as a measure of the importance of their positions. Some received letters addressed to them in the grade of the position to which they had been temporarily assigned. Their apprehension was expressed as an expectation that, if one should return home as a private, "they'll think that I've been giving them a line all the time."

Among officers rank was as uncertain as it was for enlisted men. Although the stipulated rank for the position of company commander was that of captain, in this company the commander was a first lieutenant. The only requirement for promotion to first lieutenant was eighteen months in the grade of second lieutenant. Officers were distinguished not by their relative rank, which was not so different, but the positions they held. When this company commander left the company area and the persons who identified him with his position, he was recognized only by the insignia of his rank, which was that of a very junior member of his status group. The mobility pattern among officers also tended to emphasize positions rather than rank. Just as the arrival of a new man in the platoon initiated a process of mobility, the assignment of a new officer to the regiment made it possible for a company commander or a senior platoon leader to move to battalion or regimental headquarters, as the new officer was assigned to the lowest vacancy created.

In summary, because rank so rarely corresponded with the position for which it was stipulated, it became a random factor and position was correspondingly exaggerated in significance. Authority appeared to be derived exclusively from the position occupied rather than supported by the rank of the occupant which contributed to a further deterioration in the significance of rank.

Risk, Reserve, and Ritual

The location of the rifle platoon and company in relation to the larger organization fostered the development of a defensive value system. Spatially, they were exposed to maximum risk. Socially, they were the ultimate recipients of most orders issued by higher echelons. Their value system was defensive in the sense that most of the norms that could be articulated justified resistance to the demands of the organization. Their norms tended to discourage the aggressive kind of behavior that was the ideal of the organization, and deprecated the symbols that the organization bestowed to reward such behavior. Thus united, members of the platoon comprised a group with a potential for collective action independent of orders given by the designated leaders of the chain of command.

The longer a unit was "on the line" directly confronting the enemy, the more intensive their relationship became, and the more their behavior deviated from the norms of the organization. Even the officers who lived with their platoons tended to think like their men, and to minimize their own contacts with higher echelons. Relations between the company commander and the platoon leaders became increasingly contentious. The probable response of the latter in executing orders in situations involving great risk was accordingly uncertain.

When an organization reached this stage, it was described as having "low morale" and withdrawn into reserve for "retraining." This is not to say that the senior commander would withdraw a unit for this reason, but that such conditions were usually present at the time the unit was withdrawn. The relief of a unit depended on many other factors, including the very practical one of having another unit in reserve to replace the unit withdrawn.

The reserve situation was a time for maximum impact from the larger organization with all members in range of continuous surveillance by the company and senior commanders. They were far enough away from combat to line up in parade formations, in the ideal shape of the Table of

Organization. Dwelling arrangements were such that men lived together as squads or platoons, rather than as *ad hoc* formations determined by the size of the "living bunker" on the line. The officers lived together as a group rather than sharing bunkers with the men of their platoons, as they had done on the line.

Administrative activity predominated through the day. Property shortages were accounted for, replacements received and assigned. Improvised personnel situations which had been kept loose and flexible on the line were now brought up for reconsideration and if affirmed, became solid arrangements. A training program was carried on which stressed adherence to correct tactical doctrine as compared to improvised solutions to real combat events mentioned by members of the unit.

Withdrawal to reserve also limited the commander's range of judgment. On the line, the commander was relatively isolated from control by the larger organization. He was expected to make decisions in terms of his personal judgment, without reference to the higher echelon. Since he controlled the channels of communication to other units and echelons, negative information about his decisions could be effectively contained. But in reserve, as in garrison, units were in close and constant contact with each other. A decision by one commander with respect to a particular form of delinquency immediately became a factor in his evaluation by superiors and status peers. Accordingly, his area of discretion was sharply reduced.

This spatial arrangement enabled the next higher echelon to impose on the company a condition of "command saturation." The shortened lines of communication permitted more detailed stipulation of organizational activities in the form of standard operating procedures, routine compliance reports, and official policies. In the place of the environment of creative freedom existing on the line, the commander was now required to become a manager, executing in mechanical routine the decisions originally formulated by higher echelons. His competence here was evaluated in terms of his knowledge of a large number of routine operations and gimmicks, and a general avoidance of ambiguous situations in which the rules could not be applied.

In this environment a ceremonial combat emerged in the form of the garrison *contest*. The norms guiding competing commanders were derived from real combat situations, and the ideals of the organization remained those of the combat crisis. But the measures of achievement were the only ones available in the reserve location. Two or more commanders were confronted with an opportunity to be comparatively evaluated by a higher commander. Extraordinary judgment or effort, analogous to their behavior in a combat crisis, was presumed necessary to excel other commanders. Members of the unit, in turn, had to be induced by persuasive techniques to provide the commander with material that could be used as measures of competence. The situations utilized for the contest were typically those in which only manipulative techniques were appropriate, such as athletic events or contributions to charities.

Each subordinate commander assumed that a relative superiority in the outcome of the contest would be evaluated by the higher commander as evidence of greater competence in inducing collective effort among the members of his unit, although such an assumption was rarely stated explicitly. The event was represented to members of the unit as an opportunity to demonstrate collective superiority over competing units. Since the subordinate commander represented his unit to superior commanders, the collective achievements of the unit became a measure of the competence of the subordinate commander.

The move from positions on the line to the reserve location was accompanied by a shift from instrumental to expressive or ceremonial activities. An awareness of their relationship to combat activity was maintained only by such rituals as the parade formation, while actual experiences in combat were evaluated as good or bad in terms of the degree to which they coincided with tactical doctrine. The intensity of interpersonal relationships declined with the removal of risk and the need for mutual dependency, and because of transfers within the company. The solidarity of the company as a whole declined when they lost their identity and distinctive activity by merger with the larger organization.

Solidarity and the Larger Organization

Contacts between the company and higher echelons were intensified in the reserve location, but even on the line the company was almost completely dependent on the larger organization for supplies. The sentiments regulating the use and disposal of supplies or "property" differentiated between the company as a component unit and as a social system.

The organization itself provided two kinds of supplies: those which were used up rapidly ("expendable") such as food and fuel, and those used by a succession of persons, such as weapons and vehicles. The second type, referred to as "property," was strongly identified with authority, in the sense that it belonged to the organization and was only "lent" to the person using it. This identification was fostered by making the commander personally responsible when property was lost or damaged. Officers were graded on efficiency reports in terms of their "cost consciousness."

When some items of property could not be accounted for, the responsible officer had two possible courses of action. First, he could attribute the loss to the negligence of the user and require that the cost of the item be deducted from the enlisted man's pay. The advantage of this method was that the "Statement of Charges" did not pass through command channels. After signature by the man admitting responsibility for the loss, it was merely forwarded to the personnel officer at the division rear echelon where the necessary action was taken. Second, the responsible officer could originate a "Report of Survey." Such action ordinarily used for major expensive items, or when individual responsibility could not be fixed, indicated that the loss was attributed to combat action or other "fair wear and tear."

The Report of Survey was a last resort, however, because it passed through command channels, involving an investigation by an officer from a higher headquarters and an explicit evaluation of the responsible officer's behavior in relation to property. Usually the investigating officer determined that the property was lost without negligence. The company commander was then excused from responsibility and replacement items issued. Less frequently but always possibly, the company commander could be found responsible because of the inadequate supervision of supply accounts, lack of good judgment in property utilization, or "poor leadership," because men had abandoned their equipment wantonly. Thus the Report of Survey was a risky venture in relation to the larger organization. The objective became one of minimizing deficiencies in supply accounts, not because this was in conformity with the organization's ideals, but because it reduced the chances of involvement with the next higher echelon.

The enlisted man primarily responsible for property within the company was the supply sergeant. He was the only person who left the company area frequently, meeting supply sergeants of other companies at supply points and depots. These colleagues were united by a system of "scrounging." Whenever the company moved into a new area, items abandoned by the previous unit were recovered and turned into the supply room. In traveling from one unit to another he found other apparently discarded or carelessly guarded equipment. When a property discrepancy developed in his own company, he had a "barter bank" with which to approach the supply sergeants of other units.

"Scrounging" was illegal. It violated procedures stipulated by the organization for revealing discrepancies and for disposing of surpluses.

It protected supply sergeants as colleagues from having to reveal a shortage to their company commanders. Since the exchanges always took place between supply sergeants as enlisted men, the chain of command was not involved. However, company commanders tolerated and often encouraged scrounging because it was a simple way to keep the supply accounts in good condition for inspections by higher echelons and reduced the need for initiating Reports of Survey.

There was a contrasting set of attitudes toward "personal property." The contrast originated in the fact that organization property was identified with the chain of command and could be "shared" only in a very formal sense. The physical environment of the company on the line, dominated by proximity to enemy observation and fire, necessarily limited the amounts and kinds of personal possessions that could be retained. There were few sources for such goods with no post exchange or native store regularly available. New items of a personal nature could be obtained only from home, or by bringing them back from Japan.

Formal rules against theft of personal property were reinforced by an elaborate system of attitudes regulating the use and disposal of all such possessions regardless of their value. These items either had to be carried by the owner, or left unguarded in his bunker. The only protection for such property was the honor of every person who had access to it.

Opposed to this conception of personal property, however, was the norm of "sharing," generated in a bleak environment where possessions were scarce. Packages from home derived their unique significance from the fact that they were so easily shared. Packages symbolized all personal property and formed the basis for the development of a ritual relating it to the combat situation.

For example, one man said:

> If a guy didn't share, maybe some day he'd be in a tough spot and the buddy would remember it and think about when you didn't make an offer. You don't always have a chance to do a favor in combat, but if you share everything, you can be pretty sure that your buddy will remember it if you need help.

Another man, who had been identified by others as a "dud," said:

> Even though a guy has been treating you pretty rough, he'll offer you something from his package and it helps you to forget what he said about you. Just like at home, you'd try to make up with a guy by buying him a beer. When you pass a package around you show that everyone is your buddy.

The discrimination between organization and personal property reflected a differentiation between the chain of command and the system of buddy relations. Organization property was considered an aspect of the authority system which could be manipulated to defend the company from intervention by higher echelons. Personal property was associated with the norm of sharing and strengthened the system of interpersonal relationships.

SOLIDARITY AND MILITARY EFFECTIVENESS

What was the relationship between solidarity and military effectiveness?

The primary basis for solidarity in the platoon and company was the recognition of mutual risk. A set of norms so regulated their behavior as to minimize that risk. On this basis buddy relationships were established and maintained. The effectiveness of the sanctions available to the chain of command depended on their meaning in a context of risk. Officers as a status group maintained their independence insofar as they could remove or protect themselves from the consensus induced by mutual risk.

Traditional explanations which neglected the significance of risk were examined. Thus individual identification with the larger unit did not appear to enhance effectiveness because there was little awareness of the existence of such a relationship. Nor was effectiveness increased by peer emulation of persons who had received awards for conforming to organizational ideals. Such attributes of masculinity as aggressiveness and initiative also appeared to have minimal influence on effectiveness.

At this point it would appear that solidarity and the effectiveness demanded by the organization were not compatible. There were, however, some aspects of solidarity which converged with the objectives of the organization and promoted effectiveness.

First, the organization permitted the norms of the buddy system to define the limits of effectiveness. The minimum contribution was that which fell below the standards exemplified by the dud. The maximum effort was that of and beyond the actions of the hero. Within this range of expected behavior, the larger organization was able to function within predictable limits.

Second, events which reinforced the soldier's relationship to some meaningful element of the larger society—especially his family—correspondingly strengthened his relationship to the organization. In a sense, the infantryman communicated with his family through the organization. The symbols understood by the family were those of the organization (such as rank), not of the buddy system. The organization also provided symbolic evidence of the soldier's career in the unit, factors which would be of greater significance to his peers in the larger society than among his buddies in the organization.

This may be one reason that "mail call" is of such critical importance in combat, and to a lesser extent, in military service generally. Letters represent the soldier's major contact with the social unit that reinforces his desire to serve faithfully and under great hardship. The conception of his role as a citizen of a community or member of a family was influenced by the letters written him by persons whose evaluations of him were very important, or by the clippings they enclosed with their letters. When the time for rotation approached and he anticipated the reaction of his family and civilian friends, he became increasingly aware of the symbols that he had previously deprecated with his peers.

Third, status group solidarity enabled the organization to maintain control at the level of greatest risk: the rifle platoon. On the line, officers were isolated from their status peers. When sharing the risks and hardships of their men they tended to develop solidarity with them and to support deviations from the norms of the larger organization, although their ultimate loyalty to the organization was effectively maintained. Technical competence as commanders was identified with status group solidarity. Concrete and ceremonial evidence of their affiliation with the organization as a whole was continuously provided. Since the duration of their exposure was limited, acts of valor and dedication to the ideals of the organization could be expected to enhance their chances of moving to positions of less risk.

THE KOREAN CONFLICT AND LIMITED WAR

The Korean Conflict had four characteristics which might be expected to recur in a situation of limited war; the effects of induction and personnel assignment policies, the compact age distribution, individual personnel rotation, and the use of native troops as "fillers" in American platoons.

Effects of Induction and Personnel Assignment Policies

Induction and enlistment quotas were filled primarily with men recently graduated from high school, rather than from an age-diversified manpower pool. Since the available manpower far exceeded the demand for replacements, occupational and educational deferments were relatively easy to obtain, as individuals or as categories. Among the select group who were ultimately inducted or enlisted, personnel assignment policies introduced an additional screening effect which tended to make echelon populations resemble social classes in the larger society. Persons with highly specialized and consequently scarce skills were assigned to echelons of minimal chance of their loss to the organization. Men assigned to the rifle company were most likely to lack highly valued social attributes (usually associated with educational experience), a deficit which often reflected their original position in the larger society.[10] This provided another potential basis for consensus and solidarity in the combat situation.

Compact Distribution

The relative youth of the population resulted in a homogeneity of attitude and behavior which might have differed if each platoon had included an age distribution comparable to World War II combat units. The emergence of the term "bug out" during this period is probably a reflection of a subculture of late adolescence. Similarly, the norm of minimizing risk may have been an analogue of "playing it cool." In future situations it may be expected that the norms of the predominant age group of recruits will have a significant effect on the social system of combat units.

An extremely youthful population has another implication for the stability of the organization. There were fewer members engaged in the Korean Conflict than in World War II who had prior experience in civilian leadership roles. There was also a corresponding lack of awareness of affiliation with reference groups in the larger society, other than the family, and a lack of mature role models with whom younger troops might identify.

Personnel Rotation

Individual personnel rotation provided each man with an easily calculated terminal point in his combat exposure. In the absence of explicit national goals—for example, "Victory" in World War II—such a policy was probably essential. It also facilitated the adjustment of replacements because there was rarely much discrepancy in seniority between "old men" and "new men." In the platoon which the author observed, the senior men had been assigned nine months earlier, the three junior men within the month that his observation of them began. At that time, only one-third of the men had been with the platoon more than four months.

Socially the policy was ineffective and disruptive. The risks of combat were not spread more extensively through the society because the policy required only the induction and exposure to combat of a relatively larger number of men with the same social attributes. Personnel with the initial fortune of being assigned to rear echelons remained longer but remained in place, without the expectation comparable to World War II of being levied as replacements for infantry units. Within infantry units the policy resulted in the continued presence of men who were to a large extent "new men" in the process of being tested for membership.

Use of Native Troops as "Fillers" in American Platoons

The use of native troops created a situation in which American units often appeared to be cadres of native soldiers through which Americans rotated rapidly.[11] Since the policy of rotation was not applicable to them, the ROKs stayed longer. Although none held leadership positions, the ROKs were the "old men" of the outfit. Had they been able to communicate, they would have been a significant element in the social system of the organization. Reports of their greater passivity in combat might have been a reflection of a relatively advanced adaptation to the norms of the combat situation.

CONCLUSION

Buddy relationships were the basic element of infantry social organization in the Korean Conflict. As the first major American experience in limited warfare, it has predictive value for future situations in which infantry is employed, for this type of military engagement has unique characteristics which fall most heavily on infantry units. "Limited" warfare implies that the survival of the society is not immediately threatened, and accordingly only a fraction of the available resources, including men, must be committed. Yet ideals must be formulated for which some few men will be willing to make a total sacrifice. With the manpower pool supporting the conflict far exceeding the demand for replacements, there are relatively fewer who must bear the battle, and correspondingly less motivational support from the larger society.

Combat situations in conditions of limited war will have many of the characteristics of the reserve location or garrison. Each engagement will be brief and require the commitment of only a small fraction of the available forces at any one point in time. However, the time span in which these engagements occur will be protracted, generating new problems for military organization. Anticipation of risk will be a more prominent consideration than actual risk resulting from participation in an active exchange of hostilities. During these prolonged expectant intervals, continuous training will be conducted to maintain a high state of readiness.

Such conditions tend to invert the usual ratio of combat units committed to those in reserve or not committed. We have noted that the transition from combat to reserve had two principal effects. First, the decline in actual risk encountered was accompanied by a corresponding deterioration in mutual dependency among buddies. Second, the standardization of activities under conditions of command saturation assimilated the identity of the smaller unit into that of the larger. Consequently, there was more acceptance of the norms of the larger organization and less resistance to activities demanded by it.

Thus major changes may be expected in contemporary leadership values. Combat situations and involvement with an external "enemy" will provide an infrequent and unreliable basis for symbolic recognition. New types of rewards must be developed, based on achievements within the organization. The subsequent allocation of such rewards will generate internal activities like those of the garrison contest in which simulated, symbolic, and group-based techniques are the only appropriate means for inducing collective effort.

NOTES

1. Little, R. W., "Collective Solidarity and Combat Role Performance." Unpublished Ph.D. dissertation, Michigan State University, 1955.

2. Appleman, R. E., *South to the Naktong, North to the Yalu: U. S. Army in the Korean War*. Office of the Chief of Military History, Department of the Army, Washington, 1960, pp. 385–389.

3. A valorous act and an award for the act were separated by an administrative process which often appeared arbitrary. First, getting an award was dependent on being "put in" for it by the company commander, usually at the suggestion of the platoon leader. Hence, whether or not the act was recognized by the organization depended on whether it was defined by someone in the chain of command as exceptional behavior. The intervening administrative process often discouraged the submission of names for awards. Second, quotas of awards were often allocated by the organization for the purpose of stimulating the recognition of valor. However, the quota system resulted in a monthly redefinition of valor. When such awards were presented in ceremonies they were described as being "handed out" with the implication that it was a routine distribution.

4. Marshall, S. L. A., *Men Against Fire*. William Morrow and Co., New York, 1947, especially pp. 54–56. Marshall does not take into consideration two factors that could be of major practical significance in restricted firing behavior. First, the conditioning effect of marksmanship training, with emphasis on hitting a specific target with a limited number of rounds (cartridges). Second, the problem of am-

munition resupply in an attack. Rounds expended can only be replaced by personnel who move out of dug-in defensive positions, or by risking the chance that ammunition bearers will not catch up with the assault.

5. Stouffer, Samuel A., and others. *The American Soldier: Studies in Social Psychology in World War II.* Princeton University Press, Princeton, N. J., 1949.

6. Shils, Edward A., and Morris Janowitz, "Cohesion and Disintegration in the Wehrmacht in World War II," *Public Opinion Quarterly,* vol. 12, Summer, 1948, pp. 280–315.

7. Mauldin, Bill, *Up Front.* Henry Holt and Co., New York, 1945.

8. Collective defiance most often occurs in combat as a passive refusal to move. It is legitimated when the organization describes a unit as being "pinned down." At this point the organization recognizes a collective definition of the probability of survival as being less than the chances of death and wounding, and the futility of invoking sanctions.

9. Janowitz, Morris, "Changing Patterns of Organizational Authority: The Military Establishment," *Administrative Science Quarterly,* vol. 3, March, 1959, pp. 473–493.

10. Mayer, A. J., and T. F. Hoult, "Social Stratification and Combat Survival," *Social Forces,* vol. 34, December, 1955, pp. 155–159.

11. Two other types of native personnel were less frequently encountered. Elements of the Korean Service Corps, a noncombatant branch of the Korean Army, were often assigned to labor details in the company area. They did not become integral members of the American units as the ROKs did. There were also native civilian laborers, employed by the company as mess attendants and paid by voluntary contributions. Because they wore discarded combat uniforms, they were often mistaken for ROK soldiers.

DETERIORATION OF MILITARY WORK GROUPS UNDER DEPRIVATION STRESS*

Richard W. Seaton

The interior of Greenland today is simply an elevated, unbroken plateau of snow, lifted from five thousand to eight thousand and even ten thousand feet above the level of the sea; a huge white glistening shield some twelve hundred miles in length and five hundred miles in width, resting on the supporting mountains. It is an Arctic Sahara, in comparison with which the African Sahara is insignificant. For on this frozen Sahara of inner Greenland occurs no form of life, animal or vegetable; no fragment of rock, no grain of sand is visible. The traveler across its frozen wastes . . . sees, outside of himself, and his own party, but three things in all the world; namely, the infinite expanse of the frozen plain, the infinite dome of the cold blue sky, and the cold white sun— nothing but these. The traveler, too, across this frozen desert knows that at no time during his journey are the highest rocks of the mountain summits below him nearer than from one thousand to five thousand feet down through the mighty blanket of snow. Such is the interior of Greenland. . . .[1]

MODERN TRANSPORTATION has opened the polar regions to the military as potential areas of operations. There is probably no other part of the earth where men and equipment are tested by such extremes of climate and terrain. In military doctrine small units continue to form basic task groups in northern latitudes, and these units should have capacity for dismounted movement. In order to collect data on human performance in the polar regions under conditions of limited supply, the U.S. Army Quartermaster Corps studied the consequence of the under-feeding of work teams in the Arctic during the summer of 1960.

* This paper is based on research conducted by the U.S. Army Quartermaster Research and Engineering Command, Natick, Massachusetts, under Polar Project 60-1. The basic data and methodological basis of analysis are to be found in a report of the Quartermaster Food and Container Institute for the Armed Forces, *Hunger in Groups: An Arctic Experiment*, Quartermaster Research and Engineering Command, 1962 (QMCIAF Report No. 34–62). The viewpoints reported are solely those of the author and are not to be construed as reflecting policy or conclusions of the Department of the Army.

The aims of the test were fourfold. The first was to obtain physiological measures of men performing hard work under conditions of undersupply. The second aim was quantitative investigation of the subjective feelings frequently reported by men who have undergone underfeeding in survival situations. The third goal, which is the concern of this report, was to determine how tasks and the stress of deprivation affect the social behavior of working groups.

A fourth aim was satisfaction of curiosity. In everyday life, groups are rarely as arbitrarily formed, as isolated, and as constrained as those in the Greenland experiment. These experimental groups were *rarae aves*, such as one might encounter on life rafts at sea, in POW camps, or among guerrillas. Opportunity to see how they developed and maintained social characteristics in the face of hard work and hunger was intriguing to the civilian scientists charged with the conduct of the experiment.

EXPECTATIONS

The literature on polar regions includes many informal accounts of the stress of deprivation.[2] These are supplemented by accounts of stress in other settings, for example, in concentration camps.[3] However, little experimental evidence has as yet been accumulated on the social-psychological effects of deprivation stress on working groups of men.[4] Some survivors of deprivation conditions have reported sexual fantasy, chilling, irritability, or *anomie*, as personal feelings accompanying food shortage, while others have not mentioned these reactions. Social conditions in working groups have been observed to change when they are subjected to external stress, and these changes have been confirmed by Torrance in his studies of simulated survival groups.[5] But the effects of different kinds of stress—(1) uncertainty, (2) task, (3) deprivation, or (4) threat—have not been experimentally established.

One model of group response to stress can be thought of as an adaptation syndrome. An increment in external demand or a threat against a collective resource mobilizes available resources and increases structural differentiation in the group.[6] This may be done at the cost of not fully meeting other normal maintenance requirements in the group. If adequate progress is made in achieving work goals or reducing threat, activity can return to supportive functions and the capacity of the group to satisfy the requirements of its members is enhanced. If the increase in external demand stress is large or if support activities must be deferred for a long time, some change in existing structure and organization may be necessary before an equilibrium is reestablished. Old obligations are dropped in favor of more pressing needs of members or requirements of external press. This enforced flexibility of organization may weaken the original formal structure, which thus may be retained only in part after the release from stress.[7]

Accordingly, from this point of view, given the onset of stress from task demands, groups can usually mobilize protective resources via (1) restricting and reordering of communication, (2) reaffirming formal power, (3) display of affect and socioemotional support for members engaged in task performance, and (4) reassertion of group goals. Minor adaptations of this variety are ever present in ongoing working groups[8] and the consequence may even be to increase group cohesion.

But the social effects of uncertainty or threat stress may be different according to a second model. Uncertainty or threat imposed on individuals, especially when differentially imposed, can reduce the willingness of members to be concerned about or to contribute to group tasks and supportive functions. Unless threat against individuals is perceived as soluble by group efforts, it induces a decline in the group's ability to mobilize its resources. Group integration decreases even while the task structure and organization of the group may remain ostensibly stable. Members may need support from their group but they are too pressed by their own worries to reciprocate support. Since group membership becomes less satisfying, affect declines and hostility may increase. Membership being less valued, members may attempt to leave, thereby further weakening the group.

Food deprivation of individuals should operate the same way in groups as does threat against individuals, except that since the need is real rather than potential, its impact enhances members' self-concern at greater cost to concern about group action. Subjective consequences of hunger, such as irritability and weakness, will also contribute to the weakening of group access to resources of its members. Irritability implies that social exchange has potential negative consequences; subjective weakness means that even if group members are pressured to contribute to group ends, they will feel they can afford to give only a little energy because they have little to give.[9] Like disease, hunger should be a stress most conducive to attrition of social units. Group punishments for deviant, selfish, or inadequate behavior are likely to be of little avail on tired, miserable men, and even application of sanctions requires energy which members may not be willing to supply. No matter how well structured, or how adaptable, a group faced with hunger stress is presumably threatened with disintegration.

THE EXPERIMENTAL PLAN

a. Design

The field experiment consisted of two cycles or repetitions which partly duplicated each other. Each cycle had two test periods, or phases. In each cycle four small teams each of five men were established. Each cycle began with members of the teams becoming accustomed to living and working with co-members during a preliminary control stage. Before and during the control stage of the first cycle, the work consisted of learning how to camp on the Greenland icecap and how to march on snowshoes with field equipment. In the control stage of the second cycle, subjects were already acclimated to icecap treks, however, team membership was shuffled and time allowed for members of the resulting new teams to become accustomed to one another.

In the first experimental phase of each cycle, a ten-day cross-country trek was begun. On this trip, two of the four five-man teams were on full rations, which meant they could eat approximately 4,800 calories daily if they wished. The other two groups were restricted to half this amount. Within these two ration levels, one team had the more difficult task of carrying personal gear in rucksacks on their backs with only team living equipment (tent, stove, and so on) on the two sleds they pulled; the other team with the easier task carried no personal equipment but instead piled all gear on their two sleds while marching. During the first five-day phase of either cycle, all teams were marching outbound from their base camp, moving roughly abreast beside a marked trail over the icecap leading to the coast. A wagon train housing observers and administrative personnel moved parallel with them. At the end of the first ("outbound") phase of either cycle the teams reversed direction and marched back to the base camp. At the same time, teams switched methods by which they transported personal gear and equipment, teams first carrying personal gear on their backs now carrying it on sleds, and vice versa for those who started out with gear on sleds.

The second cycle, beginning shortly after return to base camp at the end of the first ten-day trek, started with a trading of team member subgroups between the two teams which had been on low rations, paralleled by a comparable trading of members among the two teams which had been on full rations. Once again a five-day control stage of exercises around the base camp began, to enable the groups to become physiologically comparable and socially stabilized. Then a second ten-day trek began, this time with groups previously on full rations now on half-rations, and vice versa. The same switch-around of team transport methods took place midway on this trek as on the first one.

Thus two specific kinds of stress were independently varied within the generally unhappy context of man-hauling in the Arctic. The first was a deprivation stress, involving underfeeding of subjects. The daily deficit imposed was measured by comparing the number of calories consumed daily by subjects on limited rations with calories consumed by full-fed subjects doing the same work. The underfed subjects consumed practically all of the 2,400 calories issued daily, while full-fed subjects consumed about 1,500 calories more (a total of 3,900 calories). Full-fed subjects did not gain weight on this diet, while underfed subjects lost weight at a rate of about a half-pound daily, which is to be expected on a 1,500 calorie daily deficit.

The second major independent variable was task difficulty, as determined by method of carrying rucksacks on backs or sleds. By means of respirometers worn by the subjects at certain periods while marching, a measure was taken of the difference in energy demands of the two pack-carrying methods. The difference was slight. Over a six-hour man-hauling day a 170-pound subject would expend only about 150 calories of additional energy using the more difficult pack-carrying method. This is only a 4 per cent differential in terms of the 3,900 calorie daily expenditure estimated for these subjects.

Two other variables were artifacts of the experimental circumstances. These were time within cycles, and time between cycles. Time within cycles was divided into two phases. The prevailing wind made the second phase in each cycle more difficult; accumulated fatigue also produced added strain. On the other hand, the second ten-day cycle was easier than the first, both because subjects were more acclimated and because the weather took an exceptionally favorable turn.

b. Procedure

Twenty soldiers from the U.S. Army Quartermaster Field Evaluation Agency at Fort Lee, Virginia, were selected as participants. The men were not volunteers and took part in subsequent strenuous test activities as soldiers under military orders; nor were they specially selected for competence, experience, or interest in Arctic work. Their average age was twenty and typically they had about one year's Army experience. During Virginia's June heat, they were trained in the rudiments of living and moving about on snow and ice with various kinds of equipment; then they were flown to the coast of Greenland, equipped with Arctic gear and transported by wanigan train 180 miles inland and 7,000 feet up on the interior of the icecap. Since the wanigan train averaged about two miles per hour, the trip inland to an under-ice military base (Camp Fistclench) took about five days.

Following a week's orientation, acclimation and training, the four teams of five men each moved out for ten-day periods to bivouac on the icecap at night. From Camp Fistclench they progressed at a rate of eight miles a day toward Camp Century, an under-ice installation about 100 miles from the edge of the icecap at an elevation of 6,000 feet. On the sixth day of this downhill leg, they turned about and backtracked uphill for five days to Camp Fistclench.

Between the two camps there is a sledging trail marked by flags every mile. This is the main supply route to Camp Fistclench. In the first cycle the four test groups marched approximately abreast, parallel to this trail and some small distance to the north of it (Figure 1).[10] During clear weather the teams were spaced at approximately 100-yard intervals. They were allowed to lag or lead one another by as much as 200 yards while underway; if the longitudinal gap became greater, the lead groups were ordered to reduce speed to allow lagging groups to catch up.

Trailing behind each pair of teams were one or two "weasels" (small tracked cars) manned by auxiliary enlisted men who would have served as replacements had disability required any of the team members to drop out. The weasels, equipped with short-range radio, were a safety factor in the event of a sudden blizzard. They also carried such test equipment as might be needed on the trail and were used to carry observers from the mobile test center to the marching teams.

The trail procedure was standard for man-hauling sledges in the Arctic. One man broke trail. Two men followed in a split harness pulling a sled, followed by the last two men, also pulling a sled. The men in these three positions were rotated during breaks approximately every twenty minutes, so that each man filled each position about the same length of time.

Since the work on snowshoes was arduous, frequent breaks were taken. At noontime, the men dug a shallow trench to eat in, using their sleds for a windbreak (Figure 2). At this time each day they answered questionnaires (Figure 3). Again in the evenings they completed questionnaires or were interviewed (Figure 4).

At the close of a day's march, the teams closed in toward the trail and formed camp around the mobile test center (Figure 5). This mobile center was made up of a train of box cars on sled runners (wanigans) pulled by a tractor in which the scientific observers and support party lived and performed indoor work. Once each day the train advanced eight miles along the trail and marked the termination of the daily march.

Stringent controls were maintained over safety factors. After preconditioning exercises at the base camp in central Greenland, eight

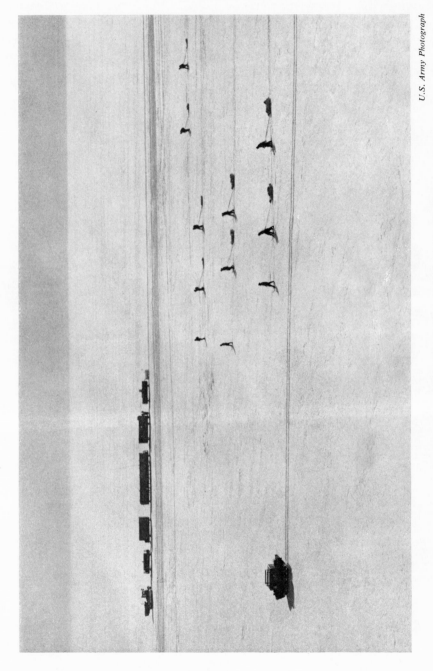

FIGURE 1. Teams of Soldiers Trek Across the Endless Icecap

Only the tractor train containing a laboratory and supplies breaks the monotony of the trackless waste.

FIGURE 2. Digging the Noon Trench

FIGURE 3. Filling out Questionnaires at Noon-time

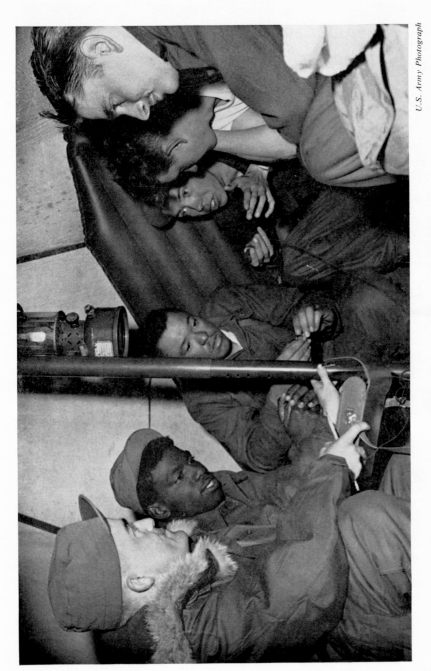

FIGURE 4. Being Interviewed in Tents in the Evening

FIGURE 5. An Evening's Camp

subjects were screened out of the experiment for various reasons of unfitness; the remaining twenty subjects were young and hardy. The level of food deprivation imposed was of moderate order and of short duration; no changes in morphology other than moderate fat loss could be expected. Physical performance capacity usually does not deteriorate under moderately short-term underfeeding. A medical aid man accompanied each trek, and a medical doctor was available to provide advice by radio or to visit the units in the field by helicopter on short notice. Weather on the icecap in July and August, when the experiment was run, is usually relatively benign; blizzards and "white-outs" are rare. The project was under the direct control of a highly experienced civilian Arctic specialist assisted by members of his staff. A radio equipped vehicle accompanied marching troops at all times. A measure of the success of safety controls is the fact that, among the 20 subjects who started the experiment, all finished the scheduled sequence.

QUALIFYING FACTORS

The setting of this experiment, the social condition of its subjects, and the research methods necessarily shaped the data obtained. Central features in the experiment were the compulsory nature of subjects' assignment, the lack of autonomy of the groups, the particular expectations and information of the groups, the shared group deprivation, the group interdependency, and the isolation and sterility of the environment.

a. Compulsory Groups

Soldiers were assigned to be test subjects in the Greenland experiment as part of their duty. The men were not keen about taking part in an experiment in the Arctic. It was realistically presented to them as a military-type exercise to learn about the Arctic environment. When they learned that the independent variable was ration intake and that no compensatory leave for the required strenuous duty could be promised, they were even less enthusiastic. When assigned to groups, they discovered that they had not been paired with their buddies. The results were generally to produce disaffection of members from the prescribed goals and relatively low initial intermember reciprocity. Admittedly, men in ordinary work groups commonly associate with co-workers not by choice but because they have to make a living. Such working groups, however, are not ordinarily bounded by the absence of alternative associations, as was true for the icecap test groups. Sick call, although used frequently in earlier stages of the experiment, could provide but temporary withdrawal. Thus the constraints on subjects in this study differ from the constraints of moral suasion and identification with abstract scientific aims which characterize subjects in other laboratory studies of stress.[11] At the same time, the men were aware of their central importance in a military-type experiment and understood that they were undergoing stress so that other soldiers might be better prepared against it. Not one of the men gave up before the end of the experiment.

b. Lack of Autonomy

Members of a group typically resent and resist changes imposed from outside.[12] The periodic imposition on the test teams of changes in activity (and method of activity) emphasized their complete, almost artificial, lack of autonomy. The daily distribution of food to individuals by test administrators removed control by the teams over allocation of a key resource. The arbitrary quality of team existence was reinforced when members were switched between cycles, and informally established, cooperative practices thereby threatened.

Thibaut and Kelley point out that, since compulsion leads to resistance,

> By sharing their hostility toward the oppressors, the members may experience both an increase in affiliative outcomes (mutual respect and affection) and a "rising moral pride" from having repudiated the impulse to give in to their captors. These gratifications may be sufficient to sustain the members even when the objective probabilities of their being able to crash the social barriers (escaping, revolting) are extremely low.[13]

The test team in the Greenland study that received highest evaluations from its members was one in which hostility to and disobedience of test requirements were most overt; this team was able to accomplish a number of sensational food-stealing raids (most of the goods were apprehended before consumption).

c. Expectations and Information

Informal cooperative practices evolved in the test groups despite their lack of control over (a) membership, (b) allocation of resources, and (c) goal selection. This may be due in part to the initial low expectations team members had. An extended briefing held before the start of the test helped to disillusion subjects of hope that they would have anything but a hard time. Bass, Thibaut and Kelley, and Stogdill[14] each point out that since groups are evaluated by members in terms of how much they support or assist members' expectations, low expectations may permit favorable evaluation of impoverished groups.

The briefing also helped to eliminate surprise from the environment. Teams began with thorough information about the external set of rules to be followed, the precise sequence of test conditions which they and others would follow, and the demands of the environment. They knew that with organization they could cope with these rules and demands. Thus the stress imposed was a task stress with a relatively low component of anxiety.

d. Shared Group Deprivation

The stresses imposed on teams were common to all members. Formal leaders had to man-haul with the other members. All men in a team fared equally well in the food they had; the confining conditions of living on the icecap did not allow any man to accumulate surpluses in resources which might become objects for competition. The differential resources leaders had were limited to official support and better access to information from the wanigan train. These conditions seemed to favor cooperation rather than competition. "Where all members have similar positions and similar access to resources, differences in status cannot become permanent."[15]

e. Group Interdependency

A factor favoring growth of integration in test teams was the interdependency of members on their teams for survival. Housing, warmth, and transport were available to members only through joint efforts. Inefficient coordination meant cold wind pouring under the tent flaps at 3:00 a.m., a stove that would not cook, or sore muscles from erratic tension on man-hauling ropes. This physical dependency was no doubt supplemented by psychosocial dependency under stress, such as Schacter[16] has examined: "Hunger likes company." However, the close interdependency within teams (such that, for example, if a man rolled over in his sleeping bag others probably had to move too) throughout the daily twenty-four hours probably was a large factor in the growth of interpersonal consideration and respect. A member socially rejected by his teammates could not be kicked out of the team but his lot could be made unhappy. There would be no place to which he might turn for even temporary succor. Other teams could not accept him, the control wanigan would not, and the environment offered nothing. Consequently, the test teams almost totally dominated the lives of their members in all phases that were not under rigid experimental control. This favored cooperation among members.

f. Sterile Environment

During the treks the teams were kept as isolated from each other (and from high-ranking visitors) as possible. The test was classed as an isolation experiment, and visits by outsiders were minimal. Social exchange between the teams was actively discouraged. A reinforcing factor here was the fatigue of the teams and the fact that when not marching they tended to want to spend as much time as possible in sleeping bags in their own tents.

The wasteland outside the circle of team activities was blank. It enforced total intimacy as one Arctic explorer has vividly reported:

> Some aspects of the intimacy of sledging life have not any parallel else-where; no, not even in marriage. (I am thinking at this moment of the sanitary arrangements when we lay up in a blizzard, perhaps for days together, in a tent which was so small that we covered the whole floor space when we lay down.) It is common knowledge that there is usually discord when two or three men are forced to live together in the unrelieved possession of each other's company. In our case you must square and cube the strain of unbroken intimacy. . . .[17]

Rose Coser suggests that extended face-to-face observability can make role-conflicts more severe.[18] Even without role-conflict, men retain a need for privacy and for the expression of personal acts that are con-ventionally tabooed. In the norms developed within the icecap teams, necessarily there came to be considerable tolerance of much normally tabooed private behavior.

Beyond forcing the men into unrelieved intimacy, the environment probably had direct effect on their vivacity. There was a dearth of things to talk about and little external stimulation to which men could share reactions. The arrival of a mail helicopter would perk them up briefly, but with its departure talk would disappear too. Interviews with the observers came to be a valued source of social intercourse, and ratings of hostility to observers declined over time. A trip to the wanigan on sick call or other routine duty was the only occasion when a man could escape his fellows and so be in a position to bring back news to them. Lindsay[19] noted that in the Arctic interpersonal exchange becomes a heavy effort; high spirits dissipate; humor becomes sarcastic: "One's reflections were neither purposeful nor constructive, at any rate after the first few days—merely dull, heavy thoughts, as dull and heavy as the day's work." Through its effects on communication, the monotony of the setting probably had a hampering effect on the development of integration in the test teams.

RESULTS

Civilian scientists accompanying the experimental units obtained a variety of concurrent measures. Some measures verified presumed characteristics of the independent variables (for example, food intake, energy demands of tasks); others related to effects of the experimental treatments on subjects' physiology, subjective feelings, and social relationships. Some measures were quantitative and observational (for example, frequency of visits to sick call); others necessarily were subjective and attitudinal (for example, level of hunger). During each experimental phase, subjects completed four different questionnaires, at different times.[20] Responses to these provided the bulk of the social-psychological data obtained in the experiment. Owing to the small sample size inevitable in experiments in the far North, response differences are considered statistically significant when reliable at the .10 level or better. Treatment contrasts discussed in the text of this section on results are statistically significant at the .10 level or better, by analysis of variance or appropriate nonparametric test, unless otherwise stated.

a. Personal Feelings

Subjects' reported sense of daily fatigue increased markedly and reliably under the 1,500-calorie daily deficit imposed over ten-day periods, relative to the fatigue levels of full-fed men (Table 1). Laboratory tests have shown that man's work capacity under such caloric deficit does not notably deteriorate.[21] The sense of fatigue accompanying hunger accordingly in one sense is not based on "reality." However, even if their capacity for work remains intact, hungry men will resist work; in this sense their fatigue is real enough. It is as though the "threshold for tiredness" has dropped so that any given increment of work seems more tiring. Thus the small differential in daily energy expenditure imposed by the two tasks of pack-carrying on their backs was hardly reflected in fatigue ratings of full-fed men but was more clearly indicated in repeated reports of underfed men; this interaction was significant.

TABLE 1. AVERAGE RATINGS OF DAILY TIREDNESS

Rations	Task		Average
	Sleds	Backs	
High	4.70	4.85	4.77
Low	5.25	6.25	5.75[a]
Average	4.97[a]	5.55	5.26

[a] Differences significant at the .10 level; throughout, all differences reported as significant are at least at the .10 level.

Going on sick call is a form of absenteeism associated with stress in the work setting, or a manifestation of poor adjustment in stressful environments.[22] Among teams on the icecap, going on sick call meant more work for teammates and therefore probably weakened a man's standing in his group. On the other hand, sick call is a time-honored device for evasion in the military and probably was viewed as such among the test subjects.

In Table 2, entries from the medical corpsman's sick log are classified by the test variables. Men on low rations put in significantly more appearances at sick call than did their opposite numbers.

TABLE 2. APPEARANCES AT SICK CALL

Rations	Task	Cycle I		Cycle II		Average
		Phase 1	Phase 2	Phase 1	Phase 2	
High	Sleds	3	3	2	2	2.50
High	Backs	9	2	3	—	3.50
Low	Sleds	8	—	6	2	4.00
Low	Backs	9	4	5	4	5.50
Average		7.25	2.25	4.0	2.0	

The initial phases of both cycles had higher rates than the second phases, and rates were higher in the first cycle than in the second. There is a clear congruence between the pattern of sick call visits and the pattern of stress.

Underfed subjects correspondingly rated themselves reliably higher in terms of suffering more from minor physical ailments. Self-ratings of irritability were also significantly higher in underfed groups. On the other hand, expected higher awareness of cold, sexuality, thirst, time-dragging, and other phenomena reported in the literature on hunger did *not* emerge from self-reports of underfed as contrasted with full-fed subjects.

b. Sociability

The term "sociability" can refer both to the volume and to the content of interaction. Two items on different questionnaires in the present experiment concerned the volume of talking in groups. On both questions, ratings of level of talking in teams varied significantly with feeding level; underfed teams reported reliably less talking. Representative data from one of the talkativeness questions appear in Table 3. In addition to the hunger effect, the data show two other reliable trends. First, there was more talk reported in the later of the two cycles. In the later cycle, subjects encountered easier weather, could march faster, and had fewer health difficulties (Table 2), so that strains of environmental requirements were eased; with decreased discomfort, and less energy required for work, interaction rose. There was also significantly less talk reported when subjects were back-carrying their packs rather than pulling them on sleds (the easier task). Notably, however, there was no reliable interaction between the stresses of hunger and task in terms of their effect on talkativeness.

TABLE 3. RATINGS OF TALKATIVENESS IN TEAMS

Cycle	Phase	High Rations		Low Rations		Average
		Sled	Back	Sled	Back	
I	1	5.80	4.40	4.80	4.80	4.95
I	2	6.20	4.80	4.40	3.00	4.60
II	1	4.80	5.40	5.80	4.40	5.10
II	2	5.80	4.80	5.40	5.80	5.45
Average		5.65	4.85	5.10	4.50	5.02

A sign of strain in a group may be a decline in humor, or the rise in sarcastic, ironic, and complaining notes in humor. Increasing frequency of nonfunny kinds of humor has been noted by observers among fasting men in laboratories, among patients in wards for serious cases, and among experimentally deprived laboratory groups.[23] Subjects in the present research were asked about good laughs during the hour preceding the noon break. Since there was not much communication during this period, humor ratings were low. They were a full scale point lower, however, among hungry groups than among full-fed groups.

Subjects were also asked about "bitching." This form of communication is often directed outside of groups and is complaining, querulous, or sarcastic in tone. It is the type of behavior sometimes classified as "hostility toward the outgroup" in group dynamics researches. Subjects' agreement with the statement, "We do a lot of bitching," rose a full scale point under the hungry condition; no comparable trend, however, was noted between the two task (pack-carrying) conditions.

c. Group Atmosphere

Hostility toward outgroups is one measure of group atmosphere. Of all the various questions about their dislikes (which were generally overtly rated low), items querying levels of hostility (a) toward other teams and (b) toward the scientific observers were rated highest by the subjects. However, no significant differences attributable to the independent variables of time, task difficulty, or hunger stress emerged from data on these two hostility dimensions.

Average ratings on each of 17 different items[24] tapping hostility within groups were very low; that is, the 20 subjects tended to score their own teams very favorably in terms of various intragroup criticisms queried by the 17 items. Comparison was made between average ratings of these 17 critical items by team members under the more arduous back-carrying method of load transport, as opposed to average ratings of the same members when using the easier sled-carriage method. More favorable mean ratings toward their own groups on 15 of the 17 items were obtained from subjects in the more difficult condition; that is, under greater workload stress the team members were less critical of their own teams than when they were under less workload stress.

In contrast, subjects when in groups under hunger stress on the average rated a majority (12 out of 17) of these critical items more unfavorably than when they were full-fed. Similarly, less favorable mean ratings on 13 of the 17 items were obtained from subjects when their fatigue was prolonged into the second (uphill, upwind) phase of each cycle. These differences were significant, in that binomial expansion under the null hypothesis indicates two-tailed probability for either of these two distributions is less than .10. Thus the contrast between the negative effects of increased hunger and the positive effects of increased workloads is clearly reliable evidence against an assumption that the two kinds of stress have the same effects.

Some 15 positively toned items referring to the social atmosphere in teams generally received ratings toward the top of the seven-point rating scale. Very high ratings were obtained on items referring to task cooperation and helpfulness (for example, "Members of the team work well together as a group"; "Somebody in the team is always ready to give me a helping hand"; and the like). No systematic differences attributable to ration level, time, or task difficulty emerged in response to these positively toned items. Further, ratings of respect for own teammates both collectively and individually were obtained from another set of items referring to "preference," "performance," and "liking"; here again, ratings were very high and as high in more stressed groups as in less stressed groups. Illustrative data are shown in Table 4.

TABLE 4. PERCEPTIONS OF CHANGE IN TEAM PERFORMANCE

Change	Packs on Sleds	Packs on Backs	Full-fed	Underfed
	(N = 40 ratings under each condition)			
About the same	18	11	13	16
Worse	2	3	3	2
Improved	20	26	24	22

d. Sociometric Structure

Matrices of responses to five items producing sociometric rankings of team co-members on different attributes[25] were analyzed to ascertain if hungry teams had more cliques than well-fed teams. Since a prerequisite to cliques is mutuality, a count of direct reciprocal choices was made in each matrix.[26] None of the experimental conditions shows any systematic effect on the frequency of mutual choices. According to this measure of group cohesion,[27] hungry groups were as cohesive as full-fed groups.

Luce devised a matrix technique whereby indirect choices of the type "A chooses B who chooses C; so A chooses C" are accounted for in cliques of size three, four, and so on.[28] The number of indirect cliques of size three open to individuals in teams was computed for each of the five matrices according to the method proposed by Luce. Resulting values were related to the patterns of direct mutual two-person choices.[29] By this method "exclusion" (that is, a team member receiving no direct choices) is a measure of low cohesion. There were more "exclusions" among all choice matrices formed by hungry groups than among choice matrices formed by full-fed groups. This was notably so for first and second choice nominations on the "work with closely" and "helpful and sympathetic" attributes. No comparable systematic differences in clique formation in matrices emerged from the two other stress factors (time and task) considered in this experiment.

e. Leader Status

Hohn has developed a Hierarchy Index which measures intragroup agreement on sociometric rankings of status dimensions.[30] Greater hierarchization implies improved agreement as to the informal leaders. In general, status agreement on the four sociometric items was as high in underfed groups as in full-fed groups. The other two stress factors (time within cycles and load-carrying task) did not appear to affect intrateam agreement on the sociometric dimensions measured. The evidence indicates that under the setting of this experiment, the onset of added hunger and work stress did not upset the degree of consensus on sociometric rankings of task-related statuses.

Formal leaders often suffer risk of displacement of status when environmental pressures on their group increase. Where cliques are found in small groups, observers have noted that formal leaders tend to be excluded. Since hungry groups were observed to form clique patterns and exclusions on sociometric dimensions, the expectation was that the formal leaders in hungry groups would be likely to suffer decline in status on these dimensions. This proved to be the case. Evaluation of formal leaders on the sociometric attributes "work with most closely," "weight and influence," and "good answers to team problems" showed in each case a decline (significant at the .10 level under the median test) in status among leaders of hungry groups as compared with full-fed groups. There were similar but not reliable trends toward lower status among formal leaders of hungry groups on the sociometric dimensions "helpful and sympathetic" and "good leaders next year."

However, a consistent maintenance of hierarchy (dispersion of sums of rankings) among hungry groups was noted as measured by Hohn's index values. Thus, generally it appears that informal leaders were partly able to accumulate the status lost by formal leaders in the hungry groups.

In contrast to the depressing effect of hunger stress on leader status, other stress factors (time and task) showed no such consistent or reliable effect. Leaders further showed no consistent loss in sociometric status over time within experimental cycles with hunger condition held constant.

f. Sociometric Stability

In both phases within cycles of this experiment, subjects ranked all of their co-workers in four sociometric items. The stability of subjects' rankings of peers over successive phases within cycles was estimated for the two feeding conditions.[31] In no case did the instability values among hungry teams exceed those obtaining among full-fed teams. Indeed, there was a trend toward less stability among the full-fed teams on three of the four sets of sociometric rankings.

g. Factors in Sociometric Judgment

The possibility that hunger might change the criteria by which peers in groups were evaluated on various attributes was investigated by means of factor analysis. Responses to six sociometric items were included in the analysis.[32] The two matrices of correlations (one for each feeding condition) among the six sociometric items were factor analyzed and rotated by the varimax method. The first factor emerging had heaviest loading in the two sociometric items providing data on power differentiation; it was termed "authority." The second factor appeared predominantly in correlations with ratings of peers as future team-mates; it was termed "congeniality." The third factor clearly referred to "sympathy."

In both feeding conditions, the "authority" factor accounted for about 36 to 38 per cent of the total covariance. The two feeding conditions varied, however, in the loadings of the remaining two of the first three factors. These two factors ("congeniality" and "sympathy") accounted for almost all remaining covariance in the hungry condition; however, in the full-fed condition, other factors in addition to the first three were required to account for the whole of covariance.

The implication of this analysis appears to be that the multi-dimensional structure of relationships was simpler in the hungry teams where the three attributes—authority, congeniality, and sympathy—almost wholly shaped sociometric scores. Among full-fed teams, however, the evaluative structure was more complex, so that, for example, a man otherwise unauthoritative, uncongenial, or unsympathetic could be judged favorably as a working partner or as a potential leader. It would appear that members of full-fed groups had more planes of relationship on which to compete, show excellence, and establish some form of status. Among hungry groups, a man lacking high authority, sympathy, or congeniality was less valued in sociometric choices.

h. Post-Test Appraisals

During personal interviews conducted a week after test completion, men were asked to compare the two teams on which they served in terms of talk, good feeling, and the like (Table 5). These retrospective judgments confirm other findings indicating diminished interaction, affect, and integration among the hungry groups. The response pattern to items on "bossing" and "strong leadership" reflect the strain on leadership indicated in subjective reports obtained during the experiment.

Individual sociometric choices among the entire assembly of twenty subjects, on the attributes "preferred on next team," "good performer," "helpful and affectionate," and "popular" were obtained after conclu-

TABLE 5. CHOICES BETWEEN UNDERFED AND FULL-FED TEAMS ON CERTAIN ATTRIBUTES[a]

Teams	More Talking	More Bossing	More Good Feeling	Better Organized	Lonelier	Stronger Leader
Underfed	6	13	4	5	11	11
Full-fed	12	4	15	14	2	8
Total	18	17	19	19	13	19

[a] Frequencies add up to fewer than 20 because one man missed his interview and because some respondents could not make a choice between the two teams on some attributes.

sion of the experiment (Table 6). Since each man served with a different subgroup of team co-members when underfed and when full-fed, the number of post-experimental nominations he received from subjects in the subgroup with which he served only while underfed could be compared with the number he received from subjects in the subgroup with which he served only when full-fed.

No systematic differences are to be observed in the frequencies with which subjects were nominated by underfed co-members or by full-fed co-members. It would appear that experiencing underfeeding with a companion did not markedly affect one's judgment of him favorably or unfavorably, and indicates the limited after-effect of the experiment.

TABLE 6. POST-EXPERIMENTAL NOMINATIONS OF SUBJECTS BY UNDERFED AND FULL-FED CO-MEMBERS

Source of Nominations	Preferred as Teammate	Performance		Affectionate		Popular
		Good	Poor	More	Less	
Underfed Co-members	12	11	16	16	8	13
Full-fed Co-members	16	5	11	22	8	11

DISCUSSION

From the existing literature on groups under stress it can be argued (1) that there is a tendency to disorganization in groups under stress; (2) that this tendency is offset by efforts toward building up a more clearly defined task and power structure; (3) that more successful groups have more differentiated structure; (4) that structure-building effort reduces informal exchange and humor; (5) that reduction of informal exchange and humor leads to potential disaffection among members and latent hostility to formal leaders; (6) that this disaffection is suppressed under task demands and is directed outward; and (7) that after removal of stress, restructuring and socioemotional exchange are likely to become manifest.

In the general stress context of the Greenland icecap, certain of these anticipated phenomena emerged. Average ratings of intragroup relations, group atmosphere, and group performances were generally very favorable, while expressed hostility to outsiders was moderately high.[33] At the same time, reported talk and humor rates were modest. Formal leaders generally were sociometric stars, and consensus on sociometric hierarchies was clearcut and stable. An easing of working conditions took place in the second of the two replicate cycles, and with this change subjects reported generally less fatigue and hunger, less consensus and less stability in sociometric hierarchies, less hostility toward outsiders, more humor and talk, and more overt argument.

Within this context, increments in duration of stress between phases, and in workload, produced certain common trends. Subjects on the average went on sick call more often under the greater stress conditions; they reported more fatigue and hunger, less talk and humor, less overt intragroup disagreement, and more satisfaction with team performances. These changes with increased stress within cycles were generally opposite those accompanying decreasing stress from the first to the second of the two cycles.

There were some differences in response to the stress of underfeeding as compared to task stress. Talk and humor suffered much more drastically during hunger than during other forms of stress. "Bitching" and discontent within groups were rated higher in subjects' reports. Underfeeding had more serious effect on sick call rates than did an increment in load-carrying difficulty. There was equivalent sociometric stability and equivalent hierarchization under the two feeding conditions, but formal leaders were not ranked as high in status on sociometric dimensions during underfeeding and were partly displaced by informal leaders. While the number of reciprocal choices in two-choice nominations did not change systematically under hunger or other stress, the factorial basis of these choices apparently included fewer dimensions in the underfeeding condition.

Most notable, however, as distinct effects of hunger were the emergence of cliques accompanied by sociometric isolates. These suggest a type of reaction specific to deprivation: a narrowing of relationships. The hungry men seemingly were too tired and irritable to accommodate interaction even with four others; certain members became sociometrically ignored while bonds with others remained strong. This seeming inability to tolerate multiple kinds of relationships with even four others would account for the observed overt resistance to formal leaders' attempts to organize cooperative work patterns among the five team members despite clear advantages of such in terms of comfort and energy requirements. In the same manner, hungry teams were post-experimentally described as "bossy."

Often implicit in discussion of effects of stress on groups is the presumption that increased member dissatisfaction and intragroup hostility disrupt organization and effectiveness and lead to the breakdown of groups into cliques. Some varieties of the expected social phenomena appeared under the hunger condition. Yet one negative finding suggests that group breakdown is not a simple process of releasing interpersonal hostilities. No measure of subjects' respect for or congeniality with co-members as individuals showed a reliable decline under hunger stress in this experiment or after it. Instead, with very little interaction energy because they were tired and weak, members found it was better to restrict reciprocity to just one or two co-members. Schacter has shown that hungry men display greater need for social support than full-fed men.[34] With interaction resources very limited, men would reasonably choose to develop support relations with just one or two others rather than expose themselves to demands for reciprocity from all members; yet abstract valuation of all members might well remain high despite lack of interaction with them.* Data in this study suggest that primary groups under deprivation disintegrate not through a process of creating social isolates. Instead, there is a level of stress which first results in the men restricting their relationships to two-person systems or groupings.

Corollary to this process are the mechanisms for maintaining order in hungry groups. Communications to deviants, and application of sanctions against deviant members irritable with hunger, require energies which hungry men feel they lack. There is, accordingly, less control in hungry groups. The observers in Greenland were impressed by a number of instances in hungry teams when physically able men, shirking their share of the work, were allowed to continue their defections without reprimand from others, while others did the work for them. Seemingly the latter found it easier to perform physical work than to engage in attempts at compelling shirkers to work harder. Likewise, the information on factor structure of sociometric judgments is suggestive. With less talk, with a narrower range of interpersonal relations, the hungry subjects also seemed to have more limited planes of reciprocity.

The evidence of this study suggest that hungry groups were more primitive and immature, and unable to sustain extended or specialized relationships. Thus contrast should be made between external task stress in groups versus internal deprivation stress on group members. It is one thing to increase the external burden on groups relative to constant resources (skills, energy, communications structures); it is another to weaken group potential by attacking internally its resources. As long as group facilities are maintained and member energies periodically replenished, moderate increases in external demand will not damage group

---

* EDITOR'S NOTE: The parallel and independent observation of Lt. Col. Roger W. Little on reaction to stress in primary groups in Korea is most striking. See his paper in this volume.

structure and its ability to function. Usually, however, external stresses continued over time lead to depletions of group resources which cannot be immediately replaced. Then, like food-deprived teams, the group becomes more primitive, less able to satisfy the social and physical needs of its members at the same time that these needs are accumulating. To relieve stress-derived social needs, members revert to particularism (for example, cliques) in associations; extended hierarchies of relationships on multiple value planes are weakened.

SUMMARY AND IMPLICATIONS

In a situation of high demand from an inhospitable external environment, compulsory groups were subjected to increments of stress involving (1) prolongation of task over time, (2) a more difficult work method, and (3) deprivation (underfeeding). In the test situation, subjects' ratings of their own groups' and individual peers' performances and desirability remained very favorable throughout the experiment with accompanying hostility to outsiders. The work stress increments (prolonged task and more difficult work method) and the deprivation stress (underfeeding) did, however, jointly tend to produce common phenomena among subjects, including increased frequencies of visits to sick call, reduced talking, less humor, more fatigue and more irritability.

In contrast to the work stress increments, the underfeeding stress uniquely produced more pronounced changes in groups, including sociometric downgrading of formal leaders, more "bitching" and less satisfaction in groups, and sociometric underchoosing of isolated peers. Sociometric rankings remained as differentiated and as stable over time in underfed groups as in full-fed groups. Factor analysis of sociometric scores suggested a less complex factor structure underlying the valuation of peers in the underfed as compared with the well-fed groups.

An explanation of these phenomena was sought by postulating individual energy resources as essential to the maintenance of group integrity. Despite their problems, full-fed groups were able to maintain a stable social organization and effective patterns of authority under conditions of high external demand. Food deprivation, however, apparently attacked group organization by depriving members both of energy and of the capacity to interact on group problems. The most striking empirical finding was the emergence of diadic cliques as the basis of social organization under these conditions of deprivation. The effect was equivalent to one that might be produced in a laboratory by progressively breaking down communication links between members of a group until only an aggregate of two-person units remained. The hungry teams tended to become collective confederations of subunits rather than organic federations. In this sense, the absolute level of member's energy appears as a prime asset, serving as a fundamental resource of groups which enables them to function in order to achieve group goals. But we are still dealing with a form of human or social organization and not with an aggregation of social isolates. Military operations under extreme conditions require command and direction as well as support, and this experiment gives a somewhat clearer picture of the structure of small groups that emerge and persist under this particular type of stress.

NOTES

1. Peary, R. E., *Northward Over the "Great Ice."* Frederick A. Stokes Co., New York, 1898, p. xxxiv.

2. For example, Lindsay, Martin, *Sledge: The British Trans-Greenland Expedition.* Longmans, Green and Co., London, 1935; Freuchen, Peter, *Arctic Adventure: My Life in the Frozen North*, Farrar and Rinehart, New York, 1935.

3. For example: Ambrière, Francis, *The Long Holiday*, Ziff-Davis Publishing Co. Chicago, 1948; Bettelheim, Bruno, "Individual and Mass Behavior in Extreme Situations" in Maccoby, E. E., T. M. Newcomb, and J. E. Hartley, editors, *Readings in Social Psychology*, 3d ed., Henry Holt and Co., New York, 1958, pp. 300–310; Keith, A. N., *Three Came Home*, Little, Brown and Co., Boston, 1947; Cohen, E. A., *Human Behavior in the Concentration Camp*, W. W. Norton and Co., New York, 1953.

4. Benedict, F. G., W. R. Miles, Paul Roth, and H. M. Smith, *Human Vitality and Efficiency Under Prolonged Restricted Diet*, Carnegie Institute, Washington, 1919; Keys, A. B., and others, *The Biology of Human Starvation*, University of Minnesota Press, Minneapolis, Minn., 1950, 2 vols.; Murray, E. J., and others, "The Effects of Sleep Deprivation on Social Behavior," *Journal of Social Psychology*, vol. 49, 1957, pp. 229–236.

5. Torrance, E. P., "What Happens to the Sociometric Structure of Small Groups in Emergencies and Extreme Conditions," *Group Psychotherapy*, vol. 10, 1957, pp. 212–220; Torrance, E. P., "The Behavior of Small Groups Under the Stress Conditions of Survival," *American Sociological Review*, vol. 19, 1954, pp. 751–755; Torrance, E. P., R. LaForge, and R. Mason, *Group Adaptation in Emergencies and Extreme Conditions*, Randolph Air Force Base, Office for Social Science Programs, Air Force Personnel and Training Research Center, Texas, 1956 (Tech. Memo. OSSP-56-2).

6. Torrance, E. P., "A Theory of Leadership and Interpersonal Behavior Under Stress" in Petrullo, Luigi, and B. M. Bass, editors, *Leadership and Interpersonal Behavior*, Holt, Rinehart, and Winston, Inc., New York, 1961, pp. 100–117.

7. Torrance, E. P., "Leadership in the Survival of Small Isolated Groups" in Walter Reed Army Institute of Research and National Research Council, sponsors, *Symposium on Preventive and Social Psychiatry*, Government Printing Office, Washington, 1958, pp. 209–327.

8. Blau, P. M., "Formal Organization: Dimensions of Analysis," *American Journal of Sociology*, vol. 63, 1957, pp. 58–69.

9. In point of fact, moderate short-term underfeeding has little or no effect on physiological performance capacity.

10. During the trek in the second cycle, both sides of the trail were used, two teams on each side.

11. Keys, A. B., and others, *op. cit.*, p. 914; Libo, L. M., *Measuring Group Cohesiveness*, University of Michigan, Research Center for Group Dynamics, Institute for Social Research, Ann Arbor, Mich., 1953, p. 6.

12. Stogdill, R. M., *Individual Behavior and Group Achievement: A Theory, The Experimental Evidence*. Oxford University Press, New York, 1959, p. 287.

13. Thibaut, J. H., and H. H. Kelley, *The Social Psychology of Groups*. John Wiley and Sons, New York, 1959, p. 182.

14. Bass, B. M., *Leadership, Psychology and Organizational Behavior*, Harper and Bros., New York, 1960, p. 42; Thibaut, J. H., and H. H. Kelley, *op. cit., passim;* Stogdill, R. M., *op. cit.*, p. 281.

15. Klein, Josephine, *The Study of Groups*. Routledge and Kegan Paul, London, 1956, p. 18.

16. Schacter, Stanley, *The Psychology of Affiliation*. Stanford University Press, Stanford, Calif., 1959.

17. Lindsay, Martin, *op. cit.*, p. 206. Apropos of Lindsay's parenthetical remark, observers noted that subjects using the common team latrine always carefully covered up their output with snow in token effort to reduce total intimacy.

18. Coser, R. L., "Insulation from Social Observability and Types of Social Conformity," *American Sociological Review*, vol. 26, 1951, pp. 28–39.

19. Lindsay, Martin, *op. cit.*, p. 165.

20. Although no two items had the same wording, the questionnaires overlapped considerably in terms of topics queried, so as to gain quasi-independent replications of responses. Typically, subjective responses were made on a rating scale. To reduce bulk of the questionnaire burden, a labeled seven-point "levels" rating scale was evolved which was commonly applied to many items referring to subjective judgments and feelings. Sociometric rankings were also obtained.
   Subjects' ratings were treated as interval data for purposes of analyses of variance. The 79 degrees of freedom in rating scale data on a typical question dimension were partitioned into 15 degrees of freedom allocated to the four dichotomous variables—Ration, Task, Cycle, and Phase—and to their first- through third-order interactions; the remaining 64 degrees of freedom were allocated to error. As is implicit in the section stating design relationships, individuals in this experiment were statistically regarded as cyphers subjected both to physical treatments of time, ration and task, and to social-psychological treatments by subgroups. Accordingly, analysis of variance of the hundred or more scaled subjective response dimensions could not properly be extended to covariance analysis.
   Differences of one scale point in mean ratings usually were significant at the .01 level. For example, each of the four questionnaires asked subjects to rate degree of hunger. Hunger ratings generally were high, averaging above 5.0 on the seven-point scale; responses of full-fed subjects averaged about 4.3, while responses of underfed subjects averaged above 6.0. Differences of this order were highly reliable statistically. There was also a significant trend to lower hunger ratings (less hunger) in the second cycle, and to higher hunger ratings in the second phase within each cycle. Variations in subjects' ratings of their enjoyment of specific canned food items corresponded closely to these statistically reliable trends in hunger ratings.
   In other instances, nonparametric tests were used to test significance; for example, if seven out of eight teams revealed a characteristic directional shift in

sociometric attributes over time, this could be tested against expansion of the binomial reflecting a null hypothesis. In still other cases (for example, certain observational data), no statistical test was appropriate because no conceptual alternate population existed—that is, the data represented the universe of events. In all events, the limited size of this experiment dealing systematically with stress in the field makes it advisable that trends, even where conventional statistical reliability criteria are not obtained, be noted.

21. Buskirk, E. R., "Standard Work Tests in Man: Some Illustrative Results" in Spector, H., J. Brozek, and M. S. Peterson, editors, *Performance Capacity*, U. S. Army Quartermaster Food and Container Institute for the Armed Forces, Chicago, 1957, pp. 115–131.

22. Melbin, Murray, "Organizational Practice and Individual Behavior: Absenteeism Among Psychiatric Aides," *American Sociological Review*, vol. 26, 1961, pp. 14–23; Mechanic, David, and E. H. Volkart, "Stress, Illness Behavior, and the Sick Role," *American Sociological Review*, vol. 26, 1961, pp. 51–58; Eilbert, L. R., and Robert Glaser, "Differences Between Well and Poorly Adjusted Groups in an Isolated Environment," *Journal of Applied Psychology*, vol. 43, 1959, pp. 271–274; Janowitz, Morris, *Sociology and the Military Establishment*, Russell Sage Foundation, New York, 1959, pp. 73 ff.; French, R. L., "Sociometric Status and Individual Adjustment Among Naval Recruits," *Journal of Abnormal and Social Psychology*, vol. 46, 1951, pp. 64–72.

23. Franklin, J. C., and others, "Observations on Human Behavior in Experimental Starvation and Rehabilitation," *Journal of Clinical Psychology*, vol. 4, 1948, pp. 28–45; Fox, Renée, *Experiment Perilous: Physicians and Patients Facing the Unknown*, The Free Press, Glencoe, Ill., 1959; Kelley, H. H., "Communication in Experimentally Created Hierarchies" in Cartwright, Dorwin, and Alvin Zander, editors, *Group Dynamics*, Row, Peterson and Co., Evanston, Ill., 1953, pp. 443–461.

24. These items and others, both positively—and negatively—toned were derived from Zimmer, H., *A Test Program for Two Antarctic Expeditions: 1956–1959*, Georgetown University Medical Center, Washington, 1958.

25. The five items concerned: (1) weight and influence of members' opinions and ideas in the group as a whole (rank all co-members); (2) most helpful and sympathetic co-members (name two); (3) members' contribution of good answers to team problems (rank all co-members); (4) members with whom respondents worked most closely (rank all co-members); and (5) members' potential as good leaders on another team in the following year (rank all co-members).

26. For these purposes, ranks one and two were counted as choice. When the number of choices is two, the maximum number of mutual choices possible in five-man groups is five; this occurs in the circular structure A-B-C-D-E-A. Such a structure occurred only once among the eighty matrices (five questions × four teams × two cycles × two phases) examined. The median number of reciprocals in a given rank matrix was about three, and this was almost invariant over different questions.

27. Proctor, C. H., and C. P. Loomis, "Analysis of Sociometric Data" in Jahoda, Marie, Morton Deutsch, and S. W. Cook, editors, *Research Methods in Social Relations*. Dryden Press, New York, 1951, pp. 561–585.

28. Luce, R. D., "Connectivity and Generalized Cliques in Sociometric Group Structure," *Psychometrika*, vol. 15, 1950, pp. 169–190.

29. Where the pattern of direct mutual choices in the matrices "excluded" an individual (as in a matrix containing a four-person chain or four-person circle) or pair of individuals (as in a matrix containing a three-person clique), the number of indirect-linkage clique formations was low. The extent that indirect interlocking choice systems supersede direct mutual choice patterns is one operational measure of integration (see North, R. C., H. E. Koch, and D. A. Zinnes, "The

Integration Functions of Conflict," *Conflict Resolution*, vol. 4, 1960, pp. 355–374). Thus a count of the number of matrices in the experimental conditions characterized by direct-choice triad cliques or four-person chains and circles formed an inverse measure of integration.

30. Hohn, F. E., *Some Methods of Comparing Sociometric Matrices*, University of Illinois, College of Education, Bureau of Research and Service, 1953, Technical Report No. 5. The Hierarchy Index, *h*, is defined as the ratio of observed variation in column sums of full rank matrices to the maximum possible variation. Index values for the matrices of rankings derived from four of the five sociometric items (the "helpful and sympathetic" item was unsuitable for treatment in terms of Hohn's Index because only partial ranks were obtained) were generally high, indicating good agreement among members within teams on power and task leadership. Most extreme differentiation (that is, most intersubject agreement in rankings) was found in the "weight and influence" item.

31. The procedure used was one in which differences between corresponding assigned ranks are squared and summed. Higher values imply less stability of ranks. The obtained sums of squared differences between individuals' rankings of peers on successive phases were ordered about their median for each of the four questions.

32. In each of the two feeding conditions, column sums of ranks were correlated among the four items calling for a full ranking of team members. (See note 25.) The mean of rank matrix column sums for these items was a constant $\frac{n(n-1)}{2}$ for rank matrices from all teams. A fifth item required only two choices among a subject's four teammates; the two choices provided were identified as ranks 1 and 2 and to their sum was added 6, representing an arbitrary sum for unnamed ranks, to complete column sums. A sixth item called for ratings of preference for individual teammates as future teammates. Since the means of rating matrices varied from team to team, column sums of each matrix were stabilized by identification as deviations from their mean.

33. Both Gerard in his study and Eren and Auld in theirs have noted that conditions of high interdependence against external threat and compulsion are likely to lead to increased normative taboo against criticism of co-members, especially to outsiders. See: Gerard, H. B., "The Effects of Two Dimensions of Disagreement on the Influence Process in Small Groups," *Human Relations*, vol. 6, 1953, pp. 249–271; Eren, T. D., and F. A. Auld, *A Study of the Thematic Apperception Test Stories and Sentence Completion of Subjects in Operation Hideout*, U.S. Navy Submarine Medical Research Laboratory, New London, Conn., 1954, Report No. 243.

34. Schacter, Stanley, *op. cit.*, pp. 96–97.

Part Five

**CAREER COMMITMENT AND
RETIREMENT**

Part Five

CAREER COMMITMENT AND RETIREMENT

THE MILITARY PROFESSION in the United States has changed from a small and relatively isolated social group to a large body with elaborate and complex ties with civilian society. Before World War II professional career commitments were formed early and tended to be fixed and lifetime, if only because of the lack of opportunity to transfer to civilian employment. In this sense, the military profession has completed its transformation. Large numbers of officers resign from the military after a limited number of years of service. Many more complete their professional military careers after twenty years of service while still in their early forties, and they must find a second career.

Thus personnel must reaffirm their career commitment at various points in the course of their military service. Is it to their advantage to continue toward a twenty, or possibly thirty, year career or will earlier resignation assist their transfer into civilian society? These career decisions have long operated for enlisted men; the new element is that officer personnel must face them. The result is that the armed forces must continually seek to strengthen professional commitment among those men whom they seek to retain. For the student of military organization the factors associated with career commitment and the consequences of the retirement system in the profession have become an additional dimension of analysis.

Military retirement benefits include not only the retirement pay and fringe benefits of medical services and the like, but also the skills that a military career develops. And contrariwise, there are significant barriers to retirement employment—legal and informal as well as the sheer lack of knowledge and limited civilian contacts that work against him after a prolonged period of military service.

Like all professions, monetary considerations are important; and in the past, the special advantages of military retirement, provided that lifetime (which was thirty years of active duty service) was a powerful career incentive in weighing the alternative opportunities outside of the armed forces. But the expansion of civilian retirement programs and the emergence of the typical twenty year career have weakened these monetary attractions that operated in favor of the military. The military profession has always relied on and continued to emphasize nonmonetary rewards—style of life, honor, group loyalty, and public service as elements in building career commitments. To this end, it is to be expected that each armed service would emphasize the importance of its service academies in training officers with enduring career commitments. And it was to be expected that after World War II, each of the armed services would press for an expansion of its academies to meet its personnel needs. But, at the same time, it is obvious that manpower requirements cannot be met even from an enlarged service academy. The sources of manpower must include men—both officers and enlisted personnel—who enter the services to complete obligated tours of duty and who find the prospect of the military career to be attractive and rewarding enough to make it a relatively long-term commitment.

In assessing the variables strengthening and weakening career commitments, the cross-sectional sample survey becomes a most useful research instrument. It is not that the attitudes expressed represent precise estimates of career intentions. It is rather that the data to be presented from the survey use the individual officer or enlisted man as the source of data and therefore it is possible to place these problems of commitment and retirement in a broad organizational setting. Thus the findings indicate that the popular assumption that the military academies produce men with strong professional career commitments is, by and large, correct. But these data likewise indicate that career commitments are fashioned by the actual career opportunities available to the individual officers. The commitments of the military academy graduate likewise are fashioned in good measure by his career opportunities; and this is the case both positively and negatively for other classes of officers.

Moreover, it is not the attraction of civilian employment opportunities per se that weaken career commitment. Those officers who actually have and who feel that they could find civilian employment easily are not necessarily those with the weakest attachments to the military profession. The core of the problem centers on whether they believe that they are currently being employed effectively by the armed forces. Career opportunities and job satisfaction build career commitments;

where these attitudes are not developed by actual experiences, professional commitments can be weakened.

But the issue of career commitment is closely tied to a vast generational transformation within the armed services. The World War II expansion—both in officers and in enlisted personnel—is producing for the first time large numbers of men who have completed twenty years of service and this retirement flow will continue into the future. The magnitude of the problems is new in United States experience. The incorporation into civilian society of these retired professional soldiers, officers and enlisted men, presents basic issues of domestic policy, and will influence the social position of the military profession. It is essential to recognize that in the early 1960's the country is still in the early and first phases of an ever enlarging flow of retirees.

The available evidence indicates that for these men a minority are experiencing an actual decrease in economic standard of living at the period of their prime productivity and maximum family responsibilities. The federal government, the armed forces, and the service associations have displayed a sensitivity to their problems of transition. The available and ongoing research data indicate the type and magnitude of efforts required from the point of view of the constabulary force. Yet a basic issue hinges on the still unanswered question of whether retirement experience will assist or complicate both recruitment and career commitment.

CAREER OPPORTUNITIES AND COMMITMENTS AMONG OFFICERS

Mayer N. Zald and William Simon

A MERICAN PARTICIPATION in World Wars I and II and in the Korean Conflict required a vast influx of officer personnel recruited through channels other than Annapolis and West Point. The maintenance of an enlarged military establishment during the Cold War, with its worldwide political as well as military involvements, and the modern technological revolution, with its demand for a wide range of specialist skills, have required a fundamental "democratization"[1] of the officer recruitment base.

Even though higher command posts disproportionately recruit Academy graduates, the services have turned to in-service training of selected enlisted men (Officer Candidate School) and to college graduates serving their military obligations (Reserve Officer Training Corps) to fill their overall officer requirements.

The transformation of the military establishment in size, in technology, and in tasks has had a profound impact on the social matrix of the officer and on his career. First, the homogeneous, relatively intimate officer corps has been destroyed; the size and heterogeneity of the corps has led to a more impersonal, complex, and bureaucratized military establishment. Second, the technological complexity of weapons and delivery systems and the political involvements of the military have led to a proliferation of professional skill requirements; the young officer must learn much more than military leadership. In the present military establishment, officers must often master skills which essentially train them for civilian as well as military occupations. Third, the relative isolation of the military from civilian life has broken down; more civilians have experienced military life, more military personnel have been involved with civilian educational institutions and are presented with civilian career opportunities.

There are differences in the extent to which these trends have affected each of the services, depending upon rates of expansion and contraction and on changing technologies and military missions. In particular, the

Air Force, as compared first to the Navy and second to the Army and Marine Corps, can be considered the most "modernized" service,[2] although all of the services have been transformed.

The broadening of the social base of officer recruitment, the proliferation of professional skills, and the changing tasks of the military have presented military managers with dilemmas in the recruitment, training, and retention of career officers. How much should the Academies be expanded? What subjects should be taught at the Academies? What proportion of the lower ranks should be Academy graduates? Should OCS and ROTC graduates be counted on for full socialization and competence to man the elite command positions? Has the "civilianization" of the military led to weaker career commitments? Finally, and most important of all, how is commitment to a military career fostered during a period of peace, in the absence of a homogeneous, segregated, and intimate officer corps?

The purpose of this paper is to explore a body of empirical data dealing with commitment to a military career, unique in that it supplies a questionnaire sample survey of the entire active duty corps of the services. The data for this study were originally collected in February, 1961, as part of a larger study of the attitudes of officers and enlisted men toward military retirement plans, conducted for the Senate Armed Services Committee. The study is reported in *A Study of the Military Retired Pay System and Certain Related Subjects:* A Report to the Committee on Armed Services, United States Senate, by the Study Committee of the University of Michigan, July 6, 1961 (Government Printing Office, Washington). This secondary analysis is concerned only with the officer sample. Each service took an essentially random sample of officers through the rank of Colonel. In the Air Force and Army this was a strictly random sample; in the Navy it was a two-stage sample— first units were picked and then samples drawn from within units. Since the distribution of units is classified information, no further details were provided. We have no reason to believe the samples were biased, but inasmuch as each service made up and distributed its own questionnaire, slight differences in wording of questions sometimes occurred. We are interested in three broad lines of analysis of career commitment: (1) differences between services and sources of commission (Academy, Officer Candidate Schools, and Reserve Officer Training Corps); (2) reasons for career choice and career investment; and (3) impact of actual career experiences. First, are there service-wide differences in commitment to a military career? For instance, has the greater transformation of the Air Force led to weaker or stronger levels of commitment and to different patterns of value than are found in the Army, Navy, and Marines? On the basis of both popular images and the actual tasks and structure of the services, we might expect both a stronger commitment to a military career in the Navy and Marines and a commitment based on more intrinsically military than self-oriented values. Furthermore, since the services differ in their dependence on the Academies, ROTC, and OCS, as sources of officers, we will be able to examine the consequences of these differences for career commitment in each of the services.

Our second theme involves the question of the consequences of military career choice and professional rewards on career commitment. A military career, as any other career, can be conceived as a set of crucial choices. A young man, by virtue of his values and the available opportunities, enters an occupational pipeline. If the occupation permits gratification of values relative to other possible opportunities (whether the values be specific to the military, for example, "defending my country," or general to the society, for example, salary and "fringe benefits"), the officer is likely to remain in the service. Tenure in service is rewarded by certain rights to both pension and position. Thus the officer develops an investment in his career and a commitment to the military social system. In our analysis, we will attempt to untangle these various components of commitment.

Our third line of analysis, a subsidiary of the second, will examine selected aspects of the impact of career experience and civilian career alternatives on commitment. Where the second line of analysis examines reasons for entering a military service, the third will focus closer on later career experiences. Any career choice must be continually reinforced or it tends to disintegrate. Of the factors relating to career experience, we will focus on the officer's perception of the utilization of his skills by his service and the transferability of his skill to civilian employment.

In the first section of the paper we examine some of the basic parameters of military careers and career commitment. What are the differences between services, in reliance on different sources of commission? How do the rank structure, the relation of education to rank, and length of service influence career commitment? In the second section we examine the relation of career motives to later career commitment. Here we will investigate the impact of original career intention—full career or minimum obligated duty—as well as reasons for joining the service on career commitment. In the third section we discuss the effect of selected career experiences on career commitment.

MILITARY STRUCTURE AND CAREER COMMITMENT

Career opportunities for any given officer exist in a matrix provided by the structure and organization of his service. The services differ in their uses of Academy or non-Academy officers, in their rank structures, in their requirements for promotion, and in the rate at which they have expanded and opened up new opportunities. Before examining officer commitment to the military, let us look into service differences and similarities in type of commission of personnel, rank structure, education and length of service of personnel. These variables represent the service-wide parameters of careers.

The differences in rate of expansion have forced some of the services to a heavier reliance on non-Academy personnel. The percentage of officers who have entered each service by means of Academy, ROTC, or OCS commissions is shown in Table 1.[3] These data, of course, reflect past recruitment policy, not the emerging military establishment.

TABLE 1. DISTRIBUTION OF ACTIVE DUTY OFFICERS, BY
TYPE OF COMMISSION, FEBRUARY, 1961[a]

Officer	Army	Air Force	Navy	Marines
		(Percentages)		
Academy	11	4	33	11
ROTC	48	27	28	31
OCS	41	69	39	58
Total	100	100	100	100
Number of cases	5,494	9,445	2,110	587

[a] These data, like all other quantitative data in this paper, are drawn from the Sample Survey of February, 1961.

As expected, it is very clear that the Navy is most dependent on the Academy for its officer recruitment; one-third of Naval officers, 11 per cent of Army officers, and only 4 per cent of Air Force officers were Academy graduates. On the other hand, the Air Force has been most dependent on its own direct training facilities. Of the four services, the Army has depended heavily on its college training program; 48 per cent of the Army officers were commissioned through the ROTC, whereas none of the other services commissions as much as one-third of its officer corps from this source. The overriding fact is that clearly the Navy has relied more on its traditional source of recruitment—the Naval Academy. In part this pattern is a result of the greater stability of the Navy over the past thirty years as compared with both the Army and the Air Force. Proportionately, its expansion during World War II was the lowest; its contraction following World War II and expansion during the Korean Conflict was more gradual.

The patterns of recruitment of the *emerging military* are reflected by the distribution of officers by type of commission for the period 1957 to 1961. (See Table 2.) The reliance on Academy graduates is much more similar for the services, ranging from 11 per cent for the Navy to 5 per cent for the Air Force. While there is still a slight tendency for the Navy to be more dependent on Academy personnel than the other services, the major difference between services now is in their utilization of ROTC and OCS personnel. Both the Army and the Air Force have decreased their dependence on OCS sources of recruitment in favor of ROTC personnel, while the Navy has markedly increased its dependence on in-service OCS training, and the Marines have maintained a strong

TABLE 2. DISTRIBUTION OF ACTIVE DUTY OFFICERS FOR PERSONNEL COMMISSIONED 1957–1961, BY TYPE OF COMMISSION

Officer	Army	Air Force	Navy	Marines
		(Percentages)		
Academy	8	5	11	7
ROTC	82	64	36	37
OCS	10	31	53	56
Total	100	100	100	100
Number of cases	1,727	1,733	955	269

emphasis on in-service OCS training. Within the past several years, the Navy initiated a program of officer training for enlisted men in special technical fields which contributes OCS officers. This program assumes that these officers will not be promoted to senior officer grades. Even this program represents a modern technique to maintain a traditional approach. It is a mechanism that allows the Navy to adapt to technological change while it reserves to Academy personnel the upper ranks of command.

The next step in describing the structure of the officer corps is to note the relationship between rank and type of commission. Data on differences in the rank structure of the services by type of commission are available for the Air Force, Marines, and Navy (Table 3). We have used terminology common to the Army, Air Force, and Marines to describe rank. Rank structure represents the military counterpart to the occupational stratification system. A young officer at the bottom is likely to

TABLE 3. DISTRIBUTION OF RANK, BY TYPE OF COMMISSION

Rank	Air Force			Navy			Marines		
	Academy	ROTC	OCS	Academy	ROTC	OCS	Academy	ROTC	OCS
	(Percentages)			(Percentages)			(Percentages)		
Colonel and Lt. Colonel	17	7	15	31	4	6	17	16	15
Major and Captain	46	29	68	47	29	25	58	24	31
First and Second Lieutenants	37	64	17	22	68	70	23	59	53
Not ascertained							2	1	1
Total[a]	100	100	100	100	101	101	101	100	100
Number of cases	411	2,561	6,473	709	582	829	67	186	334

[a] Some columns add to more than 100 per cent because of rounding.

be very aware of the extent to which he has chances of promotion to the upper ranks, depending on his service and type of commission. Reading across the top row of Table 3, it is clear that the development of the Navy has led it to promote few ROTC (4 per cent) and OCS (6 per cent) personnel to the ranks of Colonel and Lieutenant Colonel, while about one-third of Academy graduates have reached these ranks. On the other hand, both the Marines and the Air Force have in the past promoted about as high a proportion of OCS personnel as Academy personnel to the upper ranks. We would expect the Army rank structure to parallel the Marines and Air Force.

The simplest interpretation of these data would be that the Air Force and Marines have more open opportunity systems than the Navy, but such an interpretation is oversimplified. Rank structures are sharply affected by length of service and therefore, indirectly, by the rate of

TABLE 4. DISTRIBUTION OF RANK BY TYPE OF COMMISSION (MAJOR OR ABOVE) OF AIR FORCE AND NAVY OFFICERS ENTERING SERVICE BEFORE 1948 AND BETWEEN 1948 AND 1953

Period	Air Force						Navy					
	Academy		ROTC		OCS		Academy		ROTC		OCS	
	Per Cent	Number of Cases	Per Cent	Number of Cases	Per Cent	Number of Cases	Per Cent	Number of Cases	Per Cent	Number of Cases	Per Cent	Number of Cases
Pre-1948	100	122	93	234	64	3,176	99	338	95	67	94	121
1948-1954	13	95	5	396	3	699	33	133	12	121	15	66

service expansion, contraction, and retirement. If one service has followed a policy of "force-outs" while another permitted officers to remain in middle ranks for long periods of time, career opportunities of lower grade officers would be affected by the mere quantity of long tenure officers. A more direct examination of the openness of career opportunities to non-Academy personnel is provided by the data relating length of service to rank presented in Table 4. (Since only an exceptional officer commissioned between 1948 and 1953 would have been promoted to the rank of Lieutenant Colonel by 1961, we have used attainment of the rank of Major or above for this analysis.)

These data show the strong conditioning of rank structure by historical circumstances, as well as by service personnel policies. If the Navy were a "closed" system, regardless of length of service, there would be few upper rank officers (Major or above) recruited through OCS and ROTC. But the data show that any Navy officer entering before 1948 and staying in service, no matter what his source of commission, was likely to rise at least to a rank equivalent to Major. Thus if an OCS or a ROTC officer survives the Navy's force-out policy his chances for promotion parallel the Academy graduate's up to the rank of flag officer.

By way of contrast, the development of the Air Force led it to develop a bulge in the middle ranks of the officer corps; thus both older OCS officers and younger officers of all types were less likely than Navy officers to rise to Major or above. No matter what the source of commission, the Air Force officer entering between 1948 and 1953 and staying in service was less likely than the Navy officer commissioned in this period to be promoted to the rank of Major or above. But Navy tradition still shows itself in these data, since among the officers entering between 1948 and 1953, 33 per cent of Annapolis graduates, as compared to 12 per cent of ROTC and 15 per cent of OCS graduates, had been promoted to the rank of Major or above by 1961.

While these data indicate that career mobility is conditioned by the overall structure of ranks, length of service and type of commission, it might be supposed that a fourth variable, education, also affects the attainment of higher rank. Although education is related to the attainment of rank, the relation is complex, especially for officers with more than four years of college education.

Table 5 presents the percentage of officers with a bachelor's degree or more by type of commission. Almost all Academy and ROTC officers indicate they have graduated from college.[4] On the other hand, OCS officers in the Army and Air Force typically have not finished college (22 per cent have received degrees), while Marines and Navy OCS personnel typically have finished college (64 per cent and 87 per cent, respectively). Since we know that higher education tends to be a prerequisite of higher occupational status in the civilian world, we might expect amount of education to be related to rank in the military as well.

TABLE 5. OFFICER EDUCATIONAL ACHIEVEMENT (BACHELOR'S DEGREE OR MORE), BY TYPE OF COMMISSION

Service	Academy		ROTC		OCS	
	Per Cent	Number of Cases	Per Cent	Number of Cases	Per Cent	Number of Cases
Army	99	622	93	2,623	22	2,249
Air Force	95	411	97	2,561	22	6,473
Navy	97	709	96	582	87	829
Marines	98	67	98	186	64	334

However, this way of expressing expectation may be misleading. In the civilian world, better-paying and more prestigious occupations tend to require more education. But we do not know whether *within* an occupation, for example, corporate management, higher education is related to greater financial rewards, or to higher rank. Let us look at the data for the military. Since in most cases the military requires fairly high education for commission, we compare the rank attainment of officers who have taken graduate work with those holding a college degree or less. Within this framework our data indicate that amount of education beyond college has only a slight relation to rank. For instance, 70 per cent of Air Force OCS officers with *less* than a college degree entering before 1948[5] attained the rank of Major or above, while 78 per cent of OCS officers with postgraduate work attained the rank of Major or above; the difference is slight. In the Navy the data also indicate only a slight tendency for those with postgraduate work to be more quickly advanced to upper ranks: among Academy officers entering between 1948 and 1953, 39 per cent of those with postgraduate work were the equivalent of Majors or above, while 29 per cent of those with a college degree or less reached this rank. Thus advanced graduate work has had only a slight relation to the attainment of higher rank. This may not be so in the future as some graduate training becomes more and more the case.

In fact, in a technologically advanced military establishment, we might expect formal education to become an increasingly important determinant of rank. If Academy officers are more likely to desire or to be encouraged to take graduate training, they will have a further advantage in the competition for promotion. The data presented in Table 6 show the proportion of officers entering the service before July, 1953, who have taken a year or more of graduate training. (The data are presented for officers with more than eight years of service only,

TABLE 6. GRADUATE EDUCATION,[a] BY TYPE OF COMMISSION
AMONG OFFICERS COMMISSIONED BEFORE JULY, 1953

Service	Academy		ROTC		OCS	
	Per Cent	Number of Cases	Per Cent	Number of Cases	Per Cent	Number of Cases
Army	55	418	35	824	11	1,896
Air Force	54	217	32	635	16	4,877
Navy	50	471	18	188	38	187
Marines	40	40	28	60	26	144

[a] Any schooling beyond the Bachelor's degree (not including specifically military schooling, e.g., infantry training).

since, if they had any intention of taking graduate work, most of this group would have completed their training.)

As shown, Academy officers in all services are more likely than others to have taken advanced training.[6] They not only have entered the service with an elite commission, but also have obtained training which further equips them for higher ranks. Navy and Marine OCS officers are more likely than Army and Air Force OCS officers to have obtained advanced training. On the other hand, a much higher proportion of Army ROTC than Navy officers have taken advanced training (35 per cent of the Army ROTC officers, compared to 18 per cent of Navy officers). More education implies greater civilian as well as military opportunity and may be related to career commitment. The important point here, however, is that Academy officers have more education than others.

CAREER COMMITMENT

Military career structures set the limits for individual opportunity, but they do not necessarily determine individual commitment to a career. Career commitment is the degree of attachment to military values and to a position in military service. Maximally, career commitment involves loyalty to the service and devoted pursuit of military goals, while a minimum definition of career commitment is the willingness of officers to remain in service. This latter definition, the one used here, focuses on the extent to which an individual is willing to commit his occupational life to a military career[7].

Our measure of extent of commitment, the crucial dependent variable of this study, is based on the following question:

"As of today, what are your plans for your Army (Air Force, Marine, Navy) career?"

a. I prefer to remain on active duty indefinitely or until retirement.
b. I prefer to remain on active duty only until I complete my present commitment.
c. I would prefer to separate immediately.
d. I am undecided.

Since the proportion of respondents choosing alternatives b, c, and d is relatively small, the three categories are collapsed in the analysis and considered indications of weak commitment.

The percentage of officers who intend to stay in service (alternative a) for each type of commission within each service is presented in Table 7. If we just looked at the "total" column, we would conclude that officers in the Army and Air Force are more committed to the military than those in the Navy and Marines: the percentage with strong career commitment ranges from 84 per cent in the Air Force, 76 per cent in the Army, 64 per cent in the Marines to 53 per cent in the Navy. We might then further conclude that the services *in general* differed in their ability to offer satisfying career opportunities. However, further examination of the data in Table 7 indicates that such a conclusion is premature. The "total" figures are a resultant of the proportion of officers in each service with different types of commission. No differences are found between services which are systematic across all three types of commission.

Let us examine differences *between types of commission* across all services and *within a single type* of commission across the four services. It is clear that a larger proportion of Academy than other personnel are

TABLE 7. OFFICERS WITH STRONG CAREER COMMITMENT,[a] BY TYPE OF COMMISSION

Service	Total		Academy		ROTC		OCS	
	Per Cent	Number of Cases	Per Cent	Number of Cases	Per Cent	Number of Cases	Per Cent	Number of Cases
Army	76	5,494	82	622	58	2,623	93	2,249
Air Force	84	9,445	80	411	61	2,561	93	6,473
Navy	53	2,120	83	709	36	582	40	829
Marines	64	587	79	67	53	186	63	334

[a] "I prefer to remain on active duty indefinitely or until retirement."

highly committed in all four services; four-fifths of Academy personnel are committed to careers. It is also clear that ROTC personnel are less committed than Academy personnel, with the Navy ROTC personnel having the smallest proportion strongly committed (36 per cent) and the Air Force having the largest proportion strongly committed (61 per cent). On the other hand, OCS personnel vary from a large proportion having strong career commitment in the Army and Air Force (over 90 per cent plan to stay in service) to under half in the Navy (40 per cent).

These data lead to several conclusions. One, the services do not differ in their ability to tie Academy graduates to a military career—Academy officers in all four services tend to be more committed than others and roughly to the same extent. Two, relative to Academy and OCS officers, far fewer ROTC personnel have a commitment to a military career; this tendency is strikingly pronounced in the Navy, but exists in all four services. The third, and most interesting, is the case of the OCS officers, who vary from having the highest proportion intending to stay in service in the Air Force and Army (higher even than the Academy personnel) to a very low proportion in the Navy. It is important to recognize that OCS and ROTC officers are more committed in the Air Force and Army than they are in the Navy and Marines; it is among them and not among Academy personnel that the problem of building career commitment presents the greatest challenge to the military manager. We would suggest, and later analysis will show, that these results are partially a product of higher perceived career opportunities in the Army and Air Force.

The data on career commitment are not fully interpretable until length of service is taken into account, for the military retirement system offers important rewards to the career soldier. Furthermore, because the services are partially dependent on officers who are only fulfilling military obligations, a crucial choice point comes within two to four years after joining a service. At this point, the potential careerist is separated from the man who is serving an obligated term. On the other hand, officers who have stayed in service longer lengths of time have survived the force-out system, devised to produce for the services competent and age-graded personnel. Therefore the differences in commitment we have shown might only reflect, for instance, that at the time of this survey the Air Force and Army ROTC personnel on the average had longer lengths of service than their counterparts in the Navy and Marines. The first panel of Table 8 presents the relationship of commitment to type of service among officers with under four-and-one-half years of service, and the second panel presents the same relationship among officers serving more than four-and-one-half years. Making this distinction, these data indicate that almost all officers who stay in longer than four years (after the crucial choice point) have high commitments. Among officers with more than four-and-one-half years of service, over four-fifths intend to stay in service. The only systematic difference among officers with longer service is that Army and Air Force OCS officers show a slightly higher proportion with strong commitment than do Navy OCS officers. On the other hand, among the officers with less than four-and-one-half years of service, the differences among Academy, ROTC, and OCS officers are quite striking. About three-fifths of Academy officers in their first tour of duty are committed to careers, while less than one-third of ROTC officers have high commitment. But the most important conclusion to be drawn is that, even controlling for length of service, the services differ in their abilities to develop career commitment among younger personnel. Navy and

TABLE 8. OFFICERS WITH STRONG CAREER COMMITMENT, BY TYPE OF COMMISSION AND LENGTH OF SERVICE

Service	Commissioned After July, 1956						Commissioned Before July, 1956					
	Academy		ROTC		OCS		Academy		ROTC		OCS	
	Per Cent	Number of Cases	Per Cent	Number of Cases	Per Cent	Number of Cases	Per Cent	Number of Cases	Per Cent	Number of Cases	Per Cent	Number of Cases
Army	62	130	31	1,428	78	169	87	485	84	1,195	95	2,065
Air Force	65	112	37	1,229	78	608	84	294	87	1,262	96	5,680
Navy	61	142	16	381	21	574	88	559	81	193	85	246
Marines	57	19	23	100	28	150	88	48	87	79	91	182

Marine ROTC and OCS officers as compared with Army and Air Force ROTC and OCS officers are less committed to a military career. Differences in perceived opportunities and actual force-out policies are clearly at work.

Inferentially, it would appear that Army and Air Force OCS officers, with their lower education, have become embedded in a career, while civilian opportunities beckon the Navy and Marine OCS officers (who have higher education). But such an explanation does not account for differences in commitment among ROTC personnel, who have college education in all the services. Again, this may be a function of differences in the opportunities perceived as provided by the services. In the next two sections we will attempt to examine the reasons for joining the services and the career experiences that might help us explain in more detail the differences between officers recruited through different channels.

MOTIVATIONS FOR MILITARY CAREERS

The choice of any occupation is based on a complex set of factors. Career choices are compounded of rational decisions, psychological identifications, family traditions, and interpersonal and opportunity networks. Historically, military career choices in American society have not competed in the marketplace of occupational opportunities. On the one hand, to a greater extent than is true of most occupations, military career choices have been nourished in family and regional tradition. On the other hand, military career choices, at least in the popular image, have often been taken in refuge from the rigors of the open society. Furthermore, whereas entrance into most occupations of middle-class status is usually relatively voluntary, entrance into the officer corps is in some cases one step from coercion, representing avoidance of conscription or of enlisted-man status rather than a positive choice. When the choice is a free one, it represents a choice of a disciplined and dangerous career seemingly isolated from the major values of American society. Choice of a military career may stem from a greater range of motivations than most occupations, and we might expect initial motivation to have a greater impact on later career commitment than in most professions. Although our data do not permit us to analyze in depth the relation of career motivation to career commitment (for instance, we have no data on family tradition or social background), we do have data on the officers' conscious motivations for joining the service.

In examining the career plans of the officer when he entered service, we are essentially attempting to assess a simple notion that might account for the findings presented in the preceding section; namely, that the proportions intending to stay or leave reflect the fact that officers entering through different recruitment channels have different initial career plans and values. While we do not deny that initial career plans and values vary, we believe that officers undergo a number of career experiences which fashion commitment.

To discover initial career plans, this question was put to officers:

"When you first entered the Army (Navy, Marines), what were your military career plans?"

a. Intended to make the Army my career.
b. Intended to stay in the Army a while longer than my obligated tour.
c. Intended to serve a minimum tour (or wartime "duration plus six months").
d. Hadn't thought about it.
e. Was undecided and waited to see how well I'd like the Army.

The relations of present career plans to original intentions of a military career are set forth in Table 9 on page 273.[8] These data indicate that original career intentions have some, but not a pervasive, relation to later career plans. Only among Academy officers are initial intentions to follow the military profession linked to career plans. The Academy officers again show great similarity in all services, in that three-fourths of those with strong commitment (staying in service) assert that they originally intended a military career. More interesting, one-half who are now planning to leave originally planned a military career.[9]

Very few Academy personnel originally planned a minimum tour of duty. Although men may initially attend the Academy only to secure an education, by the time they are commissioned they are interested in a military career. The percentage who planned a minimum tour never rises above 8 per cent in any of the services. This would seem to be clear evidence that the 15 to 20 per cent of Academy officers who plan to leave or have vague plans (weak commitment) are people whose career experiences have not been satisfactory. But the important conclusion to be drawn is that for officers commissioned after attending the Academy there is a relatively high degree of consistency between original plans and career experience; a few seem to have been disillusioned, but most found what they sought.

A different picture emerges for ROTC and OCS officers who have strong commitment and who were brought to their careers by historical accident, not by voluntary choice. As we would expect, a much larger proportion of ROTC than Academy officers, whether or not they had strong or weak commitment, initially had doubts or were not planning a military career. More of those who plan to stay than of those planning to leave had original plans to stay, but most ROTC personnel planning to stay have in some way found careers that they had not anticipated. Only in the Marines do most of the ROTC officers who are staying (63 per cent) say they had planned a military career.

The effect of career experiences and career opportunities is most forcibly demonstrated, however, among OCS officers. First, OCS officers have stronger career commitments than ROTC officers. (See Tables 7 and 8.) But the data indicate that the percentage of OCS personnel who originally planned a military career was lower than or at best equal to the percentage of ROTC officers. Second, one-half of the Army officers now planning to stay tell us that they originally planned only a minimum tour. This is a much higher percentage than in either the Navy or Marines, yet it is the Army which has the highest proportion of OCS personnel planning military careers. Third, a similiar proportion of Army OCS personnel who are staying to those who are leaving originally had plans for a military career (21 per cent and 24 per cent, respectively; see Table 9). At least for the Army OCS, initial plans seem to have little to do with later plans. This is less true for the Marines and Navy OCS where no more than 10 per cent of those who are leaving originally planned a career. Still, a majority of OCS personnel who are staying in all three services did not originally plan to stay.

In summary, then, although Academy officers initially planned a career, original military career intentions have only a slight relationship to later career commitment for ROTC officers and no relation to OCS officers' later career plans. OCS officers are much more likely to become highly committed than ROTC officers, even though, if anything, on entering they begin in a less committed position. Is it possible, however, that those who plan on staying had different values when they entered than those who plan on leaving? Is it not the substantive values a man holds and not his original plans that are important in determining career commitment? Our data permit a partial answer to this question. Respondents were asked,

> "What were the two most important reasons for your original entry on active duty into the Marine (Army, Navy) corps?"

Thirteen alternatives were presented:

1. Was drafted, ordered to duty.
2. Travel, adventure, new experiences.
3. Preferred Army (Navy, Marines) to other military branches.

4. Army (Navy, Marines) career opportunities looked better to me than civilian life.
5. Education and training for a civilian career.
6. Pay, allowances, and fringe benefits.
7. Security of Army life (steady job and fringe benefits).
8. Wanted to take advantage of G.I. Bill in later civilian life.
9. Patriotic feelings and National Defense.
10. Interested in the outdoor, active life.
11. Liked flying and aviation (ships, boating).
12. None of the above.
13. Can't remember.

The alternative responses listed above range from essentially coerced choices (drafted) to those extrinsic to the military profession such as

TABLE 9. INITIAL CAREER INTENTIONS AND CAREER COMMITMENT, BY TYPE OF COMMISSION

Service	Academy		ROTC		OCS	
	Commitment		Commitment		Commitment	
	Strong	Weak	Strong	Weak	Strong	Weak
	(Percentages)					
ARMY Initial Intent						
Army career	78	52	38	14	21	24
Wait and see	16	36	28	45	17	17
Minimum tour	4	8	26	30	52	46
Unclassified and no answer[a]	3	5	8	11	11	13
Total	101	101	100	100	101	100
Number of cases	810	112	1,513	1,110	2,100	149
NAVY Initial Intent						
Navy career	74	53	32	5	26	5
Wait and see	16	39	47	61	33	58
Minimum tour	7	3	13	30	30	30
Unclassified and no answer[a]	3	5	9	5	11	7
Total	100	100	101	101	100	100
Number of cases	587	122	210	372	334	495
MARINES Initial Intent						
Marine career	72	50	63	17	32	10
Wait and see	17	36	30	53	34	54
Minimum tour	8	7	4	26	24	27
Unclassified and no answer[a]	4	7	3	3	10	10
Total	101	100	100	99	100	101
Number of cases	53	14	99	871	208	125

[a] Unclassified: "Hadn't thought about it" and "A while longer than my obligated tour."

security and G.I. Bill, to those intrinsic to the image of the military adventure, patriotism, and military career preference.[10] The analysis of the relation of these values to career commitment is of interest largely because we find few systematic differences between services and types of commission that are meaningfully related to commitment.

The percentage of officers offering a particular reason for joining, by type of commission and service, is presented in Table 10.[11] Broad differences in the initial motivation of officers entering the different services emerge from these data. The percentages presented in the "total" column indicate, first of all, that the Army has been more dependent on a conscripted officer corps than the other services (33 per cent for the Army as compared to 2 per cent and 1 per cent for the Marines and Navy).

TABLE 10. REASONS FOR JOINING AND CAREER COMMITMENT,
BY TYPE OF COMMISSION

Reasons for Joining	Academy		ROTC		OCS		Total
	Commitment		Commitment		Commitment		
	Strong	Weak	Strong	Weak	Strong	Weak	
	FIRST AND SECOND CHOICE OF REASONS GIVEN (Percentages)						
"Drafted, ordered to duty"							
Army	2	3	37	23	45	39	33
Navy	1	2	2	1	2	1	1
Marines	9	–	–	3	1	1	2
"Wanted Security —Pay, Fringe benefits"							
Army	21	19	19	9	11	11	14
Navy	16	11	12	5	13	4	10
Marines	11	–	18	28	9	3	14
"Liking the life style of the Military"[a]							
Army	38	37	32	28	24	23	29
Navy	46	46	42	38	38	57	44
Marines	32	27	35	34	55	24	40
"Wanting Military Career"[b]							
Army	39	29	36	27	31	30	32
Navy	43	36	51	67	75	77	61
Marines	65	92	61	73	88	86	80

[a] "Travel, adventure, new experience, like the outdoor activity and life, flying and aviation, boats and ships."

[b] "Joined the Army (Navy or Marines) in preference to other service." "Military career opportunity looked better to me than civilian life."

A second type of military career choice is represented by the person who does not especially value the goals or life style of the military, but who does value it as a way of earning a decent living, of gaining job security; he joins for extrinsic reasons. For this person the military career represents, to some extent, an alternative to the rigors of civilian competition and instability—the military is seen as an alternate route to civil service security, or to a relatively satisfactory salary. However, in all three services, the proportion entering for extrinsic reasons (security, pay, fringe benefits) is relatively small—no more than 15 per cent give security and pay as their reasons for joining.

To this point, we have presented reasons for joining which essentially represent values unrelated to the basic goals and life style created by the military establishment. One might expect, however, that Navy and Marine personnel and Academy graduates in all services would place much greater emphasis than others on intrinsic motives for joining; that is, they would value the military for itself or for the way of life attached to the military.

A larger proportion of officers tell us they joined for intrinsic rather than extrinsic or minimal commitment reasons; the proportion never falls below one-third. Between the services, differences again emerged: far fewer Army officers joined for intrinsic reasons than Navy and Marine officers. Forty per cent of Marine officers and 44 per cent of Navy officers, as compared to only 29 per cent of Army officers, chose responses pertaining to military life style as their reason for joining. Similarly, 80 per cent of the Marines and 61 per cent of the Navy officers, as compared to only 32 per cent of the Army officers, joined the service because they specifically wanted a career in their particular branch. This is the only point in the data analyzed in this paper on which across-the-board, interservice differences were found. However, even though the Army to a lesser degree than the other services capitalizes on intrinsic motivation, the important and striking conclusion to be drawn from Table 10 is that these service-wide differences do not make much difference to later career commitment. Strength of commitment turns out to be unrelated to reasons for joining as measured by the question.

Let us examine the relation of reason for joining and career commitment by type of commission, as well as by service. Being drafted has limited effect on later career commitment. Among Army ROTC and OCS officers, a sizable proportion do say they were drafted (23 per cent and 45 per cent, respectively). But these Army ROTC and OCS officers reveal a higher proportion who say they were drafted among those intending to stay than among those planning to leave. Undoubtedly this reflects the wartime conscription and therefore longer length of service among those with strong commitment. The important point, however, is that an essentially coerced entrance into the military is not incompatible with later commitment to a military career. Although a person may remain in service in order to receive a pension and the status he has achieved, these data indicate that men do not choose the military to *gain* security or pay. No more than 28 per cent (Marine ROTC, weak commitment) in any one category tell us they joined for fringe benefits and pay. Furthermore, although those staying in service are more likely to say than those planning to leave that they joined for extrinsic reasons (seven out of nine comparisons), the percentage differences are not great, never rising above 10 per cent. Officers may later find security in the military, but during this period officers did not join the military seeking it.[12]

Finally, we can examine the relation of career commitment to intrinsic reasons for joining. One might expect, for instance, officers joining for intrinsic reasons to be more committed than those coerced or joining for extrinsic reasons. Navy and Marine officers do show high intrinsic motivation, but we know from our previous analysis (Tables 7 and 8) that the level of Academy commitment does not vary between services, while commitment is stronger among Army ROTC and OCS personnel than among Navy and Marines entering through the same channels. The data in panels 3 and 4 of Table 10 reveal no systematic differences among the strong and weak commitment groups. Sometimes a larger proportion of the strongly committed joined for intrinsic reasons, sometimes a larger proportion of the weakly committed, but no systematic pattern emerges.[13]

To summarize, even though these data show variations between services and to some extent between types of commission, the data indicate that, in general, substantive reasons for joining bear no relation to later career commitment.

What, then, do we conclude from this analysis of initial career plans and motives? Basically, while we find that initial career plans are predictive of the commitment of Academy officers, they are not predictive of the later plans of ROTC and OCS officers. Furthermore, we have been unable to find a pattern of substantive values that relates to later career plans.

Thus, more than to initial motives, we must look to the career experiences that tie a man in or disengage him from a career. These are partly historical accidents—being recalled to active duty from reserve status, for instance—but they are also based on his job and life satisfactions.

THE IMPACT OF CAREER EXPERIENCES

Occupational choice is often made with only slight knowledge of the gratifications and deprivations which various occupations afford. Moreover, choice may be made as much an escape from a negative alternative as an approach to a positive one. An occupational choice transforms itself into a career line only after initial expectations are confirmed or not confirmed. Of course, historical circumstances may lead a person into a career in which he builds considerable investment in staying with an occupation mainly for extrinsic reasons. For many military officers, especially ROTC and OCS recruits, career choices have been facilitated by a peculiar combination of the "carrot and the stick"; on the one hand, many have been almost coerced into the military establishment, on the other hand, as they have devoted years to the service, their investments have rapidly risen. Not only are there career "payoffs" such as pensions, but for many there are the rewards of work, status, satisfying interpersonal relations. This is especially true for the OCS officer. More than other officers in the military, he has found a career and status which his educational level might not allow him to attain in the civilian world.

Career commitment, as defined here, depends not only on the officer's perception of rewards or deprivations from his present work situation but also on a comparison to relevant civilian alternatives. Thus commitment represents a balance between the perceived gratifications and deprivations of military and of civilian life. A great range of gratifications and deprivations may be found in any occupation; salaries, interpersonal relations, intrinsic task satisfactions, and geographic location, to name but a few, may all contribute to career commitment or disaffiliation. We focus largely on two factors related to career commitment, perception of skill utilization in the military and perception of civilian alternatives. Since officers entering service through different channels differ in their marketable skills and in their values, commitment should vary greatly, depending on whether officers perceive their skills as being highly utilized and whether they perceive good civilian alternatives.

Let us look first at the relation between officer perception of the utilization of skills and career commitment. The officers were asked, "How much do you feel the Army (Navy, Marines) has utilized your skills and abilities?" Although the question is not phrased specifically in terms of present job assignment, it is here interpreted as one measure of basic or underlying job satisfaction. The percentage of officers staying or leaving who feel their branch has utilized their skills and abilities "a great deal" is given in Table 11. It can be seen that within each service and type of commission the proportion who feel their skills have been utilized is higher among those planning to stay than among those planning to leave; thus perceived skill utilization would seem to be a factor in the degree of commitment to a career. Again we find no systematic differences between services. Army OCS indicate higher skill utilization than Marine or Navy OCS, but there are no differences between Marine, Navy, and Army ROTC and Academy officers.

More important, Academy personnel in the three services who are planning to leave (weak commitment) are in general less dissatisfied with the utilization of their skills than are ROTC and OCS people who are leaving. Approximately 40 per cent of Academy personnel with weak commitment feel their skills are utilized as compared to under

TABLE 11. SKILL UTILIZATION AND CAREER COMMITMENT, BY TYPE OF COMMISSION

REPORTS "SKILLS UTILIZED A GREAT DEAL"

Service	Academy				ROTC				OCS			
	Commitment				Commitment				Commitment			
	Strong		Weak		Strong		Weak		Strong		Weak	
	Per Cent	Number of Cases	Per Cent	Number of Cases	Per Cent	Number of Cases	Per Cent	Number of Cases	Per Cent	Number of Cases	Per Cent	Number of Cases
Army	67	510	46	112	59	1,513	22	1,110	76	2,100	57	149
Navy	68	587	37	122	59	210	22	372	66	334	26	495
Marines	57	51	43	14	64	99	10	87	70	209	26	123

20 per cent of ROTC and 25 per cent of OCS officers. The exception is the Army OCS personnel who are leaving; they are more satisfied with skill utilization than Army Academy personnel. Thus Academy officers who have weak career commitment are, to a lesser degree than the others, escaping from an undesirable situation.

These data also indicate the general dissatisfaction of ROTC personnel. In five out of six cases (the exception is Marine ROTC officers who are planning on staying), the percentage of ROTC personnel who feel that their skills and abilities are being utilized is lower than among either Academy *or* OCS personnel in comparable commitment categories.

The data, of course, may be influenced by length of service. The officer who has been in service a long time may answer in terms of general career satisfaction. But this possibility must be balanced by the fact that the officer of long service has higher rank and has probably been given an assignment compatible with his skills and interests. It is true that the longer the length of service, the greater the likelihood of an officer's feeling that his skills have been utilized. For instance, 87 per cent of Marine ROTC officers who have been in service fourteen years or more feel that their skills are being utilized a great deal, compared to 64 per cent of those in service between thirteen and seven years, and only 20 per cent of those in service less than seven years. Again, among Navy Academy people, the percentage saying "utilized a great deal" for these same length-of-service categories are, respectively, 70 per cent, 66 per cent, and 51 per cent. However, even within similar length-of-service categories, lack of skill utilization is related to weak commitment. Data relating length of service, skill utilization and career commitment among Army OCS officers are presented in Table 12. (These data are presented rather than some other group because Army OCS gives us a large enough base for statistical analysis.) The data indicate

TABLE 12. SKILL UTILIZATION, LENGTH OF SERVICE, AND
CAREER COMMITMENT AMONG ARMY OCS OFFICERS

REPORT "SKILLS UTILIZED A GREAT DEAL"

Commitment	14 years or more		13 to 7 years		Less than 7 years	
	Per Cent	Number of Cases	Per Cent	Number of Cases	Per Cent	Number of Cases
Strong commitment	76	429	61	325	49	754
Weak commitment	62	50	46	24	20	412

clearly that skill utilization is perceived to be lower among those with low commitment at each length of service level. The difference between strong and weak commitment groups does not fall below 14 per cent.

Perception of skill utilization is a rough measure of present job satisfaction, but, by itself, low job satisfaction is not a sufficient condition to give up a military career: in the absence of reasonable alternatives, even the person who feels his skills are not being utilized is likely to remain in service.

To measure perception of ease of access to comparable civilian positions, respondents were asked, "If you were soon to leave the Army, how difficult do you think it would be to find a job equal to your present one (equal as to pay, satisfaction, benefits, challenge, etc.)?" The proportion who believe it would be easy to get a comparable job by type of commission and commitment are presented in Table 13. The "Difference" columns in Table 13 present the percentage of difference between

TABLE 13. ACCESS TO COMPARABLE CIVILIAN JOB AND CAREER COMMITMENT, BY TYPE OF COMMISSION

REPORTS "VERY EASY" OR "FAIRLY EASY"

Service	Academy					ROTC					OCS				
	Commitment				Difference Per Cent	Commitment				Difference Per Cent	Commitment				Difference Per Cent
	Strong		Weak			Strong		Weak			Strong		Weak		
	Per Cent	Number of Cases	Per Cent	Number of Cases		Per Cent	Number of Cases	Per Cent	Number of Cases		Per Cent	Number of Cases	Per Cent	Number of Cases	
Army	51	510	71	112	20	46	1,513	79	1,110	33	31	2,100	56	749	25
Air Force	47	330	48	82	1	44	1,567	82	994	38	32	6,016	79	457	47
Navy	36	587	56	122	20	32	210	79	372	47	39	334	68	495	29
Marines	47	53	26	14	21	35	99	79	87	42	28	209	63	125	35

high and low commitment. It should be pointed out that, as phrased, the question is two-edged: answers to it reflect both the valuation of present jobs and the assessment of civilian opportunities. Thus interpretation of these data must take into account both the loyalty and military identification implied by perceiving little possibility of comparable jobs in the civilian world and the transferability of skill involved in perceiving easy access to comparable jobs.

It could be argued that those with low career commitment are more likely to believe it is easy to get comparable civilian jobs. But note that even among those staying in service from one-third to one-half of the officers believe it would be easy to get a comparable job. They are not staying in service because they perceive no opportunity in the civilian world. As a general rule, however, a larger proportion of those who are leaving perceive easy access to comparable jobs than among those who are staying. More interesting than this general finding are the differences found between types of commission. The fact that there is less difference between Academy officers with strong and weak commitment than among others (an average of about 17 per cent for Academy officers, 40 per cent for ROTC officers, and 33 per cent for OCS) reflects, on the one hand, that outside jobs are easier to secure for Academy than OCS officers who are staying and, on the other hand, that Academy officers who are leaving are less negative about the military than ROTC officers, especially the younger ROTC officers. This interpretation is also supported by the fact that except for Naval Academy graduates, Academy officers who are staying are slightly more likely than ROTC and OCS officers who are staying to think it is easy to get a civilian job.

Comparison of Navy and Army Academy officers is revealing. Whether they have high or low commitment, Naval Academy officers are less likely than their peers in the Army to view comparable jobs as easy to obtain. This is not a function of length of service, since both the Navy and the Army have similar proportions of Academy graduates with long lengths of service. Instead, it appears to reflect either or both of two interrelated factors: on the one hand, there is less "distance" and more "transferability" between Army life and civilian life. The range of tasks given to the Army in the postwar world and its contest with the civilian world have led to a strong civilianization of the Army. On the other hand, the smaller, more compact structure of the Navy leads Academy officers to develop a greater identification with the military career per se. Evidence for this last statement is based on a comparison of data in Tables 11 and 13. Among those staying in service, a similar proportion of Army and Naval Academy officers feel their skills are being adequately used, yet Naval Academy graduates are less likely than Army graduates to believe they can easily get comparable jobs. That this same difference exists for Army ROTC and Navy ROTC officers who are staying in service gives further support to this interpretation. In other words, Naval Academy officers seem to have stronger links to their military careers.

The perspectives of ROTC officers provide a useful contrast to those of Academy officers. In all services, ROTC officers with weak commitment see comparable jobs as easily obtained; four-fifths of those with weak commitment, a higher proportion than among any other category believe they can easily get good jobs. Their own skills and training are eminently suited for the civilian world and they have a positive distaste for military careers.

Finally, there is a slight tendency for OCS officers with strong commitment to be more pessimistic than others about their chances of obtaining comparable jobs (except among Navy OCS officers, the most educated group). For instance, only 31 per cent of Army OCS officers who are staying feel they could get comparable jobs, while 46 per cent of Army ROTC who are staying and 51 per cent of Academy officers in this category feel they could get comparable jobs. Whereas ROTC graduates seem to be running from the military establishment, OCS officers seem to have few comparable alternatives.

These data on the perception of the availability of comparable jobs and on skill utilization begin to untangle the factors leading to the decision to stay in the service. Career commitment is a function of the individual's career investment, his sense of professional satisfaction, and his alternatives in civilian occupations.[14]

Many ROTC and OCS officers enter the service with little or no commitment to a military career, but while the military provides the OCS officer with more meaningful experience and a higher status than his civilian alternative would, the military does not provide ROTC officers with a viable alternative. On the other hand, although the Academy graduate has relatively easy access to good civilian jobs, much like the ROTC officer, his training and identification are more likely to lead him to find professional satisfaction in the military.

CONCLUSION

This discussion has attempted to identify the factors associated with career commitment. The analysis led to an examination of the structure of career opportunities provided by the services. Within this framework we examined the social-psychological bases of career commitment. The services differ in rank structure, in reliance on Academy, ROTC, and OCS personnel for upper ranks, and in opportunities for promotion. However, although service-wide differences in career commitment exist, they are a result of these differences in sources from which officers are drawn. Only when service was joined with type of commission were differences in career commitment found: Academy recruits are highly committed in all services, while OCS and ROTC personnel are more committed in the Army and Air Force than in the Navy and Marines. Our strongest findings relate to the variations in commitment of officers entering through different commission channels. This is partly linked to the historical development of the services, leading to the massing of OCS and ROTC with large career investments in the Air Force and Army. But the differential career commitments of OCS, ROTC, and Academy personnel is also based on the career payoff opportunities that are provided to people with higher and lower education and on the ease of access to satisfying jobs in the civilian world.

Our analysis demonstrates the utility of a combination of "macro-" and "micro-concerns" in analyzing professional careers and military careers, in particular. On the one hand, we have attempted to set our analysis in the framework of the historical changes that have been wrought in the military establishment. On the other hand, we have looked at careers on the social-psychological level as being in a perpetual state of choice.

Possibly, however, the most important problem posed by our data is the role of career experience in developing a military commitment. The services cannot be dependent on Academy personnel only to man their officer positions. More than 50 per cent of the officer corps consists of officers who do not make a positive choice of careers; instead, they join to fulfill a military obligation or without any clearcut commitment (ROTC), or they join the officer corps only after serving as enlisted men (OCS). The turnover costs of maintaining a short-term, uncommitted officer corps are tremendously high, although the expense may be balanced by the maintenance of a reserve for emergency call-up.

Any attempt to create greater career commitment must recognize that all of the channels of recruitment do not guarantee equal commitment to substantive military tasks. Our data were not adequate to explore the questions about professional values raised in the introduction. However, the findings of this study are compatible with an overreaching generalization about the transformation of military career socialization: if in the past intensive Academy training was necessary and sufficient for the development of the skills and heroic identifications required for command, today such training is inadequate to recruit the range of professional identifications and personnel needed to man the services. Although the services may continue to be dependent on Academy graduates for filling elite positions, even the Academy graduate must be continually led to develop new skills and identifications. The fundamental transformation of the recruitment base of the officer corps, however, requires that the services develop new ways of building commitment to military goals regardless of source of commission. Our data suggest that the services must be as much concerned with career experience as they are with career recruitment in building these commitments.

NOTES

1. In *Man and Society in an Age of Reconstruction*, Karl Mannheim argues that all elite professions in industrial society will undergo a "democratization," that is, a broadening of the social base. He raises the question of the problem of transmitting social values when the institutions inculcating these values are no longer experienced by the vast majority of professionals. See Mannheim, Karl, *Man in Society in an Age of Reconstruction: Studies in Modern Social Structure*, Kegan Paul, London, 1940.

2. Although the Marines do not have "service" status equal to the Air Force, Navy, or Army, for the purpose of this paper we will refer to Marine Corps as a service. Marine officers live their military life within the branch, therefore, for analyzing career commitments we will treat it on a par with the three other services.

3. We have excluded from our analysis Warrant officers and those receiving either National Guard or Direct Commissions. Warrant officers and officers with National Guard commissions represent a small proportion of the total and our sample did not provide a large enough number for statistical analysis. Officers with Direct Commissions are a diverse group, representing both battlefield commissions and selected professions (such as medical doctors). To have relatively homogeneous groups for analysis, we restricted ourselves to the major types of commission.

4. The wording of the alternatives in the question on education permitted the respondent to choose among those linked to degree attainment *or* to years of schooling. The fact that a small percentage of Academy and ROTC officers answered that they had not completed college degree requirements probably reflects their participation in speeded-up college programs.

5. Since rank is strongly dependent on length of service, analysis of the relation of education to rank can only be made by comparing officers with varying education who have served equal lengths of time; because of sample size, this requirement considerably restricts our analysis.

6. In a personal communication, Louis Morton has suggested that these data do not reflect the Navy's practice of sending officers to the Naval Post-Graduate School, Monterey, California, while Army and Air Force officers take graduate training at the best of civilian universities. This practice on the part of the Army and Air Force tends to break down the barriers between the civilian and military worlds.

7. A fundamental problem of the analysis in the remainder of this paper is that our data are drawn from people who are now in the service. The ideal design for the

study of career commitment is that of longitudinal cohort analysis including men who never become officers and those who leave the service, as well as those in the service. No such data are available.

8. Alternatives a, c, and e are presented in Rows 1, 3, and 2, respectively, of Table 9, which gives the percentage of those staying or leaving in each category of initial intent. Alternative b, ". . . a while longer than my obligated tour," and alternative d, "hadn't thought about it," are lumped with respondents who did not answer the questions, since there were so few of them and since the categories lacked analytic usefulness.

9. We recognize that people may not recall their original intentions, thus distorting the data. It is likely that distortion occurs in the direction of cognitive consistency; that is, among Academy people planning to stay, it is likely that fewer originally planned to. But accepting this principle, more who are now leaving would say they had originally not planned a military career. Rather than try and account for distortion processes, we accept answers as veridical.
Throughout the remainder of the paper we deal with a set of interrelated questions that involve rationalization and potential distortion process. Nevertheless, these data represent the only systematic body of data available on the topic.

10. When we first began working with these data, we tried to develop types of commitment from the two choices the officers made. For instance, a person who selected as reasons for joining "adventure" and "patriotism" was classified as committed for intrinsic military reasons, while someone who chose salary and security was seen as committed for extrinsic reasons. A careerist type and a minimal committed type (drafted) were also constructed. Mixed types were created out of those who showed a combination of responses, for instance, adventure and drafted. The typology proved unproductive and was consequently abandoned.

11. We have selected for presentation alternatives that range from coerced choices to intrinsic motivation. The analysis is intended to be illustrative. Data on the other alternatives would not substantially change our conclusions.

12. Of course, since extrinsic reasons tend to be socially disapproved by many, our data may understate the extrinsic motivation for military careers.

13. We have not presented data relating to choice of "patriotism" and "National Defense," two other intrinsic reasons for joining. These reasons are likely to be given by older officers who were commissioned during the war. Controlling by length of service, they are not related to commitment.

14. A different and more direct approach to the factors related to career commitment is to examine the reasons given for staying or leaving. The officers were presented with a list of alternative reasons for staying or leaving similar to that used for reasons for joining, presented earlier. The leaving alternatives listed such factors as "family considerations," "can't choose location," and the like. Though the form of the question prohibits detailed analysis, some analyses of these data, not presented here, tend to support our interpretation of the meaning of military careers to officers with different types of commission. For instance, 23 per cent of Army Academy officers with high commitment checked "A chance to contribute to National Defense," while only 13 per cent of ROTC officers and 11 per cent of OCS officers checked this answer. On the other hand, 56 per cent of Army OCS officers checked "Security," while only 35 per cent of Academy officers and 37 per cent of ROTC officers checked such responses. One sees in these data the slightly greater goal commitment of Academy officers as compared with ROTC and OCS personnel.

SEQUELS TO A MILITARY CAREER: THE RETIRED MILITARY PROFESSIONAL

Albert D. Biderman

THE ROLE of retired U.S. military personnel in civilian life raises broader questions now than in the past. As compared with any previous time, there are presently far more retired military men with far greater involvement in more varied nonmilitary pursuits for greater proportions of their lives. These circumstances are likely to be more pronounced in the immediate future and will continue indefinitely.

The personnel structure of our armed forces assumes that a considerable proportion of all who successfully embark on a military career will have half or more of their productive lives remaining at the time they are forced to leave the military. Present and proposed personnel systems for the armed forces assume that military retirees will be able to find and pursue satisfactory second careers in the civilian world, even when their numbers are substantial.

Large-scale military retirement in the United States is still too recent and insufficiently studied to have provided an adequate test of this assumption. The retired military population of the future, furthermore, will differ markedly from that of the present and recent past in such key respects as rank, age, educational attainment, military experience, and physical health. First, let us examine the recent and future growth of the retired military population and some major changes in its composition.

Numbers

Chart 1 illustrates the rapidity with which the retired military population of the United States is growing. The number of persons receiving retired military pay has more than doubled in the past ten years; the total is now over 350,000. The year 1963, however, apparently marks the peak of the *rate* of increase. Chart 2, showing the number of actual or projected retirements from active duty, 1956–1970, reflects the movement through the personnel system of the World War II "hump." We are now approaching the twentieth anniversary of the peak of World War II mobilization and this "hump" of World War II entrants is

CHART 1. PROJECTED NUMBER OF MILITARY PERSONNEL
RECEIVING RETIRED PAY, BY TYPE OF RETIREMENT

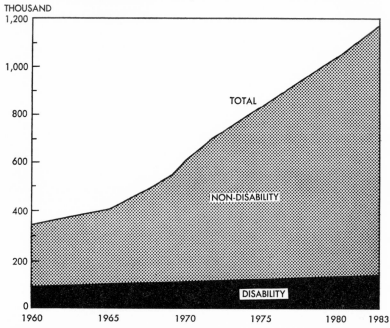

SOURCE: Glenn, Joseph B., Consultant, Office of the Assistant Secretary of Defense, "Report on Revised Estimates of the Future Numbers of Military Retired," presented at the Conference on Needs for Knowledge Regarding the Military Retirement Problem, Washington, D. C., April 30–May 1, 1960.

reflected in the plateau evident for the next several years in Chart 2. The growth of the military retired will continue into the indefinite future, however, if force levels are sustained. In 1979 it is expected that the one million figure will be reached.

Nondisability

Two marked changes in the composition of the retired military population are evident. A decade ago, persons retired for disability accounted for almost half of the total. As shown in Chart 1, however, disability retirements have remained at an almost constant level, while nondisability retirements have grown rapidly. The large majority of current retirees are in the nondisability category. (See Chart 2.)

Disability retirements constitute a complication for interpreting the available data in relation to questions about military and second careers. Many of those receiving disability pay spent only relatively brief periods in active service. Typically, these retirees resemble the pensioned veteran

CHART 2. NUMBER OF RETIREMENTS AMONG MILITARY PERSONNEL
ON ACTIVE DUTY, BY TYPE OF RETIREMENT

NUMBER
OF PERSONS
ANNUALLY

Fiscal Years 1956–1961, Actual
Fiscal Years 1962–1970, Projected

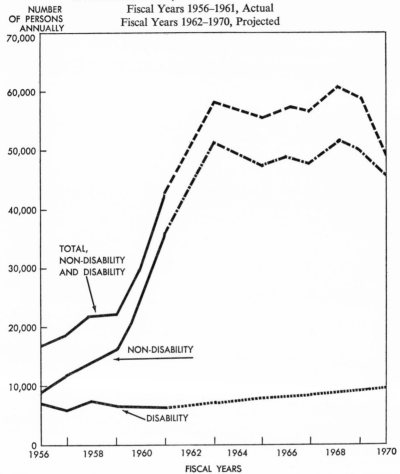

FISCAL YEARS

more than the retired professional soldier. Others, however, were also
eligible on the basis of length-of-service when they retired. Indeed, a
marginal decision faces some men on leaving the service as to whether
to elect to receive all or some of their benefits from the Veterans
Administration, in lieu of military retired pay, or some combination of
retired pay and veteran's pension. It is probably the case that a disability
is more likely to be revealed when a man is ready to leave the service
than at an earlier time. From the perspectives of the present paper, the
interest is primarily in those disability retirees who are like length-of-
service retirees in having had a commitment to at least twenty years of

service and whose post-career employment opportunities are not seriously circumscribed by physical disability.

Enlisted Men Now the Majority

A second major change in the composition of the retired military population is the rapid rise in the proportion of enlisted personnel. Until the Korean Conflict, military retirees were predominantly officers, but the rate of enlisted retirements is and has been growing rapidly. (See

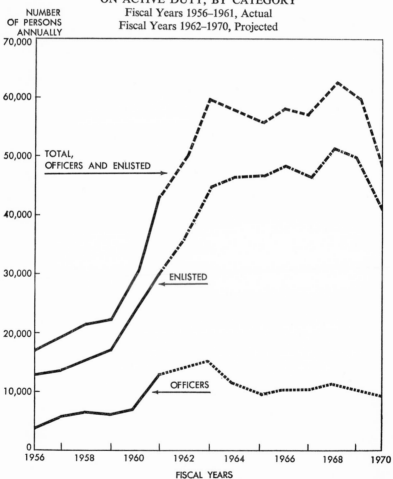

CHART 3. NUMBER OF RETIREMENTS AMONG MILITARY PERSONNEL
ON ACTIVE DUTY, BY CATEGORY
Fiscal Years 1956–1961, Actual
Fiscal Years 1962–1970, Projected

Chart 3.) Well over four times as many enlisted men will be retired during the next few years as officers. Information about post-retirement careers collected to date, however, deals almost exclusively with retired officers.

Age

The most salient characteristic of the military retired population is its relative youth. The average age at retirement for nondisability retirees is about forty-five years. About one-third of all persons receiving non-disability retired pay at the present time are under forty-five. During the next ten years, nine out of ten persons on the retired lists—new and old—will be under sixty. Projections for 1968 and 1983, and the actual age distribution for 1958, as shown in Chart 4, illustrate the relative youth that will characterize the future population as compared with the past. Although the projections that have been made to 1983 show an aging pattern in comparison with the current decade, a concentration in the active years is expected to characterize the entire twenty-year period.

Retired Pay

The retired military population is defined in some of the statistics which are presented as those persons receiving retired pay. This fails to include all persons who have completed a military career. A few (but an unknown number) regular officers are not included because they waive all retired pay in order to meet provisions of the Dual Compensation Act; other individuals find it to their advantage to receive veteran's disability compensation in lieu of retired pay.

The availability of statistics reflects the focus of policy and political concern on the issue of pay. As an identifiable budget item, it is a formidable figure for congressman and taxpayer. The total annual disbursements for military retired pay are already in excess of one billion dollars.

Representative Carl Vinson has argued against proposed amendments that would add to the cost of retired pay. He said that, even without the changes adopted by the House in May, 1963, the cost of military retired pay would be $3 billion in 1970 and $6 billion in 1983. Increasing these costs, he claimed, sows the seed that will destroy the whole program.[1]

The magical figure of one billion dollars per year was a milestone which led to a reexamination by the Congress and Defense Department of the entire military retired system. The beginnings of this reexamina-

CHART 4. PROJECTED NUMBER OF MILITARY PERSONNEL RECEIVING RETIRED PAY, BY AGE

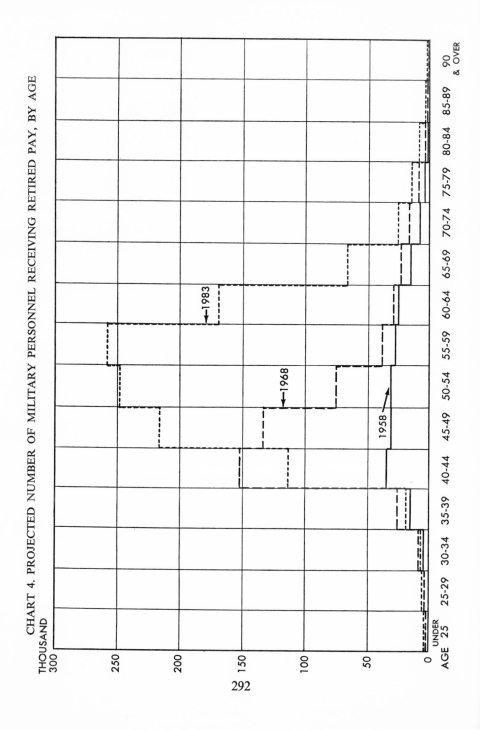

tion took place in 1961 when the one billion threshhold was near at hand. As part of this reexamination by Senator John Stennis' subcommittee of the Senate Armed Services Committee, a group of the faculty of the University of Michigan was commissioned to undertake a survey of military retirement. The writer is indebted to them for much of the data on which this present paper is based. The Michigan group, in addition to considering the highly professional actuarial data developed by Joseph Glenn of the Department of Defense, brought to bear information on other retirement systems and undertook sample surveys of retired officers and of current active duty officers and enlisted men. Its report is referred to here as the Michigan study and the research as the 1961 survey.[2]

Although the sum of all retired pay appears substantial to congressmen as an item of the national budget, the monthly check received by most beneficiaries of retired pay is seldom sufficient to be accepted by the recipient as the sole source of his income. Usually, it is not even acceptable as the major source of income. The average retirement income of an enlisted retiree is about $165 a month and for the officer about $325. Even if the individual were inclined to spend half of his active years in leisurely hunting and fishing, few could afford to do so. Table 1 shows the distribution of income among those responding to the

TABLE 1. INCOME FROM EMPLOYMENT, 1961 SAMPLE SURVEY OF MILITARY RETIREES

Type of Employment	Under $4,000	$4,000 to $6,000	$6,000 to $8,000	$8,000 to $10,000	$10,000 and Over	Not Ascertained	Total	Number of Cases
			(Percentages)					
Operate my own business	48	19	14	6	12	1	100	155
Personnel	14	33	43	10	0	0	100	21
Sales	46	26	14	7	5	2	100	354
Engineering	7	17	30	21	23	2	100	269
Other business	27	32	18	11	11	1	100	378
Federal government	8	37	34	14	6	1	100	366
State government	29	52	14	2	3	0	100	106
Local government	33	40	16	7	3	1	100	103
College teaching	30	40	19	2	7	2	100	43
School teaching	29	53	16	1	0	1	100	90
Doctor, dentist, or lawyer	23	5	7	11	52	2	100	44
Other	38	37	13	5	6	1	100	368
More than one job	24	24	13	13	26	0	100	79

SOURCE: U.S. Congress, Senate, 1961, pp. 2–41.

TABLE 2. EXAMPLES OF MILITARY RETIRED PAY FOR PERSONS
RETIRED AFTER MAY 31, 1958[a]

Pay Grade	Rank	Years of Service	Monthly Pay
0–9	Lieutenant General	30	$1,175
0–8	Major General	30	1,012
0–7	Brigadier General	30	881
0–6	Colonel	30	738
0–5	Lieutenant Colonel	27	523
0–4	Major	26	409
E–7	Sergeant, 1st Class	23	201
E–6	Staff Sergeant	23	166
E–5	Sergeant	24	144
E–4	Corporal	25	118

[a] After September 1, 1964, rates were increased.

1961 Michigan survey and Table 2 presents examples of pay rates for various ranks and periods of service.

The need to work is heightened by the family responsibilities of retirees. The average number of dependents of military personnel with between twenty and thirty years of service is slightly over three. Watson found that two-thirds of recently retired Air Force officers have dependent children,[3] many of whom are in the costly years of secondary school or college. (The particular stage of the family cycle at which military retirement takes place may contribute to orientations toward teaching as a second career, which will be discussed later.) Table 3 shows the distribution of dependents for the officers responding to the Michigan survey. (The average number of dependents does not differ greatly as between officers and enlisted men of equivalent length of service.)

TABLE 3. NUMBER OF DEPENDENTS, 1961 SAMPLE SURVEY OF
MILITARY RETIREES

Number of Dependents	Per Cent
None	3
One	29
Two	22
Three	24
Four	12
Five or more	10
Total	100
Number of cases	3,168

SOURCE: U. S. Congress, Senate, 1961, pp. 2–12.

The Second Career

As a consequence of these basic background characteristics, "retirement" in its traditional sense of leaving remunerative employment will hardly be applicable to the large majority of the retired population at any time in the foreseeable future. Pamphlets presented to those leaving the service having titles such as "Changing Your Career" (Army) or "Your New Career" (Navy) more accurately denote the transition.

Most of those retiring from the armed forces are seeking a second career. Among the Michigan sample, 70 per cent of the nondisability cases were working full time, as were 48 per cent of the disability retirees. (See Table 4.) An additional 3 per cent were in school and 10 per cent held part-time jobs.

TABLE 4. EMPLOYMENT AMONG RETIRED OFFICERS RELATED TO DISABILITY, 1961 SAMPLE SURVEY OF MILITARY RETIREES

Employment Status	Working Full-time	Working Part-time	Not Working	Not Ascertained	Total	Number of Cases
	(Percentages)					
Retired for physical disability	48	14	37	1	100	521
Not retired for physical disability	70	9	21	—	100	2,638

SOURCE: U.S. Congress, Senate, 1961, pp. 2–16.

Prospective changes in the age and rank distributions, and the great increase in the proportion without disabilities, suggest that larger percentages of the retired will be in the labor force in the future than at present. This expectation is confirmed by small sample surveys conducted subsequent to Michigan the study. Watson found that 14 per cent of recently retired Air Force officers were unemployed as compared with 45 per cent of those retired for six or more years.[4] Collings found in a survey of 416 Army officers who retired on the West Coast subsequent to 1961 after twenty years or more of active duty that more than 95 per cent had sought jobs or entered schools.[5]

Component

Projected retirements also show a decrease in the proportion of nonregular personnel in the immediate future. This trend, along with other changes mentioned earlier, is shown in the summary table of projected retirements to 1970 (Table 5).

TABLE 5. PROJECTED NUMBER OF RETIREMENTS AMONG MILITARY PERSONNEL ON ACTIVE DUTY, 1963–1970

Fiscal Year	Total	Officers					Enlisted Men				
		Total	By Component		By Type of Retirement		Total	By Component		By Type of Retirement	
			Regular	Other	Nondisability	Disability		Regular	Other	Nondisability	Disability
1963	58,202	14,662	6,194	8,468	13,160	1,502	43,540	42,440	1,100	37,461	6,079
1964	56,107	10,771	5,330	5,441	9,252	1,519	45,336	44,086	1,250	38,915	6,421
1965	54,524	9,365	4,889	4,476	7,839	1,526	45,159	43,859	1,300	38,458	6,701
1966	56,871	10,053	5,195	4,858	8,502	1,551	46,818	45,557	1,261	39,881	6,937
1967	56,122	10,531	5,864	4,667	8,954	1,577	45,591	44,347	1,244	38,373	7,218
1968	60,788	10,793	6,427	4,366	9,213	1,580	49,995	48,793	1,202	42,581	7,414
1969	58,450	10,126	7,303	2,823	8,579	1,547	48,324	47,159	1,165	40,811	7,513
1970	48,073	8,750	6,525	2,225	7,247	1,503	39,323	38,195	1,128	31,772	7,551
"Normal," for an active force of present size with current retention rates:	51,776	8,593	4,453	4,140	7,120	1,473	43,183	40,414	2,769	35,356	7,827

SOURCE: Office of the Assistant Secretary of Defense, Manpower, January 11, 1963.

In the years beyond the table's range and not included in "retirements from active duty" will be the delayed retirements of the many non-active duty reservists who first entered the service at ages eighteen to thirty-five during World War II and the Korean Conflict and who will be reaching the age at which they become eligible for retirement benefits under Title III, PL 810. These reservists who did not remain on active duty are again a different type from the men retiring after twenty or more years of active duty with whom this paper is concerned. Our data sources are slightly obscured by the presence of a very small number of these Title III retirees in the survey data on which we must currently rely as well as in our early charts based on numbers receiving retired pay. A total of 4 per cent of the Michigan sample were Title III, PL 810 retirees.[6] For only a few categories do we have information giving a clue to the manner in which these quite civilian senior citizens affect various distributions of background characteristics and post-career pursuits that we are considering here.

Education

Recent years have witnessed many efforts on the part of the armed forces to elevate the educational level of personnel. These efforts will doubtless be reflected in future retirement cohorts. Table 6 shows the far higher level of educational attainment among current active duty officers as compared with the sample of retired officers surveyed by the Michigan group. While educational attainments among noncareer officers serving periods of obligatory service may distort the comparison somewhat, the table nonetheless conveys an impression of the order of magnitude of the expected change.

TABLE 6. EDUCATIONAL LEVELS OF RETIRED OFFICERS IN 1961 SAMPLE SURVEY AND OF ALL ACTIVE DUTY OFFICERS, FISCAL YEAR 1961

Educational Level	Active Duty Officers[a]	Retired Officers[b]
	(Cumulative percentages)	
Graduated from college	56.8	27
Completed 2 or more years of college	75.3	45
Some college	85.1	60
Graduated from high school	99.3	86
Total Commissioned Officers	100.0	100

SOURCES:
[a] Dept. of Defense, Office of the Secretary of Defense, *Selected Manpower Statistics*, February 1, 1963. Mimeographed.
[b] U.S. Congress, Senate, Committee on Armed Services, *A Study of the Military Retired Pay System and Certain Related Subjects*. Government Printing Office, Washington, 1961.

Fundamental Military Changes

More fundamental changes in the nature of the armed forces will also be reflected in characteristics of the military retired. The five hypothetical lines of change around which Janowitz organized his study of the professional soldier are peculiarly pertinent:[7]

1. changing organizational authority from a basis of domination in the direction of greater reliance on initiative, persuasion, and manipulation;
2. narrowing skill differential between military and civilian elites;
3. broader basis of officer recruitment;
4. changes in career patterns permitting entry into the broader elite grouping on the basis of competent performance of routine and technical functions, but access to an inner elite on the basis of innovating perspectives;
5. changing patterns of indoctrination toward developing broader social and political perspectives and greater critical capacity and orientation.

Each of these major lines of hypothetical change implies a lessening of the distinctiveness of the military calling and corresponding ease of integration into civilian roles of persons who have been shaped by a career in the military. The problems involved in this integration, however, are placed in sharper relief if we consider the direction from which the military institution has been changing.

The second-career concept has implications diverging from various widely held conventional, ideal-typical conceptions of the military institution. Implicitly and explicitly, these conceptions constitute the theses of which Janowitz's hypothetical changes are the antitheses. At the risk of overworking stereotypes and overstressing an ideal type that has seldom been very closely approached by historical cases, let us consider some cardinal features of these conventional, ideal-typical conceptions of the military institution.

1. Total, Isolated Institution. The military is a total institution. Work, play, eating, sleeping, worship, education, nursing, and burial all tend to take place within the institution and in the company of fellow members. Symbolic as well as physical and interactional arrangements foster isolation from the larger community.

2. Organizational Identity. Membership in the organization implies a total role; that is, relatively few aspects of behavior and personality are matters of indifference to the organizational identity. The area of behavioral prescription is broad. Processes of recruitment, initiation, indoctrination, dress, ritual, and so forth create and sustain a special identity. Self-identification as a soldier is a salient personality feature.

3. *Esoteric Profession.* This identity is a professional identity. As in the case of other traditional professions, the institution exerts a monopoly claim to a practice—in the case of the military, mass violence and certain related symbolizations and ceremonials. As a practice concerned with fundamental values—life and death, the sanctity of the state—it involves strong sacred and mystical elements. The practice is an esoteric one also with respect to its elaborate skill and technological components.

4. *Life-Long Status.* The professional identity is life-long. An honorific title identifies the person and remains a mode of address in intra- and extrainstitutional contacts throughout life.

5. *Hierarchical Organization.* The title reflects rank in the precisely articulated hierarchical structure of the organization. The various dimensions of status, such as income, deference, and authority, are finely equilibrated as between one another and from situation to situation. Incumbents of each of the sharply graded levels of status possess broad areas of authority over lower grades.

6. *Class Status.* The military profession has stood in a class or caste relation in the social structure of most societies. In western culture, there is the aristocratic tradition of the officer as a gentleman (and sometimes a *déclassé* definition of the common soldier). This class position is associated with a considerable degree of economic independence by virtue of recruiting from landed wealth. A considerable degree of hereditary occupational transmission is implied.

7. *Ethos and Ideology.* An elaborate ethos and a traditionalistic ideology reflect these features of the organization.

Contemporary changes in the military institution involve attenuation of each of these characteristics of its "militariness."

Continuity and Discontinuity

The very existence of the second-career pattern is a manifestation of the extent to which the military institution currently departs in various respects from tradition. The greater the loss by the military institution of distinctive attributes and isolation, the easier, presumably, will be the accommodation of its members to the second-career pattern. At the same time, this accommodation is strained by the needs of the military institution as a whole and of retirees themselves to preserve many of their distinctive features and much of their unique identity.

Were the lives of military personnel spent in a world as completely parochial as that of military men of former times, the problems of large-scale retirement would present far more pressing problems than they do at present. Recent years have seen an increasing immersion of military men and their families in the economic and social life of the community. A look at their complaints about the "whittling away" of fringe benefits provides some index of the extent to which the housing, buying, recreation, and medical care of military families are now met through civilian facilities. The rosters of officers of civic and recreational organizations in several areas of concentrated military settlement reveal another form of participation. In considering broad changes, the relevance for this particular group of the general movement toward a mass society, such as the expanded role of mass media and a partial erasure of all sub-cultural differences, should not be neglected.

The work world of the soldier has also become less exclusively military. The civilian contractor and the civil servant are partners in more and more military enterprises—sometimes, the senior partner. Occasionally, the effectiveness rating that influences eligibility for promotion has been made by a civilian supervisor rather than a military commander. The overlap works both ways. Many military assignments involve duties hardly distinguishable from counterparts in the civil economy; civilian scientists and other civilian experts perform many tasks central to such special military functions as weapons development, planning, and intelligence.

Neither in concept nor effect, however, does the present-day military retirement system imply a complete breaking away from the total institutional pattern. The regular retiree and his dependents remain a part of the "military family." Data on place of residence of retired personnel suggest that "staying in the family" is an important factor in post-retirement location. Table 7 shows that half of those currently retired are located in only four states: California, Florida, Texas, and Virginia (a shift toward greater concentration by this index over the only previously available data).[8] States representing 23 per cent of the national population include 58 per cent of the military retired.

Presumable factors in this concentration are the desire to have access to military facilities, such as hospitals, clubs, golf courses, commissaries, and exchanges; the desire to continue associations with familiar people; or simply the appeal of the familiar.[9] Evidence was found in the Michigan survey that concentration in favored locations may aggravate the second-career problem. Unemployment in this sample was exceptionally high among retired officers in each of the states (except California) in which large numbers of retirees reside.

TABLE 7. PERCENTAGE OF U.S. POPULATION IN STATES HAVING
A CONCENTRATION OF MILITARY RETIRED PERSONNEL

States	Military Retired[a]	U.S. Population[b]
	(Cumulative percentages)	
California	27	9
Florida	37	12
Texas	45	17
Virginia	50	19
District of Columbia	52	20
Washington and Oregon	57	22
Hawaii and Alaska	58	23
All others	100	100

SOURCES:
[a] U.S. Congress, Senate, 87th Congress, 1st Sess., Committee on the Armed Services, *A Study of the Military Retired Pay System and Certain Related Subjects*, Appendix 2, July 6, 1961, p. 11.
[b] U.S. Dept. of Commerce, *Statistical Abstracts of the United States*. Government Printing Office, Washington, 1962, Table 6.

The relative significance of various factors as determinants of post-retirement location is not known, but the problem is regarded as serious enough to be a subject of major attention. On April 2, 1963, the Defense Department announced the launching of a study on problems of health care for retired personnel.[10]

There is apparent in this situation an asymmetry between the subjective orientations, identification, and dependence of retirees on the military system and the limited extent to which, by law and administrative practice, a corresponding obligation is legitimate on the part of the armed forces. An illustration is the existence of a small concentration of retired military families in Hot Springs, Arkansas, whose choice of the location had been motivated in no small measure by the excellent military general hospital at Hot Springs. This hospital, however, was closed down. The needs of the military retired population are regarded for the time being as irrelevant in justifying the continuation or expansion of other military facilities, such as commissaries.

Ambivalence Regarding Retention of a Special Identity

While in many contexts the military man must stress the distinctiveness of his calling, the second-career problem places emphasis on its nondistinctiveness. In discussing Department of Defense policy on the military retired at a Conference on Military Retirement sponsored in 1963 by the Air Force Association and the Department of Labor, Assistant Secretary of Defense Norman S. Paul stated:

To properly understand this aspect we should *not* think of today's career military service as a separate and distinct profession, per se. Rather it is the bringing together of many professions as well as technical skills in an organized and coordinated effort toward a common goal. It is this broad diversity of capabilities within the overall military profession which is often overlooked by large segments of American business.

The fact is, there are probably few military skills which do not have some transference value for civilian occupations. The main difficulty appears to be in translating skills and experience gained in a military setting into specific civilian terms so that they can be "matched up" with employer needs.[11]

An even more radically civilian perception was presented to the Conference by Assistant Secretary of Labor James J. Reynolds, who described the military commanders of the great ICBM bases as "men who have graduated from our academies and have had great courses in great institutions of learning and are well equipped to step immediately into positions of responsibility in industry. . . ."[12]

This civilian's concept of a thorough transformation of the military leader into the "military manager" or "military technologist" of Janowitz's typology may not grate too harshly against military ears in the context of a discussion of second careers in which it was presented.[13] As extreme a claim of nondistinctiveness, however, would still sound strange coming from a military professional, if only because such an avowal of the substitutability of military for industrial expertise might be held to apply both ways. Too much stress on the adaptability of military personnel to civilian pursuits—the "there's really no difference" approach—may tend to undermine the peculiar features of profession, identity, and mystique on which the distinctive claims of the military rest. This is particularly true at a time when its special claims to expertise are being challenged by the increasingly significant roles of civilians for various defense activities.

Recomputation

The ambiguous status of the retiree *vis-à-vis* the military is linked to the question of method of computing retired pay. This issue has produced years of legislative controversy concerning the military retired. It is the principle of "recomputation"; that is, the question of whether retired pay should be "recomputed" to reflect changes in active duty pay, as opposed to the alternative principle that retired pay should be readjusted to reflect changes in the cost of living. The Michigan study group recommended that the cost-of-living principle be used in the future. Since military pay increases in recent years have been heavier in the higher ranks, the financial stake in recomputation is greatest among those retired in the rank of colonel/captain or higher. The processes of legislative compromise created a situation in which persons retired after the 1958 pay bill received retired pay at the new higher rates, while those retired earlier were granted a cost-of-living increase. Arguments in the controversy center on this perceived anomaly, on the "breach of contract with the men who led our forces in two great wars," and, from the other side, on the threat to the system posed by the high cost of recomputation and the argument that those least in need received the greatest increases. The traditional origin of recomputation in the concept of the individual's status in the organization and its hierarchical ordering as life-long seemingly lost much of its persuasive relevance during the 1963 congressional consideration of recomputation. In public discussion, the retired regular's life-long status, as evidenced by such things as possibility of recall in emergencies and being subject to court martial, received no mention. There is a decided trend, in various respects, toward defining the retiree more in the manner of the pensioner or annuitant whose connections with the institution are severed than in accordance with more traditional concepts of the retired soldier.[14] In October, 1963, recomputation was explicitly abandoned as a permanent principle when the first thorough revision of military pay since 1958 was signed into law. The 1963 law adopted in essence the cost-of-living principle recommended by the University of Michigan committee (U.S. Congress, Senate, 1961). It requires the Secretary of Defense to adjust the pay of all military retirees to accord with increases in the Cost of Living Index of the Bureau of Labor Statistics. This is to be done in each year that the Index shows an increase of 3 per cent or more since the last retired pay increase.

Barriers to the Use of Special Military Expertise

In large measure, the need in discussions of second careers to minimize differences between the military person and the civilian stems from the highly restricted opportunities for second-career pursuits that draw on peculiarly military skills and attitudes. Partly involved is the fact that the institution which the retired military man must leave possesses that near-monopoly over its highly esoteric function noted in our characterization of the ideal type. This may be contrasted, say, with the professor whose retirement from a given university does not necessarily preclude his teaching at some other school or engaging in some other academic pursuit.

Law and proprieties also operate to exclude many officers from second-career jobs that are most closely related to their peculiar training and abilities. These jobs are civilian positions in the federal establishment, particularly in the Department of Defense, and in the vast world of contracts servicing the defense establishment. The barriers are essentially three:

(a) Dual office and dual compensation laws;
(b) Conflict of interest legislation and proprieties;
(c) The desire to "make it on my own as a civilian" and attitudes stigmatizing "trading on one's rank" and "influence peddling."

a. Dual Office and Dual Compensation Provisions for Retirees

The Dual Office Holding laws, the first of which was passed in 1894, provide that no person may hold two federal offices at the same time if the salary attached to either is $2,500 a year or more. A retired regular is considered to be still holding office in the armed forces. (Retired reservists are not so considered.) Retired enlisted men, as well as officers retired for line-of-duty disability, were excluded from the law in 1924. In addition, the Dual Compensation principle, in effect, restricts the combined pay of a federal job and retired pay to a total of $10,000 for retired commissioned officers, except those retired because of a disability "incurred in combat or by an instrumentality of war."

There are a variety of statutory exemptions of specific jobs from these acts, however, including a number apparently aimed at rendering a single individual employable in a specific job, that indicate the necessity of passing a law to provide for employment of these officers even when the field may be devoid of other eligibles. Nevertheless, according to data developed by the Michigan survey, the effect of these statutes on retired officer employment is substantial. In answer to a question asking whether either of these laws affected their employment opportunities, 44 per cent of the retired officers responded affirmatively. It should be noted that the population from which the sample was drawn included larger proportions of persons exempted from these provisions (because of reserve status or disability) than will be the case in the future if the laws remain unchanged.

The Michigan survey found that 12 per cent of the sample were employed by the federal government. Among active duty personnel surveyed as a part of this study, about 35 per cent of the officers were indifferent to dual office and dual compensation provisions because they did not expect to work for the federal government after retirement.

These laws have been the subject of strong attack in recent years both from military groups and from agencies that are frustrated by their inability to fill critical jobs with highly qualified retired officers. Robert E. Hampton, Civil Service Commissioner, has pointed to the need in the federal government for retired military people trained in the medical, scientific, and technical fields.[15]

An administration-proposed bill would wipe out all existing dual office and dual compensation provisions for future retirees and, except for exempted combat-disabled persons, institute a uniform limitation on combined retired and civilian pay for all retired personnel, including enlisted.[16] The retiree employed in the civil service would receive the full salary for his position plus the first $2,000 of his retired military pay and 50 per cent of any remaining retired pay. The bill would strip most retirees of some advantages they enjoy in the civil service that are particularly thorny points for the major opponents of change—the organizations of civil servants. These current advantages of the military retiree are his ability to apply his active military service toward seniority and, in most cases, to claim various civil service preferences accorded veterans.[17]

b. Conflict of Interest

The utilization of the special skills and knowledge of the military retiree is directly counter to the doctrine of "conflict of interest." A broad and blunt statement of this principle was made by the report of Representative F. Edward Hébert's subcommittee of the House Armed Forces Committee which investigated the employment of retired officers by defense contractors: "We think it unethical and unconscionable for a person to have anything to do in private life with a subject with which he was directly concerned while in public employment."[18]

No other aspect of military retirement has received more public attention than this matter of "conflict of interest." Various honorific features of the military role that followed from the nature of its central tasks lead the military office to be regarded as peculiarly incongruous with the vigorous pursuit of self-interest, particularly money interest. A feeling that an impure contamination of a role has taken place is more likely to be experienced where a military officer is believed to have used his public office to private advantage than in the case of the civilian official. The judicial office illustrates a similar attitude toward conflict of interest where the office has a sacred quality.

These traditional views are strong, but they run counter to contrary principles that relate to the state of continuous semi-mobilization. Under present conditions, the principle of full and efficient use of "human resources" has arisen along with ideas relevant to times of greater scarcity of opportunity. The interpenetration of the public and private sectors has also complicated application of the principle.

These considerations were reflected in the report by a committee of the Association of the Bar of the City of New York on the conflict-of-interest question:

> The problem of most employment restrictions must be weighed in the context of the interpenetration of the private and governmental segments of the economy. In the earlier days, the government and the private company were regarded as opposed or at least completely separate, and no need was recognized for having a man outside the government with the experience gained inside the government.
>
> With the growth of government and the technological explosion of the twentieth century such a view has been becoming unthinkable. Today, we definitely need a maximum flow of information between the government and the outside and most employment restrictions tend to build a wall between them.
>
> It is a source of comfort to no one in this country, if an experienced military scientist or technical expert is forced by conflict-of-interest rules to take up truck farming or to sell life insurance when he leaves the government service.[19]

Again, in the case of conflict of interest, there is a complex array of statutes and administrative regulations restricting the retired military officer in work in the world of government contracts. "Selling" to the government receives special emphasis in both law and attitude.[20]

Nonetheless, a considerable number of military retirees are employed in defense industry. The proportion so employed is doubtless considerably smaller than the impression that might be gained from the heavy attention the matter receives in the press. The Hébert subcommittee's survey of the employment of retired officers found that about 1,500 officers were employed by the large contractors, who account for about 80 per cent of the total annual contracting of the government. There were 261 retired general or flag officers among this group.

Current stereotypes regarding the roles played by retired officers in these industries derive from the fact that the persons who receive the most public attention at and after retirement are those who received the most attention before. These, of course, are usually the top senior officers—chiefs of staff, the major commanders, and directors of key projects, such as General Leslie R. Groves. Outside of major government posts and the large foundations and universities, almost the sole locus of jobs corresponding to the military positions these men occupied is the major industrial and business institution. Rare indeed is the large private business that is not, in some way, involved in defense. Long

lists of retired general officers and their positions in business and government, such as that contained in C. Wright Mills' *The Power Elite*, prove
only that: (a) military officers, including senior officers, retire at fairly
young ages; (b) they tend to live long and vigorous lives; and (c) there
is some status equilibration between their first and second careers.[21]

To argue from such facts to the contention that there is undue military
influence peddling or undue militaristic influence must rest on evidence
of these officers' activities in civilian positions. The Hébert subcommittee's hearing and report adduce some relevant evidence, although the
hardly model efforts of data collection, analysis, and presentation make
this evidence chaotic and nondefinitive at best.

One set of data presented by the subcommittee relates to the pay
received by officers retired in grades of lieutenant colonel or above who
work for the large defense contractors. For firms, the medians of pay
received by these retirees range from $500 to $1,650 per month, with
$900 being the approximate median of the medians among all the major
firms tabulated. A tabulation of the data on industrial pay presented
by the committee for retired three- and four-star officers employed by
the 100 largest defense contractors (see Table 8) shows that of the 38
officers in these senior categories, almost half were paid $15,000 or less
per year. Five retired generals and admirals earned over $40,000 a
year, but an equal number earned under $6,000.

Interpretation of these data must remain ambiguous as among the
following possible alternatives: (a) either a large proportion of the
retired officers employed by industries work only part-time or they work
for relatively low pay in comparison with industrial executives; (b)
retired senior officers generally have little influence to sell, or they are
not generally selling such influence as they have, or they usually are
selling the influence they have very cheaply; (c) the data are faulty, in not

TABLE 8. INDUSTRIAL PAY OF THE RETIRED THREE- AND
FOUR-STAR MILITARY OFFICERS EMPLOYED BY THE 100
LARGEST DEFENSE CONTRACTORS

Industrial Pay (nearest thousand)	Number of Officers
Over $40,000	5
$26,000 to $40,000	5
$16,000 to $25,000	10
$ 7,000 to $15,000	13
$ 6,000 and under	5
Total	38

SOURCE: U.S. Congress, House, 1960, p. 160.

reflecting emoluments other than pay and in not revealing income from other work.

Given the specific statutory provisions, it is hardly surprising that the committee failed to develop testimony of retired officers engaged in any clearcut activity involving "selling" to the armed forces. Indeed, in breaking down the scope of duties of retirees employed by contractors, in only ten of the more than 1,400 replies did the duties involve "selling" to anybody.[22] Of course, the same cannot be said of activities that are calculated to generate sales—and in the case of defense work, defense sales—for what other purpose is there to industrial activity?

The Hébert philosophy would bracket all these activities into the prohibited category: "These three steps—proposal, development, and production—are links in a chain. Each is a part of a sale. . . . A chain begins when the first link is forged. . . ."[23]

Existing measures and proposals relating to avoidance of conflict of interest include cooling-off periods to render obsolete "inside dope" from which an officer might profit, the formulation of a code of ethics by the Department of Defense, disclosures of hiring required in bids and proposals, and the disclosure by retired officers of their employment and duties.[24]

c. Ethics

As long as retired officers are not forced by law literally to go out to pasture—and it is unlikely that the public would be prepared to bear the costs in retirement pay to permit this—some retirees will secure jobs in which very fine lines of propriety must be drawn to define "conflict of interest." The lines are as likely to be violated out of unselfish as selfish intent—by the high officer who in private employment continues to press for those lines of development he has always regarded as vital to the national interest; by desires among all concerned that scarce knowledge and talents should not be wasted.

Attitudes among retired officers themselves may be a more powerful control against "conflict of interest" activities than ambiguous statutes about "selling" to one's service or a formalized code of ethics. Despite (or perhaps because of) the attitude of superiority to the civilian that is said to be a product of military indoctrination, many retired officers possess a strong desire to "make it on one's own" in the civilian world.[25] There is also sensitivity to the view common in the civilian community that the military man leads a sheltered and uncompetitive life, rises by time-serving, and would not quite be able to "hack it" in the competitive arena of business. Informal norms also operate in this direction, particularly among the very senior retirees who comprise a small and sufficiently linked group to possess some primary group characteristics. To have one's fellows saying, "He traded on his stars," or "He's become an influence peddler," is something many officers presumably are powerfully motivated to avoid.

It is apparent that the possibility of such taint leads some officers to eschew the easiest and most direct paths to employment. Some of the activities in which retired military officers are engaged, such as their frequent enrollment as full-time students and shunning of defense related employment, can be understood in terms of the man's desire to show that he can compete in the civilian world on its own terms and on his own merits. The nonactivity of a few senior retired officers may also be traceable to the difficulty of finding any congenial pursuit which is altogether free of the possible allegation, just or unjust, that they are trading on the status, contacts, or "inside dope" they had as soldiers. Implicit feelings about the separateness of the two worlds—one sacred, the other profane—underlie some of these attitudes.

The Enlisted Man and Conflict of Interest

The concepts of conflict of interest and unjust exploitation of status, by both law and custom, are less applicable to retired enlisted men. Indeed, it is regarded as a "good thing" if they are able to use their military training and experience to profit in a civilian career. It is doubtful whether any businesses (other than some supplying NCO clubs and messes) have sought to exploit the old saw, "It's really the sergeants who run the Army." Probably, there are yeomen who are as vast repositories of "inside dope" as some admirals. However, enlisted personnel are not exempted from the statutes prohibiting action during the two-year cooling-off period on matters with which the person was "directly connected" during his service.

Job Motivations

Despite the preoccupation with selling in discussions of "conflict of interest," the matter appears actually a tangential one insofar as the large majority of retirees are concerned. It is tangential not only because few of the personnel are at the levels of influence that have achieved notoriety, but also because selling is very low among the job interests of retirees.

At a 1960 conference, representatives of organizations involved in counseling and job placement of retired officers reported an intense and almost uniform aversion toward sales jobs on the part of their clientele.

As Janowitz pointed out at this conference, however, the image of sales to which retirees might be reacting was that of selling consumer goods, not producer goods. In the world of interindustrial contact, as well as in some variety of government procurement, he stated, "sales" work involves the kinds of logistical, technical, and interpersonal negotiatory problems that resemble military managerial activity more closely than they resemble sales as traditionally conceived.[26]

TABLE 9. OFFICERS' ANTICIPATED OCCUPATIONS AFTER LEAVING SERVICE, 1961 SAMPLE SURVEY OF ACTIVE DUTY OFFICERS

Anticipated Occupation	Officers			
	Army	Navy	Marine	Air Force
	(Percentages)			
Haven't thought much about it	4	6	6	2
Have thought about it, but have no definite plans	20	26	27	20
Have thought about it, and probably will engage in:				
My own business	12	9	7	13
Personnel management	5	3	5	2
Sales	4	3	5	3
Engineering	5	5	4	6
Other business or managerial	9	9	9	8
Flying	2	1	2	2
Government service	8	2	2	6
College or university teaching	6	6	6	8
Teaching other than college	8	6	10	7
Scientific and research	3	3	1	3
Several of the above	6	10	8	10
No work, just retire	1	1	1	1
Other	7	10	7	9
Total	100	100	100	100
Number of cases	3,980	4,746	1,481	3,484

SOURCE: U.S. Congress, Senate, 1951, pp. 3–24.

In surveys of active duty officers about their post-retirement job intentions, the category "sales" ranks very low. Between 3 and 4 per cent of prospective officer retirees indicate that they are considering entering such an activity, and less than 2 per cent of the enlisted men. (See Tables 9 and 10.) Preferred or not, selling is more prominent among the kinds of work being performed by those presently retired than in the intentions of those to be retired in the future. About 11 per cent of the currently retired—15 per cent of those employed—reported they were engaged in saleswork in answering the Michigan question-

TABLE 10. ENLISTED MEN'S ANTICIPATED OCCUPATIONS AFTER
LEAVING SERVICE, 1961 SAMPLE SURVEY OF ACTIVE DUTY MEN

Anticipated Occupation	Enlisted Men		
	Army	Navy	Marine
	(Percentages)		
Haven't thought much about it	5	5	5
Have thought about it, but have no definite plans	20	19	17
Have thought about it, and probably will engage in:			
Attending college	13	16	15
My own business	11	9	11
Managerial work	2	1	2
Sales	2	2	1
Clerical work	2	2	1
Skilled craft (electrician, plumber, etc.)	8	14	12
Technical work (electronics, X-ray, etc.)	6	6	3
Teaching	1	1	1
Farming	4	4	4
Government service	13	9	12
Factory work	3	2	3
Professional (doctor, lawyer)	1	1	2
Other	8	4	7
Will probably not work	1	a	1
Don't know what kind of work	a	5	3
Total	100	100	100
Number of cases	4,442	3,914	4,993

a This alternative was not offered on the questionnaire.

SOURCE: U.S. Congress, Senate, 1961, pp. 3–25.

naire. (See Table 11.) Moreover, the low status of selling may be due in part to an accurate image of the economic return for retired military personnel. Retirees working in sales had the lowest distribution of income from employment of all categories of work tabulated by the Michigan survey. (See Table 12.) The low figures for sales may be due to the fact that it is a frequent form of part-time work.

Janowitz has contended that public service orientation is an important basis of the choice of a military career; that military professionals tend to be recruited from subcultures with strong traditions of public service motivation; and that the career itself reinforces such motivations.[27] The reported aversion to sales jobs as a second career would follow, as would a preference for employment of a public service character, insofar as can be judged from the categories used by the Michigan study to tabulate type of job. The expressed job interests of active duty personnel

TABLE 11. PRESENT OCCUPATIONS, 1961 SAMPLE SURVEY OF
MILITARY RETIREES

Type of Occupation	Per Cent
Operate my own business	5
Personnel	1
Sales	11
Engineering	8
Other business (please specify)	12
Work in federal government	12
Work in state government	3
Work in local government	3
College teaching	1
Public school or private school teaching	3
Doctor	1
Dentist	*
Lawyer	*
Other (please specify)	12
More than one job	3
Not ascertained	1
Not employed at present time	24
Total	100
Number of cases	3,168
OCCUPATIONS OF THE 24 PER CENT CHECKING "OTHER BUSINESS" OR "OTHER"	
Professional and technical	4
Managers and officials	5
Clerical workers	4
Skilled workers; foremen	3
Semi-skilled and unskilled workers	1
Service workers	2
Farmers	1
Other, or not ascertained	4
Total	24

Source: U.S. Congress, Senate, 1961, pp. 2–6.

who have clear intentions lean more heavily in the direction of such jobs. (See Tables 9 and 10.)

The largest single class of public service employment, as seen in Table 10, is in the federal service, so that, as we have indicated, the barriers to federal employment of retirees restrict real choices markedly. These barriers are not present to positions in state and local civil services. Six per cent of the retirees in the Michigan sample, excluding teachers, were employed in nonfederal civil service. Since many functions similar to federal ones are exercised at these levels, these representations may be regarded as small. Apart from the more obvious areas of direct transferability, such as civil defense, police, city management, correction, public health, and public works engineering in which the utilization of retired military personnel is well established, other local government

TABLE 12. EMPLOYMENT INCOME RELATED TO MAJOR MILITARY SPECIALTY, 1961 SAMPLE SURVEY OF MILITARY RETIREES

Major Military Specialty	Employment Income (Percentages)					Not Ascertained	Total	Number of Cases
	Under $4,000	$4,000 to $6,000	$6,000 to $8,000	$8,000 to $10,000	$10,000 and Over			
Clerical; personnel; administration	33	36	15	9	6	1	100	382
Medical and other professions	28	20	13	7	32	0	100	82
Pilot	31	22	18	11	17	1	100	147
Line officer	29	38	17	7	9	—	100	309
Staff officer	25	38	23	8	6	0	100	106
Supply; Quartermaster; transportation; logistics	28	31	21	12	8	0	100	334
Ordnance; maintenance; repair, machinist	35	34	22	4	4	1	100	276
Signal corps; communications; electronics	20	29	18	20	12	1	100	242
Engineer	21	23	28	10	17	1	100	195
Research and development; other technical specialties	25	29	26	9	11	0	100	116

SOURCE: U.S. Congress, Senate, 1961, pp. 2–38.

313

functions would seem to present opportunities for high transfer of skill and knowledge.

A possible barrier to second-career employment in local government is the difficulty the older person has in moving into an established bureaucracy. The seniority system, as in the military, is a powerful determinant of position and emoluments in such organizations. The likelihood that retirees would tend to select occupations in which seniority does not play a significant role is thus great.

Insofar as higher-ranking retirees are concerned, appointive positions in state and local government might constitute rewarding second careers. Two major paths toward such positions are political and social connections. From the first, the military man was barred while on active duty. With respect to the second, Janowitz persuasively argues that in recent decades, military leaders in the United States have not been effectively integrated into local civilian elite groups.[28] The case is quite different from that of the retired British officer, discussed by Abrams, who possesses more elaborate integration with "the establishment" through family ties, common education, and intimate patterns of social intercourse.[29]

Teaching as a Second Career

Of all aspects of the second-career placement of military personnel, by far the greatest amount of attention has been given to their utilization as teachers. The congruity of this career with the public service image may account in part for this special emphasis. The first impetus came in 1957 from a report of the President's Committee on Education Beyond the High School. Attention to the shortage of teachers of science and mathematics in the post-Sputnik context was also important. The utilization of retired personnel in education has been studied by the National Education Association, the American Council on Education, the National Science Foundation, and the Defense Department.[30]

The central role of education and training in the military suggests at least face validity for education being a natural second career for many military leaders. Janowitz cites a survey of Army command and staff school graduates which revealed that these men had spent an average of one-third of their careers in schools or in training. Many command and staff tasks involve teaching roles: training troops, briefing crews, and so on.

A number of efforts have been made to ascertain the potential existing among present and future retirees for filling teaching jobs. The National Science Foundation, following one of the suggestions of the President's

Committee on Education regarding possible untapped sources of potential teachers, sponsored a survey of 8,800 retired officers to determine their possible interest in teaching science or mathematics. Among approximately 2,600 responding, 42 per cent indicated that they were interested, and an additional eight per cent expressed possible future interest. (Among those responding to this questionnaire, 11 per cent were already teaching.)

A Department of Defense sample survey in 1959 of officers who were within four years of retirement produced the following results:

> Of the 37,024 total respondents—11,643 (31.4 per cent) stated they were positively interested in a teaching career; 13,161 (35.6 per cent) said they might be interested.
> Of the 24,804 who stated interest—15,624 (63.0 per cent) had bachelor degrees or higher; 22,216 (89.6 per cent) were age 50 or below; 1,959 (7.9 per cent) possessed or had possessed a teaching certificate.[31]

If we look at the jobs retired officers now hold, however, we find only very small numbers are teaching. The Michigan survey reported one per cent teaching in colleges and universities and 3 per cent in private and public schools.

The continuous elevation of educational qualifications of officers makes for a larger number of persons eligible to teach among each successive retirement cohort. The active encouragement of teaching as a second career may also be producing increased interest in the field. Small-sample surveys restricted to officers who have retired more recently than most of those included in the Michigan study show much higher percentages in the educational profession. Collings reported that 7 per cent of the retired Army officers responding to his questionnaire were teaching.[32] Massey's survey of graduates of the Naval Academy who retired in 1960 found over 22 per cent were in teaching or educational administration.[33]

Despite the face validity of the idea of high transferability of interest, training, and experience to careers in education, it is easy to identify many obstacles that confront a retired officer seeking a teaching job. Education, particularly public education, is as rigorous as an institution can be about matters of formal credentials. As the Defense Department's guidance pamphlet, *Teaching: A Second Career*, points out:

> The small number who possessed teaching certificates, the 37 per cent who did not have bachelor's degrees, and the extended length of time most respondents have been absent from academic classrooms indicate that preparatory education will be required in most instances to transform these personnel into adequately prepared instructors.[34]

Is the lure of this profession great enough to lead the retiree to finance himself for a year or two in school? As expected, teaching was one of the more poorly paid occupational categories among retirees now working.

Some programs have been instituted and others proposed to help the interested officer surmount the hurdle of qualifying for a teaching job. The National Science Foundation assisted programs at two universities specifically for the purpose of preparing retired military personnel to teach science and mathematics. Both report high success. Other schools have solicited students from among the retired group. The Omnibus Education Bill submitted by the Administration to the Congress in 1963 would authorize appropriations to help universities establish graduate training programs to train retired military and others for second careers in elementary and secondary teaching (Sec. 321(5), HR 3000, 87th Congress).

The American Council on Education, at the request of a Defense Advisory Committee on Education in the Armed Forces, undertook a survey of higher educational institutions to ascertain the availability of teaching positions for retired military officers. The replies, as a rule, indicated that military background per se would prejudice hiring neither favorably nor unfavorably. There is also some positive regard for the prospect of the male retiree entering the excessively feminine world of primary and secondary education. Given the very short sojourn in teaching of the typical female product of a teachers college, the prospect of many years of service from the typical military retiree should also be attractive to both teacher training institutions and employing schools.

A statistical estimate of the potential of the retired military as a supply of teachers, based on data relating to interest, qualifications, and place of residence, concludes that only in a very few localities such as Washington, D. C., would there be more than a handful of retired military officers in any school system in the future.[35] Military retirees as teachers will not provide a great relief in teacher shortages, nor do they offer any threat of "the militarization of the schools."

Specialists and Generalists

As expected, the Michigan survey found that officers who had pursued certain specialized careers tended to secure higher paying jobs in civilian life. (See Table 12.) With the exception of ordnance maintenance, and personnel administration specialties, the specialized officer fared much better in the employment market than the line officer. The professions, communications, and electronics specialists, in particular, were more frequently found in the higher paying jobs. Collings reports generally parallel findings among the 311 recent retired Army officers he surveyed, with the major exception of ordnance specialists.[36] The 17 such specialists among his respondents were second in ranking of incomes by branch of the Army, exceeded only by Medical Corps (physicians).

The career management systems of the armed forces, with rotation of assignments and graded increases in responsibilities, tend to produce a large concentration of officers whose preparation and credentials are more appropriate to general managerial tasks than to highly specific and technical ones. Preparation as a generalist may be fine if one is a retired general and a candidate for an executive post in a large corporation, but it can prove to be a difficulty for the field grade officer who has difficulty in identifying any salient qualifications in his background.

Enlisted Retirees

In this respect the enlisted man may be better off, in that he usually has a more specific vocational identity in the armed forces. There is a dearth of evidence regarding the proportions of enlisted retirees who find it easy or difficult to place themselves in satisfactory second-career jobs. The lack of evidence leads to expression of contradictory surmises. On the one hand, it is suggested that the placement of enlisted personnel really does not constitute a great problem because of the earlier age at which they usually retire and the more specialized technical training and experience they have had relative to the officer. On the other hand, there is the view that the enlisted rather than the officer constitutes the more severe problem because of the sheer numbers involved; because of the difficulties that persist in equating military jobs to civilian requirements; and because of obstacles confronting the hiring of older men.

A limited survey of retired Air Force enlisted personnel undertaken in 1959 is the only source of systematic information.[37] It was found that about three-fourths of the 945 respondents (from among 2,700 in the original mailing) were or had been employed after retirement. About half of those employed were working in jobs similar to those they had performed in the Air Force. About half reported they were doing work requiring the same level of skill as their Air Force jobs.

A major problem for the retired enlisted men may be lack of effective organization (there is an active association of members of the Fleet Reserve [Navy and Marine Corps], but various attempts to organize an association of retired NCO's representing all services paralleling the Retired Officers Association have not been highly successful).[38] Other organizations, the civil servants' associations and labor unions, are unlikely to look with favor on significant entries from this group into the fields they regard as their province. Indeed, competition in a declining labor market from men whose retired pay allows them to work at lower than prevailing wages may be viewed as a threat by organized labor, particularly in fields such as aerospace industry, which may be particular targets of job-seeking by military trained technicians.

It is noteworthy that the problem of military retired employment tends to evoke quite different attitudes on the part of the civilian from those in the case of the war veteran concerning employment and reemployment. This is true despite the fact that the current nondisability retiree is a veteran of two wars and the Cold War. There are attempts to enlist patriotic motivation to support the placement of retirees in second careers. These appeals are invariably made by civilians, however.[39] It may be said that such efforts will be measured as successful if they so much as cancel out negative attitudes toward the peacetime soldier and fears of unfair competition for jobs.

Status Maintenance

The most common question asked about the military retiree is: "How well off is he as compared with his situation in the service?" Earlier (see Tables 1 and 2), the relevant data from the Michigan study on retired pay and income from employment were presented. On a number of counts, however, these data provide only a very limited answer to the question, if we consider the underlying interests of those who pose it.

With respect to the simple matter of income maintenance alone, the study did not provide a distribution of disposable income from all sources for those currently retired. Collings concluded that the average retired Army officer in his sample, who was employed, was somewhat better off in terms of income than he had been in the service, if the mean of active duty pay and allowances is compared with the mean total of retired pay and earnings from a civilian job after retirement.[40] Taking medians, rather than means, however, the average man was found slightly disadvantaged. (See Table 13.) Collings' averages for income from civilian jobs are quite similar to those of the larger Michigan study, although the average retired pay of his sample was considerably higher than that of the Michigan sample.

Even if we had similar data on a more exhaustive sample than those reported in Collings' study, we would still lack a definitive answer to the question of income maintenance. The transition from a military to civilian status involves a broad change of life style, as well as a mere change of job. There is some controversy about the money value of

TABLE 13. COMPARISON OF PAY BEFORE AND AFTER RETIREMENT
FOR RETIRED WEST COAST ARMY OFFICERS (MEAN AND MEDIAN)[a]

Source of Income	Mean	Median
Retired pay	$ 487	$446
Civilian job	574	499
Total Civilian Pay	$1,061	$945
Active Duty Pay and Allowances	$ 941	$960

[a] Adapted from Collings, K. J., "Employment of Retired Military Officers in the West Coast Area: A Pilot Study." Unpublished Master's thesis, University of Washington, 1963.

various fringe benefits that active people enjoy and the value of the residual ones that retirees who locate near military facilities can continue to utilize.

Even more difficult are questions that may be raised about the relative dependence upon the cash nexus of the military, as opposed to the civilian style of life. A questionnaire study of retired officers conducted in 1956 yielded a consensus that the money demands of retired life were lighter because of "its slower pace."[41] The few and atypical respondents in this study, however, make it hazardous to extrapolate the generalization to current and prospective retirees.

For many of the questions raised about military retirement, an assessment of the subjective satisfaction or dissatisfaction of retirees with their situation is more important than objective figures of income. From either the sociological perspective, or that of evaluating the adequacy of the retirement system toward encouraging recruitment and retention, a pertinent question is: "How many feel that they have had a fair deal, a bum deal, or a plush deal?" Here, too, the difference between style of life before and after retirement is presumably important. To what extent, for example, do the loss of personal contacts and movement out of the integrated and structured social world of military life thrust the military family toward more extensive use of market mechanisms for equivalent satisfactions?

In considering the subjective aspects of the problems of maintenance, examination of the nature and levels of expectation and aspiration is crucial. To what extent, for example, do military personnel feel that they are deferring some of their aspirations until after the completion of military careers? How many are content now because of the expectation that their retirement pay will make possible a gratifying post-retirement life? Some greater satisfaction from family life might reasonably be regarded in this deferred category by the soldier, and more so, by his wife, who looks forward to the time when the family is freed from the disruptions of temporary duty and changes of station, and the separations associated with sea and foreign duty.

The adequacy of the second career, however, is the focal problem in evaluating the congruence of expectations and aspirations, with the actualities.

Anticipations and Actuality

It is a consistent finding of many surveys of servicemen that they regard their military experience as of great value. In questionnaire studies conducted by the Bureau of Social Science Research among basic trainees, it is found that raw recruits at the beginning of their obligatory service overwhelmingly believe that the time they spend in the service will be advantageous, rather than disadvantageous, for their civilian careers. There is some objective support for these beliefs. According to Feldman, the most recent data from the current population survey of the Bureau of the Census show that for the year 1962 employed veterans enjoyed a substantial advantage in earnings over nonveterans.[42] For full-time, year-round workers, age thirty-five to forty-four, the median income of World War II veterans was $6,758, but only $5,644 for nonveterans. While this difference is doubtless affected in the veterans' favor by the armed forces selection standards and by educational benefits enjoyed by veterans after discharge (and, in the other direction, by the possibilities for nonveteran "head starts" during manpower shortages), Feldman argues that in-service training certainly has played an important role in the difference. Wool describes the magnitude of service education and training programs and discusses the very limited existing information regarding potential transferability of the resulting skills to civilian job demands.[43] Each year armed forces schools offer between 2,000 and 3,000 different courses and, excluding flight training and the professional education of officers in civilian institutions and staff schools, nearly $1 billion annually is expended on this training.

The career soldier, too, generally attaches high value to his service experience. Indeed, the Michigan study found that a large number of officers report that military skills helped them a great deal in civilian work, and the majority found their experience at least of some value. (See Table 14.) If we compare ratings of those already retired of the application of their military skills to civilian jobs (Table 14) with ratings by those approaching retirement of the applicability expected (Table 15), we find the actuality much lower than the anticipation.

TABLE 14. JUDGMENT OF USEFULNESS OF MILITARY SKILLS IN CIVILIAN JOB, 1961 SAMPLE SURVEY OF MILITARY RETIREES

Usefulness	Per Cent
Helped a great deal	37
Helped somewhat	20
Helped very little	10
Did not help at all	14
Have done little or no work since leaving the active military service	15
Not ascertained	4
Total	100
Number of cases	3,168

SOURCE: U.S. Congress, Senate, 1961, pp. 2–8.

TABLE 15. ANTICIPATED UTILIZATION OF MILITARY EXPERIENCE IN CIVILIAN LIFE, 1961 SAMPLE SURVEY OF ACTIVE DUTY PERSONNEL

Utilization	Officers			Enlisted Men		
	Army	Navy	Marine	Army	Navy	Marine
	(Percentages)			(Percentages)		
Will probably help a great deal	63	58	53	32	48	42
Will probably help somewhat	25	30	31	23	21	23
Will probably help very little	4	6	7	10	7	10
Will probably not help at all	2	2	3	20	12	17
Have no idea how much it will help	6	4	4	15	12	8
Not ascertained	–	–	2	–	–	–
Total	100	100	100	100	100	100
Number of cases	3,980	4,746	1,481	4,442	3,914	4,993

SOURCE: U.S. Congress, Senate, 1961, pp. 3–16.

The survey of recently retired Annapolis graduates conducted by Massey was primarily oriented to comparing expectations and actual experiences regarding civilian employment.[44] On all of the items used—unemployment, difficulty in finding first job, income, and value of service skills in post-retirement employment—Massey found that these officers held overly optimistic expectations.

The impression of armed services retirement counselors is consistent with the survey data comparisons above that indicate a considerable inflation of expectation over reality about the ease with which a retiree is likely to find a job that will make good and remunerative use of his

TABLE 16. ANTICIPATED EASE OF EQUALING MILITARY JOB IN CIVILIAN LIFE, 1961 SAMPLE SURVEY OF ACTIVE DUTY PERSONNEL

Anticipated Ease	Officers				Enlisted Men			
	Army	Navy	Marine	Air Force	Army	Navy	Marine	Air Force
	(Percentages)				(Percentages)			
Very easy	21	20	15	17	33	21	31	18
Fairly easy	27	25	23	27	27	31	22	35
Fairly difficult	28	30	30	34	14	19	17	31
Very difficult	12	14	21	15	9	10	11	9
Don't know how difficult it would be	12	11	11	7	17	19	19	7
Total	100	100	100	100	100	100	100	100
Number of cases	3,980	4,746	1,481	3,484	4,442	3,914	4,993	3,117

Source: U.S. Congress, Senate, 1961, pp. 3–18.

322

skills. They report that the person usually goes through a process of scaling down his levels of expectation and aspiration during the period immediately before and after his retirement, as he comes into realistic contact with the occupational world.[45]

Not that anxieties do not exist among men approaching retirement, for as Table 16 shows, fewer than half of the officers (although somewhat more of the enlisted men) expect to have an easy time finding a job that will match their service job in general desirability. As Table 17 indicates, however, relatively few expect to be worse off financially. Neglecting their retired pay, almost half of the officers and well over half of the enlisted men expect civilian jobs to equal or better their military pay.

TABLE 17. ANTICIPATED EARNINGS IN CIVILIAN LIFE: AMONG MILITARY PERSONNEL WITH FIFTEEN YEARS OR MORE SERVICE, 1961 SAMPLE SURVEY OF ACTIVE DUTY PERSONNEL

Anticipated Annual Earnings	Officers			Enlisted Men		
	Army	Navy	Marine	Army	Navy	Marine
	(Percentages)			(Percentages)		
Much higher than I was making in the (Service)	8	8	6	19	15	12
A little higher	19	16	12	23	23	26
About the same	27	20	21	22	21	17
A little lower	21	19	32	8	9	18
Much lower than I was making in the (Service)	6	8	11	1	1	4
Have no idea	17	27	18	25	29	22
Will probably not work after I leave the (Service)	2	2	—	2	1	1
Not ascertained	—	0	0	—	1	—
Total	100	100	100	100	100	100
Number of cases	2,086	2,126	632	692	648	510

SOURCE: U.S. Congress, Senate, 1961, pp. 3–21.

Implications for Recruitment and Retention

We have alluded only briefly to the significance for the defense establishment of the second-career pattern. How retirees fare in civilian life may have consequential effects on the armed forces. Feedbacks from retirement patterns are more likely to be significant if the increase in the numbers of retirees leads to greater attention to them as a group and to greater stereotyping. Thus if great numbers of retired personnel have to accept civilian jobs of low pay and prestige, this may have important consequences for the morale, public image, and recruiting ability of the armed forces. On the other hand, if a widespread impression arises, correct or incorrect, that these retirees have an undeserved "soft touch," or are subsidized in such a way as to compete unfairly for jobs in the civilian labor force, there will also be adverse consequences for the armed forces. Among the latter would be additional pressures for changes in the retirement system.

In responding to survey questions, few career personnel rate retirement benefits high among the factors that led them to choose a service career. The Michigan study group reasoned that this did not necessarily imply that it was not an important factor in recruitment, since retirement security might very well be taken for granted as an aspect of this life career. The past, furthermore, is not an adequate guide to the future with respect to the significance of retirement matters for recruitment and retention. Yet the images of the attractiveness of retirement that may affect recruitment and retention of servicemen in the near future will probably be influenced by the retirement experiences of these quite dissimilar World War II entrants, just as the latter's images of retirement as an officer or soldier were influenced by a military generation quite unlike themselves.

One cannot be absolutely sure that retirement may not come to be defined as a negative matter, rather than an inducement of the career, because of the high possibility of having to establish a new career when one is approaching forty and the certainty of this step by age fifty-two. It can be assumed, however, that whatever its specific content, there is likely to be more consciousness of the retirement matter in the future than in the past. This may have some consequence for qualitative aspects of recruitment. For example, some might look for a favorable consequence if the second-career aspect of a military career led to a greater selection of persons with the kind of self-confidence and tolerance for imperfect security that allowed them to be sanguine about early retirement at modest pay. The concept of a two-step career also implies attitudes about the consonance of the military profession with civilian ones that depart markedly from the conventional image outlined at the beginning of this paper.

Official Cognizance of the Retiree

Despite its acknowledged importance and possible consequences for recruiting and retention, the second-career problem has been approached by the armed forces in an indirect and tentative manner. Paradoxically, both the concept of the retiree as severed from the institution and that of not being fully severed from it have contributed to the inability of the armed forces to approach the matter directly. Since the retiree "has left" the service, his occupation is regarded as a private matter of no official concern (so long as it is within the law). The second-career problem is "outside the mission," so to speak.

At the same time, the fact that the military definition clings to the retiree gives the armed forces less freedom of action in assisting retirees to find civilian jobs than is possessed, say, by a business firm or university which operates with a mandatory retirement system, or even that exercised sometimes toward civil servants dismissed because of reductions in force. Sensitivity about public attitudes, we believe, has produced some anxiety regarding possible charges of "the military feathering its own nest" were the military establishment to attack the matter too vigorously.

The armed forces have also been more concerned with retention than with separation. Giving too much attention, and particularly too early attention, to preparing men for post-retirement employment, it was feared, might be encouraging men to retire or simply diverting their attention from the main business at hand.[46] As of 1963, preretirement counseling is not undertaken until the terminal processing phase of the last assignment.

Second-Career Assistance

For a number of years, each of the services has maintained a Retired Activities Section at the service headquarters level to assist retired members and those about to retire. In addition to providing information about the maze of laws and regulations applicable to retirement, these sections conduct and coordinate programs for counseling men regarding their second career. As Assistant Secretary Paul emphasized in describing these activities:

> This program does not include any activities relating to job hunting or job placement for the military retiree. This is an area in which we believe the Department of Defense should not become involved.
>
> Furthermore, the needs of this group are so diversified that the Department could not, within current resources, establish the national machinery required to match job opportunities and the applications on the scale required. Therefore, it is the policy of the Department of Defense to provide the United States Employment Service of the Department of Labor, through its affiliated local employment offices throughout the country, all assistance possible in order to make its services available to the military retiree. . . . The Department of Labor has the main governmental responsibility to assist personnel being separated from active duty in obtaining civil employment.[47]

These arrangements were originally established in 1956, arising in large measure from initiatives taken by a group of Navy officers. Beginning with the Navy, counseling and placement services were established, using the agency of the Professional Division of the Labor Department, operating through the Professional Office of the District of Columbia Labor Service. Until 1959, the District of Columbia office was the national center for military retiree placement. At that time, a West Coast center was added. In 1963, with growing attention to the needs for providing preretirement counseling, six more centers were slated for addition to this professional office system.

British Services Resettlement Service

Very similar problems have faced all of the World War II allies, including the Soviet Union. Although definition of the problem and formal arrangements for handling it in Great Britain have been very similar to the American case, it has involved considerably more intense activity in Britain.[48] A detailed discussion of the British case is given by Abrams.[49] He writes:

> The successful resettling [of retired officers either after 20 years of service or by age 55] remains the outstanding challenge to those who would create a modern military profession in Britain. And since 1957 the machinery of resettlement has developed as dramatically as the career pattern itself. The heart of this apparatus remains the "service" provided by the Ministry of Labour since 1949. But this has now been invested with new prestige and strengthened by a network of contacts with powerful figures in the services, private industry, and the government. Prior to 1957 the imagined stigma of the "Labour Exchange" still weighed heavily against the service, no more than 25 per cent of retiring officers being willing to make use of it. Nor perhaps was the record of placings likely to encourage even those officers not troubled by any sense of indignity of using the service.
> In 1957, however, the service took a new lease on life.

Abrams describes in detail the extensive network and vigorous activity of the organization that emerged. This was primarily a three-sided affair. A new government post, Director of Resettlement, was created to coordinate the activities. The newly retired Vice Chief of the Air Staff took this post. The second leg was an Advisory Board representing key figures of industry and commerce. Finally, according to Abrams, "The Ministry of Labour has managed, albeit unintentionally, to conquer the myth of its own slightly low-class personality by working alongside and in cooperation with the influential and very respectable Officers' Association."[50]

Sir Frederic Hooper, managing director of Schweppes, Ltd., who has headed the Advisory Board, provided vigorous leadership to the Resettlement Service.[51] His interest is perhaps indicated by the selection as a symbol of the Schweppes product the bearded Commander Whitehead, who also symbolizes the retired British officer turned dignified salesman.

Since its inception, the Resettlement Service has carried on a major propaganda campaign to create an atmosphere favorable to the easy transfer of ex-officers to industrial positions.

> Soldiers had to be convinced that employment of an attractive nature was available. Employers had to be persuaded that the services could provide high quality and easily trainable personnel. This has been very largely an ideological matter on both sides—to break down pictures of blimpishness among civilians and to dislodge ingrained but outmoded conceptions of status among officers. . . . Twelve regional committees have been set up, "each chaired by a distinguished local industrialist whose name carries great weight in his respective region." The Director of Resettlement has addressed many "gatherings of leading industrialists," Rotary Clubs, Chambers of Commerce, etc., as well as approaching the leading authorities of all the nationalised industries and corporations such as atomic, coal, transport, B.B.C. and the like, to remind them of the new material on the labour market and to get concessions for the ex-regular where possible. Opportunities were "sought and obtained" to persuade employers by means of the press, radio, and television. . . . The "job finder" of the Officers' Association visited over 900 employers in the year 1958–1959.[52]

These British activities were not restricted to propaganda, however:

> Substantial grants, the so-called Golden Bowler, have been provided by way of compensation for premature retirement over and above the normal retired pay and terminal grants. . . . These tax-free capital payments are matched by smaller grants to officers retiring normally during the run-down period in recognition of the fact that they have to compete for jobs with the prematurely retired. A series of training and "re-orientation" schemes have been set up to introduce the officer to civilian life. A number of articles and pamphlets have indicated the sort of jobs officers may reasonably expect and the best means of pursuing them. Ministry of Labour officials have toured service establishments talking to officers about civilian employment. And something remarkably like a military pressure group has emerged in Parliament to voice the problems and aspirations of the retired officer. Debates on general defense issues have been diverted to wring assurances of sympathy for the plight of officers from Ministers.[53]

Increasing Attention in U.S.

A more frontal approach to retired employment in the United States is developing. The Air Force Association meeting billed as the First National Conference on the Utilization of Retired Military Personnel is a case in point. It was complete with a message from the President, and earnest speeches by a variety of high-level government and industrial officials. Underlying these addresses was the assumption that the second-career matter was not a problem that would take care of itself. Funds, legislation, early counseling and career planning, retraining programs, and programs of public and industry information were all envisioned.

A particular target of the active staff work being undertaken by the Air Force Association is the provision of retraining funds for retiring military personnel under the Manpower Development and Retraining Act and the National Defense Education Act. AFA has also pressed for Labor Department studies of the utilization and retraining needs of retired military personnel.

The AFA publicity-oriented entry into the second-career problem contrasts somewhat with the quieter activities of the Retired Officers Association. The latter has been an active participant in the Labor Department's placement program and runs its own placement activity, which it says handles about 20 inquiries from applicants daily. It achieves such public notice as it gets, however, largely in connection with its positions on pay legislation.

Career Continuity

The AFA conference also witnessed a step away from the policy of deferring official cognizance of the second-career matter to the moment of retirement. Assistant Secretary Paul stated:

> In many cases, the personnel concerned are informed of their separation from active duty by as much as a year ahead of time, and in most cases it is at least six months prior to the date of release. Therefore, we believe that we should now revise our thinking and arrange for the United States Employment Service representative to brief our people at an earlier date. In this way, the retiree will be better able to prepare himself to meet the requirements of the civilian labor market.[54]

As of 1963, the objective is to provide second-career counseling at least six months before retirement. Where possible, it is intended that professional employment counselors of Labor Department centers visit bases to provide this counseling. Current thinking in the Defense Department envisions eventually that counseling occur two years prior to retirement, insofar as the separation of the individual can be sufficiently foreseen. Those responsible for providing second-career help reiterate the importance of channeling information to personnel well before retirement. They conclude that most personnel do very little during their active duty careers to plan and prepare themselves for post-retirement employment. Some military figures, however, continue to oppose early second-career counseling.

Are the Military and Civilian Worlds Antithetical?

The traditional opposition within the armed forces toward encouraging members to concern themselves with early planning for a second career rests on an assumption that orientation toward civilian life is incompatible with a proper military orientation. This assumption has some similarity to that common among civilians regarding the disparate nature of the two worlds. There exists also the fear that if training and experience in the service gives the soldier a readily marketable skill, he is likely to succumb to the high-paying temptations of private industry. This fear was heightened in the mid-1950's by concern in the Air Force about the loss of skilled enlisted technicians to industry. In certain key occupations, attrition among technicians led to dismay in the service that its training schools were serving more to produce a skilled work force for industry than to meet its own needs. A Bureau of Labor Statistics survey in 1952, for example, revealed that one-third of all civilian electronics technicians had received all or part of their training in military technical schools.[55]

While these problems of retention in the face of competition from industry are doubtless of consequence for selected occupational areas, findings of recent research are not completely consistent with the assumptions of conflict underlying the wariness toward training and civilian career counseling that might "encourage men to retire prematurely."

The Michigan group's survey of active duty personnel yielded the highly pertinent data shown in Table 18. In Appendix 3 of the report their findings were discussed in these words:

> When thinking about the possibility of transferring their Army training and experience to civilian life, those officers who feel that these skills are very transferable more often tend to remain in the Army, while those who feel that their training and experience will help "very little" or "not at all" more often are thinking of leaving the Army. In short, those officers who intend to leave the Army are not predominantly men who have developed valuable skills in the Army that are transferable into lucrative civilian jobs. Rather, the intention to leave the Army is associated with a feeling of lack of development of skills and abilities. Those who intend to leave are people with a feeling of waste in this area. They have not utilized the skills they had nor developed any others which they feel will help them in civilian life, and therefore appear to be eager to leave the service. Development of a meaningful, purposeful skill, then, would seem to be one way of insuring a commitment that keeps an officer in the military even though he feels the skill could be utilized in civilian life.

TABLE 18. UTILIZATION OF MILITARY EXPERIENCE IN CIVILIAN
LIFE RELATED TO ARMY CAREER PLANS: AMONG ARMY
OFFICERS AT DIFFERENT CAREER STAGES

Career Stages	Utilization of Military Experience			
	A great deal	Somewhat	Very little; not at all	No idea
	(Percentages)			
A. *Less than two years of service*				
Remain indefinitely or until retirement	24	10	4	18
Undecided or separate after present commitment	76	90	96	82
Total	100	100	100	100
Number of cases	*184*	*172*	*50*	*17*
B. *Five to ten years of service*				
Remain indefinitely or until retirement	80	59	44	84
Undecided or separate after present commitment	20	41	56	16
Total	100	100	100	100
Number of cases	*371*	*156*	*45*	*38*
C. *Ten to fifteen years of service*				
Remain indefinitely or until retirement	93	83	78	96
Undecided or separate after present commitment	7	17	22	4
Total	100	100	100	100
Number of cases	*297*	*98*	*23*	*44*

At the same time it should be noted, as indicated in the right-hand column of Table 18, officers who had "no idea" about the value of their military skills for civilian employment were as highly committed to the service as those who regarded their experience as highly useful.

Watson, using a different approach, reached conclusions consistent with the Michigan group's findings.[56] The focus of his study of retired Air Force officers was to test directly the hypothesis that there was conflict between identification with the military institution and adjustment to civilian life after retirement. His general conclusions were the reverse. He found that officers who had high "identification" with the military institution, as measured by the questions in his index, tended to have higher civilian occupational adjustment than those with low military identification. This relationship was due to the prevalence of both higher identification with the military and better occupational adjustment among the more recently retired officers in his sample, as against those who had been retired for six or more years.[57]

An examination of Watson's data suggests that the relationship may be due to the role of education. Education, particularly possession of the bachelor's degree, is increasingly a factor in success in both the military and civilian worlds. To a much greater degree than in the case of retirees of past years, the recent officer with low education would have been disadvantaged in both his military and civilian careers, while the college-educated officer would be more in tune with both worlds.

It is clear that there is no one-to-one correspondence between the qualities given the highest rewards in the military and in the civilian area. Many very specifically trained technicians—the computer programmer, for example—can anticipate far higher civilian income than men who had more general training and skills. Table 19 shows the imperfect correlation of civilian income and military rank of retired officers responding to the Michigan survey.

Statistically, however, there seems to be considerable association between the possession of qualities that make for success in a military career and those that lead to more successful adaptation to the civilian occupational world after retirement. Further, there is some indication in data such as Watson's that this is becoming increasingly the case. A

TABLE 19. EMPLOYMENT INCOME RELATED TO RANK, 1961 SAMPLE SURVEY OF MILITARY RETIREES

Rank	Under $4,000	$4,000 to $6,000	$6,000 to $8,000	$8,000 to $10,000	$10,000 and over	Not Ascertained	Total	Number of Cases
			(Percentages)					
General, Admiral, Colonel, and Naval Captain	26	18	14	10	31	1	100	338
Lt. Colonel and Commander	30	26	18	12	11	3	100	548
Major and Lt. Commander	26	34	21	11	6	2	100	613
Captain and Naval Lieutenant	27	35	25	7	6	—	100	346
First Lieutenant and Lieutenant j.g., Second Lieutenant, and Ensign	26	31	28	6	6	3	100	85
Warrant Officers	30	40	20	7	2	1	100	431

SOURCE: U.S. Congress, Senate, 1961, pp. 2–34.

considerable correlation between rank and income from employment has been found in all surveys. Collings further found that Regular Army officers generally earned considerably more in civilian jobs than did retired reservists.[58] He also reports that length of service was positively correlated with income from employment in the first job after retirement. The most directly comparable data in the Michigan survey, unlike Collings', show a disadvantage in delays in retirement beyond the twenty-year point. The discrepancy may be due to the restriction of Collings' sample to recent retirees. A factor may be a greater representation in the recent sample of reservists or former reservists who did not wish to retire, but whose eligibility for continued active duty depended upon qualifications, particularly education, that also proved relevant for civilian occupations. Possession of a bachelor's degree was important, for example, in a reservist's being accepted for integration into the regular component.

Social Integration

There is also little information on how the retired fit themselves into the communities in which they settle—the extent to which they move into wider social circles or retain exclusivity; the degree to which various dimensions of their civilian status are as well equilibrated as was true in military life, and, where disequilibration occurs, as it assuredly must, how they adapt to it.

The limited data developed by Watson suggest that the prevailing patterns involve continued psychological identification with the military institution, as manifest in discussing military affairs with friends, a desire for close contacts with a nearby military base, continued reading of military periodicals, and representing one's service to the civilian community.[59] He found, however, that these ties need not interfere with integration into the civilian community; in fact, they appear to facilitate it. Relatively few of his respondents reported that most of their social activities were with other military personnel—active duty or retired—or that available military facilities were the major determinant of their choice of a locality in which to settle. Only in those cases in which the continued military identification did involve the continued dependence on the military manifest in choice of location and of friends, along with feelings of status deprivation upon retirement—a composite of items Watson labeled "low civilian identification"—did he find a poor adjustment to civilian life. "Low civilian identification" affected both occupational and social adjustment adversely.

The social and occupational integration of the military retiree constitutes a valuable perspective for examining the nature of the military institution in American life and the evolving nature of the social role of the military professional. Most of the evidence available suggests that the military role is not as distinctive as is frequently supposed, and that only peripheral changes of life style are demanded for the social and occupational integration of the retiree.

As in the case of most roles, however, military roles are not developed by the institution and its members without regard to the definitions and expectations of others in the society. The growth of the military retired population is one of a number of developments increasing the involvement and visibility of the military professional in civilian society. Presumably, this may tend to increase the influence of civilian definitions upon military roles.

Politics

We have not attended in this paper to a topic of considerable public attention—political activity by retired officers. In comparison with Great Britain, retired officers are not particularly numerous or prominent in American political life. Abrams writes about the British situation:

> In reply to a Conservative statement in the House of Commons in June, 1956, that there was "some anxiety among officers, particularly brigadiers," about postservice employment, a Labour speaker asked whether this was to be taken to mean that there was now "no room in the ranks of the *normal* occupation of ex-Brigadiers"—namely, on the Conservative back benches.[60]

While a former military leader has fairly frequently become President of the United States, the lack of strong local identifications and ties has restricted access to office and activity in political organization in our strongly federalistic system. Ex-military leaders are more likely to be in the public eye in either national elder-statesman roles, as typified by General Lucius Clay, or in roles removed from the mainstream of political life, as exemplified by the deviant, ideological politics of General Walker or Admiral Crommelin.

The classic anxiety of the political scientist regarding the politics of a displaced class, or of the sociologist regarding the downwardly mobile, does not seem to be broadly applicable now to the military retiree. Its relevance in the future will depend not only on the fate of retirees in a second career, but also on the broader evolving patterns of recruitment and career management in a context of changing military technology.

NOTES

1. *New York Times*, May 8, 1963.

2. U. S. Congress, Senate, Committee on Armed Services, *A Study of the Military Retired Pay System and Certain Related Subjects.* 87th Congress, 1st Sess. Government Printing Office, Washington, 1961.

3. Watson, J. H., "A Study of Social and Occupational Adjustment in Relation to Civilian and Military Identification of United States Air Force Retired Officers." Unpublished Ph.D. dissertation, State College, Mississippi, 1963, p. 45.

4. *Ibid.*

5. Collings, K. J., "Employment of Retired Military Officers in the West Coast Area: A Pilot Study." Unpublished Master's thesis, University of Washington, 1963.

6. One additional complication in interpreting the data is the "length of service" eligibility of numbers of those presently retired and retiring in the near future based on "constructive service." "Constructive service credit" involves the counting of time during which no actual creditable service was performed in the case of various categories of officers, such as older men who entered service during World War II and who were "integrated" into regular components subsequently, and certain professional categories who receive constructive service for their advanced educational standing at the time of their entry.

7. Janowitz, Morris, *The Professional Soldier: A Social and Political Portrait.* The Free Press of Glencoe, New York, 1960, pp. 8–12.

8. Biderman, A. D., "The Prospective Impact of Large Scale Military Retirement," *Social Problems,* vol. 7, 1959, pp. 84–90.

9. Biderman, A. D., *ibid.,* and Biderman, A. D., *Needs for Knowledge Regarding the Military Retirement Problem: Summary Report of a Conference Held in Washington, D. C.* Bureau of Social Science Research, Inc., Washington, 1960.

10. U. S. Department of Defense, News Release, April 2, 1963.

11. U. S. Department of Labor and the Air Force Association, *Proceedings: The First National Conference on the Utilization of Retired Military Personnel,* Air Force Association, Washington, 1963, pp. 5–6.

12. U. S. Department of Labor and the Air Force Association, *ibid.,* p. 8.

13. Janowitz, Morris, *op. cit.,* pp. 21ff.

14. U. S. Congress, Senate, 1961, *op. cit.*

15. U. S. Department of Labor and the Air Force Association, *op. cit.,* p. 29.

16. H. R. 12721, 87th Congress. These provisions were enacted into law subsequent to the preparation of this paper.

17. U. S. Department of Labor and the Air Force Association, *op. cit.,* pp. 30–31.

18. U. S. Congress, House, Subcommittee for Special Investigations of the Committee on Armed Services, *Employment of Retired Commissioned Officers by Defense Department Contractors.* 86th Congress, 1st Sess. Government Printing Office, Washington, 1960, p. 20.

19. Association of the Bar of the City of New York, *Conflict of Interest and Federal Service.* Harvard University Press, Cambridge, Mass., 1960.

20. Califano, J. A. "Limitations on the Employment of Retired Naval Officers," *JAG Journal,* November, 1957, p. 2; Clinard, D. M., and J. A. Foltz, "Retirement and the Law," *JAG Journal,* June-July, 1959, p. 3; Neely, W. E., and R. W. Canady, "Restrictions on Post-Retirement Employment: Recent Developments and Trends," *Retired Officer,* July-August, 1963, pp. 29–31.

21. Mills, C. W. *The Power Elite.* Oxford University Press, New York, 1959.

22. U. S. Congress, House, 1960, *op. cit.,* Appendix 4.

23. U. S. Congress, House, 1960, *ibid.,* p. 15.

24. The constitutionality of the conflict of interest statutes and of the employment registration procedures used by the Department of Defense to enforce these statutes have been made the subject of a test case before a U. S. District Court. (See "The Taussig Case," *Retired Officer,* March-April, vol. 19, 1963, pp. 15–16.)

25. U. S. Department of Labor and the Air Force Association, *op. cit.,* pp. 37–40.

26. Biderman, A. D., 1960, *op. cit.,* p. 10.

27. Janowitz, Morris, "Civil Roles of Retired Military Professionals." Unpublished paper read at Conference on Needs for Knowledge Regarding the Military Retirement Problem, Washington, D.C., 1960.

28. Janowitz, Morris, *The Professional Soldier, op. cit.,* pp. 207–211.

29. Abrams, Philip, "Democracy, Technology, and the Retired British Officer" in Huntington, S. P., editor, *Changing Patterns of Military Politics.* The Free Press of Glencoe, New York, 1962.

30. U. S. Department of Defense, 1961, *op. cit.,* p. vi.

31. U. S. Department of Defense, 1961, *ibid.*

32. Collings, K. J., *op. cit.*

33. Massey, R. J. "A Survey Study of the Integration of Retired Naval Academy Graduates into the National Economy." Unpublished report, The Armed Forces Management Association, 1963.

34. U. S. Department of Defense, 1961, *op. cit.,* p. vi.

35. Boegel, T. J. "The Potential Resource for Teachers From the Ranks of Retiring Military Personnel." Unpublished Ph.D. dissertation, St. John's University, Jamaica, New York, 1961.

36. Collings, K. J., *op. cit.,* p. 78.

37. Garrett, D. G., "Retirement Experiences and Employment Status of United States Air Force Retired Enlisted Personnel." Unpublished Master's thesis, University of New Mexico, 1961.

38. A recently organized group—the NCO Association of the United States— recruits actively among retired enlisted men, as well as among those on active duty. A job register for retirees is one of its advertised benefits.

39. See, for example, U. S. Department of Labor and Air Force Association, *op. cit.,* pp. 8, 16, 23–24.

40. Collings, K. J., *op. cit.*

41. Committee of Retired Army, Navy and Air Force Officers, *Retirement from the Armed Forces,* 2d ed. Military Service Publishing Co., Harrisburg, Pa., 1958.

42. Feldman, Sidney, "Employment Outlook for Veterans," *Employment Security Review,* vol. 30, 1963, pp. 6–8.

43. Wool, Harold, "The Armed Services as a Training Institution" in Ginzberg, Eli, editor, *The Nation's Children,* Columbia University Press, New York, 1960; and Wool, Harold, "The Changing Pattern of Military Skills," *Employment Security Review,* 1963, vol. 30, pp. 27–32.

44. Massey, R. J., *op. cit.*

45. Biderman, A. D., 1960, *op. cit.*

46. See remarks of Assistant Secretary of Defense Paul in U. S. Department of Labor and Air Force Association, *op. cit.,* 1963, pp. 6–7.

47. U. S. Department of Labor and Air Force Association, *op. cit.*, p. 6.

48. Despite prevalent impressions to the contrary, the premature retirements of officers in Great Britain following the *Defence White Paper* of 1957 did not involve resettlement problems of an entirely different scale of magnitude in relation to total labor force as compared with the American case. During the critical period 1958–1963, the *White Paper* foresaw 25,000 officer retirements. In the similar period, over 50,000 U. S. officers were retired. In the United States, retirements of 10,000 officers a year will be sustained over a long period.

49. Abrams, Philip, *op. cit.*, p. 163.

50. *Ibid.*, p. 164.

51. Great Britain, Ministry of Labour and National Service, *Resettlement Advisory Board Progress Report 1957–1959.* H.M.S.O., London, 1958.

52. Abrams, Philip, *op. cit.*, p. 164.

53. *Ibid.*, p. 165.

54. U. S. Department of Labor and Air Force Association, 1963, *op. cit.*, p. 7.

55. Quoted by Harold Wool, 1963, *op. cit.*

56. Watson, J. H., *op. cit.*

57. Watson's data also reveal that those with higher military identification more frequently indicated that they had made plans for their retirement while they were still on active duty than those with less military identification.

58. Collings, K. J., *op. cit.*

59. Watson, J. H., *op. cit.* See also Watson, J. H., "A Study of Characteristics and Military Identification of United States Air Force Retired Officers," unpublished Master's thesis, State College, Mississippi, 1961.

60. Abrams, Philip, *op. cit.*, p. 151.

Part Six

BIBLIOGRAPHIC GUIDE

SELECTED LITERATURE OF REVOLUTIONS AND COUPS D'ETAT IN THE DEVELOPING NATIONS

Moshe Lissak

COUPS D'ETAT, REVOLUTIONS, AND POPULAR REVOLTS are by no means a new issue of study and research by students of society and history. Very often these subjects emerge as the core of famous works by historians, political scientists, and sociologists. Classical scholars such as Karl Marx, Max Weber, Karl Mannheim, Arnold J. Toynbee, Pitirim Sorokin, and more recently, Hannah Arendt and J. Talmon, have made major contributions either to the understanding of one revolution in particular, or to outlining the basic patterns and stages of revolution in general. Western society is primarily if not exclusively the historical background referred to by these and other scholars. The great dramas of the "glorious" revolution in England, the American revolution, the French and Russian revolutions, the unification of Italy, and to a lesser extent, the various coups d'état in the Balkan countries at the end of the nineteenth century and the beginning of the twentieth century served as stimuli for many more writers on the subject. These revolutions became an integral part of the history of western society and consequently the intellectual realm of historians and political scientists. Sociologists in the past, by contrast, have almost entirely neglected this field of research.

The emergence of national movements in Asia and Africa and the social ferment in many Latin American societies after World War II was followed by a renaissance of interest of social scientists in these historical phenomena. The establishment of new states and the crystallization of new nations accompanied by radical social upheavals created a fresh challenge for the sociologists, anthropologists, and political scientists. Social scientists became aware that the study of problems confronting the developing countries in their effort to establish new social institutions might not only contribute to the understanding of the events themselves but revitalize, as well, sociological theory of social change. Conceptual issues such as political modernization, nation building, and the like became almost *sine qua non* of the growing literature dealing with these subjects.

The rapid and abrupt changes occurring in these countries and the absence of historical documentation have made research a difficult task, if one wishes to draw conclusions based on a thoughtful and cautious analysis. It is no wonder, indeed, that some aspects of the issues in question, and frequently some central aspects, have not yet been treated systematically as, for example, the relation between party and administrative organization in the new nations, or the relation between technological changes in the organization of production and social changes.

One of the most neglected fields is the comparative study of the role of the military and para-military organization in the process of consolidation of the developing societies. While coups d'état and popular revolutions became an integral part of the political processes of many countries in the Middle East, Southeast Asia, and Latin America, research on these topics has been conducted, in general, on a case study basis.

The aim of this annotated bibliography is to present a sample of the studies published in recent years that refer directly and indirectly to problems of the position of the military in the social and political process in the developing countries. It should be emphasized that this bibliography is to be considered only as a selected guide for several reasons: (a) The bibliography refers solely to materials published in English and to a lesser extent in French. It does not include the studies in Spanish (dealing with the Latin American context). No attempt was made to examine the German studies. (b) The bibliography does not include governmental documents or other sources which might serve as documentary material for sociological analysis, but is confined mainly to studies published in professional periodicals and to books with sociological relevance though not always written by sociologists or political scientists per se. (c) Books or articles dealing with the general historical background of the societies are not presented unless they referred directly or indirectly to problems of military-civil relations. (d) We confined ourselves chiefly to works written since the 1940's and referring to the peculiar problems of the new nations emerging since then, and to the Latin American countries in this period.

The overview of the issues as presented by this bibliography makes possible consideration of some of the basic problems and variables involved in the analysis of factors conditioning intervention of the military in politics in the developing societies. Most studies refer, sometimes indirectly and under various titles, to the problem of modernization and its bearing on social groups and their orientation toward social change. At times, however, implicitly or explicitly, modernization is perceived and identified with the democratic and pluralistic type of society that has emerged in Europe and the United States. Even the distinction between "western" and "nonwestern" types of modernization does not provide us with a better basis for conceptualizing the potential differences in development. Progress could be made by further knowledge about the forms and processes of modernization in specific institutional spheres, as, for example, in political organization, political and cultural communication, and the stratification patterns. Second, and most important, one should study the different configurations of modernization as they interrelate the various institutional spheres, which might lead eventually to a more significant distinction between the existing types of modernization, and the avoidance of descriptive terms as "western" and "nonwestern."

The emergence of different configurations of political and social structure in the process of modernization is presumably a result of the diverse circumstances of revolutions and coups d'état, that is, the problem of unevenness in social change. In other words, synchronization of change in the different sectors of the society is not usually found in these countries. While changes take place in various spheres, they differ in intensity and range when one particular social system is the object of analysis, or when a comparison is made between several societies. Japan is a society where initial, quite radical changes in the political and economic structure were accompanied by surprisingly limited changes in the stratification structure, in family composition, and in the basis of legitimacy. This pattern of change is not found in many new nations or underdeveloped countries. Ample evidence is already available on the impact of demographic factors and the stratification patterns on the political and economic "progress" of new and developing nations. The role of Islamic religious institutions in the Middle East and the institutionalization of violence in Latin America are cases in point.

Systematic study in this direction might provide empirical indices for the understanding of "functional constellations of change," that is, the combination of changes which would not severely undermine the whole social structure or lead to a stalemate in the process of change. Indeed, Deutsch,[1] Lerner,[2] and Almond[3] make preliminary contributions when they suggest indices of economic, political, and cultural development. However, a great deal of arbitrariness may be found in the definition and classification of countries according to indices suggested by various authors.[4]

The main reason for emphasizing this issue in the context of compiling a bibliography on coups and revolutions is as follows: There is apparently an important relationship, though certainly complicated, between the synchronization of social change and the mobilization of manpower, and material resources for realizing national political and cultural objectives. One of the conclusions to be drawn from the literature is that in many cases the crises and difficulties in economic mobilization supply immediate conditions for intervention in politics by the military, who claim to have special devices for overcoming the crises of mobilization.

All military elites do not respond to the challenge of mobilization in the same way. Aside from the general problem of the social circumstances in the new nations and developing countries which are conducive to a confrontation between military and civilian elites, the following specific questions may be raised: (a) What is the cause of the emergence of various types of military elites in terms of different attitudes toward political power, and the means of influencing the decision-making process? (b) What are the various techniques and devices used by the military to assume power? (c) How does the military manage to consolidate its power? (d) Under what circumstances can a peaceful and effective institutional transfer of power back to civil authorities take place? A few examples of the factors mentioned in the literature that deal with the military and society will give the reader a general impression of the trend of studies in this field. The most frequently mentioned factors are, for example, the extent of the economic development of the society and general possibilities for mobility; the type of civilian bureaucracy emerging or existing in the society; the range and character of the political organization; problems of internal and external security; the absence of middle-class or other types of intermediate links between the alienated sectors of the society; the character of civilian control on the military; and the extent of similarity between the ideology prevalent in the society and the ideology of the military.

Another group of factors is concerned with the internal structure of the military establishment, or the military as a social system. In this context the main items are: the degree of professionalization of the officer corps and the enlisted men, the combat experience, the experience and functions fulfilled by the Army in the colonial period, and types of careers prevailing in the military elites. The social composition of the Army, the range and character of nonmilitary roles assumed by the military before the coups or the revolutions, especially in the economic, political, and cultural spheres seemed to be important factors. In some cases the Army appears as an almost self-sustaining system, providing its own educational and indoctrination programs, establishing its own economic institutions, and in some cases its own political organization. The development of these nonmilitary roles not only improves the chances of succeeding to political power, but even more important, they improve chances to consolidate power after takeover.

Success of the military in realizing its political objectives and fulfilling its pledge of economic mobilization, in the recent past, have been the exception. Thus the study of factors bearing on the failure, as well as the study of conditions under which a peaceful and institutional transfer of power to the civilians may occur, is no less important than the study of factors leading to coups and revolutions. In tracing the causes of military ineffectiveness in solving economic and organizational problems some studies referred to another important factor, that is, the applicability of "military skills" in handling the complicated social and organizational problems of the society at large.

It is doubtful whether military men are qualified to adjust to new patterns of communication, to assume a role of arbiter between conflicting social groups, to accept gradual progress, to suffer setbacks, and to solve complicated economic problems. In many cases it is simply the "western" structure of the military, so well preserved by the military elite, which became an obstacle to the new-role adjustment of political leaders. These roles involve participation in a complex and difficult process of supply and demand of political support. At times, in such entangled situations, the inclination of the military is to resort to force. But when the Army resorts to force and eliminates two-way communication the military has further contributed to its inability to assist a constitutional government through a period of gradual change. During this process of disruption, internal splits in the Junta are often inevitable and coups and counter coups often ensue.

Success or failure in solving the problems of political and social modernization are not only attributed to the military establishment. More general processes in the society, the emergence of a middle-class, trade union leadership, and professional elites, are emphasized by many studies as basic requirements. These middle-stratum groups, while serving as new centers of identification, are able to provide the military elite with the technical and ideological guidance needed for carrying out the ambitious plans of economic and social modernization of the society.

NOTES

1. Deutsch, Karl W., "Social Mobilization and Political Development," *American Political Science Review*, vol. 55, September, 1961, pp. 493–514.

2. Lerner, Daniel, *The Passing of the Traditional Society*. The Free Press, Glencoe, Ill., 1958.

3. Almond, Gabriel A., and James S. Coleman, editors, *The Politics of the Developing Areas*. Princeton University Press, Princeton, N. J., 1960.

4. See discussion on the problem of synchronization of changes in Eisenstadt, S. N., "Sociological Aspects of Political Development in Underdeveloped Countries," *Economic Development and Cultural Change*, vol. 5, July, 1957, pp. 289–307.

BIBLIOGRAPHY

1. ABDEL MALEK, ANOUAR, *Égypte Société Militaire*. Éditions du Seuil, Paris, 1962. Analysis of the sociological character of the military regime in Egypt which includes the role of the Army in the industrial development of Egypt, the decline of the "ancienne bourgeoisie," and the emergence of a new ruling class. Efforts to develop a national ideology are also discussed.

2. ALBA, VICTOR, "The Stages of Militarism in Latin America" in Johnson, J. J., editor, *The Role of the Military in Underdeveloped Countries*. Princeton University Press, Princeton, N. J., 1962, pp. 165–184. Description of three stages in the history of Latin American militarism: (1) the *caudillos*, 1810–1912; (2) the conservatives and the demagogues, 1918–1958; and (3) the recent period, characterized by the young technocratic element.

3. ALEXANDER, ROBERT J., *The Perón Era*. Columbia University Press, New York, 1951. Account of the social forces in Argentina during the Peron era. Techniques by which Peron consolidated his power are discussed and analyzed.

4. ALEXANDER, ROBERT J., *The Bolivian National Revolution*. Rutgers University Press, New Brunswick, N. J., 1958. Analysis of the historical background of the 1952 revolution in Bolivia. The status of the Indians, organized labor, and the fight against militarism are some issues discussed.

5. ALEXANDER, ROBERT J., "The Army in Politics" in Davis, Harold E., editor, *Government and Politics in Latin America*. The Ronald Press Co., New York, 1958, pp. 147–166. Account of the causes and methods of military intervention in political life. Treatment and analysis of factors limiting militarism and changes in the role of the army itself.

6. ALEXANDER, ROBERT J., *Today's Latin America*. Doubleday Anchor Books, Garden City, N. Y., 1962, pp. 173–188. Deals with the origins of military intervention in politics, twentieth-century militarism, change in the nature of the military, and changes in the position of the military in the Latin American countries.

7. ANDRZEJEWSKI, STANISLAW, *Military Organization and Society*. Routledge and Kegan Paul, London, 1954. Examination of relations between military organizations and social structures. Analysis of the relations between warfare organization and

stratification, the size of political units and their cohesion, patterns of subordination and hierarchy, and so on.

8. ARCINIEGAS, GERMÁN, *The State of Latin America.* Alfred A. Knopf, New York, 1952, chaps. 6, 7, 8, 17. History of military and civil relations in Peru, Venezuela, and Bolivia. Concluding chapter on the armies of Latin America and the international scene.

9. ARNADE, KURT CONRAD, "The Technique of the Coup d'État in Latin America" in Christensen, A. N., editor, *The Evolution of Latin American Government,* Henry Holt and Co., New York, 1951, pp. 309–317; also *United National World,* vol. 4, February, 1950, pp. 21–25. Various techniques of coups d'état in terms of preparation, organization, and performance.

10. ASHFORD, D. E., "Politics and Violence in Morocco," *Middle East Journal,* vol. 13, Winter, 1959, pp. 11–26. Discussion of the origin and social character of the Moroccan Army of Liberation and its relations with the Istiqlal leaders and the Royal Army.

11. BADEAU, JOHN S., "A Role in Search of a Hero: A Brief Study of the Egyptian Revolution," *Middle East Journal,* vol. 2, Autumn, 1955, pp. 373–384. Account of the problems confronted by Egypt in its attempts to achieve a constitutional form of government.

12. BADEAU, JOHN S., "The Revolt Against Democracy," *Journal of International Affairs,* vol. 13, no. 2, 1959, pp. 149–157. Cites the failure of the parliamentary regimes to provide a bulwark against western control, to include newly developing political groups in the government, and to be an instrument for social progress as the main factors for the intervention of the military in political life.

13. BADGLEY, JOHN H., "Burma's Political Crisis," *Pacific Affairs,* vol. 31, December, 1958, pp. 336–352. Description of the internal conflict in the AFPFL and the eventual internal split, the threat of civil war between the political partners, and the military reaction to it.

14. BADGLEY, JOHN H., "Burma's Military Government: A Political Analysis," *Asian Survey,* vol. 2, August, 1962, pp. 24–31. Discussion of the historical and immediate causes of the 1962 coup d'état, with special attention devoted to the military ideology.

15. BADGLEY, JOHN H., "Burma: The Nexus of Socialism and Two Political Traditions," *Asian Survey,* vol. 3, February, 1963, pp. 89–95. Deals with the political-ideological foundation of the military in Burma. The author describes the means by which the military seeks to aggregate its power by utilizing nonwestern secular symbols and methods of rule. Details about the policy of the Revolutionary Council are included.

16. BENDA, HARRY J. "Non-Western Intelligentsias as Political Elites" in Kautsky, John H., editor, *Political Change in Underdeveloped Countries: Nationalism and Communism.* John Wiley and Sons, 1962, New York and London, pp. 235–251. Typology of non-western societies and elites, with special consideration of the intellectual elites in which the military elite is included.

17. BERGER, MORROE, *Military Elite and Social Change: Egypt Since Napoleon.* Center for International Studies, "Research Monograph No. 6," Princeton University Press, Princeton, N. J., 1960. Consideration of the role of the military as a direct and indirect agent of social change in Egypt. A historical analysis covering the Mohammad Ali era to the military regime since 1952.

18. BINDER, LEONARD, "The Modernization of Egyptian Political Culture" in *Political Culture and Political Development,* forthcoming. Presentation of the process of modernization in the political culture of Egypt through description and analysis of (1) social stratification, with special reference to the Egyptian elites, including the military; and (2) the pattern of decision-making and the process of political communication between the military and the Egyptian people. Consideration of the basis of a new legitimacy and the stages of power consolidation.

19. BLANKSTEN, GEORGE I., *Ecuador: Constitutions and Caudillos.* Publications in Political Science, vol. 3, no. 1. University of California Press, Berkeley, 1951. Analysis of the political instability of Ecuador through examining the parties system of election, the type of national administration, legislature, and judiciary. Includes a chapter on types of *caudillos,* their motives, and patterns of action.

20. BLANKSTEN, GEORGE I., *Perón's Argentina.* University of Chicago Press, Chicago, 1953, especially chap. 13. A short history of the Argentine armed forces and their internal structure and professionalization. Deals with the circumstances resulting in Perón's rise to power.

21. BLANKSTEN, GEORGE I. "Revolutions" in Davis, H. E., editor, *Government and Politics in Latin America.* The Ronald Press Co., New York, 1958, pp. 119–146. Types and anatomy of revolutions in Latin America with some short case studies as examples (Mexico, Guatemala, and Bolivia).

22. BONNET, GABRIEL, *Les Guerres Insurrectionnelles et Révolutionnaires de l'Antiquité à Nos Jours.* Payot, Paris, 1958. Discussion of political, social, religious, and economic antagonisms causing insurrections. Classifies types and analyzes the power and the weakness of insurrections and counter-insurrection movements.

Data based on wars and insurrections from antiquity to the Algerian War.

23. BRINTON, CRANE. *The Anatomy of Revolution.* Rev. ed. Prentice-Hall, Inc., New York, 1952. Comparative study of the Cromwell, American, French, and Russian revolutions. Analyzes the structural weaknesses of the old regimes, and the types, stages, and consequences of the revolutions.

24. BRUCE, JAMES, *Those Perplexing Argentines.* Longmans, Green and Co., 1953, London, chap. 23. Cites four reasons for the political influence of the Argentine Army: (1) training; (2) discipline and organizations; (3) patriotism; (4) ruthless determination to have power.

25. BUTWELL, RICHARD, "Civilians and Soldiers in Burma" in Sakai, R. K., editor, *Studies on Asia.* University of Nebraska Press, Lincoln, 1961. Description of the social background of the military and political elite in Burma, focusing on the deterioration of political stability.

26. BUTWELL, RICHARD, "The Four Failures of U Nu's Second Premiership," *Asian Survey,* vol. 2, March, 1962, pp. 3–11. Discussion of the major failures and errors in judgment of U Nu's government that eventually engendered the assumption of power by the military.

27. CALLARD, KEITH, *Political Forces in Pakistan, 1947–1959.* Institute of Pacific Relations, Vancouver, B. C., Canada, 1959. Presentation of the political forces in Pakistan and analysis of the factors contributing to the deterioration of democratic institutions. Comparison of the emergence of the military elite as a new political elite with the decline of the professional politicians who led the national movement to independence.

28. CARACTACUS [FREDERICK J. SNELL], *Revolution in Iraq.* Victor Gollancz, London, 1959. Survey of public opinion in Iraq before and after the revolution, and description of the social and political conditions leading to the 1958 revolution.

29. CARLETON, ALFORD, "The Syrian Coups D'État of 1949," *Middle East Journal,* vol. 4, January, 1950, pp. 1–11. Report on the internal and external political and social conditions leading to the series of coups in Syria in 1949.

30. CHORLEY, KATHERINE. *Armies and the Art of Revolution.* Faber and Faber, London, 1943. Conditions of insurrections and role of armies in the consolidation of revolutions. Presentation of theory of relations between the armed forces and the state, and of the contrast between theory and practice. Reference to the major revolutions and insurrections since the eighteenth century.

31. COLEMAN, JAMES S., AND BELMONT BRICE, JR., "The Role of the Military in Sub-Sahara Africa" in Johnson, J. J., editor, *The Role of the Military in Underdeveloped Countries*. Princeton University Press, Princeton, N.J., 1962, pp. 359–406. Survey of the development of the military establishment in various countries of Sub-Sahara Africa, distinguishing between the colonial and post-independence armies and different patterns of development in the ex-British and ex-French territories, and examining the political orientation of each new state and its impact on military organization and training.

32. CROZIER, BRIAN, *The Rebels: A Study of Post-War Insurrections*. Chatto and Windus, London, 1960. Comparative study of postwar insurrection and mass-movement rebellions in Algeria, Vietnam, Cyprus, Kenya (Mau Mau), Greece, Cuba, Indonesia, and Burma. Also deals with the uprisings against Communist rule in Tibet, Hungary, and East Germany.

33. DAALDER, H., "The Role of the Military in the Emerging Countries." Publication of the Institute of Social Studies, The Hague, Minor Series 1, 1962. A short paper on the rise of the military as a modernizing force. Positive and negative contributions by the military to the process of development are noted.

34. DARLING, FRANK C., "Marshall Sarit and Absolutist Rule in Thailand," *Pacific Affairs*, vol. 33, December, 1960, pp. 347–360. History of the coups d'état in Thailand, with detailed discussion of the 1957 coup d'état. Background data on the major social and economic problems of Thailand.

35. DAVIS, HAROLD E., "The Political Experience of Latin America" in Davis, H. E., editor, *Government and Politics in Latin America*. The Ronald Press Co., New York, 1958, pp. 2–25. Analysis of the political heritage of Latin American countries, with conclusions about the prospects of democracy in Latin America.

36. DAVIS, KINGSLEY, "Political Ambivalence in Latin America" in Christensen, A. N., editor, *The Evolution of Latin American Government*. Henry Holt and Co., New York, 1951, pp. 224–246; also *Journal of Legal and Political Sociology*, vol. 1, October, 1942, pp. 127–150. Conditions and prospects of political and social democracy in Latin America. Analysis of the value of ethical equality, the opportunity to advance public education, the organization of the economy, and the class structure, with emphasis on the breaking points leading to revolution.

37. DEVILLERS, PHILIPPE, *Histoire du Viêt-Nam de 1940 à 1952*. Éditions du Seuil, Paris, 1952. History of the Civil War in Indonesia and

analysis of the factors leading to the victory of the Viet-Minh revolutionary forces.

38. DOZER, DONALD MARQUAND. "Roots of Revolution in Latin America" in Christensen, A. N., editor, *The Evolution of Latin American Government*, Henry Holt and Co., New York, 1951, pp. 293–308; also *Foreign Affairs*, vol. 27, January, 1949, pp. 274–288. Consideration of historical tradition, official defalcation and malfeasance, personal ambitions, and inflexible constitutions as secondary factors of revolution in Latin America, the main factor being the social pressures seeking an outlet in violent change.

39. DUPUY, T. N., "Burma and Its Army: A Contrast in Motivation and Characteristics," *Antioch Review*, vol. 20, Winter, 1960–1961. Analysis of the factors underlying the transfer of power from U Nu to General Ne Win in 1958, with special reference to the social characteristics of the military and its top officers.

40. EDWARDS, LYFORD P., *The Natural History of Revolution*. University of Chicago Press, Chicago, 1927. Sketch of the essential problems and indication of problematic research issues. Deals with preliminary symptoms of unrest and advanced symptoms of revolution and its cycles: rise of radicalism, reign of terror, return to normality, and the next revolution.

41. EL-BARAWY, RASHED, *The Military Coup in Egypt*. The Renaissance Bookshop, Cairo, 1952. Description of the historical background leading to the military coup of July, 1952, in Egypt by a devoted partisan of the revolutionary regime.

42. ETZIONI, AMITAI, "The Israeli Army: The Human Factor," *Jewish Frontier*, vol. 26, November, 1959, pp. 4–9; also vol. 27, January, 1960, pp. 9–13. Description of the social organization of the Israeli Army, its interrelations with Israeli society, and the causes of its *esprit de corps*, against the background of the structure of Israeli society.

43. FALL, BERNARD B., *The Viet-Minh Regime*. Institute of Pacific Relations, Vancouver, B.C., Canada, 1956. Study of the internal social and political structure of the Viet-Minh regime in historical perspective, most specifically with the strategy and tactics of operations, and political wing of the Army, and its ideological and psychological warfare, and the organization of the armed forces and economic problems.

44. *Far Eastern Economic Review*, "Rebirth of a New Nation" (editorial), June 9, 1960, pp. 1161–1163. Analysis of the economic situation in Pakistan that provided, according to this source, the most important incentive for the military coup.

45. FEITH, HERBERT, "Indonesia" in Kahin, George McTurnan, editor, *Governments and Politics of Southeast Asia*. Cornell University Press, Ithaca, N.Y., 1959, pp. 155–230. Examination of the political process in Indonesia and of the basic causes of political instability.

46. FEITH, HERBERT, *The Wilopo Cabinet, 1952–1953: A Turning Point in Post-Revolutionary Indonesia*. Monograph Series, Modern Indonesia Project, Department of Far Eastern Studies, Cornell University, Ithaca, N.Y., 1958. Description of the basic changes in the constellation of political power among the major political parties, the President, and the Army.

47. FINER, S. E. *The Man on Horseback: The Role of the Military in Politics*. Pall Mall Press, London, 1962. A contribution to the typologies of military-civil relations in countries of high, low, and minimal developed political culture. The book deals especially with the predisposition of the military to intervene in political life; levels, modes, and results of intervention.

48. FITZGIBBON, RUSSELL H., *Uruguay: Portrait of a Democracy*. Rutgers University Press, New Brunswick, N. J., 1954. Focuses on the emergence of Uruguay as a democratic state—a deviant case in the Latin American political scene—and on parties, the electoral systems, the power of the press, and a system of liberal education as the main foundations of Uruguay's democracy.

49. FITZGIBBON, RUSSELL H., "Revolutions: Western Hemisphere," *South Atlantic Quarterly*, vol. 55, July, 1956, pp. 263–279. Examination of the revolutionary mass parties in Latin America, especially the Aprista and Accion Democrática parties of Peru and Venezuela and their counterparts in other Latin American countries.

50. FITZGIBBON, RUSSELL H. "The Revolution Next Door: Cuba," *Annals of the American Academy of Political and Social Science*, vol. 334, March, 1961, pp. 113–122. Account of the causes of the Cuban Revolution, with special reference to the role of Castro as a charismatic leader. Analysis of the Cuban Revolution as a social movement and of the problem of institutionalization.

51. FLUHARTY, VERNON L., *Dance of the Millions: Military Rule and the Social Revolution in Colombia, 1930–1956*. University of Pittsburgh Press, Pittsburgh, 1957. Political analysis of the period of social upheaval and revolution in Colombia. Argues that the recent military dictatorship has paradoxically contributed toward democracy.

52. GERMANI, GINO, AND KOLMAN SILBERT, "Politics, Social Structure and Military Intervention in Latin America," *Archives Européennes de Sociologie*, vol. 2, no. 1, 1961. Systematic comparative study of twenty Latin American countries in terms of civil-military relations, classifying the countries according to economic structure, stratification system, degree of cultural and economic homogeneity, identification with national symbols, and extent of regional differentiation in terms of economic and social variables. Six main stages of military relations are distinguished, and a typology of military-civil relations is suggested.

53. GILLESPIE, JOAN, *Algeria, Rebellion and Revolution*. Ernest Benn, London, 1960, especially Part III. History of the Algerian national liberation movement and its army, including the structure of the FLN, the army, and its strategy and tactics.

54. GOMEZ, R. A., *Government and Politics in Latin America*. Random House, New York, 1960. The meaning of revolutions in the specific social context of Latin America, with discussion of some of the structural and social characteristics of the army and the cult of violence.

55. GROSS, FELIKS, *The Seizure of Political Power*. Philosophical Library, New York, 1958, Parts I, IV. Part I: The relations between power and culture and types of power transfer (nonviolent and violent). Part IV: Various means of struggle against seized power. Empirical data drawn from the Russian Revolution and Communist activities in Europe to 1956.

56. GUTTERIDGE, WILLIAM, *Armed Forces in New States*. Institute of Race Relations, Oxford University Press, New York, 1962. Brief general introductory discussion of the functions of armed forces in new states, and a more specific survey of the problems of the public's attitudes and the recruitment to the armed forces in the states of Commonwealth Africa.

57. HALPERN, BEN, "The Role of the Military in Israel" in Johnson, J. J., editor, *The Role of the Military in Underdeveloped Countries*. Princeton University Press, Princeton, N.J., 1962, pp. 317–358. Inquiry into the historical roots of military organization and ideology in the Zionist movement, with discussion and analysis of the role of the army in present-day Israel.

58. HALPERN, MANFRED, "The Middle Eastern Armies and the New Middle Class" in Johnson, J. J., editor, *The Role of the Military in Underdeveloped Countries*. Princeton University Press, Princeton, N.J., 1962, pp. 277–316. Comparative study of military roles in Middle East countries, with analysis of the change in the Army's

traditional role in terms of social changes occurring in the Middle East, with special emphasis on changes in the military role from a praetorian guard to an advanced guard. Consideration of the Army's special characteristics as a political instrument and the circumstances of intervention.

59. HANRAHAN, GENE Z., *The Communist Struggle in Malaya.* Institute of Pacific Relations, Vancouver, B.C., Canada, 1954. Historical study of the strategy and tactics of the Communist revolutionary movement in Malaya, tracing the origins and early development of Malayan communism, its activities in World War II, and its revolutionary course in the postwar years.

60. HOLT, P. M., *A Modern History of the Sudan.* Weidenfeld and Nicolson, London, 1961. Historical survey of the Sudan from the arrival of the Arabs till the army coup and military government, including a short description of the background to the abortive coup in 1959.

61. HUNTINGTON, SAMUEL P., *The Soldier and the State.* Harvard University Press, Cambridge, Mass., 1957. Comparative, historical, and theoretical analysis of the relationship between the military institutions and the state, with case studies of the military in the United States, Germany, and Japan.

62. HUNTINGTON, SAMUEL P., "Patterns of Violence in World Politics" in Huntington, S. P., editor, *Changing Patterns of Military Politics.* Free Press of Glencoe, New York, 1962, pp. 17–50. Discussion of violence in world politics, with special reference to revolutionary wars and to reform coups and modernization.

63. JANOWITZ, MORRIS, "Military Elites and the Study of War," *Conflict Resolution,* vol. 1, March, 1957, pp. 9–18. Delimitation and analysis of the roles of the four major models of political-military elites: the aristocratic, the democratic, the totalitarian, and the garrison-state models.

64. JANOWITZ, MORRIS, *The Military in the Political Development of New Nations: An Essay in Comparative Analysis.* University of Chicago Press, Chicago, 1964. Comparative analysis of military-civil relations in more than 50 new nations, based on two major assumptions: (1) the common societal context of the military in new nations (the military operating in societies which are confronted with uniform political, economic, and social requirements); (2) the organizational features of the military condition that limit the capacity of the military profession to exercise political power.

65. JOHNSON, CHALMERS, "Civilian Loyalties and Guerrilla Conflict," *World Politics*, vol. 14, July, 1962, pp. 646–661. Critical analysis of the literature dealing with the various forms of guerrilla and counter-guerrilla warfare.

66. JOHNSON, JOHN J., *Political Change in Latin America: The Emergence of the Middle Sectors*, Stanford University Press, Stanford, Calif., 1958. Comparative study of the emergence of the middle-class sectors in Argentina, Brazil, Chile, Mexico, and Uruguay, discussing and analyzing the new position of the officer corps in this context in the respective countries.

67. JOHNSON, JOHN J., "The Latin American Military as a Politically Competing Group in Transitional Society" in Johnson, J. J., editor, *The Role of the Military in Underdeveloped Countries*. Princeton University Press, Princeton, N.J., 1962, pp. 91–130. Historical survey of military-civil relations in Latin America, focusing on the social organization of the military in various periods and its relations to various social classes. Analysis of the function of the military as an instrument of modernity, especially in the economic-industrial field.

68. KAHIN, GEORGE M., *Nationalism and Revolution in Indonesia*. Cornell University Press, Ithaca, N.Y., 1952, especially chaps. 6, 9, 14. Examination of the role of the military and armed groups in (1) the internal politics of the Revolution until the first Dutch military action; (2) the internal struggle for power from Renville through the Communist rebellion; and (3) the Unitarian movement.

69. KENNEDY, MALCOLM, *A History of Communism in East Asia*. Frederick A. Praeger, New York, 1957. Outline of the chief developments in the rise of nationalism and the spread of communism in South East Asia, covering events from 1850 until ten years after World War II.

70. KHADDURI, MAJID, "The Role of the Military in Middle East Politics," *American Political Science Review*, vol. 47, June, 1953, pp. 511–524; reprinted in "The Army Officer: His Role in Middle Eastern Politics" in Fisher, S. N., *Social Forces in the Middle East*. Cornell University Press, Ithaca, N.Y., 1955, pp. 162–183. Argues that the nostalgic longing in the Middle East for a "strong" regime, the Islamic way of life and divine system, the unhappy experiment of the new generation with democracy, the absence of any significant middle-class, and the Israeli War are the factors underlying the emergence of military regimes in the Middle East.

71. KHADDURI, MAJID, *Independent Iraq, 1932–1958*. Oxford University Press, London, 1960. A history of the Iraqi national movement. Trial and error in self-government and the recurrent pattern of coups d'état are the main themes. The structure of the Iraqi Army and the social and ideological characteristics of the officers are analyzed.

72. KILNER, PETER, "A Year of Army Rule in the Sudan," *World Today*, vol. 15, November, 1959, pp. 430–441. Account of the circumstances leading to the takeover by the Sudanese Army and a survey of its record during its first year in power.

73. KLING, MERLE, "Towards a Theory of Power and Political Instability in Latin America" in Kautsky, John H., editor, *Political Change in Underdeveloped Countries, Nationalism and Communism*. John Wiley and Sons, New York, 1962, pp. 123–139. Advances a theory for explaining the three main characteristics of Latin American instability in politics: (1) its chronic existence; (2) its association with limited violence; and (3) the lack of basic shifts in economic, social, or political policies.

74. KLING, MERLE, "Cuba: A Case Study of a Successful Attempt to Seize Political Power by the Application of Unconventional Warfare," *Annals of the American Academy of Political and Social Science*, vol. 341, May, 1962, pp. 45–52. Comparison of the traditional coup d'état of Latin American politics with the Cuban Revolution which involved protracted military warfare and sweeping social and economic changes.

75. LACOUTURE, JEAN AND SIMONNE, *L'Égypte en Mouvement*. Éditions du Seuil, Paris, 1956, Part II. Discussion of the social and political structure of Nasser's regime, mainly through depicting the career of Nasser and his fellow revolutionists.

76. LANCASTER, DONALD, *The Emancipation of French Indochina*. Oxford University Press, New York, 1961, especially Part III and Appendix 2. History of Indochina from the advent of the Europeans to the consolidation of the partition between North and South Vietnam.

77. LASSWELL, HAROLD, "The Garrison State," *American Journal of Sociology*, vol. 46, January, 1941, pp. 455–468. Makes a distinction between the "specialist on bargaining" (the businessman) and the "specialist on violence" (the soldier). Analysis of the patterns of political and social regulation of these types of elites.

78. LERNER, DANIEL, AND RICHARD D. ROBINSON, "Swords and Ploughshares: The Turkish Army as a Modernizing Force," *World Politics*, vol. 13, October, 1960, pp. 19–44. Analysis of the

role of the military in Turkey since the establishment of the republic, and a discussion of the army as initiating political, economic, and educational reform.

79. LIEUWEN, EDWIN, *Arms and Politics in Latin America*, Frederick A. Praeger, New York, 1960; also a summary, "Militarism and Politics in Latin America" in Johnson, J. J., editor, *The Role of the Military in Underdeveloped Countries*, Princeton University Press, Princeton, N.J., 1962, pp. 131–164. A comparative study of military functions and roles in Latin American societies, analyzing the changes of roles in the military after describing the crumbling of the traditional order and the emergence of new types of social revolutions. A chapter concerned with the military aspects of the Latin American policy of the United States.

80. LIEUWEN, EDWIN, "The Military: A Revolutionary Force," *Annals of the American Academy of Political and Social Sciences*, vol. 334, March, 1961, pp. 30–41. Examination of the history of Latin America in terms of military domination, either directly or by assuming the role of arbiter among civilian contestants, of internal and external politics. Discussion of the Army's primary role as leading the first revolution emphasizing social and economic reforms.

81. LINARES, O. S. V., "The Etiology of Revolutions in Latin America," *Eastern Political Quarterly*, vol. 4, June, 1951, pp. 254–267. Account of the major factors conditioning the revolutions in Latin America; for example, (1) divergence between constitutional prescription and governmental practice, (2) the respect of rulers toward oppositions, and (3) the absence of a powerful middle class.

82. LIPSET, SEYMOUR M., "Some Social Requisites of Democracy: Economic Development and Political Legitimacy," *American Political Science Review*, vol. 53, March, 1959, pp. 69–105. Not related directly to the problem of military-civil relations, but concerned with the requisites of democracy, especially with economic conditions and type of legitimacy. Comparative discussion of the Latin American scene and the European societies, followed by the theoretical presentation.

83. LISSAK, MOSHE, "Social Change, Mobilization and Exchange of Services Between the Military Establishment and the Civil Society: The Burmese Case" in *Economic Development and Cultural Change*, forthcoming. Analysis of the "unorthodox" functions and activities of the military in Burma, proposing theoretical framework for military-civil relations in under-developed countries.

84. LITTLE, TOM, *Egypt*. Ernest Benn, London, 1958, chaps. 14–23. Description of the emergence of the Free Officers in Egypt, the planning of its coup, execution, and the consolidation of its power.

85. LOEWENSTEIN, MARK, "The Presidency Outside the U. S.: A Study in Comparative Political Institutions," *Journal of Politics*, vol. 11, August, 1949, pp. 447–496. General account of the development of Latin American presidencies, their classification and evaluation.

86. MACKIE, J. A. C. "Indonesia's Government Estates and Their Masters," *Pacific Affairs*, vol. 34, Winter, 1961–1962, pp. 337–360. Deals with the transfer of the Dutch estates into state ownership. The emergence of a new managerial elite and the role of the regional military authorities in management of the estates are given detailed treatment.

87. MANCHESTER, ALAN K., "Brazil in Transition," *South Atlantic Quarterly*, vol. 54, April, 1955, pp. 167–176. Consideration of the major differences between the Vargas and the pre-1930 periods, emphasizing the role of the Brazilian Army in political and social transition.

88. MARSHALL, CHARLES B., "The Military in Pakistan." Unpublished. Discussion of (1) the impact of parliamentary and viceregal traditions during the preindependence period on the political structure of Pakistan, and (2) the place and role of Islam as a unifying power. These issues provide a frame of reference for explaining the accession of the military to power in Pakistan.

89. MUS, PAUL, *Vietnam Sociologie d'une Guerre*. Éditions du Seuil, Paris, 1952. Sociological analysis of Vietnam's social and cultural structure, focusing on the social and ideological forces involved in the Civil War.

90. NEWMAN, K. J., "Pakistan's Preventive Autocracy and Its Causes," *Pacific Affairs*, vol. 32, March, 1959, pp. 18–34. Presentation of the military assumption of power as a conclusion of a historical process beginning with the British Parliament's Government of India Act of 1935.

91. NEWMAN, K. J., "The New Monarchies of the Middle East," *Journal of International Affairs*, vol. 13, no. 2, 1959, pp. 157–168. Comparative study of the military regimes of Egypt, Iraq, and Pakistan in terms of each respective regime's aims and ideology.

92. OSANKA, F. M., editor, *Modern Guerrilla Warfare*. The Free Press of Glencoe, New York, 1962. Collection of papers dealing with modern guerrilla warfare, primarily concerned with the military

and political aspects of the guerrilla warfare. Contains a comprehensive bibliography.

93. PARET, PETER, AND JOHN W. SHY, *Guerrillas in the 1960's*. Frederick A. Praeger, New York, 1962, especially chaps. 3 and 4. Comparative study of guerrilla warfare theory, with data based on guerrilla warfare in China, Algeria, Cuba, Indochina, and so on, concentrating on communism and insurrection, the integration of political and military leadership, and the tasks of counter-guerrilla actions.

94. PAUKER, GUY J., "The Role of Political Organizations in Indonesia," *Far Eastern Survey*, vol. 27, September, 1958, pp. 129–142. Discussion and analysis of the failure to integrate Indonesians' political organization into one national movement, highlighting the neglect of organizational efforts to reach the intermediate stratum of society as the main cause. Discussion of the role and the prospect of the Army to overcome this obstacle.

95. PAUKER, GUY J., "Southeast Asia as a Problem Area in the Next Decade," *World Politics*, vol. 11, April, 1959, pp. 325–345. Discussion of the prospect of political, economic, and social progress in Southeast Asia, of the problem of synchronization among social, economic, and political forms of changes. Analysis of the role of the military as an alternative elite to the Founding Fathers, whose influence and power are diminishing.

96. PAUKER, GUY J., "The Role of the Military in Indonesia" in Johnson, J. J., editor, *The Role of the Military in Underdeveloped Countries*. Princeton University Press, Princeton, N.J., 1962, pp. 185–230. Discussion of the origins of the officer corps, its combat experience, and the ideology and pattern of civil-military relations developed in Indonesia.

97. PETTEE, GEORGE S., *The Process of Revolution*. Harper and Bros., New York, 1938. Comparative study of major modern revolutions (French, Russian, and so on), defining and classifying the phenomena of revolutions in terms of change of personnel and social and cultural features, focusing on the prerevolutionary society and its crises leading to the showdown of the old elite with the revolutionaries.

98. PIERSON, WILLIAM W., AND FEDORICO GIL, *Governments of Latin America*. McGraw-Hill Book Co., New York, 1957, chap. 6. Discussion of the various explanations of the dictatorships in Latin America, presenting such factors as inheritance of social customs and political habits, illiteracy, economic conditions.

99. PORTER, CHARLES O., AND ROBERT J. ALEXANDER, *The Struggle for Democracy in Latin America*. Macmillan Co., New York, 1961. Analysis of the forces in Latin America favoring and opposing democracy.

100. PREWETT, VIRGINIA, "The Mexican Army," *Foreign Affairs*, vol. 19, April, 1941, pp. 609–620. History of the Mexican Army, analyzing the process of transformation it has been undergoing both in mission and in organization.

101. PYE, LUCIAN W., *Guerrilla Communism in Malaya*. Princeton University Press, Princeton, N.J., 1956. Case study of the Malayan Communist Party, focusing on the relationship between the general experience of Malayan Chinese who became Communists and their attitude toward what they considered the sphere of politics, and analyzing the process of recruitment and indoctrination.

102. PYE, LUCIAN W., "Armies in the Process of Political Modernization," *Archives Européennes de Sociologie*, vol. 2, no. 1, 1961; also in Johnson, J. J., editor, *The Role of the Military in Underdeveloped Countries*, Princeton University Press, Princeton, N.J., 1962, pp. 69–90. Discussion of (1) the political implications of the army as a new social institution in new nations undergoing social change, and (2) the military as agent of modernization.

103. PYE, LUCIAN W., "The Army in Burmese Politics" in Johnson, J. J., editor, *The Role of the Military in Underdeveloped Countries*, Princeton University Press, Princeton, N.J., 1962, pp. 231–252. Analysis of the political split, the social gap between the politicians and administrators, the social background of the officer class, its relations to the civilian elite, and other issues.

104. RAPOPORT, DAVID C., "A Comparative Theory of Military and Political Types" in Huntington, S. P., editor, *Changing Patterns of Military Politics*. The Free Press of Glencoe, New York, 1962, pp. 71–100. Proposes a typology of nations: (1) the praetorian state, (2) the civilian and military polity, and (3) the nation-in-arms.

105. SAYEED, KHALID B., "Martial Law Administration in Pakistan," *Far Eastern Survey*, vol. 32, May, 1959, pp. 72–79. Comparison of the structural and social features of the political parties, civil service, middle class, and the military.

106. SCAFF, ALVIN H., *The Philippine Answer to Communism*. Stanford University Press, Stanford, Calif., 1955. Political and sociological analysis of the Huks rebellion in the Philippine republic,

covering the combination of military force and constructive programs that was a salient feature of the Philippine government's strategy against the Communist rebels.

107. SHILS, EDWARD, "The Military in the Political Development of the New States" in Johnson, J. J., editor, *The Role of the Military in Underdeveloped Countries*. Princeton University Press, Princeton, N.J., 1962, pp. 7–68. Consideration of (1) the determinants of political development in new nations, emphasizing gaps in the social structure and the internal cultural conflicts; and (2) the alternative courses of political development of which one is the "modernizing military oligarchies."

108. SPEIER, HANS, *Social Order and the Risks of War*. George Stewart, New York, 1952, chaps. 18, 19, 20. Discussion of social types of war, militarism in the eighteenth century and class structure, and total war.

109. STOKES, WILLIAM S., "Violence as a Power in Latin American Politics," *Western Political Quarterly*, vol. 5, September, 1952, pp. 445–468. Study of the nature of political power and the methods of achieving authority in Latin America.

110. STOKES, WILLIAM S., *Latin American Politics*. Thomas Y. Crowell Co., New York, 1959, especially chaps. 7, 13, 14, 15. Survey of the social institutions like the stratification system, the family and educational institutions, the church, and political structure, discussing in this context the phenomenon of violence and the history of militarism in Latin America.

111. TANHAM, GEORGE K., *Communist Revolutionary Warfare*. Frederick A. Praeger, New York, 1961. Presentation of the Viet-Minh military doctrine and military organizations.

112. THOMPSON, VIRGINIA, "Governmental Instability in Siam," *Far Eastern Survey*, vol. 17, August 25, 1948, pp. 185–189. Survey of the economic and financial troubles and corruption leading to the November, 1947, coup.

113. TINKER, HUGH, *The Union of Burma*. Oxford University Press, New York, 1961. History of modern and independent Burma, surveying social, political, and economic aspects of present-day Burma, and including a history of Burmese Army.

114. TINKER, HUGH, *India and Pakistan: A Political Analysis*. Frederick A. Praeger, New York, 1962. Comparative study of the political and the public services of India and Pakistan, with a section dealing with structural and social aspects of the military establishment in the two countries.

115. VAGTS, ALFRED, *A History of Militarism*. Rev. ed. Meridian Books, New York, 1959. Analysis of the idea and nature of militarism and its patterns from the feudal society until the post-World War II period, dealing especially with the development and militarization of mass armies, the military and politics, and the post-1918 militarization of society.

116. VAN DER KROEF, JUSTUS M., "Instability in Indonesia," *Far Eastern Survey*, vol. 26, April, 1957, pp. 49–62. Analysis of the causes and circumstances of the frequent revolts by dissident army officers against the central Indonesian government.

117. VAN DER KROEF, JUSTUS M., "Indonesia's Military and the State," *Far Eastern Economic Review*, vol. 24, May, 1958, pp. 683–686. Description of the specific role of the Indonesian Army in movement for national independence by tracing the historic origins and development of the Army, and discussion of the problems of private armies, para-military organization, and the civil control.

118. VAN DER MEHDEN, F. R., AND C. W. ANDERSON, "Political Action by the Military in Developing Areas," *Sociological Research*, vol. 28, Winter, 1961, pp. 459–479. The paper deals with types of military regimes as constitutional caretakers and revolutionary forces and with causes of coups in Asia, Africa, and Latin America.

119. VATIKIOTIS, PANAYIOTIS J., *The Egyptian Army in Politics*. Indiana University Press, Bloomington, 1961. Discussion of the transformation of the military group into a ruling elite, suggesting theoretical considerations about the role of the military in the underdeveloped countries in general and the Muslim countries in particular.

120. VATIKIOTIS, PANAYIOTIS J., "Dilemmas of Political Leadership in the Arab Middle East: The Case of the United Arab Republic," *American Political Science Review*, vol. 55, March, 1961, pp. 103–111. Discussion of the political theory of the Egyptian officer corps, the use of Islam as an instrument of national policy, and the effort to synthesize between Islam and socialism.

121. VIGNEAU, JEAN, "The Ideology of the Egyptian Revolution" in Laqueur, W. Z., editor, *The Middle East in Transition*. Frederick A. Praeger, New York, 1958, pp. 129–144. Study of Egyptian military leaders' ideologies and their application in the constitution and political framework (the national union and the parliament).

122. WHEELOCK, KEITH, *Nasser's New Egypt: A Critical Analysis*. Frederick A. Praeger, New York, 1960. Consideration of the

consolidation and entrenchment of the military regime, analyzing the problems of agrarian reform, education, and social development, economics and industrialization, and foreign policy.

123. WHITAKER, ARTHUR P., "The Pathology of Democracy in Latin America" in Christensen, A. N., editor, *The Evolution of Latin American Government*, Henry Holt and Co., New York, 1951, pp. 248–270; also *American Political Science Review*, vol. 44, March, 1950, 101–118. Historical study of the pathology of democracy in Latin America, dealing mainly with such factors as literacy, urbanization, the problem of the middle class, and party organizations.

124. WHITAKER, ARTHUR P., *The United States and Argentina*. Harvard University Press, Cambridge, Mass., 1954. Political analysis of Peron's rule in Argentina, with a historical introduction, focusing on the means by which Peron consolidated his power

125. WHITAKER, ARTHUR P., *Argentine Upheaval*. Frederick A. Praeger, New York, 1956. Political analysis of the direct and indirect factors causing the fall of Peron's tyranny, including detailed analysis of the roles of the various power groups, especially the military, in the revolt of June 16.

126. WILSON, DAVID A., AND HERBERT P. PHILLIPS. "Elections and Parties in Thailand," *Far Eastern Survey*, vol. 27, August, 1958, pp. 113–119. Survey of the electoral system of Thailand and the basis of political power, discussing the relations among the three main groups in the Thai society: the royalists, the military, and the civilian officials supplemented by provincial politicians.

127. WILSON, DAVID A., "Thailand" in Kahin, G. McTurnan, editor, *Governments and Politics of Southeast Asia*. Cornell University Press, Ithaca, N.Y., 1959, pp. 2–68. Consideration of the historical background, the contemporary setting in terms of the selective problems, political, economic, educational, and so on, as well as a detailed analysis of the role of the Army.

128. WILSON, DAVID A., "Thailand and Marxism" in Trager, F. N., editor, *Marxism in Southeast Asia*. Stanford University Press, Stanford, Calif., 1959, pp. 58–101. Presentation of the role of Marxism in Thai society and the character of the coups d'état, emphasizing the flexibility of the social and political structure and the relative smoothness with which one group displaced another without internal disorders.

129. WILSON, DAVID A., "The Military in Thai Politics" in Johnson, J. J., editor, *The Role of the Military in Underdeveloped Countries*.

Princeton University Press, Princeton, N.J., 1962, pp. 253–276. Discussion of the historical roots of the position of the military in Thailand, the stages of military-political relations, the Army as a political and social organization, and its congruence with the political and social system of Thai society.

130. WILSON, DAVID A., *Politics in Thailand.* Cornell University Press, Ithaca, N.Y., 1962. An analysis of political relationships in Thailand in terms of those elements of Thai politics which constitute recurrent patterns of institutional behavior. The military as a social institution shaping Thai society is analyzed in detail.

131. WOLFSTONE, DANIEL, "The Burmese Army Experiment," *Far Eastern Economic Review*, February, 1960, pp. 352–357. History of the political crises of 1958 and the achievements of the caretaker government of General Ne Win in 1958–1960.

132. WYCKOFF, THEODORE, "The Role of the Military in Latin America," *Western Political Quarterly*, vol. 13, no. 3, 1960, pp. 745–763. Theoretical analysis of types of Latin American states in terms of differences in patterns of military politics.

INDEX

INDEX